SPLASH
ONE

ALSO BY IVAN RENDALL

The Chequered Flag

SPLASH ONE

ONE

THE STORY OF JET COMBAT

IVAN RENDALL

CASSELL

Cassell Military Paperbacks

Cassell & Co
Wellington House, 125 Strand
London WC2R 0BB

A catalogue record for this book is available from the British Library

ISBN 0-304-35242-X

Cassell Military Paperbacks are available from all good bookshops or from:

Cassell C.S.
Book Service By Post
PO Box 29, Douglas I.O.M.
IM99 1BQ

Tel: 01624 675137
Fax: 01624 670923

Printed and bound by Guernsey Press.

CONTENTS

PREFACE

The jet fighter is one of the great icons of the second half of the twentieth century, a symbol of achievement, of technical excellence, of ultimate modernity, of latent military power. There is a worrisome beauty about the natural marriage between elegance and lethality, grace and brutishness, delicacy and hardness – the perfect combination of form and function. In the air, that function is clear – aggression, hunting and killing. Flying low and fast, a jet fighter's physical, menacing presence cannot be ignored: the urgent whistle of air over its skin; the shock wave, and the ear-ripping bark of the afterburner assaulting the senses.

On the ground, the air of lethality is more contained. A grounded jet fighter looks awkward and forlorn, like a caged animal, squatting on its oily undercarriage, its flying surfaces hanging limp, its clean lines broken, the gun port covered with a canvas weather guard, safety pins in the weapons and electronic countermeasures pods, evidence that they are inert. Yet even asleep, a Sabre, Jaguar, Harrier, Phantom, Falcon or Eagle holds the eye as a design classic, and that worrisome beauty is still there close up – the cared for, nurtured, spoilt feel, the expensive finish, the quality of the materials, the craftsmanship evident in the flush rivets, the highly polished canopy, the gunmetal sheen of the external instrument sensors, each carefully protected by rubber sheaths with flapping red tags to remind the pilot to take them off before flight.

The jet fighter is the peak of aeronautical evolution. The inherent extremes of its fragility and robustness are evident in the cockpit, with the hooded VDUs with touch-sensitive screens, a moulded Perspex canopy built to withstand the forces generated by flight at over twice the speed of sound, the tiny micro switches positioned under the pilot's fingertips on the moulded plastic grip on the control column and throttles, the heavy fabric and lightweight buckles of the parachute harness, the precision engineering of the ejection seat systems, the nylon leg restraint cords, bolted to the cockpit floor. Everything is obviously made out of the best materials for the job, designed and honed to perfection. Close examination shows the tell-tales signs of the violence and energy of its working environment. The matt paint of the nose cone, which hides the radar, is peeling off from daily cutting through a wall of air at high speed, the rear of the fuselage is skinned back to bare metal from the intense heat of the afterburner, the surface mottled with purple bruises.

A jet fighter looks, and is, expensive and alluring. It demands lavish care and permanent cosseting, constantly applied throughout its working life, and, like a stunningly beautiful and dangerous courtesan, it stirs conflicting emotions, swinging between desire and fear, awe and guilt, even a touch of moral confusion at finding a machine the purpose of which is so clear – to kill and destroy – so hauntingly attractive. The beauty comes from it being perfectly evolved for its function – destroying other aircraft – and its parallels in nature are creatures high on the evolutionary scale, creatures who live by killing other creatures. Their names embody that preying quality – Jaguar, Tigershark, Hawk, Eagle and Falcon – conjuring up images of quiet power and thoroughbred purity. They are machines but, like any animal bred and tamed by human ingenuity, when used for their real purpose and handled to their full extent by a real expert, their capability is awesome.

The fighter pilot, or 'driver' in modern jargon, is one of the heroes of the twentieth century, the quintessential warrior of our times, part of a small élite at the top of the tree of military prowess for whom there are only two kinds of aircraft – fighters and targets. He is a master of his craft, a perfectionist who has risen to the most exalted job in aviation by a process of ruthless natural selection in training for his ability to demonstrate a rare mixture of intellectual capacity and natural aggression, mental balance and killer instinct, modesty and profound self-belief, and competitiveness and coolness under pressure.

A fighter pilot generally fights alone. He will be part of a flight, and pilots will work together tactically, but battles are personal – duels between pilots – the outcome of which depends greatly on individual skill and understanding of a rapidly changing situation, on the ability to see any potential for advantage in a situation, how to set the agenda for the dogfight, how to become the master of the conflict and kill most effectively and surely. To achieve this the fighter pilot must have an intimate understanding of the full capability of his aircraft and all its systems and be able to get every last measure of performance out of it. He must be able to fly it at, and occasionally beyond, the limits, in the realm where instinctive and flowing thoughts and actions transcend mere skill, where mind, body and senses become an extension of the aircraft and its high-technology systems, the human mind and the computer interacting in a real combination of man and machine. In military terms, a fighter pilot must have inherited something of the courage of Achilles, the cunning of Ulysses and the spatial awareness of Nelson, while having the affinity with computer technology of a Bill Gates.

In the half-century since the end of the Second World War the face of war has changed dramatically, and at the heart of that change has been science and technology. Nuclear physics and micro-electronics have brought about changes as profound as gunpowder did in the fourteenth century and the aeroplane itself did at the beginning of the twentieth. The age of formal, international conflicts, fought by millions of men across oceans and continents, has passed. The Cold War lasted half a century but it stayed cold, and in the stasis that surrounded it an age of small-scale war was ushered in, of terrorism, of long drawn out, simmering ideological conflicts which occasionally bubbled over into short, sharp regional wars.

The period from 1945 to the present day matches, almost exactly, the age of the jet aircraft, and the development of the jet fighter has mirrored the changing needs of war in that age. It has been a Cold War weapon on a grand scale, the first line of defence against nuclear bombers and a 'gunship', doing for the superpowers what Royal Navy gunships did for the British Empire in the Victorian age – providing a means of projecting power swiftly and flexibly, influencing events by being an immediate and menacing symbol of far greater power over the horizon.

As we near the end of the twentieth century, so the future of this potent combination of man and technology, the jet fighter, is in doubt. There are those who believe that microchips will take over from fighter pilots just as surely as steam power displaced sail-makers and coachmen in the last century, and computers are replacing bank-tellers and lighthouse-keepers in the modern age. Some military thinkers and planners believe we are about to enter, or may have already entered, a new era in the development of warfare – infowar – the era of the true robot warrior, a man (or woman) safe in an underground bunker at a console, guiding his or her Remotely Piloted Vehicle (RPV) to spy on, attack or engage in aerial combat with enemy RPVs a continent away.

If the computer is about to replace this twentieth-century hero and his mount, then it will be the end of the culture which, however modern it may seem, has its origins in the skies over Flanders in 1914. There is an unbroken line of succession, in Western fighter pilot circles at least, which goes back to those origins and passes on the skills of the job from one generation to the next no less personally than a blacksmith or a cabinet-maker does to his apprentice. With that succession is a cult of perfectionism, of individualism, of supremacy, of years – whole careers – spent honing highly specialised skills few will ever have the chance to put into practice. Even those who do, and who spend whole careers in pursuit of that supreme skill, can only measure their experience of real aerial combat in minutes, seconds even.

That culture goes beyond the pilot to those who maintain, build, design and plan jet fighter programmes and, being part of that culture, they recognise that the fighter pilot and his aircraft have to be maintained as near to perfection as possible. No expense can be spared: having the best fighters and the pilots in the first place, then keeping them in the peak of fighting ability, using the latest technology, is a huge cost in human talent and cash. The objective is to win, and the price of winning a split-second fight for supremacy in an obscure patch of sky, often far from home, is whatever it takes to give the pilot an edge. It is a law as old as warfare itself: 'Nervos belli, pecuniam infinitam' (Cicero: 'The sinews of war, infinite money').

Few countries today have the industrial ability, economic resources, pool of talent or continuity to build state-of-the-art fighters and the weapons systems to go with them. Nor do they have the bedrock of experience to train their pilots to fly them to the limits of their capability. Most countries that aspire to a

4

combat-ready air force have to buy both the fighters and pilot training from the small number of countries who do have the expertise, or build fighters to an inferior standard, often copies of earlier Western or Soviet designs. Countries which do have the ability to build state-of the-art fighters – Russia, Israel, France, Britain, Germany, Italy and, soon, China – find it hard and expensive to sustain in the 1990s.

The exception is the United States. With the end of the Cold War, air power remains at the heart of US global power, just as Britain's sea power did in the last century. Just occasionally, when that power is exercised, the world gets a glimpse of the real difference between those countries who have the best men and machines and those who have second-best.

On 19 August 1981 the US Navy's Sixth Fleet was carrying out a missile-firing exercise off the Libyan coast in the Gulf of Sirte in the Mediterranean. Relations between the USA and Libya were at a low point, and throughout the previous day Libyan fighters had flown towards the firing area, challenging America's right to declare a Restricted Area so close to their coast. US Navy fighters had intercepted them, and there had been aggressive manoeuvring by both sides, but no shots were fired. Ultimately, the Libyans accepted being escorted away.

At 6.00 a.m., two F-14 Tomcat fighters took off from the carrier USS *Nimitz* to patrol the area. Leading the mission was Commander Henry 'Hank' Kleeman, CO of 41 Fighter Squadron, with his Radar Intercept Officer (RIO), Lieutenant David Venlet, in the back seat; his wingman was Lieutenant Lawrence 'Music' Musczynski, whose RIO was Lieutenant Jim 'Amos' Anderson. At 07.15 Venlet picked up a radar contact to the south, a 'bogey', aerial combat jargon for an unidentified aircraft which could be hostile but not positively identified as such. The bogey was heading for the firing area. The Tomcat pilots went to investigate, flying a 'defensive combat spread', or 'Loose Deuce', a flexible formation, about two miles apart, with the wingman slightly above and behind the leader, guarding his tail while leaving plenty of room for individual lookout, initiative and manoeuvre. At eight miles, Kleeman saw two Soviet-built, Libyan Air Force Su-22 fighters, known by the NATO codename 'Fitter'. They were flying in a far less flexible 'welded wing' formation, just five hundred feet apart on the same level, typical of Soviet doctrine of the time in which fighters were really airborne missile platforms, controlled from the ground. The 'bogeys' were now 'bandits', that is, they had been positively identified as hostile.

The two formations closed on each other rapidly. At five hundred yards Kleeman started a left-hand turn away from the Fitters, while keeping them in sight all the time, intending to reverse the turn and swing in behind them, an internationally recognised manoeuvre initiating the process of escorting them out of a Restricted Area, but also a good firing position. At about 300 yards distance, the lead Fitter fired an AA-2 'Atoll' heat-seeking, air-to-air missile head on at Musczynski. It was a very poor firing position for a 'heater', and it missed. Having lost their chance, the Libyan pilots tried to escape. They split up, the leader climbing to his right, above Musczynski, the wingman also breaking right, above Kleeman, and climbing towards the sun. As the Fitters shot overhead, the American pilots tightened their left-hand turn, rolling out after 180 degrees, putting them right behind and below the Fitters. The Americans had huge reserves of power, were fighting as a team and were perfectly positioned, while the Libyans, having split up and lost all coherence as a fighting unit, were flying away, apparently without a plan other than to try and get away.

Musczynski fired an AIM-9L Sidewinder missile at the leader. The Sidewinder is also a 'heater' but built to a far superior standard than the Soviet Atoll. As it left the rail he reported, 'Fox Two,' the NATO code indicating to his leader and to the *Nimitz* that he had fired a heat-seeking missile. (The code 'Fox One' would have indicated using a longer-range, radar guided missile, and 'Fox Three' would have indicated that the combat was even closer, using guns.) Musczynski's missile ran true, hit its target in the tailpipe and the Fitter exploded, leaving no time for the pilot to eject.

As Kleeman rolled out of the turn, the second Fitter was right in front but high, against the sun, a bad firing position for a Sidewinder whose infrared (IR) sensor might have been confused by the sun's heat. Kleeman waited a full ten seconds until the Libyan wingman had cleared the sun and was against blue sky, then he fired a 'winder.

'Fox Two,' he reported, then it hit, too. This time the Fitter did not explode for five seconds, giving the pilot time to eject.

'Splash two Fitters,' was the next report, giving the Task Force the good news.

The whole incident lasted less than a minute, and the outcome was a foregone conclusion, the result of a hopeless mismatch of aircraft and pilots. The Fitter, an ageing, single-seat, ground-attack fighter was at a chronic disadvantage against the Tomcat, a state-of-the-art, two-seat fighter, and that was without making any allowance for the huge differences in the backgrounds, training, culture and experience of the pilots.

Kleeman, Venlet, Musczynski and Anderson gave a press conference to describe their victory. The authority of their slow, precise and unemotional descriptions of the split-second decisions and instinctive reactions which had won the engagement were a classic example of the controlled aggression and understated self-confidence which is the hallmark of the modern fighter pilot. They were potent symbols of excellence, living vindications of the prowess and superiority of American fighter pilots. In their crisp white uniforms, with their youth, restrained energy and quiet professionalism they projected, as they were intended to, a reminder of the proficiency of American military power, especially air power.

The 'Gulf of Sirte Incident', as the dogfight became known, was a brief, hot moment during the Cold War, a small but classic battle in the history of fighting for command of the air and a clear demonstration of how to do it – boldly, skilfully, decisively and ruthlessly. It made headline news around the world, the first kill to a new generation of American fighters and the first time that American pilots had shot down a hostile aircraft since the Vietnam War a decade previously. It was a vivid example of modern aerial combat, while also illustrating its timeless qualities – the value of the latest technology, the advantage of flexible tactics and, above all, the decisive value of high-calibre pilots with the individual initiative to maximise any advantage to the full. It underscored the ancient axiom about warfare that the only thing more expensive than investing in the best people and the best equipment is settling for second best. Winning is about accepting that there is no such thing as second best.

October, 1997

INTRODUCTION

Kleeman and Musczynski were among the best fighter pilots in the world. Both had graduated from the US Navy's Fighter Weapons School at Miramar Naval Air Station near San Diego, California, better known by the sobriquet 'Top Gun'. The existence of Top Gun is a reminder of the simple rule that success in air warfare, to be able to fight for and maintain air superiority, is founded not only on the latest and most advanced fighters, but also on the best fighter pilots.

Top Gun is also a monument to the ability to forget, and relearn, that rule between wars as new, theoretical and usually technology-based ideas about aerial combat gain credibility, promising cheaper, more effective and more predictable alternatives to fighter pilots manoeuvring and killing each other. It was established during the Vietnam War when it became clear that one of the new central ideas of the 1950s, that guided missiles were about to take over and make the dogfight redundant, were shown to be wrong. US fighter pilots had been unable to establish mastery of the skies over North Vietnam and something had to be done about it. In 1968 America still had fighter pilots with experience going back to the Korean War and the Second World War, and they were able to teach combat skills to the next generation, re-establishing the dogfighting mentality and maintaining the unbroken line of experience that is an important factor in preserving fighter-pilot effectiveness.

That heritage is evident on the wall of Hangar One at Miramar where, following Kleeman's and Musczynski's success, small red silhouettes of Su-22s were added to the lines of similar images of MiG-21s shot down by Top Gun graduates in Vietnam.

Top Gun and, today, other courses run by the USAF with other NATO air forces are where dogfighting skills are honed and the experience of one generation of fighter pilots is passed on to the next. If they are ever scrapped it will be a sign that robot warriors are winning the argument. The most recent evidence that those lessons have not been forgotten came in 1991, in the Gulf War, which showed that the qualities needed to fight for air superiority are still there in the cockpit rather than stored in a computer, skills which manifest themselves in many different ways in the jet and computer age but which, in their essentials, date back over eighty years to the skies over France in 1915.

The invention of the aeroplane at the beginning of the twentieth century changed warfare fundamentally. From the stirrup to gunpowder and from rifled gun barrels to steam turbines, new technologies have been levers of change in the way soldiers and sailors fight each other, but the aeroplane changed the nature of warfare itself for ever. Until this century armies and navies protected their rulers, their countries and their populations by standing between them and their enemies.

Aircraft provided the means of leaping over those barriers, bypassing them, to strike directly at the heart of a nation, at its people and its industry. The aircraft of the day were very fragile and could not carry a sufficient weight of bombs to seriously damage a nation's infrastructure, but as early as 1908, just five years after the Wright brothers' first powered flight and a year before Louis Bleriot flew across the English Channel, H. G. Wells wrote in *War in the Air*, 'There is no place where a woman and her daughter can hide and be at peace. The war comes through the air; bombs drop at night. Quiet people go out in the mornings and see air fleets passing overhead – dripping death – dripping death.'

The first military aircraft were not used to bomb women and children but to spy on the enemy, and little thought was given to fighting between aircraft until both sides in the First World War sought to prevent each other's observation aircraft from crossing the trenches. Both sides realised that they would have to fight for control of the skies, just as they did on the ground and at sea. The French were the first to fit machine-guns to their aircraft, but the Germans produced the first pure-bred fighter, the Fokker *Eindecker*, the E.1, which had a forward-firing machine-gun fitted with an interrupter gear so that it could be fired through the propeller. The combination of aircraft, gun and pilot became a single, cohesive fighting machine with the pilot at the heart of the combination, the aircraft and the stream of fire which it produced being an extension of his mind and body which could be aimed at his opponent in a single flowing movement, using the whole aircraft as a weapon. The fighter has grown in size and complexity ever since, but that idea, of the pilot, his aircraft and its armament being a single fighting entity, has remained. In the Second World War the British fighter leader, Sqn Ldr Wilfrid 'Smithy' Duncan Smith, RAF, described his Spitfire as 'an integral part and an extension of [his] own sensitivity' and he told the fighter pilots under his command, 'You don't just strap yourselves in, you buckle the Spitfire on like girding on armour.'

In the same war Lt Jack Broughton, USAAF, flew the P-47 Thunderbolt, known to its pilots as 'the Jug' and the largest single-engined, propeller-driven aircraft ever to fly, weighing over 9 tons. He later flew F-80 Shooting Stars in Korea and he made his name as a wing commander and fighter leader in Vietnam, flying the largest single-seat jet fighter, the 24-ton Republic F-105 Thunderchief, or 'Thud' to its pilots. In his book, *Thud Ridge*, this pithy, fighter pilot's narrative expresses the same idea, without even thinking about it, 'The first time I strapped a Jug to me, I thought it was the biggest thing I had ever seen...'

At dawn on 1 August 1915 two British aircraft attacked the German airfield at Douai. Two E.1 pilots, Lieutenants Max Immelmann and Oswald Boelke, raced for their machines to intercept them. They climbed above the two Royal Flying Corps biplanes, then dived on them. Boelke's gun jammed and he landed to get it fixed, but Immelmann followed the attack through, firing all the way, breaking away only at the last moment. He converted his speed back into height by climbing again, then dived once more, a favourite tactic which was later named after him – the Immelmann Turn. Once again he fired from above and behind one of the British aircraft, which then went into a shallow glide and landed heavily in a field. Three weeks later Boelke shot down his first RFC machine, and a few days after that a pair of E.1s from Douai shot down an entire flight of nine French bombers.

In the weeks that followed, the idea of the fighter, combined with the aggression, enthusiasm, skill and understanding of air warfare of men like Immelmann and Boelke, gave the German Air

Service superiority over that section of the Western Front. They were the first real fighter pilots, and Boelke, in particular, came to be regarded later as the true architect of the principles of aerial combat. The German High Command had deployed the *Eindeckers* in penny numbers, a couple of aircraft attached to each *Staffel*, or squadron, to provide close protection for the reconnaissance aircraft. Boelke suggested a different approach, based on principles which he had developed on the job. He brought the fighters together in specialised fighter squadrons, *Jagdstaffeln*, literally hunting squadrons, whose job was to range over a particular area, like hunters, giving the leader the freedom to act on his own initiative, seek out the enemy and bring the combined fire power of the squadron to bear on him. He realised that the action would then split up into individual dogfights, but the effect of a surprise first pass, firing all the way, was also psychologically advantageous, putting the enemy on the back foot. He wanted to control the airspace by aggressive patrolling while the German reconnaissance aircraft did their work protected by his lethal shield.

Boelke had rare gifts of leadership and he also understood the dynamics of running a small fighting unit. In the *Jagdstaffeln*, he created a community of kindred spirits, a fraternity with its own, very particular *esprit de corps*, born of a shared experience and understanding of what they were doing – men who lived and breathed combat tactics and thrived in an exclusive, superior, competitive, fighting élite, making them personally all the keener to win in combat. Boelke's *Jagdstaffeln* were formidable, superior to anything the allies had, and French and British losses mounted in the autumn of 1915, a period known as 'the Fokker Scourge'.

German superiority was neutralised by the introduction of new French and British fighters, and in 1916 the first massed air battles took place above the battlefields of Verdun and the Somme, and with them the culture of fighter pilots as a warrior élite took shape. The advantage swung back and forth between the two sides as each introduced new fighters and pilots learnt the basic rules of air combat. Those who survived battle did so because they learned the rules on the job. They passed on what they could to newcomers, and the principal architect of air combat doctrine, and of much of its attendant culture, was Oswald Boelke. In the summer of 1916 Boelke issued his pilots with a set of eight basic rules, the first expression of a methodical approach to air fighting. They are known as Boelke's Dicta and they have, in modified form, been passed down the generations of fighter pilots ever since.

1. Secure all possible advantages before attacking.

One of the biggest advantages in aerial combat, as in most aspects of warfare, is surprise. The idea of the fighter pilot as a 'knight of the air', a heroic, chivalrous figure, facing his enemy in a duel, is nonsense. The successful fighter pilot's favourite tactic is to sneak up on his adversary from behind and shoot him in the back before he knows about it. Eighty years later little has changed: four out of five pilots who are shot down never see their attacker. Coming out of the sun, or cloud, so the enemy can't see you gives a huge advantage, and fighter pilots have always used the sun to help their attack. As recently as 1982, over Lebanon, the Israeli Air Force timed some attacks so that they could come out of the sun. An awareness of the elements, especially the wind, can lead to advantage. In the First World War the Germans were at a permanent advantage because the prevailing wind was from the southwest, blowing from the allied lines towards their lines. If they ventured over the allied lines the wind gave them an advantage on the way back to base, while the reverse was true for allied pilots. Fighter pilots use height to gain advantage: height is stored energy which can be converted to speed, which can then be used to manoeuvre to advantage. Over the years Boelke's Dicta have been given a more modern interpretation and at Top Gun his first dictum has become, 'First look, first shot, first kill' and 'Lose height, lose the fight'.

2. Always carry through an attack once you have started it.

Aerial combat is essentially an aggressive business and showing determination to fight gives a vital moral advantage. Breaking off an attack hands the moral advantage to your opponent and it will achieve nothing in any case because if you do break off and try to escape, your target will become your attacker very quickly.

3. Fire only at close range, when your opponent is properly in your sights.

When two aircraft are both travelling fast in three dimensions, hitting your opponent is difficult enough; with evasive tactics, it becomes even more difficult. To hit his opponent, the attacker has to allow for deflection, he has to lead for the time taken for his bullets to reach their target and if his aircraft is turning or side-slipping then that motion is imparted to the bullets as they leave the muzzle of the gun. Gravity also acts on the bullets as soon as they are fired. Some of these problems can be overcome by devices such as setting the gun sights deliberately high to allow for gravity but, even allowing for a perfectly judged shot along the line of sight, the bullets will still not go where they were aimed. With all these variables, the closer you were to your opponent the better, and in the First World War the best range was about twenty yards. James McCudden, one of the RFC's best tactical fighter pilots, also stressed the value of closeness when he was a fighting instructor. In action he sometimes came back to base with gruesome evidence of how close that could be, with the front of his aircraft covered in a thin film of blood. His CO would congratulate him on getting so close.

As fighter speeds have grown and armament has moved from guns to guided missiles, especially the new, long-range 'fire and forget' missiles, such as AIM-120 Advanced Medium-Range Anti Aircraft Missile (AMRAAM), so this dictum has changed. Once locked on, the missile finds its own way to the target using radar and the advantage now lies with the attacker who can fire first at maximum range, often Beyond Visual Range (BVR).

4. Keep your eye on your opponent and never let yourself be deceived by ruses.
Boelke often used what he called ruses, such as feigning battle damage and flying towards his own lines, all the time getting into the best position he could and then suddenly turning on his pursuer. Firing at too long a range was another, tempting the victim into taking evasive action, thereby closing the distance between them and letting the attacker get closer to the victim. Another ruse was to put a single aircraft in an obvious and tempting position as a decoy with a whole squadron high above, usually up sun, ready to pounce.

5. Always assail your opponent from behind.

No matter how good a pilot's lookout, dead astern is always a blind spot so the attacker has all the advantages of surprise. The rear shot also has the advantage of minimum deflection and maximum time to aim properly. It also gives the target the most problems in turning the tables since he cannot fire back until he has manoeuvred to gain some advantage.

Boelke had started his career in a two-seater, the LVG, in which the pilot flew the aircraft and concentrated on the task in hand, while the observer/gunner kept a lookout for hostile aircraft. In a single-seater, while it was superb for attacking the enemy, he found that he could not keep as good a lookout while concentrating on the attack. His solution was to fly in pairs, a leader and a wingman to guard his tail and keep a lookout. Having a wingman to cover your tail, and covering his when necessary, has been fundamental to aerial combat ever since, with variations in the distance between the two aircraft. Boelke, though he would have marvelled at the technology of the F-14 Tomcat, would have understood the 'two ship', 'Loose Deuce' dynamics of the formation which Kleeman and Musczynski flew against the Libyans.

Even allowing for all the differences between the Libyan MiGs and their US Navy opponents, the Fitter pilots put themselves at a hopeless disadvantage from the start by shooting from the head-on position with a missile which had to use a heat source, the hot area around the jet efflux, to home on to its target. It also gave the American pilots maximum opportunity to evade the missiles and put them behind. In modern fighter-pilot jargon, which uses the clock-face system of giving positions in the air with your aircraft at the centre, the short, sharp way of expressing this rule has become 'Check Six'.

6. If your opponent dives on you, do not try to escape but fly to meet it.

Showing aggression gives a moral advantage, but flying to meet any threat is good fighting tactics. Even if your turn is not completed, at least you present the most difficult target, i.e., maximum deflection. From above, your attacker has the advantage of speed, but if you complete the turn and meet him head-on then the closing speed increases and your attacker will have less time to get his shot in. The shot is in any case more difficult because it has become a head-on shot, and once you are past each other you can manoeuvre to best advantage.

7. Never forget your line of retreat.
This rule is more than simply making sure you can get home after the battle, important as that is. It encompasses the idea of spatial awareness, of having an understanding of all the forces that act on shaping the battle – the relative size and technical sophistication of the two formations, the fuel state, the wind, the cloud, the effect of altitude on the relative performance of your aircraft and your opponents' and the position of enemy ground defences.

8. Whenever possible attack in formations of four or six and when the fight breaks up take care that several do not go for the same opponent.
Attacking in large numbers inflicts maximum damage on the first pass, but once that is over, the fight will break up into individual dogfights. If two go for the same target, effort is wasted, not all enemy aircraft will come under attack and there is the danger of collision as two aircraft go for the same firing position. This rule also emphasises the importance of the high level of awareness each pilot has to have of the whole of the battle, what today is called the 'big picture'.

On 28 October 1916, while engaging in a dogfight with twelve of his squadron, Boelke fell victim to getting on the wrong side of one of his own dicta when, in the mêlée, he collided with Erwin Boehme and crashed and was killed. His dicta lived on in the squadron and by the end of 1916 its pilots had shot down 211 for the loss of 39 aircraft.

Boelke's place at the helm of the German fighter arm was taken by one of his own pupils, Manfred von Richthofen. Leadership of a fighter squadron calls for very particular qualities, all the aggression, awareness, individualism and coolness needed to do the job while at the same time being able to make the other pilots on the squadron, who have the same qualities, act as one when they need to. Richthofen had those qualities in abundance. When he took over his first squadron, Jasta 11, it had been in existence as long as Boelke's Jasta 2 but had only one enemy aircraft to its credit, and that was unconfirmed. On the day Richthofen took over, to demonstrate his own prowess, he went out alone and doubled the squadron's score by shooting down an allied machine. Within days the pilots were shooting down allied aircraft, and the only reason was Richthofen's leadership. Jasta 11 became one of the most effective squadrons on the front, the basis of Richthofen's famous 'Flying Circus'. The whole squadron revolved around him, around his personality and charisma, which developed into a personal mystique which survives today.

There are many examples of the importance of strong, aggressive leadership in making a fighter squadron effective. In the Second World War the legless fighter pilot, Sqn Ldr Douglas Bader, RAF, took command of 242 Squadron, which had been badly led in France and the CO left behind, drunk. When it flew back to Britain it had been every man for himself, and it arrived demoralised. Bader, who exemplified the aggressive qualities of the fighter pilot and fighter leader, transmitted them to the men under his command by personal example, flying a dangerous and impromptu routine of low-level aerobatics in front of them on his arrival simply to prove he was not a cripple. He then weeded out those whom he did not feel had the right stuff to be fighter pilots in war, and enthused the rest with his own views of tactics at every opportunity. He had 242 back in shape in weeks and it served with distinction in the Battle of Britain.

In parallel with the tradition of reliance on strong leadership and fighting as a team in aerial combat, there is also the tradition of the ace, the idea of a single individual who is right at the top of the tree. Richthofen was not only a leader, he was the highest-scoring fighter pilot on any side in the war – an ace. He is still a legend eighty years later as a fighter pilot and as a leader, and the two are indivisible – to lead, the leader has to be the best, an individual.

The First World War was waged by faceless masses on the ground where there was little room for individual achievement. Fighter pilots represented both individual skill and military success; they stood for quality over quantity. In the grim reality of industrialised warfare and mass slaughter which characterised that war, when people were far less restrained about celebrating military success and saw the human virtues which achieved it as positive, the fighter pilot stood out as a rather obvious heroic figure, something tangible in the way of success which soldiers on the ground, as well as civilians, could understand.

The generals needed successes which could be reported in the newspapers, and fighter pilots on both sides quickly became highly visible, national champions in a nationalistic age. An aura rose up around them, a new embodiment of the supreme warrior, a chivalrous 'knight of the air', the antithesis of the experience of the trenches. They were singled out as special and invested with glory of which the men on the ground could only dream. Pilots of observation aircraft, whose job was more dangerous and often provided valuable intelligence, could never match the way the fighter pilot captured the public imagination.

It was not just the publicity. One of the lasting themes in the history of aerial combat is that a small number of individual fighter pilots have stood out from the rest, in all wars. In the First World War 5% of fighter pilots accounted for over half the aerial victories, and in the Second World War 5% accounted for 40% of all victories. Inevitably the aces drew most attention and the idea of deliberately singling out the super-successful fighter pilot as a public symbol of martial prowess was first used by the French, who not only decorated their top fighter pilots with medals but singled them out with the sobriquet 'ace'.

The first was Eugene Gilbert, who shot down his first German on 1 January 1915 and by the summer had shot down a total of five before being shot down and killed himself: five became the threshold. Newspapers encouraged the idea, following the aces' exploits daily and giving their scores in little boxes. Men like Georges Guynemer, Charles Nungesser and René Fonck quickly took on huge public status, superstars on a par with the rock stars, top entertainers, supermodels and sportsmen of today.

Germany picked out its top scorers for particular attention too but the German High Command demanded ten victories, each one confirmed by a wreck on the ground, for which the pilot was given the informal title 'Oberkanone', literally Top Gun. Oberkanone were automatically awarded Germany's highest military honour, the *Pour le Mérite*, an exquisite, blue-enamelled medal worn round the neck and nicknamed the 'Blue Max', now part of the legend and folklore of aerial combat. Max Immelmann and Oswald Boelke were the first two pilots to be awarded the *Pour le Mérite* and Immelmann went on to be put on display in Berlin with his aircraft beside him, attracting huge crowds. Boelke was only twenty-three but his status grew and grew. One German general let it be known that he thought that the name Boelke was worth three infantry divisions. (It would be interesting to know what that did for the individual infantry soldier's moral, bearing in mind a German division of the time was 10,000 men.)

The myth became bigger than the pilot: the German High Command decided that Boelke was so valuable as a symbol of fighting prowess that he was too valuable to lose, and consequently too valuable to fight, and he was taken out of frontline service. He was personally outraged by the decision and phoned the Kaiser to remonstrate, but the Kaiser was adamant and Boelke did spend some time in 1916 touring the Eastern Front before eventually finding his way back into the air over France.

Britain deprecated the system of singling out individuals. For a time, Lt Albert Ball, RFC, aged twenty and a moody loner, was the leading scorer in the war, ahead of Boelke, but his name rarely appeared in newspapers until his death and then it was in a much more restrained way. He was a legend inside the RFC, as were James McCudden whose tally was 54 and 'Mick' Mannock, the highest-scoring British pilot. Nineteen British fighter pilots were awarded the VC, including Mannock, McCudden and Ball, and by the end of the war, using the five-kills yardstick, the British had by far the largest number of aces, but most were virtually unknown – 784, to Germany's 363, France's 158 and the United States' 110.

The man who, more than any other, symbolised the idea of the ace and the public accolade that went with it was Richthofen. His death in combat was treated as a national disaster, though it only enhanced the legend: his crashed aircraft was stripped by souvenir-hunters; free passage was granted to German aircraft to fly over the lines unmolested to drop wreaths; a fresh uniform was delivered to put on his body and he virtually lay in state, surrounded by laurel leaves and branches of immortelle, for three days before being transported to a church and buried, by his enemies, with elaborate military honours.

Whatever the view about the disparity between the treatment received by the top aces, there is no doubt that they were, in a very narrow sense, very special people. They were able, at a glance, to read a situation in the air – taking in the nature and height of cloud, the strength of wind, the position of sun, the speed, height and direction of any aircraft in the sky, whether they were friendly, likely direction of threats, the angle and height from which they would come, the relative performance of aircraft, likely trajectories of enemy fire – endlessly computing it all as it changed, while deftly finding the best position from which to make an attack. Today we call it situational awareness, and, with a huge amount of information being fed into the cockpit by data links, radar and voice communication, having a mind capable of building up a clear picture of a changing situation from scraps of information is still a vital part of the fighter pilot's mental equipment.

The qualities have remained very much the same since – courage, while clearly born in people, also comes from having honed their skills to perfection, feeling and being in control, giving a sense of being on top, infallible, somebody completely at home in combat, actually enjoying it, killers rather than superb pilots. Aces are winners, pilots who rarely, if ever, came off worst in a fight. Many of them were hit only seldom by enemy fire in fights while others quite close to them were riddled. It was a mixture of instinct, experience and luck in the early stages. If a new pilot came up against an expert on his first day he had to be exceptional, or well protected by others, to survive, and the rule on the squadrons was that the value of a fighter pilot doubled for every week he stayed alive. That is the culture which Boelke, Richthofen, Guynemer, Fonck, Nungesser, Ball, McCudden, Mannock and Rickenbacker created and passed down: no mistakes, no doubts, no fear, on top, simply the best.

After the First World War, many of the lessons of the Western Front were slowly forgotten. In 1927, the Italian General Douhet argued that aircraft had changed warfare to the extent that armies and navies would have no time to engage before aircraft would have won the war, that air power, namely bombers, alone could win wars. The emphasis shifted from fighters to bombers. Instead of using aircraft to fight for control over a battlefield, the idea of creating a third, separate force in warfare, distinct from armies and navies, gained ground. It had been made flesh when Britain created a separate air force on 1 April 1918 – the Royal Air Force, the world's first independent air force. The idea took hold in the two greatest powers, Britain and America, and in the process, the focus shifted further from the fighter to the bomber. In Douhet's mind, the offensive centrepiece was a giant machine, literally a 'flying fortress', the aerial version of the tank or the battleship, bristling with guns and carrying bombs, flying in tight formation for protection against any purely defensive fighters. The value of the fighter was downgraded, and as the speeds of fighters rose, so many air power theorists believed that aerial combat between fighters would be impossible; the RAF saw fighters as bomber killers only and evolved superbly choreographed standard forms of attack, giving each fighter pilot a place in the queue to line up behind the bombers for his turn to shoot. The idea that air superiority, fought for by fighters, would have to be achieved first, or that bombers would need fighter escorts, virtually disappeared.

It took the experience of real war to change perceptions. In 1939 neither side was prepared to unleash its bombers against the heart of nations for fear of similar retaliation. The bomber fleets were sent not against industry and the population but against military targets. On 29 September 1939 RAF Hampdens flew to Wilhelmshaven to bomb the German Navy in port; they had no escorting fighters. The first wave alerted the defences and failed to hit any of their targets. When the second wave of five aircraft arrived, fast, short-range, defensive fighters, Messerschmidt Bf 109s, were waiting and they shot down all five Hampdens. On 19 December 1939 22 Wellingtons went back to Wilhelmshaven in perfect weather: the Bf 109s shot down 10 of them and damaged all the others, 2 of them so severely that they crashed on landing. The fighter was a superb bomber killer, but the antidote was not to arm and armour the bomber but to have other fighters to hunt and kill the defending fighters, to fight for air superiority. Since all Britain had were short-range defensive fighters, escorting the bombers was impossible.

In May 1940 the German army swept through Europe, supported by 2,400 conventional bombers, dive bombers, recce aircraft and transports which played a huge part in the success of Blitzkrieg. They did so under an umbrella of nearly 1,500 fighters which made short shrift of the Polish, Danish, Dutch, Belgian, French and the small number of RAF fighters Britain sent to France. To invade Britain, the Germans had to have air superiority first. The stage was set for the Battle of Britain, a strategic battle of survival on the scale of Trafalgar, a battle for control of the skies over southern Britain. Without that control the Germans could not bomb RAF airfields or British cities in daylight, nor could they invade Britain.

The Battle of Britain remains the greatest battle for air superiority ever fought. The first targets for the German bombers were the RAF's airfields, hitting aircraft on the ground. The main targets for the RAF fighters were the German bombers, but to get at them the fighters pilots had to fight their way past the escorting Bf 109 fighters. The 109 pilots had to protect the bombers and break the resistance of RAF Fighter Command. For the first time the Luftwaffe was up against defensive fighters of similar capability, the Hurricane and the Spitfire, flown by pilots with less experience than their German counterparts but fighting close to their airfields and with the aid of radar. The battle lasted two months. The Bf 109 could escort the He 111, Do 17 and Stuka across southern England, but they were operating at the limit of their range and they could not reach London. Away from their fighter protection, the German bomber crews were as vulnerable as the RAF had been over Wilhelmshaven. Losses became unacceptably high and the Luftwaffe essentially had to give up or be slowly cut to pieces over Kent and Sussex.

The RAF won, but by a tiny margin: the Spitfire and the Bf 109 were both superb defensive fighters, with only marginal differences in top speed and rate of turn; the RAF had the advantage of fighting close to their bases and of having radar to tell them from what direction the German attacks were coming. The Luftwaffe had the advantage of numbers, around 1,500 fighters to the RAF's 700, but they were at the limit of their range and Luftwaffe pilots had recent experience of aerial combat in the Spanish Civil War. The RAF fighter pilots rediscovered the importance of dogfighting and learned from the Luftwaffe's more flexible tactics; the Luftwaffe, fresh from victory in Poland, the Low Countries and France, learned that, despite its size, a smaller, well-equipped, skilled and determined opponent could deny it command of the air. Both sides learned that the primary role of fighters was fighting for command of the air, and that without it other air, ground and sea operations on any scale were very hazardous. The basics of air warfare, that control of the skies had to be fought for, laid down in 1915 and 1916, had been relearned.

When Germany invaded the Soviet Union on the Eastern Front in 1941, the Luftwaffe spearheaded that attack too. It was a battle of quality versus quantity. The Soviet Il-2 Schturmovik ground attack fighter was produced in huge numbers, 36,000 in total, and it still holds the record for the aircraft produced in greater numbers than any other, testimony to the Soviet doctrine of putting quantity before quality. The Soviet Air Force was huge, around 15,000 aircraft, half of it deployed opposite the Germans, but it was not as technically advanced as the Luftwaffe, nor as well trained. On the first day of the attack the Germans destroyed 1,489 aircraft on the ground and a further 322 in aerial combat for the loss of two. By the end of the first week the Luftwaffe's score stood at 4,990, a third of the Soviet Air Force, for a total of 179 losses. Experience counted for a great deal and individual Luftwaffe fighter pilots collected huge tallies. The Russian policy of having huge numbers of what were second-rate fighters proved costly.

The Germans failed to reach Moscow and for two years the massive front soaked up men and materials. The Russians held the Germans at bay at Kursk where they had a large salient which the Germans planned to attack on 5 July 1943, using 800 bombers against the Soviet tank forces, escorted by 300 fighters. The Russians planned a pre-dawn strike, hitting the Luftwaffe on its airfields with a huge force of ground attack fighters and bombers. The Germans had mobile radar systems which detected the Russian aircraft in plenty of time. It was what has become known as 'a target-rich environment' for the skilled Luftwaffe fighter pilots, who shot down 120 Russians in the first encounter, a figure which reached 430 by the end of the day, with over 200 more the following day, all for virtually no loss.

From that point on the tide on the Eastern Front turned. The Luftwaffe had to withdraw many of its best units to protect its armies now facing the Allies in Italy and the bomber raids on its homeland. By 1944 it was too thinly stretched and the huge Soviet numerical advantage began to have its effect.

When the Americans came into the war in Europe in 1942, they started flying over Germany unescorted in daylight and suffered heavy losses. The tables began to turn only when the big American fighters, the P-38 Lightning, P-47 Thunderbolt and the incomparable P-51 Mustang, became available with the endurance to fight the Luftwaffe for control of the skies over Germany, opening the way for the bombers to do their work. When Göring, a veteran of Richthofen's Flying Circus, saw Mustangs protecting daylight bombers over Berlin, he realised the implications, and he is said to have remarked that he knew the war was over. The closing stages of the Second World War represented the high tide of the propeller fighter. The basic lessons, forgotten in the 1920s and 1930s, were relearned in the summer of 1940 and put into practice for the rest of the war. The fighter pilot ace re-emerged: between 1939 and 1945, on all fronts, including the Eastern Front, 1% of operational fighter pilots on all sides shot down 46% of all aircraft lost in aerial combat; in the West, 5% of pilots made 40% of kills. The value of the highly capable fighter with a highly motivated and well-trained pilot was once again recognised.

In an age, in the West at least, where military experience is limited to professionals and it has become fashionable to reject military values, the ruthless, élitist value system of the fighter pilot, which has been passed down through generations of fighter pilots from another age, is out of kilter with the populism of the 1990s. It survives because it is an essential part of winning in battle, and successful fighter pilots in the West remain highly visible heroes, masters of new technology, individualistic and talented star performers. Western air forces select their fighter pilots for competitiveness, aggressiveness, cunning, mental agility and an indefinable 'press on regardless' spirit of determination. An aspiring fighter pilot has to submit himself to years of ruthless selection, much of it at the hands of experienced fighter pilots who weed out those individuals whom they regard as not possessing that elusive combination of qualities which make up the famous *Right Stuff*. Being equal to an opponent is no good in a fighter pilot. He has to be the best and he has to believe he is the best, feel superior, be a winner – and winners, by definition, belong in élites. It may be that the manned fighter will disappear some time in the next century, just as knights on horseback did, but it would be a mistake to break the traditions of the manned fighter élites until that future is sure.

Once that culture is destroyed, breaking the link with 1915 and Boelke, McCudden, Richthofen and Mannock, it will be impossible to replace.

CHAPTER ONE

Born in Battle

The Second World War neatly divides the history of military aviation into two ages: the propeller age and the jet age. One fighter pilot whose career started in the propeller age but whose name, more than any other, is linked to the jet age is Brigadier General Charles 'Chuck' Yeager, USAF. He epitomises the timeless and modern qualities of the fighter pilot – individuality, awareness, a flexible mind, a press-on spirit, boiling aggression combined with cool-headedness and a longing to fight tempered with instinctive prudence. For years, Yeager was best known as a test pilot, the first man to fly faster than sound, and although he was well known inside the world of experimental aviation his name meant little to anybody outside the jet fighter fraternity. Today he is part of popular culture, the inspiration for Tom Wolf's book and the film *The Right Stuff* which was a celebration of the cult of the individualism and sheer guts of the fighter test pilots who became the first astronauts.

Yeager learnt his trade and made his name as a fighter pilot flying the P-51D Mustang, the last of the great propeller-driven fighters. As a young man of twenty-one he came to England in 1942 to fly daylight escort missions for USAAF B-17 and B-24 bombers from their bases in East Anglia at the height of the Allied bombing offensive against Germany. On 5 March 1944 he was shot down over France. Ever defiant and resourceful, and eager to get back to the air battle, he evaded capture and escaped through Spain. Back at base, he was told that it was standard practice, for security reasons, for evaders to be sent home to the USA. For Yeager combat in the Mustang was the ultimate experience, the ultimate high. That was what he had been put on Earth for, to fight in an aeroplane, and, as a sergeant, he appealed directly to the Supreme Allied Commander, General Dwight Eisenhower, to be allowed to stay. Ike recognised his natural aggression and made an exception.

Yeager repaid Ike on 12 October 1944 by shooting down five German fighters in a single dogfight to become that rarity, even among aces, an 'ace in a day'. His squadron only accounted for eight in the whole engagement. Yeager put his success down to what he called 'combat vision', the ability to focus at high altitude where there is little to focus on long before others did, pick out his targets and plan his attack.

His first encounter with a jet fighter was in the air. Three weeks after becoming an ace in a day, on 6 November 1944, he was leading a flight of four Mustangs home after escorting bombers to Essen. Just north of the city, flying at 8,000 feet above broken cloud, he spotted a flight of three German Me 262 Schwalbe jet fighters below, their speed and swept-back wings making them unmistakable. He dived the flight straight at them at full throttle, but as the Mustangs closed on the German jets the Luftwaffe pilots simply opened their throttles wide and sped away, obeying their standing orders which were to avoid dogfights. They were needed to attack bombers, not to indulge in jousting with Allied fighters, and although they were much faster than the Mustang, the propeller fighter was much more nimble, and in a close, turning fight the jets were at a disadvantage. Yeager and his flight were doing 450 m.p.h. when the German pilots spotted them and used their 100 m.p.h. speed advantage to leave the Mustangs standing. Yeager fired just as they were disappearing from view, and when his gun camera footage was developed, it showed he had hit the leader.

Yeager had lost touch with the rest of his flight in the mêlée so he climbed back to 8,000 feet but there was no sign of them so he headed north, expecting to find them over the North Sea.

Then, through the clouds, he spotted a German airfield with long runways. The wind was from the north so Yeager scanned the southern approach to the main runway where aircraft would be approaching to land into the wind. What he saw was a red-blooded Mustang pilot's dream: lining up with the runway, 500 feet above the ground, its wheels and flaps down, flying at about 200 m.p.h. and preparing to land, was an Me 262 jet, probably one of those he had shot at earlier.

For once Yeager had a potential speed advantage over the jet, and he immediately went into a 'split-S', rolling the Mustang on to its back and pulling through into a near vertical dive, converting his height into energy in a perfectly judged, steep, turning dive at full throttle. He pulled out low, at 200 feet and around 500 m.p.h., slightly above and behind the Me 262 and closed fast, in a perfect firing position. At 400 yards he opened fire with barely enough time for a three-second burst from the Mustang's six machine-guns. He just had time to see strikes hitting the jet's wings before he passed overhead. Seconds later Yeager was over the middle of the German airfield, just above the ground, in a hail of flak from what seemed like every anti-aircraft gun on the airfield. He pulled up hard, converting his speed back into height, zoom-climbing almost vertically back to 8,000 feet amongst the clouds. Looking back in the climb, he saw the Me 262 crash-land just short of the runway. Allied fighter pilots called it 'rat catching', deliberately seeking out German jets when they were landing or taking off, the one moment when the Luftwaffe jet pilots could not use their speed advantage. He stuck to most of Boelke's Dicta: find some advantage; attack from above; always follow through; get close before firing, and work out how to escape.

Yeager's Mustang was arguably the finest all-round single-engined, propeller-driven air superiority fighter in the world in 1944, with a level speed of 437 m.p.h., a ceiling of 41,900 feet and a range of 1,100 miles with drop tanks. It was a pure fighter, the last in the line that stretched back to the Fokker Eindecker. His opponent was the first in a new generation, the jet fighter – 100 m.p.h. faster, a comparable ceiling but half the range and less manoeuvrable. They marked the midpoint in the history of the fighter: the Mustang, the last of the great propeller fighters; the Me 262, the first of the coming jet age.

Energy, as Yeager's fight showed, is the lifeblood of the dogfight: speed can be converted into height and height can be converted quickly back into speed. Giving the fighter pilot more speed than the enemy was, until halfway through the jet age, one of the two central features in fighter design, the other being a low wing loading which makes the fighter more manoeuvrable, able to turn tighter. In the late 1920s and early 1930s, the fastest aircraft in the world were not fighters, but racing seaplanes built specially for the Schneider Cup. The RAF formed a High Speed Flight for the contest and its pilots won the trophy three times in a row in 1927/29/31, flying highly specialised Supermarine seaplanes designed by R. J. Mitchell around a series of Rolls-Royce R engines. The races were abandoned after Britain won them three years in a row, but in the process they had pushed speeds much higher and they made a huge contribution to fighter design. In 1921 the race was won at 117 m.p.h.; in 1931 it was won at 340 m.p.h., and after winning the trophy in 1931 Flt Lt G. H. Stainforth went for the world speed record and broke it at 406.94 m.p.h. By comparison, the first 200 m.p.h. fighter to enter RAF service was the Hawker Fury, also in 1931, a biplane with a top speed of 207 m.p.h.

The Schneider Cup races brought about a revolution in fighter design and all the major countries built monoplane fighters with enclosed cockpits and retractable undercarriages designed for speed. Supermarine used the Schneider Cup racers as the basis for R. J. Mitchell's finest creation, the Spitfire. Rolls Royce developed the R engine into the Merlin, the most advanced, slimline and successful piston aero engine ever built. The new fighters came into service between 1935 and 1937 with speeds well over 300 m.p.h., the fastest being the Spitfire and the Messerschmidt Bf 109 at over 350 m.p.h. Messerschmidt built what it described as a Bf 109R in which its test pilot, Fritz Wendel, set a new speed record on 469 m.p.h. in 1939; in fact, it was a pure speed machine and it was linked to the fighter for reasons of propaganda.

The quantum leap in speed which the new fighters represented led many people to believe that the absolute maximum speed had been reached, and that absolute was the speed of sound. We now know that as an aircraft moves through the air it sends a shock wave ahead of itself, like the bow wave which builds up in front of a ship going through the water. As it approaches the speed of sound the aircraft starts to catch up with its own shock waves which build up into a single shock wave perpendicular to the line of flight. At such speeds the forces exerted on the airframe were so brutal they could, and in some cases did, break up aircraft in the air. Flying close to the speed of sound was flying in the unknown aerodynamically, and some pilots pushed their aircraft beyond what they could take, with the result that they suddenly started tumbling through the air, lending even more credibility to the view that supersonic flight was impossible.

Ernst Mach, an Austrian scientist, had established that the speed of sound varies with altitude and air temperature, from 660 m.p.h. at sea level, rising to 700 m.p.h. at 40,000 feet. He devised the idea of measuring speed in relation to the speed of sound and expressing it as a percentage of the speed of sound at a given height and air temperature, a percentage known as the Mach Number after him, the speed of sound being Mach 1.

But even if speeds faster than sound were theoretically possible, another problem was finding the engine power to do it. A British scientist, W. F. Hilton, calculated that to fly faster than sound 30,000 horsepower would be needed, compared with the 2,300 of the R engine which won the last Schneider Cup. Hilton wrote that the figure 'loomed like a barrier' from which the idea of a 'sound barrier' gained popular currency, a physical barrier which could not be exceeded.

For some people the answer was the jet engine or, as it is more properly known, the gas turbine engine, which was, in theory, a much more efficient engine for an aircraft anyway. A piston engine driving a propeller becomes less efficient the faster and higher the aircraft flies, while the jet engine becomes more efficient, using less fuel mixed with the thinner air and getting a greater expansion of that air because it is very much colder at high altitudes. The problem was weight: few people believed that a jet could be produced at a weight which would make it a practical proposition. A jet engine which was light enough and powerful enough would be ideal for a fighter.

The first patent for a jet engine was taken out by a young RAF pilot, Frank Whittle, in 1930. He had set his sights on a machine which could do 500 m.p.h. at 40,000 feet, and set about raising official backing and finance to make such an engine. But the Air Ministry was so lacking in interest that it never even bothered to put the patent on the secret list. After five years without success Whittle let the patents lapse in 1935 because he could not afford the £5 to renew them.

In 1936 he put his RAF career on the line, stepping out of the mainstream to set up Power Jets Ltd, a private company backed by venture capital. He had to operate on a shoestring but by early 1937 he had a prototype, mounted on the back of a truck, which he used to test his theory. The first bench test, on 12 April 1937, nearly ended in disaster when the Whittle Unit, as it was known, ran out of control at over 8,000 r.p.m. even after Whittle had shut off the main fuel valve. The problem was that fuel had collected in the bottom of the combustion chamber which went on burning after the shut-down. It was the first of many problems which had to be overcome on limited funds, and for a long time it seemed that the sceptics might be right.

Whittle was a brilliant engineer and mathematician and persistent to a fault in pursuit of his experiments. What he lacked was the charisma and social background to shift official inertia. He also lacked the finance to do it properly, while struggling against the huge vested interests of Rolls Royce and other aero engine manufacturers, who had huge amounts of capital and reputation bound up in the piston engines, in particular the Merlin. The idea that there was a completely new way to power aircraft just around the corner, one invented, moreover, by a young, rather gauche RAF pilot, was well nigh impossible for them to contemplate. In the late 1930s they were busy re-equipping RAF Fighter Command with Hurricanes and Spitfires, the products of one recent revolution in aircraft design, both of them powered by Rolls Royce's Merlin engine, and a jet engine, even if they thought it was viable, would have been a threat to that investment by making the Merlin redundant. They were not about to see it made obsolete, and government and industry responded in the same way as sailors of sailing ships first responded to steam, or horsemen responded to the internal combustion engine, seeing it as at best an intriguing irrelevance and at worst a threat to an established way of doing things.

In Germany, Willi Messerschmidt's great rival, Ernst Heinkel, who was renowned for innovation, backed his jet engine designer, Dr Hans Joachim Pabst von Ohain, and his assistant, Max Hahn, strictly as a private venture. Ohain took out a patent in 1935 and they began work on 15 April 1936 in great secrecy in a hangar at Heinkel's Marienhe airfield near Rostock. Ohain was better financed than Whittle, and by September 1937, his first engine, the HeS 1, was running on the bench, powered by hydrogen; it was also fairly uncontrollable at first, giving 550 lb (250 kg) of thrust.

While Ohain and Whittle were testing their early prototypes in the late 1930s both the Luftwaffe and RAF Fighter Command had been increased in size in direct response to the build-up of tension in Europe brought about by Adolf Hitler who had announced a huge increase in the size and effectiveness of the Luftwaffe in 1935. Hitler appointed Herman Göring as Minister for Air and he built it up quickly into the largest air force in Europe. In the same year, the German Air Ministry, the Reichsluftfahrtministerium (RLM), was subordinated to the needs of the Luftwaffe and given the task of equipping it. Ernst Udet, a former First World War fighter pilot, who was head of the technical requirements for the Luftwaffe, was mainly interested in the immediate build-up and, although he saw the potential in jet power for the future, the first priority was inevitably propeller-driven fighters such as the Bf 109 and FW 190; by 1939 the Luftwaffe had 1,600 propeller fighters, mainly Bf 109s.

As war loomed from 1938 onwards so official interest in the idea of a jet engine increased and the pace of development quickened in both countries. The RLM was aware of Ohain's work at Heinkel, but its propulsion expert waited until 1938 to put some money into jet propulsion. When it did, it moved on from the Ohain principle, which was based on a centrifugal compressor, the same as Whittle, to the more advanced axial flow type of compressor. Ohain's engine was designated 001, then RLM awarded contracts to BMW for 002 and 003, both very advanced axial flow engines, and to Junkers for a more conservative and less powerful engine, the 004. Heinkel was also engaged to develop an axial flow engine, the 006, and later Daimler-Benz, too, the 007. At the same time RLM awarded a contract to Messerschmidt to build a fighter airframe to take the BMW engine, the idea being to have a prototype flying by December 1939.

Inside Germany there was intense rivalry between Heinkel and Messerschmidt. Heinkel started out in the lead with its own engine and an airframe to take it. The aircraft was the purely experimental He 178. By mid-1939 Ohain had produced the HeS 3b, the first jet engine actually designed to power an aircraft, which had been tested by strapping it to an He 118 prototype dive bomber, and with it Heinkel won the race to get the first jet into the air. On 24 August 1939 the He 178, powered by the HeS 8b engine, made a few hops down the runway at Marienhe with test pilot Erich Warsitz at the controls. Three days later, on 27 August, Warsitz made the first proper flight ever in an aircraft powered by a jet engine, a single circuit of the airfield. The He 178 had a top speed of 435 m.p.h., which was impressive, but it had an endurance of only ten minutes.

The first flight of a jet aircraft went largely unremarked by senior Luftwaffe officers, but that may have been understandable as they had other matters on their collective minds: three days after the He 178's first flight Germany invaded Poland, and the Second World War had started. The first demonstration to the Luftwaffe had to wait until 1 November 1939.

After three years' work, by October 1938, Whittle could show that a viable jet engine was emerging from his research. On 30 June 1939, the Director of Scientific Research at the Air Ministry saw the latest Whittle Unit, the WU.3, run and decided to act. The imminent prospect of war now gave some urgency to the project. The Air Ministry drew up specification E.28/39 for a purely experimental airframe to take Whittle's first jet engine, the W.1. It had to be able to carry a .303 machine-gun plus 2,000 rounds of ammunition, the idea even at that stage being clearly a jet fighter. The specification was issued to the Gloster Aircraft Company on 3 February 1940 and in August, at the height of the Battle of Britain, while work on E.28/39 was under way, another specification, F.9/40, was issued to Gloster for a twin-engined jet fighter.

On 2 April 1941 Heinkel produced the first prototype jet fighter, the twin-engined He 280, which chief test pilot Fritz Schafer flew at Marienhe to become the first jet aircraft, designed from scratch as a fighter, to fly. It had two HeS 8 engines which only produced 500 kg, against a design specification of 700 kg. Heinkel had learned from the He 178 that the tail wheel configuration was wrong because the jet efflux was pointed at the runway, making it difficult to build up speed, and had redesigned the He 280 with a tricycle undercarriage, with one wheel at the front giving better vision, but it could also build up speed more quickly. Realising that escaping from an aircraft at the high speeds involved would also be difficult, the He 280 also had the world's first ejection seat. The characteristics of the jet fighter were taking shape.

On 5 April 1941 a flight was arranged for RLM officials and senior Luftwaffe officers, and it was this flight that convinced them that jet propulsion was a realistic option. On 18 April Fritz Shafer raised the world speed record to 485 m.p.h. in an He 280, but the flight was shrouded in secrecy; a later prototype, He 280, reached 509 m.p.h., putting Heinkel a long way ahead of Messerschmidt.

By April 1941 Messerschmidt had three prototype Me 262s ready but no engine. BMW, whose engines were destined for the Messerschmidt, could not get the engine right. Willi Messerschmidt was eager to make progress but could do nothing, so, while he was waiting for a jet engine, he installed a Junkers piston engine in the Me 262 airframe and on 18 April 1941 Fritz Wendel made the first flight. The Me 262 was originally designed with a tail wheel so it needed no modification to take a propeller.

Five weeks later, on 15 May 1941 at RAF Cranwell, Gloster Chief Test Pilot P. E. G. 'Gerry' Sayer made the first flight in Britain's first jet aircraft, the E.28/39. The flight lasted seventeen minutes. It was twenty-one months after Germany's equivalent, the He 178, had flown.

Just before that flight, in March 1941, General Henry 'Hap' Arnold, Chief of Staff of the USAAF, had heard of the jet and made arrangements for an example of the Whittle engine, the W.1X, to be flown to the USA in October 1941. The engine was given to General Electric to build copies under licence and the Bell Aircraft Corporation was contracted to build the XP-59 Airacomet to take it. The American government and aircraft industry put real energy behind the project and a year later, in October 1942, the Airacomet was flying, long before Britain, which had supplied the engine, had a jet fighter in the air. The Airacomet was a disappointment, capable of only 413 m.p.h., and never went into service.

Messerschmidt finally received the first batch of BMW 003 engines for the Me 262 in November 1941. The original idea had been to have them in the wing roots, but they were too big and had to be slung under each wing instead. The combination was ready in March 1942 but, for safety, it was decided to keep the Jumo piston engine and propeller as well. It was a good decision for no sooner had Wendel cleared the airfield boundary on take-off than the two jet engines flamed out and he had to land on the piston engine alone; later examination showed that several turbine blades had failed in both engines.

The BMW 003 was clearly not up to the job so the design team at Messerschmidt redesigned the Me 262 to take the Junkers 004 which was less powerful but it was ready. Messerschmidt swept the wings back to balance the aircraft with the extra weight. In so doing he discovered one of the keys to high-speed flight, and one of the characteristics of the jet fighter, swept-back wings, which became a closely guarded secret. In fact, the engine was not really ready and was put into service some six months ahead of when it should have been, and there were many problems.

The first flight of Me 262 with jet engines only came on 18 July 1942. The anticipated take-off speed was 112 m.p.h. It was still a 'tail dragger' and the tail had to come up first before take-off, but during taxying trials he found it impossible to get the nose down. The problem was that the jet efflux was hitting the runway because of the nose-up attitude, then bouncing back over the tailplane which would then not respond to Wendel's movement of the control column. Wendel had an idea: touch brakes to get the tail up. It was an incredibly dangerous idea, but it worked and left the ground for a twelve-minute flight of pure delight. For all its design changes and problems, the basic design was superb and handled beautifully.

The development of HeS 8 had not gone well, and by April 1943, there being no other Heinkel engines available, the He 280 was fitted with the Junkers Jumo 004 jet engine instead, giving it an improved top speed of 559 m.p.h., initial rate of climb and service ceiling. It was tested by the Luftwaffe and found to be very fast, up to 530 m.p.h., and superior in mock combat to the FW 190, the Luftwaffe's finest propeller-driven fighter of the day. The downside was that the airframe had been built with fuel tanks based on the predicted performance of the HeS 8, which had not materialised, and with the Jumo 004 the new fighter only had two-thirds of the range. With guns and other fighting equipment added, the range would be even further reduced. To the bitter disappointment of the Heinkel team, the He 280 was passed over in favour of the Messerschmidt Me 262, largely because of the technical problems with the new engine, but there was also a feeling that Messerschmidt, who had provided the Reich with some of its best fighters, had political support.

Once the decision had been made, Adolph Galland, one of the leading aces in the Battle of Britain and, by 1943, the Luftwaffe's General of Fighters at the age of thirty, flew the Me 262 for the first time on 22 May. There were no two-seater versions so there could be no dual flight. When Galland climbed in and started up. One of the engines caught fire so, undeterred, he flew another aircraft instead, one of the prototypes which still had the tail wheel configuration. He waited agonisingly as the speed built up only slowly at first to about 80 m.p.h., when the tail came up and the speed increased to 120 m.p.h. and it started to lift off. For somebody who had flown piston-engined aircraft almost every day for years, with their attendant vibration, he was struck by the serenity of the jet engine. During his test flight he made several passes at a four-engined bomber flying near the airfield, then landed again, ecstatic, describing flying it like being 'pushed by angels'. He sent a message to Messerschmidt later, saying, 'not a step forward but a great leap forward'.

On 26 May 1943 the production prototype with a tricycle undercarriage was completed, and shortly afterwards test pilots were regularly reaching 590 m.p.h., the edge of the speed of sound, where it started buffeting and became difficult to fly. There were still problems with the engines, which really needed more development, and it was still very tricky to fly, but the potential was huge and Galland could see it. As a fighter pilot, he knew the edge it would give his men in the air, but for them to make a difference in the air war they would have to be produced in the right numbers and enough of the right kind of pilots would have to be trained to fly them. For Galland it was a matter of urgency, and in an effort to enthuse the top brass in the Luftwaffe he sent a signal to Feldmarschall Edward Milch: 'This aircraft opens up completely new tactical possibilities.'

In August there was a meeting between the Luftwaffe and the RLM about fighter production. The FW 190, the mainstay of the

Luftwaffe's Home Defence squadrons, could just about hold its own against the latest American fighters, but the Bf 109 was no longer a match for them. What was needed was a quantum leap to give the Luftwaffe fighter pilots real superiority over the Allies, and Galland could see that leap forward was the Me 262. He argued forcefully for a quarter of all fighter production, 1,000 aircraft a month, to be Me 262s. He got nowhere, and on 5 June 1943 the Me 262 was put into very limited production.

Sadly for Galland and his fighter pilots the new machine had come at a time when there was a gulf opening up between the hierarchies of the Nazi Party and the Luftwaffe. It was fundamental, and it was created by Hitler's inability to see what most of the professional airmen around him could see, namely that with the reverses in Russia, the entry of America into the war, and the RAF night bombing offensive the Luftwaffe was stretched too thinly and it had lost any qualitative edge it might have enjoyed in the early years of the war. Hitler still wanted to be on the offensive and that single wish drove his thinking; he wanted to build bombers, not fighters, which he saw as purely defensive. The reality was that there had been a fundamental shift and, whether Hitler could see it or not, Germany was on the defensive and the Me 262 represented the best defence against the Allied bombers and their fighter escorts, many of whose targets were the aircraft factories which kept the Luftwaffe flying.

German delay gave Britain time to catch up. The Air Ministry had also spread its engine-building between different aircraft companies and the engine chosen to power the F.9/40, which had been named the Meteor, was the de Havilland H.1. Michael Daunt made the first flight at Cranwell in the prototype Meteor Mk 1 on 5 March 1943. Its straight-winged design created greater drag than the Me 262 and it was 100 m.p.h. slower, at 420 m.p.h., with a ceiling of 40,000 ft. It was also less heavily armed than the Me 262 with 4 × 20 mm long-barrel Mk 2 Hispano cannon.

Meanwhile, the Americans were also catching up. In June 1943, following a conference at Wright Field, Dayton, Ohio, at which Kelly Johnson, Lockheed's chief designer, promised to build a jet fighter around the de Havilland H.1 engine in 180 days, the USAAF gave an immediate go-ahead. It actually took 145 days but there were delays with the engine and the P-80 did not fly until 8 January

1944. In testing, the Shooting Star, as it became known, was the first US aircraft to fly faster than 500 m.p.h.

On 26 November 1943 Hitler saw the Me 262 for the first time and he was very impressed. It was just what he wanted, he said, a high-speed bomber, a 'Blitzbomber', not a fighter. Out of all the jet development programmes the Me 262 was the most immediately practical as a fighter but, having built it, Hitler then frittered its advantage away in a political and philosophical debate over how to use it, a debate which went to the heart of air power doctrine, about the need for air superiority. It was not a pure debate for it had become infected with politics and personal ambition.

Galland continued to recommend mass production of the Me 262; he could see how its superior speed, allied to new tactics, could be used to cut through the fighter escorts which protected the Allies' heavy bombers. As a pilot, and as a commander of fighters, he both knew about and believed deeply in the idea that before any air operations could be successful an air force had to have air superiority, and the Mustangs were getting ever more numerous and threatening in the skies his fighter pilots were defending.

Hitler saw fighters as essentially defensive, and not very good at that either since, during 1943, the Allied bombing offensive against Germany was becoming increasingly effective. With Goebbels, his propaganda chief, and his personal and Nazi Party secretary, Martin Bormann, he wanted to hit back at Britain with lightning raids. He knew that the Allies were planning an invasion and wanted to bomb the invasion ports where troops were gathering with ships and equipment, and to attack the troops on the beaches as they landed in France.

Galland and his colleagues in the Luftwaffe knew that such raids would only be pinpricks, that the Me 262 did not have the range with anything like a decent bomb load to do an effective job, that at the high speeds of which it was capable at low level it would be an impossible platform from which to drop bombs so the pilot would have to slow down, denying it the one advantage it had – speed – and making it vulnerable to attack even by propeller-driven fighters and anti-aircraft fire.

Galland, and the other Luftwaffe generals, also knew that any bomber, to be effective, had to operate with air superiority and to have that you had to have fighters. In the Me 262 they were convinced that they had a fighter which had made the quantum leap, and if only they could have them in sufficient numbers they could do convincing damage to the Allied bombers, especially the daylight bombers.

Hitler no longer trusted the Luftwaffe. He blamed them for the indignity and the physical damage which the Allied bombing was inflicting on Germany and he undermined the Fighter Arm of the Luftwaffe, accusing them of cowardice. He had meetings which considered the future of aircraft production priorities at which the Luftwaffe was not even present; they decided to continue with tests of the Me 262 – it was not to go into mass production.

When Göring saw the Me 262 at Lechfeld for the first time he was impressed and reported favourably to Hitler. Hitler's response was to enquire if the new fighter could be turned into a bomber. He came and saw it for himself and, being assured by Göring that it could carry two 1,000 lb bombs, he ordered that a fighter bomber version be built, specifically to counter the invasion he expected in France in the spring of 1944.

Galland continued to oppose the policy, and his enthusiasm infected the rest of the Luftwaffe. He was supported by his squadron commanders and his best pilots, many of them veterans of every campaign the Luftwaffe had fought since the Spanish Civil War. Even Milch, who had been a Hitler supporter, was won over to the jet fighter camp. Secretly, the Luftwaffe generals ignored Hitler and ordered 60 Me 262 fighters, keeping only a small development cadre for bomber conversion.

By November 1943 the Luftwaffe's fighters were outnumbered 7 to 1 in its own skies and Col. Kneymeyer, the head of the Luftwaffe's air armament development, warned that something had to be done to offset the growing numerical and technical inferiority. He pointed out that the Me 262 could give the Luftwaffe's fighter pilots the edge, that having the best could be an answer. He produced a plan to concentrate the Me 262s where they could do most damage, at bases from northern France to the Netherlands in a defensive shield which would take on the Allied escort fighters, leaving the bomber streams unprotected over Germany where the propeller fighters could get at them unmolested. He was ignored in the political battle going on above his head.

The point about superiority was made even more emphatically by the arrival of the Mustang deep inside Germany in January 1944. On an escort mission to Kiel, fighter pilots of the 354th Fighter Group shot down 18 German fighters for no loss; on 11 January 1944 they shot down at least 15 and damaged 16 more. Within a month, four of the 354th's pilots were aces. By February, the Mustangs were escorting the bombers on an 1,100 mile round trip to Leipzig, their targets aircraft factories, which further debilitated the Luftwaffe. Between January and April 1944 the Luftwaffe lost over a thousand aircraft; in February alone it lost 225 pilots killed and 140 injured. Replacing aircraft was relatively easy, but good fighter pilots took a long time to train and the whittling down of the core of experienced men created a downward spiral in the fighting ability of the Fighter Arm which was impossible to reverse in wartime. At the beginning of the war a Luftwaffe fighter pilot received 18 months' training before becoming operational, including 50 hours of combat training. By 1943 the figure was down to 30 hours and the best instructors, those with the most combat experience, were all needed at the front so were unable to pass on their skills. Accidents in training grew. One course of Bf 109 pilots started out with 100 men and by the end it had been reduced to 68, the others having all died in accidents. When the new pilots arrived at their squadrons they had to learn on the job and many died in the process.

Hitler was alarmed at the progress the Allies were making, and called a meeting with the Luftwaffe. Galland told Hitler that there was a 'danger of collapse of the air arm'. He tried to point out that Britain, having fought for air superiority over its own territory in the Battle of Britain, had sustained that, and gone on to the offensive with that superiority intact while Germany was no longer really in control of the skies over its own territory. What he wanted were substantial numbers of jet fighters to break the morale of the Allied bomber crews or, put statistically, for every five Bf 109s or FW 190s he would prefer one Me 262. When Hitler realised that the Me 262 was still being developed as a fighter he flew into a rage because his orders about turning it into a fighter/bomber had been disobeyed. He anticipated the Allied invasion in the summer of 1944 and was obsessed by offensive weapons even as the bomber streams grew in number and effectiveness. He would not listen to Galland

and forbade any further development of the Me 262 as a fighter, giving the fighter/bomber version the name Sturmvogel (Stormbird) as opposed to Schwalbe (Swallow), and forbade any mention of Me 262 as a fighter. There was no mass production which still concentrated on propeller fighters and production figures for May 1944 show just 60 Me 262s against 2,580 Bf 109s and FW 190s. To use a fighter as a fighter bomber when the strength of the fighter arm was inadequate to achieve air superiority was putting the cart before the horse. Milch, who had seen that the advantage which the Me 262 might have given the Luftwaffe was being frittered away, protested and was dismissed shortly afterwards.

As a sop to Hitler, on 3 June 1944 No. III Group of Kampf-geschwader (KG) 51 was ordered to give up its Stuka dive bombers and go to Lechfeld near Munich to reform around the fighter bomber version of the Me 262. It was redesignated KG(J)51 under the command of Major Wolfgang Schenk, one of the Luftwaffe's most experienced fighter bomber pilots. Three days later the Allies landed in Normandy.

In the same month a test squadron, Erprobungskommando 262 (EK 262), was formed, also at Lechfeld, under the command of Hauptmann Werner Thierfelder. Its purpose was to train oper-ational fighter pilots to fly the Me 262 and to develop combat tactics. For example, they found that taking up formation after take-off wasted a lot of time and fuel, and that once formed up it was difficult to fly the jet with the constant throttle adjustments needed to congregate tightly which, in turn, could lead to engines flaming out. Lechfeld had wide runways and they found that for-mation take-offs, three abreast, were the best way to get airborne in a hurry. Formation take-off called for a high level of flying skill and in the air they found that a looser formation was better because, again, it called for fewer and slower throttle movements to stay in formation.

In mock combat with the Bf 109 Thierfelder and his pilots found that, as expected, due to the high wing loading of the Me 262 it could not turn as tightly as the propeller fighter and that consequently in a dogfight it would be at a disadvantage. Acceleration was also poor, and the pilots found they had to nurse the throttles very gently – any harsh movements and the engines had a tendency to 'flame out' or catch fire. Even for an expert, the Me 262 was difficult and sometimes dangerous to land. The landing speed was much higher than that of the propeller fighters and the tyres took a huge strain on touching down and sometimes burst, precipitating a collapse of the undercarriage and a crash. But for all its problems, the Me 262 was 100 m.p.h. faster than any other propeller or jet fighter; it was an interceptor, a bomber killer, not a dogfighter, and that was what Germany needed in 1944.

As an interceptor and bomber killer, the Me 262 was armed with four 30 mm, Mk. 108 cannon in the nose. Bombers such as the B-17 and B-24 could take enormous punishment and against such big, solid targets, which had limited ability to manoeuvre, a fighter pilot had plenty of time to line up for the shot and needed heavy ammunition to do maximum damage. The heavier the round the slower the rate of fire, and against another fighter, where the attacker might only get a fleeting chance at a shot, he needed a high rate of fire which meant lighter ammunition. With no propeller, the Me 262's guns could be on the centreline of the aircraft, right in the front of the cockpit, but this led to new problems. The powerful charge that sent the cannon shell on its way left huge amounts of debris in its wake, wadding and spent propellant, which flew over the windscreen. The propellant was changed, which solved the debris problem but at the expense of a huge flash that also obscured the pilot's view. To counter this, a flash guard was put over the muzzle of the gun. Trials with a 50 mm cannon in the nose were abandoned because the flash it produced was simply too blinding for the pilot. Trials also started with unguided R4M rockets, 12 under each wing, which could be fired in salvoes from well outside the effective range of the B-17's machine-guns and were designed to saturate the target. To improve the accuracy of the rockets, there were plans to drop the nose-mounted cannons and replace them with a pod of 24 R4M rockets.

Britain and Germany deployed their jet fighters in July 1944, in the immediate aftermath of D-Day, and the first operational use of the Me 262 and the Meteor happened virtually simultaneously. The first jet fighter to be delivered to an operational fighter squadron was the Gloster Meteor. Four years after the Air Ministry had issued the specification, seven Meteor Mk. 1s were delivered to 616 Squadron, Royal Auxiliary Air Force, on 21 July 1944. The squadron normally flew Spitfires, and at first the new arrivals were established as a separate High-Speed Flight.

They were just in time to take on the world's first strategic unmanned missiles, the V-1 'buzz bombs' which were first fired against London from launching sites in the Pas de Calais in France the same month. Interception was difficult as they were too fast for pilots to wait on the ground and scramble so 616 pilots flew standing patrols over Kent. On 27 July Flying Officer Watts saw a V-1, or 'diver' as RAF pilots called them, heading north over Kent and came in behind, only to have his guns jam as he tried to open fire. On 4 August Flying Officer T. 'Dixie' Dean found another flying over Tunbridge. He manoeuvred behind it, but his guns jammed too. Frustrated, he opened the throttle and flew right up alongside the V-1, eased in towards it sideways until the Meteor's left wing was underneath the V-1's right wing, then flipped his wing up, destabilising the V-1. Its equilibrium upset, the V-1 went into an uncontrollable spin and crashed in a field near Tunbridge. As Dean was celebrating his somewhat unorthodox victory, Flying Officer Roger found another V-1 over Tenterden. His guns did not jam and he hit it with a short burst of cannon fire which sent it crashing into open countryside. The squadron shot down a further four V-1s before the Allied armies overran the launching site in France.

Hitler put enormous faith in Germany's *Wunderwaffen*, such as the V-1 cruise missile, the V-2 ballistic rocket, radio-controlled air-to-ground missiles, air-to-air rockets, the Me 163 rocket-powered interceptor and a range of advanced jet fighters which would replace the Me 262. The result was that German research and development resources were spread very thinly, over too many projects to be effective, and not concentrated, as Galland wanted them to be, on fighters which he believed could really make a difference. Hitler backed new technologies, but he used his position to determine how they were used operationally in areas where he had no understanding. In 1944, as Allied bombing rose to a crescendo, he had a new idea for the jet engine, another distraction from getting the Me 262 into service. His idea was the He 162 Volksjager, the People's Fighter, one of the most muddle-headed ideas in the history of aerial combat, a politically inspired, mass-produced jet fighter in which hundreds of novice pilots would take to the skies to save

Germany from the bomber streams. It denied all the experience of what it took to be a fighter pilot even in a tried and tested machine with plenty of training, let alone with a completely new technology and an aircraft which had yet to be built.

If any further proof were needed that flying and fighting in a jet fighter took very high levels of skill, it came with the early experiences of mastering it by pilots of EK 262. Thierfelder had handpicked his pilots from the cream of the Fighter Arm, many of them with hundreds of combat experiences and many victories in the air, and even they found adapting to the new jet fighter a demanding task. The squadron was semi-operational, but the first four losses were not in combat but in crashes on training flights which killed three pilots, including Thierfelder, and injured the fourth.

One of EK 262's best pilots was Leutnant Alfred 'Bubi' Schreiber, and he made the first contact with the enemy in aerial combat involving a jet fighter in July 1944. Whenever the weather was suitable high-flying RAF Mosquitoes and Spitfires, stripped of all armament for speed and altitude, carried out photo reconnaissance missions over Germany virtually unhindered. The flights caused the German High Command intense irritation but there was no German propeller fighter that could match their 430 m.p.h.

On 26 July 1944 Flight Lieutenant A. E. Wall of 544 Sqn took off in a Mosquito from Benson in Oxfordshire to carry out a high-altitude mission over Munich; his navigator was Pilot Officer A. S. Lobban. As they neared their target area, Lobban spotted a twin-engined aircraft closing on them. Wall applied full boost to the two Merlins and expected to leave the German fighter standing.

The German fighter was an Me 262 flown by Schreiber who had at least a 100 m.p.h. speed advantage over the Mosquito. Schreiber closed in on Wall and flew alongside the Mosquito to confirm his identification, then he turned to get behind Wall. Wall broke hard right and nosed down to get every last bit of speed he could out of the Mosquito, at the same time turning to get out of Schreiber's line of fire. The Mosquito could turn much tighter than the Me 262 and Schreiber was forced to break off the attack, but he was then able to use his greater speed to position himself again, quite quickly, behind Wall. This time Schreiber opened fire from long range, about 800 yards: once again Wall broke hard and once again

Schreiber was forced to break off the attack. The two pilots repeated the process four more times, Wall using his better turning ability to get inside Schreiber's line of fire and Schreiber using his speed to get back on Wall's tail with relative ease. Evading the last rear attack, Wall actually turned so tightly that he got behind Schreiber and, had he been armed, could have opened fire.

Schreiber then tried another tactic. He dived, then pulled up at full throttle from underneath the Mosquito. This time Wall broke hard again and dived at full throttle for some cloud below, hearing two loud bangs against the underside of the Mosquito as he did so. Schreiber followed, but was just too late and lost sight of the Mosquito in the cloud. Lobban opened the hatch and looked into the rear fuselage to see that the doors had been ripped off near the hinges. Wall set course for the nearest Allied airfield, which was at Fermo in northern Italy, where inspection showed that the doors had hit the tailplane as they had come off. There was no damage from the Me 262's guns and the assumption was that Wall's violent manoeuvring had wrenched the doors off. Wall's combat report made clear the threat which the Me 262 posed for photo reconnaissance missions and that they would no longer be able to roam so freely.

The brief encounter between Wall and Schreiber marked the beginning of the age of the jet fighter. Germany's secret was out. Allied intelligence had known of the existence of the Me 262 for some time, but now they knew the jet was operational and its debut caused great concern among US and British air commanders because they had no antidote: not only was the Meteor much slower than the Me 262, it had nothing like the range to escort bombers over Germany.

On 27 July 1944 the first Sturmvogels, the fighter/bomber versions of the Me 262, went into action with Kommando Schenk of KG(J)51. Its bombload was light, just one 500 lb bomb under each wing; experiments had been carried out with a towed, 2,200 lb glide bomb, but it made the 262 unstable and was scrapped. They were based at Chateaubrun in France, close enough to carry out Hitler's lightning strikes against the advancing Allied forces, but to maintain secrecy they had to fly at 13,000 feet and their bomb aiming was so rudimentary they caused little or no damage. As the Germans retreated so, to maintain secrecy, Kommando Schenk retreated, too, to avoid their aircraft falling into Allied hands. The Allies had virtual air supremacy over their advancing armies and the Me 262 fighter bombers and Hitler's dream of stopping the invasion with jets was shown to be so completely ineffective that the Allies remained unaware for some time that the Me 262 had become operational in that role.

As a fighter, even though it was not fully operational, it was having some success. On 2 August 1944 Schreiber claimed a photo-reconnaissance Spitfire but this has never been confirmed because most of the Luftwaffe's records were destroyed by bombing. The first undoubted kill by a jet fighter in aerial combat came on 8 August 1944 when Leutnant Joachim Weber, also of EK 262, shot down a photo-reconnaissance Mosquito, killing the pilot and navigator.

The Allies got their first hard evidence of the Me 262 in combat on 15 August. A Mosquito of 60 (South African) Sqn flown by Capt Saloman Peinaar and Lt Archie Lockhart-Ross as navigator was tasked with flying from its base in Italy to photograph EK 262s at an airfield at Liepheim. As they approached the airfield Lockhart-Ross saw an Me 262 take off, then suddenly Peinaar saw another in his mirror, closing in to attack from behind. He broke right just as the German pilot opened fire and the cannon shells smashed into the Mosquito's left wing; had he broken left he would have received the full force of the fire and would undoubtedly have been destroyed. The German pilot went round again and managed to score more hits on the Mosquito, which suddenly flicked into an uncontrolled spiral dive. Pienaar managed to pull out of the dive and found that the aircraft was just flyable, using full right aileron, although the port engine was stuck at full power. The Me 262 attacked a total of ten times and each time Pienaar let the Mosquito flick into a dive to avoid the German's fire. The combat lasted an extraordinary 30 minutes, getting lower and lower until eventually Pienaar dived for cloud at 500 feet and the German pilot, by now short of fuel, broke off the engagement. Pienaar set course for Italy and was met by Spitfires over the Adriatic and escorted to San Sevro for a crash landing. Lockhart-Ross had left the cameras running throughout the combat and the Allies had evidence that the Me 262 was operating as a fighter. Pienaar and Lockhart-Ross were both awarded the DFC.

Evidence of the effectiveness of the Me 262 was mounting. On the same day Pienaar narrowly escaped, Feldwebel Helmut Lennartz of EK 262 shot down a B-17 and the next day an Me 262 shot down a P-38 Lightning on a reconnaissance flight. On 26 August Schreiber shot down another P-47 and Feldwebel Reckers shot down a Mosquito.

Hitler's policy of using the Me 262 as a fighter bomber received a setback on 28 August when Oberfeldwebel Hieronymous 'Ronnie' Lauer of JG(J)51 was returning to his base at low level and was jumped by a flight of P-47s led by Major Joe Myers, USAAF, just north of Brussels. Myers left four of his flight at 11,000 feet and went down with two others in a shallow dive, reaching 450 m.p.h., just overhauling the jet. Lauer started to jink about to avoid the US fighters and in doing so a wingtip touched the ground and he crash-landed. Unhurt, he scrambled out and ran for some trees while Myers and his two wingmen strafed the Me 262 on the ground.

Another KG(J)51 pilot was Hauptmann Hans-Cristhof Buttman. On 5 October 1944 he was flying towards Nijmegen to bomb the bridges in the city to delay the Allied advance. A flight of Spitfires from 401 Sqn RCAF was patrolling in loose battle formation above Nijmegen to protect the bridges, which the Germans had been trying to bring down for some time. It was a clear afternoon with good visibility; a member of the flight spotted Buttman's aircraft approaching from the northeast very fast at the same level, about 13,000 feet. The leader, Sqn Ldr R. I. A. 'Rod' Smith, who recognised it as an Me 262, brought the squadron round to the north, climbing slightly, then through a left-hand turn, putting the sun behind them, as the German aircraft practically flew through the formation. It continued to fly on straight and level and clearly had not seen the Spitfires.

Smith lined up for a perfect shot from Buttman's six o'clock when another Spitfire, flown by Smith's wingman, John MacKay, came into the line of fire at the last moment so Smith had to hold his fire. Then Buttman saw them and started twisting, turning and diving. Smith noticed that as he dived Buttman appeared to throttle back a bit, a tactical error when speed was his best defence. The Spitfires dived at full throttle, closing the gap, and a third Spitfire, flown by Hedley Everard, managed to get in ahead of MacKay and opened fire from 900 yards. Buttman tried a spiral dive, but MacKay got behind him and scored some hits. As Smith had pulled out of his dive at 7,000 feet he saw the Me 262 again over the outskirts of Nijmegen, now at full throttle, pulling away from the Spitfires. The Spitfire pilots all felt Buttman would escape when he made a second tactical error by pulling up into a near-vertical climb. Smith did the same, following the Me 262 up, firing all the way. Just as the speed of both aircraft began to decay rapidly, smoke and flames started to come out of the jet engines. They had been hit earlier, and as the two fighters reached the top of the vertical climb Smith was the first to stall-turn to the right. Suddenly Smith realised that Buttman, who had stall-turned a little later, would be right behind him as they both went into the dive, and he waited for Buttman's cannon shells to hit him. But the Me 262 was on fire and went into a vertical dive, dragging a huge plume of smoke until it crashed in flames just outside the town. Buttman had flown with great skill and had earned huge respect from the Canadian pilots for his courage, but he did not have the fighter pilot background and he was up against fighter pilots, albeit in slower aircraft, and the two tactical errors and lack of dogfighting experience probably cost him his life.

Hitler was finally convinced that the Sturmvogel experiment was wrong and at the end of August 1944 he authorised all Me 262s to be produced as fighters by the end of October.

The jet fighter was literally being born in battle without the time to test it properly, iron out the engine problems or develop weapons systems and tactics. The Luftwaffe was trying to evolve tactics to use the Me 262 to the best advantage with their backs against the wall, EK 262 trying to write the instruction book and be an operational fighter squadron at the same time. The Me 262s' task was to hit the bombers, but in going for the bombers their high speed was a problem: closing speeds were too high for head-on attack, and if the jet pilot slowed down he lost his main advantage – speed – and became just another target for the bomber's gunners and the escort fighters. Finding this out led to some losses. To counter the problem, EK 262 developed the Roller Coaster attack: the jets would climb up to 6,000 feet above and three miles behind the bomber stream and its escorts in a loose V-formation, the aircraft fifty yards apart. They would then dive at full throttle, cut through the fighter escorts, go 1,500 feet below the bombers, then lift the noses, killing off the excess speed, and fire into the bombers' bellies. Propeller fighters and power-operated gun turrets were no answer to fighters coming in at 570 m.p.h.

When the bomber crews and escort fighter pilots first saw the Me 262s flashing through their formations they could hardly believe their speed, and gave the jets the dismissive nickname 'blow jobs', part in awe and part in admiration. To help US aircrews adjust to the new fighters the RAF sent Meteors from 616 Squadron to bases in Britain to carry out mock attacks on B-17s and B-24s and to dogfight with US fighter pilots.

In an effort to counter the Me 262 the Americans squeezed every last drop of speed out of the combination of the reciprocating engine and propeller in the form of the Republic XP-47J, an experimental version of the P-47 Thunderbolt. In trials it reached 504 m.p.h. on 4 August 1944, becoming the first propeller-driven aircraft to fly faster than 500 m.p.h., and the Allies rushed out an operational version, the P-47M Thunderbolt, which could reach 470 m.p.h., but that was still 70 m.p.h. slower than the Me 262.

The Allies were worried about the possible effect that the Me 262 could have if it went into mass production, and Allied bombing was targeted at aircraft factories, especially those which Allied intelligence could identify as associated with jet fighter production. It had some effect: the planned number of man hours to build an Me 262 was 6,000 but, due to the bombing, they turned out to take 9,000–10,000 hours. Instead of switching production, and despite all the evidence that the jet could give the Luftwaffe the edge it needed, the RLM still concentrated production of propeller fighters to keep the numbers up to impress Hitler. Mass production of Me 262s barely got under way until October 1944 and then grew only slowly: November – 101; December – 124; January – 160; February – 280.

Allied bombing and production of the Bf 109 and FW 190 were not the Me 262's only enemies. Just as it was finding its place in the early autumn of 1944, Hitler's brainchild, the He 162 Volksjager, renamed the Salamander from a mythical creature which could walk through fire, became a further distraction for Germany's hard-pressed aircraft industry. It was an act of desperation but, with staunch Nazi Party support, a specification had been issued on 8

September 1944 and companies had to submit drawings a week later for a target date for its first flight on 1 January 1945. Heinkel was awarded the contract on 30 September for a design which was powered by an 800 lb thrust BMW engine mounted in a pod on top of the fuselage. Work began six days before the contract was awarded in an underground salt mine in the Harz mountains and it made its maiden flight on 6 December 1944 at Vienna's Schweckat airfield.

The whole programme was ill-conceived: they were expected to be produced in thousands but there were no spares and little training in maintenance. The pilots were to come from the Hitler Youth and they were to be trained on operational flying. The Salamander was extremely tricky to fly and, though there were many problems still to be sorted out, a flying display was arranged for 10 December in front of Nazi Party members and RLM officials. During a high-speed, low-level pass, the left wing came off in flight, killing the pilot, but production and testing pressed ahead. The Salamander had an endurance of only 20 minutes at low level and under an hour at high level where it could reach 522 m.p.h., Mach .75, but at that speed it started to snake badly and had to be handled very gently by the pilot, not the best characteristic for fighting in the air in the hands of an expert, let alone a novice. The plan was to build up to production of 4,000 aircraft per month by the middle of 1945, but only 275 were completed by the end of the war – none saw combat.

The Luftwaffe selected one of its top-scoring aces to command the first fully operational jet fighter squadron, twenty-three-year-old Major Walther 'Nowi' Nowotny, who had 225 aerial victories to his credit and wore the Knight's Cross with Oak Leaves, Swords and Diamonds, the highest military decoration. He was the kind of pilot of whom there were too few left. The unit was known after him – Kommando Nowotny. On 3 October 1944 it moved to bases at Achmer and Hesepe near the Dutch border, belatedly working to the plan set out by Col. Kneymeyer to use the Me 262 to engage Allied escort fighters before the bombers reached Germany. On their first day Nowotny's pilots shot down three B-24s, but on the same day the squadron lost two of its 23 aircraft to rat-catchers. The jets were so vulnerable on landing that the Luftwaffe detached a number of Bf 109 fighters to Nowotny's bases to patrol the approaches and take on any Mustangs which might be waiting to ambush the jets. In the first month it scored nineteen kills, but losses were matched one for one, many of them to accidents. On 21 October Schreiber shot down two, making him the first pilot to be considered a jet ace, but, given that he had claimed Flt Wall's Mosquito as his first and it made it to Italy, the true identity of the first jet ace cannot be determined with certainty except to say that it must have been one of the pilots of EK 262 or Kommando Nowotny.

Each success was a minor triumph for the squadron as it battled not only against the enemy but also against chronic shortages of spares, continued engine flame-outs and bursting tyres. On 1 November Oberfeldwebel Willi Banzaff, and three other Me 262s, climbed high over the Dutch German border, to over 30,000 feet, then dived on the Mustang escorts, strictly according to plan. Banzaff shot down one Mustang then swept through the bomber stream, firing as he went. By the time he came out the other side there was a horde of Mustangs on his tail, diving at full throttle with full boost. Banzaff came out of the dive around 10,000 feet and went into a climbing turn, hoping to use his speed to be able to climb away. But the Mustangs were still close enough to take advantage of his manoeuvre, cutting the corner to close with him. Several of them fired at once, setting one of his engines alight. The Me 262 went into a spin and Banzaff just managed to bale out.

The Allies could afford a war of attrition in the air – the Luftwaffe could not. Under Nowotny's command, the squadron shot down 50 Allied aircraft in its first month of operations, but it lost 26 Me 262s in the same period, more than its starting strength. On 8 November Adolph Galland flew to its base at Achmer to meet the pilots. When the air-raid sirens sounded Nowotny and Oberleutnant Gunther Wegman took off to join Leutnant Franz Schall and Sergeant Buttner who took off from Hesepe. Nowotny's engine failed before take-off but Schall and Wegman each claimed a P-47. As soon as they'd landed the sirens went again and Nowotny, Schall and Oberlfeldwebel Baudach took off. Schall shot down two more and Nowotny hit a B-24 and possibly a Mustang, then one of his engines failed and caught fire. His aircraft went into a dive. He did not manage to bale out and died when his Me 262 crashed in a field next to the airfield, in full view of the squadron. The commander

of the Luftwaffe's first operational jet squadron had died barely a
month after its formation, another victim of the Me 262 being
hurried into service.

After Nowotny's death the squadron was taken over by another
outstanding fighter pilot and leader, Col. Johannes Steinhoff, an
ace with 170 aerial victories. It was renamed Jagdgeschwader 7 and
Steinhoff introduced more training, up to thirty-five hours for each
new pilot, and he also tried a much looser formation of three
aircraft instead of the usual two pairs. This was to allow far fewer
throttle movements to stay in formation. Under Steinhoff's
command, JG7 pilots shot down 100 aircraft in a month with only
30 jet fighters on strength.

Hitler's last offensive spasm came in the freezing cold of the
Ardennes forests on 1 January 1945, and the Luftwaffe was thrown
in to support the army. The Allies were briefly caught off guard
and the German pilots destroyed 200 Allied aircraft, most of them
on the ground. By the time the Allies had reasserted control, the
Luftwaffe had lost 300 aircraft and, more importantly, 250 pilots.

Germany was slowly collapsing but the political feuding between
the Nazi Party and the Luftwaffe Fighter Arm continued relentlessly. Göring, weakened by drug addiction and increasingly dis-
tracted by his art collection, was not in touch with the reality his
pilots faced. Since the ill-fated plot against Hitler's life which had
failed, and the officers behind it summarily executed, there was a
climate of fear and suspicion, and Göring was reduced to telling
Hitler whatever it was he wanted to hear. Heinrich Himmler, head
of the SS, also wanted to control the Luftwaffe, and one of the
casualties of his intrigue was Adolph Galland who was relieved of
his command in January 1945. Having lost the argument, all he
wanted to do was to go back to being a fighter pilot, a jet fighter
pilot, but even that request was denied. Senior commanders in the
Fighter Arm protested, but to no avail, and when they confronted
Göring with their demands that Galland be reinstated Göring
accused them of plotting against him and he dismissed them as
'conspirators'. Galland and Steinhoff and a number of other like-
minded senior Luftwaffe officers were banished, some of the best
pilots and fighter commanders were sidelined in Germany's hour
of greatest need. Albert Speer intervened with Hitler and Galland
was eventually, but only partially, rehabilitated. He was finally

granted his dream – a free hand to develop his own command, a jet squadron to be known as Jagdverband, Hunting Brotherhood, JV44, for Me 262s only.

JV44 was to be deployed at Riem, near Munich, and from January 1945, once it became common knowledge that Galland was about to form a squadron, fighter pilots throughout the Luftwaffe, who felt that they had been ridiculed by the political hierarchy, wanted to be part of it.

Allied bombing reached new intensity in the spring of 1945 and Berlin became the primary target. In March 1945 there was a steady build-up of raids which culminated in the last great air raid of the war in which the Luftwaffe could still inflict serious losses. JG7 was still operating against the bomber streams, but as the Allies advanced so they had to pull further back to bases nearer Berlin. On 18 March some 1,329 heavy bombers and 733 fighter escorts attacked the city. JG7 sent 37 Me 262s to engage them – odds of 20:1 against fighters alone. A few dozen jets 'cut through the fighter screens', just as Galland had wanted them to do in hundreds. The R4M rocket firing system had just been made operational and was first used on this raid by Gunther Wegman against a B-17 which immediately went down in flames. JG7 pilots shot down 8 bombers and 1 fighter for the loss of 4 of their own number, but losses were running at 100 Me 262s a month. The rockets proved a devastating weapon but could only be deployed in tiny numbers against hundreds of bombers. By the war's end JG7 pilots had shot down 427 Allied aircraft. But the attrition rate was high and the worst day for the squadron came three weeks later, on 10 April 1945, when they put up 55 Me 262s on a single mission and lost 27 of them by the end of the day, many of them in accidents. One of the casualties was Franz Schall, whose jet crashed into a bomb crater on landing and burst into flames.

On the same day Galland met Göring for the last time. In private, Göring agreed that Galland had been right about the defence of the Reich, but by then it was far too late. Germany was finished, and JV44 became operational just as the world its commander and its pilots were pledged to defend was literally crashing around their ears.

JV44 was founded at Brandenburg-Briest where Galland had rounded up what remained of the cream of the Luftwaffe's fighter pilots: ten holders of the Ritterkreuz (Iron Cross), another ten very experienced fighter pilots and some new fighter pilots who had done very well in short careers. Gerhard Barkhorn (300), Erich Hohagen (55), Karl-Heinz Schell (72) and Walter Krupinski (197) had themselves released from the Luftwaffe's hospital. Gunther Lutzow (108), the arch 'conspirator' who was a close friend of Galland's, Heinz Bar (204), Johannes Steinhoff (176), Hans-Ekke-hard Bob (59), Heinrich Buckner, a Stuka dive bomber pilot, the only ex-bomber pilot to make it, Hans Grunberg (82), Herbert Kaiser (68), Klaus Neuman (37) and Heinz Sachsenberg (104) also joined. Others, such as Fred Heckman, tried to make it across Germany, but failed.

Much has been made of the high scores of German fighter pilots, and the Luftwaffe did produce aces like no other air force in the Second World War. Erich Hartman, the highest-scoring fighter pilot in history, shot down 352 before the war's end and, between them, the top 100 Luftwaffe aces, all of whom shot down over 100 each, accounted for 15,000 enemy aircraft. There are many reasons for this and the most obvious is that there were many more targets on the Eastern Front, where the Luftwaffe aircraft were far superior for most of the war. Another reason was that they kept on flying right through the war, not stopping to rest. They wanted to fight and that is what drove them to want to be part of JV44. They shared many common objectives, not least a desire to continue to fight for their Fatherland, but there were also personal reasons. Galland made no secret of his desire, his personal ambition, to put together a squadron of fighter pilots who would be the last fighter pilots in the Luftwaffe. What motivated Steinhoff to join JV44 was to feel the special feeling of superiority in the air which flying the jet gave him.

The squadron rarely operated with more than 16 Me 262s, largely due to the huge difficulties in maintaining them. The pilots and ground crews also had to contend with being constantly under attack, both from fighters waiting to ambush them and full-scale bombing raids directed at the airfield, which, littered with debris and bomb fragments, had its own dangers. On 18 April Galland was leading a 'Kette', a wide, loose V-formation which JV44 had developed for easy manoeuvring in the air, consisting of himself as leader, Steinhoff and Walter Krupinski. Just as Galland became airborne, and Steinhoff was about to reach flying speed and lift off behind him, Steinhoff's left tyre burst, probably punctured by a piece of shrapnel. His left wing dropped suddenly and though he tried to get into the air he was not flying quite fast enough and crashed into a bunker on the airfield boundary, his aircraft immediately bursting into flames just as Krupinski took off over his head. Steinhoff jumped out very quickly which saved his life, but he was severely burned on the hands and face.

JV44 managed to send up a flight of 11 Me 262s on 24 April, armed with R4M rockets, to intercept a large formation of USAAF Marauders heading for a munitions factory south of Augsberg. The leader was Gunther Lutzow. They opened fire from just under 800 yards and shot down two. The same afternoon a force of 74 Marauders escorted by P-47 Thunderbolts attacked an oil depot thirty miles north of Munich. This time JV44 could only manage to get six Me 262s airborne, though two had engine failure before take-off, leaving Lutzow, Krupinski and Neuman, plus an unidentified pilot to take them on. The Me 262s split into two elements of two and attacked from different angles, just as the bombers were lining up for their bombing run. This time the escorts dived on them and Lutzow was shot down and killed.

On 26 April Galland led five Me 262s to intercept a force of 60 Marauders escorted by 63 P-47 Thunderbolts on their way to bomb Lechfeld airfield. He led them above the bombers and in front, then turned to dive and meet them head-on, going straight through the formation. He turned behind it for a second attack from below, aiming to come up into the tightly packed boxes from the left flank of the formation. Edouard Schallmoser, Galland's wingman, fired a salvo of R4M rockets and was rewarded with a B-26 blowing up in the air immediately. Galland positioned himself perfectly and fired his rockets, but had forgotten to release a safety catch, so nothing happened. He switched to 30 mm cannon at the last moment and hit another Marauder, which also exploded. The guns of the Marauders were all firing at him as he came into the box, still firing and hitting a second Marauder. As he left the bomber formation the P-47 escorts attacked and hit his instrument panel which exploded in front of him, glass fragments injuring his knees. When he arrived back at Riem he found the airfield under attack by ground-strafing Mustangs, but his fuel tanks were punctured, he was very low on fuel and he had no alternative but to land in the middle of the attack. By the time he was over the threshold he had virtually no throttle control and crash-landed, struggling to get out and into a slit trench until the strafing was over.

It was Adolph Galland's last combat sortie. Heinz Bar took over command of JV44 and it continued to fight, shooting down another six P-47s before surrendering to American forces just four days before the end of the war. In its month of action JV44 achieved 50 kills with little servicing support. Bar finished the war as the highest-scoring Me 262 pilot with 16 victories, bringing his personal total to 220.

Had Galland had his way, and the Me 262 had been deployed earlier in large numbers, with the right pilots and proper training, it might have been different. Just as the Luftwaffe needed a technological edge to take on the much greater numbers it faced on two fronts, and just as it had such an edge to hand, it was denied to the Luftwaffe because the politicians failed to grasp the importance of air superiority. It was one of Hitler's great blunders, not to trust the views of his airmen. Göring should have stood up to him, but a mixture of fear and the fact that he was completely out of touch with his pilots meant that at best he wavered. Galland, Nowotny, Steinhoff, Lutzow, Schall, Bar, Banzaff, and many more knew it and fought to prove it to the last. Steinhoff put it simply: '[we were] wrongly equipped and wrongly engaged.'

Galland formed JV44 with the intention of showing that his war of words had not been hot air, that he was right about the Me 262. It was a supreme, if rather dark and complex example of the enthusiasm of fighter pilots for combat. Feeling abandoned by their masters, and with very little in the way of orders or moral or practical support, they used their own initiative and simply got on with the job. In his diary, Galland wrote, 'I feel great satisfaction to have been able to participate on active duty during the last turbulent months of the war. The knowledge that I led the last fighter unit in the greatest of all wars will always be one of my cherished memories.'

The same eagerness for aerial combat was also evident in the RAF's first jet fighter squadron, No. 616. They moved to Melsbroek in Belgium on 20 January 1945 with the new F3 Meteor, then followed the advancing Allied armies at a discreet distance. Their role was air defence, to be on standby against air attack. Unlike their propeller-driven cousins, who were free to engage the enemy over enemy-held territory, the Meteor pilots were forbidden to fly over enemy territory in case one was shot down and captured. Had either side risked its jets over the front line, there was the tantalising possibility of jet on jet combat, but it never happened because both sides kept them for the air defence role. During the Rhine crossing on 24 March 1945 the Meteors flew closer to the front line, flying ground attack missions. From 17 April Meteors were allowed to fly over enemy territory and their contribution was ground-strafing of German transport and airfields, on one occasion destroying six German aircraft on the ground. The pilots looked for aerial combat and came close on one occasion when four of them engaged a flight of FW 190s.

Before combat could start, a squadron of Spitfires, mistaking the Meteors for Me 262s, manoeuvred to attack the Meteors who then disengaged and used their speed to escape what could have become a 'friendly fire' incident. On 2 May 1945 a Meteor caught a tiny, unarmed German communications aircraft, a Fiesler Storch, in the open but the German pilot managed to evade being shot down in the air by landing, getting out, and running away. The Meteor pilot then strafed it on the ground and set it on fire.

The jet fighter had arrived. In addition to the Meteor, Britain also built the de Havilland Vampire which flew in 1944, but it was not deployed operationally. The only jet fighters to see action during the Second World War were the Me 262 and the Meteor. Germany passed on many of the secrets of the Me 262 to Japan where Nakajima built two prototypes of a jet fighter called the Kikka, but it made only two flights before the atomic bomb ended the war in the Pacific. Lockheed put an American jet engine, an Allison J-33, in the P-80 Shooting Star, which became fully operational in December 1945.

The victorious Allies flew the Me 262 experimentally but most were scrap. After the war a total of 3,545 Meteors were produced, of which 3,140 served in the RAF in many different roles, including a very successful two-seater night-fighter version, the remainder going to Commonwealth air forces and in foreign sales. The initial USAAF order for Shooting Stars was 3,500, but that was scaled down with the end of the war and the final production run was

1,731 as the F-80. From 1949 a two-seater trainer version was produced as the T-33, and over 5,000 were built which served the USAF as its standard jet trainer for twenty years. In that role, America's first jet fighter taught several generations of fighter pilots their trade.

CHAPTER TWO

A Brave New World

The Second World War was an overture to the jet age, a foretaste of the new devices and new themes that would shape warfare in the post-war world. The needs of war had produced a huge range of new technologies – from the jet engine to electronic control systems and computers, and from radar to the atomic bomb – technologies that would revolutionise warfare for the second time in the twentieth century. America had led the search for the atomic bomb, but Britain and Germany, the two original combatants, had been in the forefront of a revolution in military aviation and Germany, in particular, had applied both resources and brainpower to basic aeronautical research, making huge strides, especially in high-speed flight.

By 1945 Britain was exhausted, and its new Labour Government was preoccupied with building a welfare state at home while re-establishing the Empire abroad. At its height, during the war, the British aircraft industry had employed over 2 million people; from 1945 that was steadily cut to 140,000. Having given its jet engine secrets to the United States in 1942, in a fit of naïvety, the new government shared them with its other two wartime Allies, the Soviet Union and France. Against the wishes of the Air Ministry, the Soviet Union was allowed to buy 25 Rolls-Royce Nene and 30 Derwent, the best jet engines in the world at that time.

Germany was in ruins, its aircraft industry smashed by Allied bombing, but the ruins contained valuable secrets, nevertheless, and the four wartime Allies systematically plundered what was left. In the summer of 1945, as war turned to an uncertain peace, American, Soviet, British and French technical teams scoured Germany's scientific research stations, and what they unearthed gave them a fascinating glimpse of the future of military aviation.

The technical drawings and research data for high-speed jet fighters and bombers and electronically guided weapons conjured up a futuristic vision of air warfare with increasing levels of technical complexity and far greater lethality. In addition to the Me 262 and He 162 jet fighters, there were prototypes for many more based on three different propulsion systems – ramjet, rocket and pure jet, the products of a late conversion by the Nazis to the need for defensive systems.

In late 1944 the RLM had announced an Emergency Fighter Competition between the manufacturers for a 1,000 km/h fighter which could reach 45,000 feet with four 30 mm cannon. Heinkel, Junkers, Blohm & Voss and Focke-Wulf had each submitted a design for a single-engined jet fighter with swept wings; Messerschmidt had submitted three designs and started work on one, the P.1101, on its own initiative, a prophetic, shiny aluminium tube of a fighter with its wings swept back to 40 degrees; the engineless prototype was captured by the Americans. Another Messerschmidt fighter design, the P.1110, was designed to fly at 43,000 feet with the pilot in a pressurised cockpit. All the aircraft manufacturers had been waiting for was Germany's second generation of jet engines to be finished, particularly the Heinkel-Hirsch 109–011, which had twice the power of the Me 262's 003 and 004s.

Hitler's dreams of offensive aircraft were also in evidence. The most ambitious was the '1000 × 1000 × 1000' bomber, a jet which could carry 1,000 kg of bombs over 1,000 kilometres at 1,000 km/h. Junkers had started work on the prototype but it, too, was waiting for the new jet engines. Fortunately, Germany's research into atomic weapons was minimal so the bombs would have been high explosive.

The area where Germany was furthest ahead of the Allies was in unmanned, electronically guided weapons. Britain had experienced attack by the first strategic surface-to-surface missile, the V.1, and its successor, the ballistic V.2. The V.1 was an early ancestor of the Tomahawk cruise missiles which the USA deployed in Europe in the 1980s and which opened the attack on Baghdad in the Gulf War in 1992, and the V.2 was an early version of what became, in the late 1950s, the Intercontinental Ballistic Missile (ICBM).

As the Allies had closed in on the Reich they had found plenty of evidence of guided and unguided missiles being used for air defence. The basic V.2 technology had also been turned into Wasserfall (Waterfall), a surface-to-air, radio-controlled, anti-aircraft missile with a huge warhead which could be guided from the ground and detonated in the middle of a bomber stream; it would have been ready in November 1945. The Rhinemaiden anti-aircraft missile had a smaller warhead, but it came with its own on-board guidance system. The Taifun, a small, unguided rocket, could be fired in salvoes. The Henschel 297 radio-controlled surface-to-air (SAM) missile was nearly ready for use as the war ended. It was the beginning of a ground-based air defence system in which the Soviet Union, with its huge land mass to protect, took a great interest. Britain was working on a SAM system during the war, but it was years behind the development of the idea in Germany.

One missile which had been used in the war, and had actually sunk Allied ships, was the Henschel 293 which was launched from a parent aircraft and then guided by an operator to its target by radio control. It was the start of a line of anti-shipping missiles which culminated in sea-skimmers like the Exocet which was used against British warships in the Falklands campaign. On the drawing board was another air-to-surface missile, the Bv246 Hagelkorn (Hailstone), a glide bomb controlled by a gyroscope linked to an electronic system that followed a radio beam emitted by the launching aircraft straight to its target. The USA developed weapons that were much more advanced but used the same basic principle. They were first used in Vietnam and they were the early ancestors of the 'smart' weapons which gave the Coalition such an edge in the Gulf War.

Guided missiles for air-to-air combat were also in development, more advanced systems to replace unguided rockets like the R4Ms, which Me 262 pilots had used against Allied bombers. One of them, the X-4, was fired from the cockpit, the pilot guiding it to its target using a little control column which sent instructions down $3\frac{1}{2}$ miles of thin wire that unravelled from the fighter's wingtips.

The hardware was fascinating and valuable, if somewhat wrecked by the bombing, but the most valuable assets were the brains behind the work so the scientists became wartime booty, too. The Soviet Union captured the complete RLM archive when they occupied Berlin, they had taken large numbers of BMW and Junkers jet engines, and they comprehensively looted the Henschel and Junkers factories at Brandenburg and Dessau. As they swept up the data and the half-finished weapons they took an equally straightforward view of the people who had been developing them, simply rounding up whole design teams and shipping them from Germany to Russia.

The USA achieved the same result by a different, and rather more humane, process codenamed Operation Paperclip under which they induced German scientists to come and live and work in America, promising money and a lifestyle rather better than that they could expect in post-war Germany or the Soviet Union. Taking this approach, they finished up with two of the most influential scientists: Werner von Braun, the man who had led German long-range rocket research development; and Adolf Buseman, whose work on swept wings and high-speed flight was seminal. Germany had expended great resources and brainpower on its search for a technical edge over the enemy and, had the war lasted a year or two longer, or had those resources not been spread too thinly over too many projects to be effective, the scientists might have been able to turn the tables in the air by giving the Luftwaffe, and the anti-aircraft defences, a qualitative edge.

Seen as a whole, the full range of the booty added up to a very clear vision of the future of air warfare. For offensive purposes, there would be fast, long-range bombers which could carry a large payload, including atomic weapons; beyond that was a future based on unmanned cruise missiles and ballistic missiles that could be fired from one country to another. For air defence, there was an equally clear vision of a mixture of ground-based SAMs and high-speed fighters to attack bombers, and air superiority fighters with guided missiles rather than guns or cannon. None of the Allies had anything to compare with them.

The USA and the Soviet Union took the bulk of the spoils and used them to begin fashioning that future. They did so in the context of a new world order which was emerging at the same time, a world dominated by two superpowers, the USA and the USSR, leading two armed camps in a Europe graphically split between two ideologies – a capitalist, democratic Western Europe and a communist, authoritarian Eastern Europe, with what, in 1946, Winston Churchill called an 'Iron Curtain' between them.

The following year Bernard Baruch, a US Presidential advisor, coined the expression 'Cold War' to describe a new and distinctive world order, characterised by US–Soviet tension and the division of Germany – and much of the rest of the world – on ideological, political and economic grounds. Each had a very different idea of the future, and as soon as the war was over the two sides in that Cold War started using the secrets of the previous war to protect their own visions of the future by beating their swords into even more destructive swords, rather than ploughshares.

General Henry 'Hap' Arnold, Chief of Staff of the USAAF, was a great believer in new technology; he it was who had seen the potential of the jet engine and had immediately and swiftly arranged for Britain to share its secrets with the United States. In August 1945 he gave a lecture to Air Force colleagues at the Pentagon about the future of aerial warfare, and what he saw ahead was dominated by high technologies such as the jet engine, but particularly electronic guidance systems, unmanned weapons systems and nuclear bombs. Ultimately his vision included the idea that at some point in the future reconnaissance, strategic bombing and aerial combat would be carried out by unmanned aircraft, and that electronics would ultimately displace the pilot from the cockpit.

General Arnold's views were based on what he knew about US and British research at the time, but they were also based on the direction towards which German aeronautical research pointed. It was a very Western view. After the war the Western democracies tried to demobilise, returning their huge armed forces to normal, small, professional status. America, especially, saw high technology as a way of filling the gap left by the huge reductions in manpower in the armed forces which seemed only normal to Western societies.

The Soviet Union saw things very differently. Ever since Peter the Great, Russia had imported Western technology and its rulers, tsarist and communist, had always had an insecurity about not being able to develop it themselves. They saw technology as important, but regarded the Western emphasis on it as misguided. Russia, with a vast land mass to defend and a huge population with which to defend it, was conditioned to thinking of defence on a continental scale. Russia's military history was of huge armies of ethnically diverse people, held together by a tradition of pretty brutal militarism. Its citizens were forced to serve in the armed forces for long periods, which stunted the development of the civic, commercial and social institutions based on local and individual effort. Russians have an Asian rather than a European view towards authority – it has always been a country used to control from above, and that suited the centralised and highly planned approach of the Communist Party. The Soviet Army, Navy and Air Force inherited the Russian imperial military tradition of large General Staffs and a parallel political system, their military doctrine based on huge forces directed from above according to carefully predetermined plans with very high levels of control and not much room for initiative at unit or individual level. They had just won their 'Great Patriotic War' with 11 million men under arms, and, though there were lessons to be learned and new weapons to be built, they saw no reason to change the fundamentals of their system by embracing high technology.

In the air that military culture was very different from the Western tradition of élite forces such as the fighter arms of the RAF, USAF and Luftwaffe, traditions of personal aggression and achievement, individual flair and initiative, born in the First World War. The Soviet Air Force was huge, and while they wanted the booty from Germany, as well as the latest technology, they wanted to use it in the context of their own military system which, even though the armed forces were reduced to 5 million, was still based on size and control as its principal ingredients. As West and East prepared to equip themselves for a new age in military aviation, they did so from too very different cultures: one poor, tightly controlled, highly authoritarian with ancient military traditions and ruled by fear; the other rich, brash, self-sufficient and based on individualism and ideas of choice and freedom.

They also did so from very different starting points. In 1945 perceptions of the threat from either side of the Iron Curtain were very different. For the Western powers the threat lay in the huge Soviet Army, which was occupying half the continent of Europe under a leader for whom world domination was firmly on the agenda. That army was backed up by a huge and, in 1945, almost exclusively tactical air force, a threat similar to that which Germany had posed in 1939, but on a far larger scale. The Western priority was to replace its strategic bomber and fighter forces with jet bombers armed with atomic weapons and jet air superiority fighters, jet escort fighters and jet fighter bombers to replace the Spitfire, Mustang, Lightning and Thunderbolt. In 1946 the Soviet Union had neither a strategic bomber force nor an atomic bomb, nor did the West expect them to have either in the immediate future, so there was less emphasis on interceptors.

The view from the Kremlin was very different. Britain and the USA both had large, well-trained and well-equipped strategic bomber forces, which had laid waste to most of German and Japanese cities and industry and had just devastated two Japanese cities with a single atomic bomb each. Stalin's worst nightmare was that those strategic air forces, upgraded with jet engines and electronic aids, could attack, or threaten to attack, the USSR, a scenario for which the Red Air Force was completely unprepared. This view was endorsed by US plans for the formation of an air force completely separate from the US Army and Navy as the RAF had been since 1918. It was to be renamed the United States Air Force, USAF, rather than the United States Army Air Force, USAAF, with blue rather than khaki uniforms. When it came into being on 18 August 1947, its new Chief of Staff was General Carl A. Spaatz, USAF, commander of US strategic bomber forces during the Second World War. Worse, from the Soviet perspective, he was planning to form an air force within the air force – Strategic Air Command (SAC), dedicated to strategic bombing with jet bombers with nuclear bombs under the command of General Curtis LeMay, another bomber enthusiast. The threat looked even more real when America's first strategic jet bomber, the B-47 Stratojet, flew for the first time on 17 December 1947.

The Soviet Union had plenty of tactical fighters but no interceptors to defend itself against existing, let alone new, USAF and RAF strategic bombers, and its first priority was air defence. Creating an air defence system for a country as vast as the Soviet Union was an immense task. Western countries with short borders could afford to have small élite interceptor forces which could reach most points on their borders in minutes, but the Soviet Union needed a much larger force and in the immediate post-war period the priority was a high-altitude jet interceptor which could be built and operated in large numbers. The rule of thumb at the time was that to be effective they needed three interceptors for every one in the West.

The Soviet Union also started work on a jet bomber, but since that would take time, to fill the gap and to counter the immediate threat of SAC, it built a propeller-driven strategic bomber, the Tupolev Tu-4, a copy of the long-range US bomber, the B-29 Superfortress, the type which had been used to drop the first atomic bomb.

The first generation of jet fighters, the Gloster Meteor, the de Havilland Vampire and the Lockheed P-80 Shooting Star owed their basic design to the propeller age: they all had straight wings. The same straight-winged configuration was true of many other jet fighters on the drawing boards of all the major aircraft companies in the USA and Britain. The distinctive feature of all German jet aircraft, including the Me 262, was that they had swept wings. Most of the Me 262s were scrap but the few that had survived were carefully examined and flown by US, Soviet and British test pilots, and what they found was that the Germans had uncovered precisely what had eluded the pre-war scientists who had believed in the impermeability of the 'sound barrier'.

The secret was that the shock wave which built up in front of the aircraft as it approached the speed of sound built up over the wings first because the airflow over the wings was faster than that over the fuselage. By sweeping them back, the onset of the shock wave, and consequently its effects on the controllability of the aircraft and its physical safety, was delayed, enabling stable flight closer to the speed of sound. That simple fact, gleaned from defeated Germany, was the single most important legacy its scientists left their former enemies. Supersonic flight was clearly the goal, but building a new generation of jet fighters capable of flying closer to Mach 1 was the victor's first step in the immediate post-war period, and the Me 262 lived on in the design of US and Soviet jet fighters conceived and built in the late 1940s.

The effect was immediate. North American, which had built the P-51 Mustang, had a straight-winged naval jet fighter, the XFJ-1, on the drawing board which, as the XP-86, was also being considered by the USAAF as its next generation jet fighter. The information about swept wings, passed on in the summer of 1945, resulted in a complete redesign of the wings, sweeping them back at 35 degrees, and by 1 November 1945 the design had been accepted by the USAAF even though it meant waiting a further year for delivery of the prototype. It was powered by a Wright J-65 engine, which was based on the British Armstrong Siddeley Sapphire. It had the same effect on new bombers: once it knew about the German research, Boeing swept back the wings of what had hitherto been a straight-winged jet bomber, the B-47.

The effect of sweepback on speed is best illustrated by comparing the speed records held by the German jets and the post-war British and American jet fighters. The German records were set during the war: 623.86 m.p.h. by the swept-wing, rocket-powered Me 163 in 1941; and 624.5 m.p.h. by the Me 262 in 1944. On 7 November 1945 Grp Capt. H. J. Wilson, the chief test pilot at the Royal Aircraft Establishment, Farnborough, established the first official air speed record since 1939 at 606.25 m.p.h. in a standard Meteor Mk IV, the only modification being to fair over the gun ports. On 7 September 1946 Grp Capt. Edward Donaldson flew another Meteor Mk 4 to 615.65 m.p.h. A battle for the speed record developed between the USA and Britain using the Meteor and the Shooting Star. On 19 June 1947 Col. Albert Boyd, Chief of Flight Testing for the USAAF, flying a specially prepared Shooting Star designated P-80R, raised the record to 623.61 m.p.h. still just short of the German unofficial record set years earlier in wartime. It was not until 20 August 1947 that the German record was beaten, and that was achieved by a post-war pure research aircraft, the Douglas D-558-I, flown by Cmdr T. Caldwell, USN, who raised it to 640.60 m.p.h. On 25 August 1947, Major M. Carl, USMC, used the same aircraft to increase it to 650.78 m.p.h.

The Douglas D-558-I was a high-speed research aircraft, part of America's plans to research into speeds close to, and ultimately beyond, the speed of sound. Britain had a similar aircraft, half-built at the end of the war, the Miles M-52, which was built around a special Whittle engine with an afterburner. It had straight wings and, with implications of the German work on swept wings driving aeronautical thinking, it was cancelled. De Havilland then built a swept-wing research aircraft, the DH.108, around a Vampire fuselage. On 27 September 1946 Geoffrey de Havilland, the son of the founder of the company and its chief test pilot, crashed in the DH.108 on a high-speed test flight and was killed. The accident brought manned high-speed research flying to an end in Britain although, for a time, radio-controlled experiments continued. Britain simply could not afford the huge expense of producing a new generation of jet fighters so soon after the war, and its research and development steadily fell behind and the lead which it had enjoyed over the USA and the Soviet Union quickly evaporated.

The American and Soviet aircraft industries steadily widened their lead. Prototypes of the Soviet Union's first two jet fighters, the Yak-15 and the MiG I-300, were both flown for the first time on 24 April 1946, using engines based on the German BMW 003 and Junkers 004. The 'I' in the designation MiG I-300 stood for 'Istrebitel', the Russian for Interceptor. Building an interceptor remained the highest priority for the Russians, and the pace of development was forced ahead faster than was prudent. The MiG test pilot was Alexei Grinchik and as he pushed the speed up he experienced very severe vibration at high speed. A month after the first flight, on 24 May 1946, Grinchik was carrying out a high-speed run when the MiG went into a high nose-up attitude which he was unable to correct and it went into an uncontrollable dive. Grinchik was killed. His place was taken by Mark Gallai who continued the high-speed testing, coming close to disaster on a number of occasions. He eventually traced the problem to the jet efflux, which was too near the tail assembly and set up vibration throughout the whole aircraft. The MiG-9, as the I-300 became, was put into squadron service in December 1946 and on Mayday 1947 it was put on public display at the Tushino air show outside Moscow. Russia's first jet fighters were still based heavily on wartime designs and technology, not quite equivalent to the Meteor and Me 262, but there was great surprise in the West at what Russia had achieved in the two years since the end of the war.

The pace quickened. In America, North American's prototype XP-86, to be known as the Sabre, made its maiden flight on 1 October 1947 with George Welch at the controls. Three months later, on 30 December 1947, a Soviet test pilot made the first flight in the Soviet answer to it, the MiG-15, powered by a Rolls-Royce Nene engine. The Soviet Union had moved from the first to the second generation of jet fighters in under two years and even though details of its performance were scarce in the West, the way the Soviet Union had apparently closed the gap in jet fighters caused concern in American military circles.

In between the first flights of the Sabre and the MiG-15, an even more momentous flight had taken place over the desert in California. In the USA, a supersonic research aircraft, the Bell XS-1, had been under construction in great secrecy at the Bell Aircraft factory at Buffalo, New York, since December 1943. The fuselage was based on the shape of a .45 calibre bullet with short, stubby, straight wings, and despite the evidence of the importance of swept wings, Bell did not abandon the design. The XS-1 was rocket-powered and could not take off under its own power, and was designed to be dropped from the bomb bay of a B-29. After a series of glide flights in 1946, Bell's Chief Test Pilot, Chalmers 'Slick' Goodlin, made the first powered flight on 9 December 1946. The programme then moved to Muroc Dry Lake, deep in the Californian desert, where twenty more subsonic flights were made before the X-1 was handed over to the Air Force.

To make the first supersonic flight, the USAF chose its ace fighter and test pilot, Captain Charles 'Chuck' Yeager. He started powered flights in August 1947 and by September had built up the speed to around Mach .94, where he began to experience severe buffeting and loss of elevator effectiveness. What was happening was that the shock wave was flattening out and gripping the tailplane, making any movement of the control column ineffective. The tailplane was adjustable, and Yeager suggested making it moveable in flight, the 'flying tail' as he called it. On 14 October 1947 the X-1's fiftieth flight, Yeager attempted supersonic flight. As the speed increased beyond Mach .94 he found that he was getting elevator effectiveness back, then suddenly he was flying serenely above Mach 1 for the first time at Mach 1.06 (700.66 m.p.h.), the first man to fly faster than sound. The USAF was very anxious to keep Yeager's flight secret from the Russians, especially the way it had been achieved. Testing went on, gradually building up the speed until on 26 March 1948 he reached Mach 1.45 (959.8 m.p.h.).

A month later, on 26 April 1948, George Welch took a modified version of the prototype XP-86 to high altitude and pushed the nose down into a shallow dive. The tailplane had been modified to incorporate the lessons learned from Yeager's experience in the X-1 and the speed increased smoothly to just over Mach 1, making it the first aircraft designed as a fighter to exceed the speed of sound. In June 1948 the Air Force went public and Yeager was showered with trophies and awards.

Three years after the end of the Second World War the Cold War began in earnest. On 26 June 1948 the Soviet Union closed off road and rail links from US-, British-and French-occupied Western Germany through Soviet-occupied Eastern Germany to the divided city of Berlin. It was a crude attempt to get the Allies to leave the city. To counter the blockade, American and British transport aircraft flew thousands of sorties, carrying everything the city needed to survive. The Berlin Airlift set the tone for the Cold War – confrontation, propaganda and brinkmanship, but little or no armed conflict. The transports had fighter escorts to protect them in the air corridors to the city and occasionally the opposing fighter pilots buzzed each other and a few shots were fired, but they were warnings and both sides stopped short of actual fighting.

The Soviet Union's muscular behaviour in Europe, coupled with the victory of Mao Tse-tung's Communist forces in China, created a new atmosphere in the world and the steady running down of armed forces in the West was halted and then reversed, and the last years of the decade were marked by increasing tension between the superpowers and their allies. On 4 April 1949 eleven countries, the USA, Canada, Britain, France, Italy, Denmark, Holland, Iceland, Belgium, Portugal and Norway, signed the North Atlantic Treaty in Washington to create NATO. Western European countries felt threatened by the Soviet Union and NATO bound them together with the USA with a pledge to come to each other's assistance in time of war.

Standing up to the Soviet Union paid dividends. On 12 May 1949 the Berlin Airlift ended. The Russian leadership backed down, unable to raise the stakes without risking a confrontation with NATO. They were not ready to confront the USA, which had nuclear bombs and jet bombers, without the means to retaliate. Western policy was to contain the Soviet Union, which it saw as expansionist, to encircle it with threats, threats from the air which could come from any point of the compass. To be able to challenge the USA and NATO Russia continued development of its strategic bomber forces. The first Soviet strategic bomber was the Tu-4, a clone of the B-29, which became operational in 1947, but it only had a range of 1,500 miles, enough to threaten European targets but not the continental United States. Two jet bombers flew in 1947, the Tu-12 and the Il-22 which was put on display at the Tushino air display on 3 August 1947. Both were disappointing but they showed that the Soviet Union was putting a huge effort into developing a strategic bomber force as well as interceptors.

In response, America started to look at equipping the USAF with interceptors. In October 1948, having considered a variety of options, high capability was subordinated to immediate availability and the USAF gave the go-ahead to Lockheed to build an interim interceptor by modifying the TF-80C, the two-seater version of the Shooting Star. It was to be an all-weather interceptor equipped with on-board radar, giving it some autonomy. America's first jet interceptor was renamed the F-94 Starfire and it flew for the first time on 1 July 1949.

The F-86A, the first production model of the Sabre, entered squadron service in February 1949. It had a top speed approaching Mach 1, a great advance on the Shooting Star, but performance had been sacrificed to what many pilots felt was too much weight. The Sabre weighed 16,000 lb and much of the weight came from a list of extras such as emergency fuel pumps and self-sealing fuel tanks and a radar operated gunsight which not only added weight but was unreliable.

The MiG-15 was much lighter than the Sabre, at 11,000 lb, and most of its design features had been sacrificed to performance, particularly altitude. It was intended as a high-altitude interceptor for the long-range B-47 Stratojet nuclear bomber and had a service ceiling of 51,000 feet. It was powered by a copy of the Rolls-Royce Nene engine and without that engine it is doubtful if it would have flown at all and it would certainly not have had the performance it did. It was the result of a collaboration between Artem Mikoyan, whose design bureau had started designing fighters in 1940, and Mikhail Gurevich, a mathematician, and they relied heavily on captured German data, particularly from the Me 262 and an experimental Focke-Wulf design, the Ta 183. It was a very basic aircraft in its on-board equipment and pilot comforts, but it was simple and cheap to produce in large numbers.

Born of the same parent technologies, German aerodynamics and British engines, to look at there was little to choose between the MiG-15 and the F-86 Sabre. The MiG-15 was 10 per cent smaller than its US counterpart, but it was much lighter, giving it a rate of climb of 9,000 feet per minute, half as much again as the Sabre, though flying straight and level at 20,000 feet the Sabre was marginally faster and the Sabre's 'transient performance', its initial rate of roll, was faster, giving its pilots the ability to change direction in a dogfight more swiftly. Overall the MiG was the superior aircraft by a small margin: it could out-climb the Sabre; its service ceiling was higher; and at high altitude, above 36,000 feet, it was faster. The MiG-15 had been designed as an interceptor, but, unusually, it was also highly manoeuvrable, making it an effective dogfighter, too.

Though slightly slower at altitude, the Sabre was the better gun platform. At full speed it remained stable, while at high speed the MiG became unstable with a tendency to 'snake' from side to side, which was not very helpful to the pilot trying to get into a good firing position. The MiG's gunsight was gyro/optical, similar to those used by US and British pilots towards the end of the Second World War, and while the Sabre's radar-assisted sight was far more advanced, and when it worked it was very accurate, pilots found they could not rely on it. The two fighters had very different armament. The Sabre was built as a dogfighter, an air superiority fighter, and still carried six .50 calibre machine-guns, giving it a high rate of fire for use against other fighters. The MiG-15 was armed with two 23 mm and one huge 37 mm cannon to attack bombers. The Sabre's machine-guns could be fired for longer than the cannon, fourteen seconds compared with seven, and the machine-gun bullets had a much higher muzzle velocity, which meant they reached their target more quickly, leaving less room for error, compared with the Russian cannon which had a relatively low muzzle velocity, and a low rate of fire. Against a bomber that was fine, but against a fighter it called for excellent shooting on the part of the pilot. At altitude, where oxygen was scarce, the cannon had a specific advantage because the exploding shells would set their target alight, while the inert, lead machine-gun rounds, which in any case had less hitting power than cannon shells and did less immediate physical damage to their target, often failed to start a fire.

The Soviet aircraft industry was geared up to build huge numbers of MiG-15 interceptors, three for every Sabre built in the USA. Protecting the Soviet Union and its European empire from strategic air attack was a huge challenge for the Soviet Air Force. They had to start virtually from scratch to become a modern, effective, co-ordinated air defence system for a land mass that stretched across ten time zones, with thousands of miles of border running through areas as different as the Arctic and the Caucasus, along the Barents Sea and the Iron Curtain in Europe. It could not maintain a radar cover of its entire airspace and in the late 1940s fighters were the only defence against bombers, and 20,000 MiG-15s were ordered compared with 900 Sabres. With such numbers, it was impossible to make the fighters as capable as the Sabre, and equally impossible to select and train the pilots to the same standard as in the West. Not only that but pilots and aircraft had to fit into a tightly controlled Soviet military system. Instead of giving their fighter pilots a high degree of autonomy – allowing them to be hunters, free to decide for themselves how best to fight an air battle – the Soviet air defence system was based on the Ground Controlled Intercept (GCI) in which the pilot was vectored to his target under strict control from the ground.

The Soviet Union's next jet bomber, the Il-28, had a range of 1,500 miles and a maximum speed of 590 m.p.h., and it went into service in 1949. A massed flypast by twenty-five of them at Tushino on Mayday 1950 made a huge impact on Western observers and the impact was all the greater because, in August 1949, the Soviet Union had exploded its first atomic bomb.

Russia was still some years away from a long-range operational bomber capable of carrying a viable nuclear bomb, but it would not be long before it would be able to match the US capability, and

NATO reacted to that progress and its perceptions of the Soviet Union's intentions with new vigour. On 13 January 1949 the USAF had issued an Advanced Development Objective (ADO) for a pure interceptor, a completely new, supersonic aircraft built around an electronic control and weapons system which would carry only rockets and guided missiles as armament. It was to be known as the Ultimate Interceptor and it would have to be ready by 1954, by which time the USA believed the USSR would have a strategic jet bomber. In the meantime, the initial order for Starfires was increased threefold and as a further interim measure the Pentagon authorised an interceptor version of the Sabre, the F-86D.

The Soviet threat to US security had stirred America once again. The five years of peace since 1945 had seen the foundation of a new technical age in air warfare, but those same years of peace had laid the foundations of the Cold War. In 1950 a joint committee of the US State Department and Department of Defense was tasked with looking at the defence needs of the USA without regard to budgetary or political constraints. It reported to the National Security Council in April, recommending a large increase in US defence spending. The Report, NSC-68, was effectively a blueprint for the USA to become a military superpower, and it had far-reaching implications for the USA – one of the most immediate was a dramatic increase in the scale and pace of development in military aviation. The success of the X-1 led to a series of pure research aircraft which culminated in the manned X-15 which, just over a decade later, was travelling at speeds bordering seven times the speed of sound at 250,000 feet, the border with space, speeds and altitudes of which the German scientists who had laid many of those foundations during the Second World War could only have dreamed.

In four years Britain had completely lost its position in fighter development. Research and development flying increased in the 1950s but by the time Britain's first prototype swept-wing fighter, the Hawker Hunter, was flying in 1951 it had been overtaken in Europe by Sweden with the Saab J-29, which first flew on 1 September 1948, and by France with the Ouragan, which first flew on 29 February 1949, both of which used British engines. Frank Whittle, and his colleagues at Power Jets Ltd, who had made it all possible by doing the spadework under very difficult circumstances during the war, were crushed by the major aero engine manufacturers. Whittle would have loved to have been able to influence developments, and he had a clear vision of the future, but he was no match for the businessmen. The Americans paid the British government a paltry $800,000 for all the rights to his engine, on which the US engine industry was founded. The Russians built copies of the Derwent and Nene without paying any royalties and subsequently 'licensed' their production to other communist countries. Whittle had the vision and the practical ideas but they were always exploited by others, and he suffered nervous breakdowns as the British Government frittered away the fruits of his labours. He was promoted to Air Commodore then invalided out of the RAF and knighted in 1948, having been awarded £100,000 for all his patents and war work by a Royal Commission. In 1976 he went to live in America and died there in 1996, aged ninety-one.

The jet engine had changed the face of aviation, but as it did so the world had also changed beyond recognition. Britain and Germany were the pioneers, but it was the post-war superpowers who built the first classic jet fighters, the F-86 Sabre and the MiG-15. They were destined to meet in combat, not as anticipated in a major European war between those superpowers, but in a small regional war in colder, more obscure skies.

CHAPTER THREE

Jet on Jet

In 1950 jet fighters had been an operational reality for six years, but they had never met in aerial combat. All that changed on the morning of 8 November 1950. Communist North Korea had invaded Western-orientated South Korea on 25 July, and after initial successes the North Korean army's advance had been checked by US air power. By November US air power controlled the skies over the whole Korean Peninsula, right up to its border with China. North Korea was being supplied from China but there was a bottleneck in the supply route at Sinuiju, the temporary capital of North Korea, where everything had to pass over two bridges over the Yalu River, the actual border between the two countries. The bridges were heavily protected by anti-aircraft guns, and just over the border, at the Chinese airfield at Antung, Chinese MiG-15s were on permanent armed alert.

The bridges were a target that morning for seventy USAF B-29 heavy bombers, under UN control. Shortly after dawn, while the bombers were still 200 miles away at 18,000 feet, USAF F-80C

Shooting Star and F-51D Mustang fighter bombers attacked the anti-aircraft gun batteries at ground level, using High Velocity Aerial Rockets (HVAR), napalm and machine-gun fire. High above them, flying along the Yalu, just on the Korean side, a flight of four F-80Cs of the USAF 16th Fighter Interceptor Squadron (FIS) of the 51st Fighter Interceptor Wing (FIW) was flying 'top cover', forming a shield between Chinese airspace and the approaching B-29s.

One of the American fighter pilots was Lt Russell J. Brown. From 20,000 feet, he and his colleagues watched as six MiG-15s took off from Antung. The Chinese pilots had all the advantages. The Americans were not allowed to infringe Chinese airspace, either to fight or to bomb the airfields, so the MiG pilots could climb to operational height in safety over China, under guidance from ground radar stations which tracked the Americans, who had no radar. The Chinese pilots were very close to the sanctuary of their bases while the Americans were a long way from theirs, flying at the limits of their range with one eye always on the fuel gauge. The Russian MiG-15 was a whole generation younger than the F-80C, and outclassed it by a wide margin in all parameters – top speed, rate of climb, service ceiling, manoeuvrability and armament.

In full view of the F-80C pilots, the MiGs climbed above them to 30,000 feet where they split into pairs and started a shallow dive towards the Americans, building up speed to over 600 m.p.h., a tactic similar to the Roller Coaster developed by Luftwaffe fighter pilots in the Me 262 to attack bombers. Seeing them coming, the Americans turned to meet the attack head-on, throwing the MiGs into confusion. They broke in all directions, some passing through the American formation, firing as they went, then five of them used their stored energy to zoom-climb back up to their perch at 30,000 feet. The sixth Chinese pilot made a basic mistake: instead of climbing again, he dived for the ground. Sensing a real opportunity, Russell Brown dived after him. The F-80 was slightly heavier than the MiG-15 and, diving at full throttle, Brown managed to close the gap. He clung on until the MiG started to climb, which enabled him to cut across the bottom of the dive and close it even more. He opened fire with a five-second burst from just one of his six machine-guns – the other five had jammed. The MiG continued upwards so Brown fired again, and this time flashes of flame appeared from the MiG's jet pipe followed by thin smoke which suddenly started belching out as the aircraft flipped over into a spin and crashed into a riverbank and burst into flames; the pilot did not eject.

It was the first aerial victory by one jet fighter over another. Russell Brown's kill was all the more remarkable because the F-80C Shooting Star should not have been a match for the state-of-the-art, swept-wing MiG-15. The outcome was solely the result of the differences between the pilots, and they were the products of two very different cultures and military systems. Russell Brown, with no radar support, was lower and slower at the start of the battle, but managed to turn the tables on his Chinese opponent who had all the initial advantages. Brown moved straight into the attack, engaging aggressively, which caused confusion in his adversary who then made a mistake. Brown immediately took advantage of the error and saw the attack through to the end. The Chinese pilot's initial tactics were highly suitable against slow, lumbering bombers, for which the MiG-15 had been designed and the pilot trained, and which were their planned targets that day, but they could not get at the bombers without taking on the fighters first. To take on the fighters required individual dogfighting skills and aggression and the Chinese pilots simply did not have them.

The B-29s arrived thirty minutes later to drop incendiary bombs on Sinuiju and 1,000 lb high-explosive bombs on the Korean end of the bridges. The F-80s had done enough to keep the MiGs away but the Chinese put up a heavy barrage of anti-aircraft fire from across the border. None of the bombers was damaged, but they failed to bring the bridges down.

Korea had been divided since the end of the Second World War. It had been part of the Japanese Empire since 1905 and, with the defeat of Japan in 1945, it was divided at the 38th Parallel by Russia and the United States, who both installed leaders inclined to their side: Kim Il Sung in North Korea and Syngman Rhee in South Korea. Like the Iron Curtain in Europe, it was a division which became part of the front line in the Cold War, and in the summer of 1950, encouraged by Russia and China, Kim Il Sung's army prepared to invade South Korea and reunify the country under Communist rule.

America had not been prepared for the Cold War to suddenly

become hot. For Americans in South Korea, Sunday 25 June 1950 was reminiscent of a Sunday morning nine years earlier in Hawaii when the Japanese had attacked Pearl Harbor. They woke up to news that the North Korean Army had started to pour across the 38th Parallel and that North Korean Air Force (NKAF) Yak-9s were attacking the Republic of Korea Air Force's (ROKAF) main airbase at Kimpo and a small adjacent airfield just outside the South's capital, Seoul. The NKAF had Russian flying instructors and 132 aircraft, most of Second World War vintage: 62 Il-10 Schturmovik ground attack fighters and 70 Yak-3, Yak-7B, Yak-9 and La-7 interceptors, none of them jets. Its main military airfield was near the North Korean capital, Pyongyang, which was beyond the reach of ROKAF which consisted of 60 training aircraft only, all of US origin: L-4, L-5 and T-6 Texans. It had been US policy to keep South Korea without any offensive air capability to avoid provoking the Communists. Consequently, when the attack did come, initially the NKAF had complete air superiority.

South Korea fell under the protection of the US Far East Air Force (FEAF), which was made up of the three separate Air Forces – the 20th on Okinawa, the 13th in the Philippines and the much larger 5th Air Force based in Japan under the command of Maj. Gen. Earle E. Partridge, USAF. It did not include any F-86 Sabres – America's latest fighters were concentrated either in the USA or Europe, and the mainstay of FEAF's fighter force was the USAF's first jet fighter, the F-80C Shooting Star, backed up by its last piston-engined fighter, the F-82 Twin Mustang.

The first news of the invasion reached 5th AF HQ at 09.45. FEAF was supposed to have a high degree of combat-readiness, but General Partridge was away for the weekend so news did not reach him until 11.30 a.m. His orders were to assure evacuation of US nationals from South Korea, but not to intervene unless North Korean forces interfered with that evacuation and then, only on direct orders from General Douglas MacArthur, he could attack ground targets.

In the early afternoon of 25 June 1950, two Yak-9s flew round Kimpo on reconnaissance unopposed. At 15.00 they came back and strafed the airfield, destroying the control tower, setting a fuel dump on fire and damaging a parked USAF C-54 transport aircraft. Four more Yaks hit the small nearby airfield and destroyed seven

ROKAF aircraft on the ground, and two more Yak-9s came back two hours later to finish off the C-54.

With Kimpo under attack, Syngman Rhee implored the USA to send Mustangs for his air force and for US air power to be used against the North Koreans, but the US Ambassador's orders were to evacuate US personnel by sea from Inchon, a port to the west of Seoul; air cover for the evacuation would have to come from Japan. The F-80C jets did not have the range so it fell to relays of the very long-range F-82 Twin Mustangs who started patrolling Inchon before dawn in flights of four just below the cloud base. A single NKAF La-7 came out of the clouds at one point, guns blazing, then went back. It represented no threat to the F-82s so they stayed where they were until the freighter which had been chartered to take off the US civilians had been escorted away by US Navy destroyers.

Many other Westerners gathered at Kimpo, where the airlift got under way the following day with North Korean tanks approaching just seventeen miles from the airfield. Gen. Partridge had put together a force of twelve transports escorted by F-82s which patrolled low over the airfield while the people embarked. The F-80Cs could reach Kimpo and they patrolled to the north, the most likely approach for NKAF fighters. At midday five Yak-7s appeared and started a long dive from the north towards Kimpo, getting through the F-80C screen, but the F-82 pilots were warned and ready and shot three of them down. An hour later a larger force of eight Il-10 Schturmoviks approached. This time the F-80s pilots saw them and shot four down, but the American pilots had orders not to pursue so the other four escaped. It was the first time US jet fighters had fired their guns in anger, and the first kills for the F-80. It was also a convincing enough demonstration of American superiority to stop the NKAF intervention at Kimpo completely.

The USA was acting firmly but cautiously; it no longer had a monopoly on atomic weapons and was very careful not to provoke a wider Soviet–US war by precipitate action. With the evacuation complete, the same evening, the United Nations debated a resolution condemning the North's invasion of South Korea and supporting action to repel it. Russia could have vetoed the resolution, but it was boycotting the UN at the time so it was carried and the USA was asked to lead a force to come to the aid of South Korea.

By then, the only way the North Korean advance could be stopped was by air power.

The only air power available with anything like sufficient force to do the job was US air power in Japan. Britain had no RAF forces in the area but sent the Royal Navy aircraft carrier HMS *Triumph* with Seafire and Firefly fighters to patrol off the coast of Korea with the USS *Valley Forge*, which was equipped with Grumman F9F Panther jet fighters. The Royal Australian Air Force (RAAF) had a single squadron, No. 77, flying the F-51D Mustang, also based in Japan. With UN authority and under US leadership, the air campaign started, ranging over the whole of South Korea up to the 38th Parallel. It started with attempts to stem the supplies reaching the advancing North Korean armies in the south and at 07.30 on 28 June, B-26 medium bombers attacked the Munson railyards.

What the North Koreans feared most was the deployment of US air power on airfields in the South, and the same afternoon Yak-9s attacked Suwon airfield, further south from Seoul, destroying an American B-26 and an F-82 which had made emergency landings there. They were back a few hours later to attack a C-54 transport just as it was coming in to land, though it managed to return to Japan for an emergency landing. A third attack destroyed another C-54 on the ground but Suwon stayed open, and the following afternoon General Douglas MacArthur arrived at Suwon airfield to carry out a tour of inspection. An hour after his arrival Suwon was attacked by four Yak-9s; US fighters shot them all down.

One of the first rules of air warfare is to destroy your enemy's aircraft on the ground if at all possible, and MacArthur swiftly sought authority to attack the NKAF's bases. On 3 July US Navy Corsairs and Skyraiders, the ultimate propeller-driven attack aircraft, with RN Seafires as fighter cover, attacked Pyongyang and Onjon-ni airfields. In the course of the strikes, Ensign J. H. Plog, USN, flying a F9F Panther jet fighter, shot down a Yak-9, the first enemy aircraft to fall to the guns of a US Navy jet fighter. A second UN attack brought the total of NKAF aircraft destroyed to 110, effectively neutralising the NKAF. With nothing to resist it, the UN had complete air superiority.

US fighters and bombers then turned their attention to supporting South Korean troops in the ground war. The battle was stalled along the Han River and F-80Cs and F-82s flew ground attack missions from their bases in Japan, a difficult task for the F-80 pilots who had only fifteen minutes at most over the target area. The sorties slowed the North Korean army down but the South Korean army was starting to crumble and the Han River line gave way; Seoul fell shortly afterwards and the North Koreans kept going south.

In response, President Truman authorised the commitment of US ground troops. The US 24th Infantry Division was airlifted from Japan to Pusan, a port right at the southern tip of the Korean peninsula, on 1 August and two battalions headed north from Pusan. In two days they met South Korean soldiers retreating south towards Pusan so, instead of advancing, a defensive perimeter was established to protect Pusan. The US troops had no armour, no artillery and poor communications, and their only means of bombarding the enemy was tactical air power. Without the fighter bombers from Japan keeping the North Korean army at bay on the perimeter around Pusan, it would almost certainly have taken the port, but the line held and the USA was able to deploy more men from ships, ready for a counter-attack.

In the meantime, General MacArthur planned a bold move to outflank the North Koreans by landing from the sea at Inchon, retaking Seoul, then moving inland to cut off the North Korean supply lines. However, MacArthur needed time to plan those landings and assemble the force, and while he planned the perimeter around Pusan had to be held. With 70,000 North Korean troops on the ground with trucks, T-34 tanks, and their equipment, all with no air cover, there were many targets for the US fighter bombers, but to take advantage of the situation they needed to be based at Pusan, nearer the fighting.

The problem was getting the right aircraft in the right place, and Korean airfields, most of them grass strips built by the Japanese during the war, were not suitable for jet fighters. The USAF had a tailor-made jet fighter bomber, the Republic F-84 Thunderjet, which had the range and payload to do some real damage, but even Japanese airfields did not have runways long enough to take them. The F-80Cs were good fighter bombers, but they could not be effective with such little time over the target. The solution was to take F-51D Mustangs, which could operate from crude strips, out of storage and out of service with the Air National Guard (ANG) in the USA and fit them out for ground attack, but that would take time, and while they were waiting for the Mustangs to arrive the F-80s and the B-26 medium bombers had to hold the line.

Seventy per cent of ground attack sorties were carried out by F-80C Shooting Stars, mainly using 5 in. HVARs against North Korean armour with only minutes over the target area. The F-80C could carry two 1,000 lb bombs, but if it did so its range was reduced, making it impossible to reach the targets. USAF engineers came up with a novel solution on the spot: they took apart an external fuel tank known as a Fletcher tank and inserted it into the middle of the tip tanks, adding 200 gallons of fuel, which extended their time in the air by thirty minutes. The combination of fuel and weapons was over the normal weight limits for the F-80C but the modification was authorised and the work was carried out in Japan.

The sustained use of ground attack aircraft began to have its effect and by 8 July the North Korean army had to pause. Meanwhile, US Army engineers were working on the rough airstrips around Pusan, making them ready to take Mustangs. One very rough field, Taegu, was within a few miles of the North Koreans, and the first F-51s went to Taegu when they arrived from the USA on 14 July, the first USAF aircraft to be based on Korean soil. Many F-80C fighter pilots of the 51st Wing, nominally interceptors, converted to P-51s just to get into the fight. By mid-August there were six squadrons of Mustangs around the Pusan perimeter. It was a desperate battle, but the turning point came once the locally based Mustangs, supported by attack aircraft from the USS *Philippine Sea* off the coast, were able to increase the sortie rate with far higher bomb, rocket and napalm loads from bases only minutes away from the front line.

On 18 August the North Koreans mounted an offensive against Taegu, advancing to within twelve miles of the airfield, but the P-51 pilots held off the attack by operating round the clock for 48 hours. On 31 August the North Koreans, in an act of desperation, used human waves against the perimeter. They were met from the air and the sortie rate rose from 249 close support missions a day by Navy, Marine and Air Force fighter bombers to around 700 a day by 11 September, slaughtering thousands of North Korean soldiers. It was the high tide of the battle and air power had held the line.

The UN had built up its ground forces and the following day South Korean, US and British troops launched a counter-offensive. The North Koreans started to fall back, still pounded from the air.

Improvisation and persistence in the air and on the ground had bought enough time for MacArthur to plan the Inchon landings, which took place on 15 September, and to prepare the way. US Navy Corsairs and Skyraiders from the USS *Valley Forge*, *Philippine Sea* and *Boxer*, with RN Seafires and Fireflies from HMS *Triumph* giving fighter protection, attacked the defences. They were opposed from the air by just two Il-10s and 1 Yak-9, which had no effect. The landings were a complete success with 70,000 men, mostly US Marines, landed from the 260-ship armada. The Marines took Kimpo airfield two days later and within hours whole squadrons of USMC Corsairs had landed from the carriers to fly close support missions for the Marines heading for Seoul. By 21 September Suwon had been recaptured and the build-up of UN air forces in South Korea gathered pace. Kimpo and Pusan airfields were quickly refurbished and supplies were soon arriving by air, including three squadrons of F-80Cs at Kimpo, three more in Taegu and No. 77 RAAF at Pusan.

On 19 September the 24th Division spearheaded a breakout from the Pusan perimeter and the North Korean forces first scattered in confusion, then started streaming northwards, unprotected from air attack. Fighter bombers roamed over the countryside, looking for targets of opportunity, and destroying trucks, tanks and artillery and killing North Korean soldiers. By the end of September there were no worthwhile targets left.

UN forces retook Seoul on 27 September and the same day, MacArthur was ordered to destroy the North Korean army, pursuing it beyond the old border along the 38th Parallel to unite Korea, North and South, as one country. Kim Il Sung rejected surrender and Chou-en-lai warned the UN that it would come to the assistance of the North Koreans if the North was invaded. UN fighters started patrolling the whole of North Korea, right up to the Yalu River, and there were reports of Chinese troops along the Yalu River, but the UN enjoyed complete air superiority and under that cover its ground forces crossed the 38th Parallel and invaded North Korea.

The Chinese were put under pressure from Stalin to invade from the north, and he said that, if they did, Russia would secretly supply more MiG-15s with Soviet pilots. In October the 64th Fighter Aviation Corps, including many of their Second World War aces, was sent to Chinese airfields close to the North Korean border in Manchuria with Chinese People's Air Force insignia on their aircraft and wearing Chinese uniforms. The Soviet Air Force, despite its huge size, its emphasis on tactical fighters and on well-drilled aerial combat, had the same experience as Western air forces, and a small number of pilots had been responsible for a high proportion of aerial victories, and the SAF did send some of its best pilots. Later they were commanded by Col. Ivan Khozedub, the SAF's leading ace of the Second World War with sixty-two victories, including one Me 262, and nominated Hero of the Soviet Union three times, but he did not fly in combat for fear that he might be shot down and captured.

The airspace above the Yalu was hotly disputed. Chinese anti-aircraft batteries on their side of the river regularly fired over the border at US aircraft patrolling aggressively along it, and on 16 October they shot down a Mustang. Two days later an RB-29 on a reconnaissance flight over the area reported up to seventy-five MiG-15s at Antung. Air-to-air skirmishes started on 1 November when a B-26 was attacked by three Yak-9s with Chinese markings; the B-26's gunners managed to shoot one of them down and the others fled back to the safety of China. Later that day F-80C fighter bombers attacked Chinese Yak-9s on Sinuiju airfield, losing one to ground fire. In the afternoon four Mustangs were patrolling along the Yalu when a flight of six MiG-15s flew straight through their formation at high speed in a slashing attack reminiscent of Luftwaffe tactics over Germany, firing as they went, then turned back over the river to safety; no Mustangs were hit.

In the next few days General Partridge made repeated requests to be allowed to neutralise the MiGs by bombing their airfields on the Chinese side of the Yalu, but permission was denied, though bombing of the bridges was allowed to continue, reflecting the anxiety in Washington that China and Russia might begin a wider war against the USA.

Four days later, on 5 November, 180,000 Chinese troops crossed the Yalu without giving away their numbers. It was a spectacular failure of intelligence by the UN, and General MacArthur, believing the force to be much smaller, asked for maximum bombing effort to halt them. A raid by seventy B-29s from Okinawa was planned for 7 November, but it had to be abandoned because of bad weather. It was rescheduled for the following day, with F-80Cs as escorts, and it was that raid which brought about the first confrontation between the Chinese MiG-15 and the F-80C flown by Lt Russell Brown.

The Chinese Air Force, equipped and trained by the Soviet Union, remained in a broadly defensive posture and did not venture far from their sanctuary to carry the fight to the Americans. The US fighters kept the Chinese fighters bottled up in their own airspace, leaving the UN air forces free to bomb, even right up against the border. Most of the bridges were eventually destroyed but to little effect: Chinese and North Korean engineers built pontoons to carry the supplies instead, and once the river froze they could be moved across the ice. Strategic bombing needed strategic targets and most of those were in China, which was out of bounds, infuriating many American airmen who wanted to bomb Chinese targets, especially airfields. But this was the new world order, the world of huge power blocs, and though North Korea had been the aggressor, and China was her ally, in the context of the Cold War an attack on China could have brought in the Soviet Union and started a much wider war. It was one of the characteristics of a world divided into two armed camps who could not fight each other directly that they did so by proxy along the fault line of a divided world.

On subsequent B-29 raids the Chinese MiG-15 pilots climbed higher above both the bombers and their fighter escorts, using their superior ceiling and speed to penetrate the US fighter shield and get at the bombers, shooting several down and damaging others. Damage was slight, but the mood had changed; only weeks earlier, there had been genuine hopes that the Korean War would be over by Christmas, but now it was a confrontation between major powers and for those who realised it the air war, far from being over, had only just begun. As tension rose the US pilots renamed the sky above the Yalu 'MiG Alley'.

Up to early November, the UN had relied mainly on aircraft of Second World War vintage, which had been sufficient to cope with the NKAF and do the fighter/bomber work. The huge advantage which the MiG-15 gave the opposition, not only in performance but also in numbers, now posed a real threat to UN air superiority. The only answer was to deploy a fighter which could take on and beat the MiG-15, and there was only one – the North American F-86A Sabre. Russell Brown's landmark victory in the F-80C Shooting Star was a cause for celebration inside the USAF, but everybody knew that the venerable Shooting Star was no match for the MiG-15, and on the day of the jet victory the Pentagon decided to send Sabres to meet the new challenge in air superiority and F-84E Thunderjet fighter bombers were sent to take over the ground attack role.

On 11 November orders were received at the HQ of the 4th FIW at Wilmington, Delaware, to prepare to move to Korea. Three days later the commander, Col. Bruce Hinton, USAF, and his pilots and aircraft embarked on an aircraft carrier to take them across the Pacific; they arrived in Japan on 28 November. The Sabres had been sealed in protective cocoons against the weather while they were transported across the Pacific and some had suffered corrosion damage on the way. Once they were in Japan it took a few days to take them out and service them, ready for combat, including painting black and white 'invasion stripes' round their fuselages. The Sabre and the MiG-15 were very similar in appearance and the stripes were to avoid any F-80C, F-51D or F-84E pilots mistaking them for Chinese fighters.

On 17 December the Sabres ventured into 'MiG Alley' for the first time, a flight of four led by Bruce Hinton. On the way north, Hinton mimicked the speed, altitude and tactics of the slower F-80s, hoping to lure the MiGs up for a fight. Chinese radar spotted them and the MiGs duly scrambled from Antung. When the Sabres reached the Yalu they turned east, flying along the river at 20,000 feet. Hinton's wingman saw the four MiGs first, below the Sabres, a mile away and still climbing. Hinton heard the warning, then his radio went dead. The rest of his flight did not hear the order he gave which signified they were about to fight: 'Baker Flight, drop tanks.'

His own long-range tanks dropped away, lightening the Sabre, and he opened the throttle to full power. In the hectic prelude to combat, the fighter pilot could not just slam the throttle open; early jet engines had to be coaxed gently and skilfully to full power or they could 'flame out' if the pilot failed to get the mixture of fuel and air just right. Hinton separated from his flight as the MiGs split into two pairs, one of which crossed below and in front of him in a wide right-hand climbing turn, trying to get into a firing position behind him. Hinton rolled into a right-hand turn himself, trying to get on the inside the MiGs' turn and on to their tails. He nosed down a bit, the Machmeter showing Mach .95, well over the normal limit, but he needed to convert his slight height advantage into a little bit of extra speed to close on them.

The leading Chinese pilot was still climbing and falling back slowly, trying to get above and behind Hinton, but his wingman had levelled out in the turn, the tactic being to lure Hinton into concentrating on the No. 2 while the leader manoeuvred higher into a good firing position behind Hinton. It was shaping up as a classic turning battle, everybody trying to get on each other's tail, precisely the kind of dogfight for which the idea of wingmen was invented – to cover the lead aircraft as it goes for the kill. But Hinton was alone; he was both attacker and target, with no wingman to cover his tail.

Hinton was sandwiched between two superior enemy fighters in a high-speed turn in 'MiG Alley'. He was also a colonel in the United States Air Force, a veteran of the Second World War and a fighter pilot in his element. At 500 yards he fired at the Chinese No. 2, and saw strikes, but no fire. The MiG continued to fly in a tight level turn, giving his leader every possible opportunity to get into a better firing position. But Hinton stuck with his target and fired again. This time the Chinese pilot made an unforced error: he put out his speed brakes, killing off speed very quickly, possibly in an attempt to force Hinton to fly past him. The gap closed suddenly, then he made another error: he changed his mind and put the brakes in again. Hinton was still there, closer now, and he fired another five-second burst straight into the MiG's tail pipe from right behind. Bits of the MiG's engine flew off and it slowed a bit but continued to fly. Hinton could hardly believe it but, heedless of the danger which the leader still might pose, he flew right up alongside the MiG looking for damage, then drew back to a safe distance and fired again. More bits flew off the MiG and this time it rolled over on to its back, went lazily into a spin and fell out of the sky. Hinton did not follow it down, but twisted and turned in the cockpit, trying to find the leader, but the sky was empty, with no MiGs or Sabres to be seen.

The Chinese leader had clearly decided not to fight: one reason may have been the wind. The high-level wind over northern China and Korea at that time of year blows steadily eastwards, from west or northwest, away from Chinese airspace towards Korean, giving aircraft flying east up to a 100 m.p.h. speed advantage. The dogfight had taken them east already, and if the MiG's pilot had flown further east, deeper into UN airspace, he would have had to fly against the wind on the way back to the safety of Chinese airspace.

The 4th FIW Sabres took over the job of patrolling at height over the Yalu, and on 22 December eight were patrolling at 30,000 feet when they were bounced by a flight of sixteen MiGs; one of the Sabres was hit immediately and went down, and a fierce dogfight developed. Outnumbered two to one, the American pilots shot down six of the MiGs for no further loss. The fight had a salutary effect on the Chinese and for the next seven days the Sabres patrolled unchallenged. On 30 December a flight of 16 Sabres was attacked by 36 MiGs but the MiGs broke it off once two of their number had been damaged. In December as a whole the Sabres destroyed eight MiGs plus two probables and seven damaged, for the loss of one Sabre – a kill ratio of 8:1 in their favour.

On the ground it was very different. By the middle of December the UN forces were in headlong retreat. On 16 December the Chinese army came out into the open and started streaming along the roads in open country, once again easy targets for the Thunderjet, Shooting Star and Mustang fighter bombers. However, as the Chinese advanced so the fighter bomber squadrons had to retreat from airfields which might be overrun. The MiGs were still bottled up by the Sabres close to their bases in China so the UN still had air superiority over the battlefield, and as the Chinese army went south, often in the open, it did so without air cover. The fighter bombers made good use of the opportunity to attack the massed Chinese armies out in the open, using HVAR, machine-guns and napalm, and they inflicted an estimated 33,000 casualties, forcing the Chinese under cover again which slowed their progress. The communists had 700 Chinese and 500 Russian fighters not far away, but they made virtually no use of them over the battlefield, partly because they were fearful that they would be severely beaten in the air by US pilots, and partly because to launch air attacks on the UN from inside China might have provoked a bigger US response.

The headlong retreat by UN forces had a poor effect on morale which took another knock when the Eighth Army commander, Gen. Walton, was killed in a road accident. His replacement was the highly regarded Gen. Matthew B. Ridgeway, commander of Allied airborne forces in the Second World War. He was in place by the end of the year with a new policy – to get the Chinese out of South Korea and re-establish the status quo.

As Ridgeway took over so bad weather kept the UN air forces on the ground for the rest of December, allowing the Chinese and North Koreans to continue their advance relatively unmolested from the air. Then on 1 January 1951 the skies cleared and the fighter bombers could go to work again on the road to Seoul where the communist troops were massed to retake the capital. In five days they inflicted 8,000 casualties, but the Chinese were prepared to spend soldiers' lives on a huge scale to advance without air cover while reluctant to see their aircraft advance too far forward and tangle with the Sabres in order to protect the men on the ground; they took Seoul on 14 January.

The Sabres had to evacuate Kimpo and move further south to Suwon, putting them even further away from MiG Alley; some even went back to Japan from where they could not reach it at all. The Chinese offensive petered out seventy miles south of Seoul, where Ridgeway had established his last line of defence, with about a third of South Korea in Chinese hands. To hold the line, let alone advance further, the Chinese army would have to have air support, but the Chinese People's Air Force (CPAF) did not have the range to support the Chinese army on the ground. They had 450 MiG-15s, and a plentiful supply of Il-10 Schturmovik ground attack fighters, but they knew the Il-10s would be slaughtered by the US fighters without air superiority and there were no bases inside Korea from which the MiGs could operate with the same sanctuary which they could from their bases inside China. To get the UN out of Korea the Chinese generals knew they would have to mount an air offensive so a plan was evolved to fight for air superiority over northwestern Korea, break the UN hold on the area, then repair the airfields so the Il-10s could use them to land, arm and refuel, go south to their targets, then transit back through them to safety in China, all under the MiG umbrella. They started rebuilding Sinuiju airfield, just inside the Korean border, and Pyongyang much further south, and denying these airfields to the Chinese became a major job for the UN F-84s, F-80s and F-51s.

The Chinese air offensive began on 21 January. Two formations of MiGs crossed the Yalu; one flight of twelve attacked four F-80s and shot down one of them. The other flight attacked eight F-84s which were attacking bridges over the Yalu, shooting down one of the Thunderjets but losing one of their number to the CO of the Thunderjet squadron.

The UN counter air offensive began on 23 January when a flight of 33 F-84 Thunderjets took off from Taegu, right in the south, and flew the full length of the peninsula to Sinuiju. Eight of the F-84s strafed the airfield while 25 flew top cover at 20,000 feet. At that altitude they had an advantage over the MiGs, especially in turning. As expected, the MiGs came up to defend Sinuiju, and tried to tempt the Thunderjets up, but without success. The strafing F-84s finished the attacks then joined the top cover patrol and a huge dogfight developed at around 20,000 feet. The F-84 pilots accounted for four confirmed kills, two of them to Lt Jacob Kratt, with a further three probables and four damaged, all for no losses. An hour later 46 F-80s attacked Pyongyang airfield with guns, rockets and bombs. They did not need the fighter cover because it was too far south for the MiGs to venture. The Chinese air offensive had failed.

On the ground Ridgeway counter-attacked on 7 March and retook Seoul a week later. With Kimpo retaken for the second time, the Sabres came back from Japan to Suwon, then Kimpo, and were able to reach back into MiG Alley, carrying the fight to the enemy and penning the MiGs up against the border again.

The fighter bomber war was becoming an all-jet war too. Without air superiority above them, the communist soldiers surrounded their vehicles with anti-aircraft guns, 12.7 mm machine-guns and 37 mm cannon, and from March 1951 it was clear that the speed of the jet fighters gave them the edge. The Mustangs were still doing great damage on the ground but they were increasingly vulnerable to ground fire and Gen. Partridge asked for F-80C and F-84E replacements for the ageing F-51 Mustangs.

On 22 April the Chinese launched their spring offensive with the objective of isolating, then taking, Seoul again. They put 70 divisions, over 500,000 men, into the battle. Ridgeway made extensive use of minefields and artillery against the huge numbers of advancing Chinese infantry, and also made maximum use of the air superiority; he had to call in fighter bombers as flying artillery. The 27 Fighter Escort Wing (FEW) was equipped with F-84 and fragmentation bombs which burst into a hail of shrapnel above the ground. They were unopposed in the air and could pick and choose their targets. On 23 April UN air strikes accounted for 2,000 Chinese casualties. In one incident two F-80s caught around 200 Chinese soldiers in the open and attacked with 260 lb fragmentation bombs, then followed up with machine-gun fire and HVAR rockets. Virtually none of the Chinese soldiers survived.

On 26 April it appeared the offensive had been checked, then three days later it was renewed with a final Chinese push for Seoul. It was a battle between flesh and steel, reminiscent of the First World War: human waves ranged against modern munitions, even more so as the ground fighting stabilised into a delicate equilibrium along the much-violated border at the 38th Parallel. The front settled down to trench warfare, while above them fighter pilots fought to control the airspace so that attack aircraft and artillery could do their work without hindrance. Steel won. In advancing thirty-five miles in the face of heavy bombardment, the Chinese and North Koreans lost 70,000 men in a week; on 30 April they started pulling back.

With air superiority over the peninsula, the UN fighter pilots continued to prevent the Chinese from rebuilding airfields further south by constant pressure. By early May Sinuiju airfield had largely been rebuilt and it was ringed with anti-aircraft defences, making it the best-defended target in North Korea. On 9 May a huge UN attack lasting forty-five minutes by waves of F-80Cs, F-51Ds and Navy Corsairs smashed it up again while Sabres, F-84Es and Navy Panthers held the MiGs at bay; all the UN aircraft returned to base.

That was the pattern which developed: the Sabres leant on North Korea, rather as the RFC and French had leant on the Germans over the Western Front, never giving up the battle for superiority, always being on the offensive in order to defend their airspace. Like the First World War, the pilots who fought individual battles were singled out for particular attention and became individual heroes in an otherwise faceless war. One such man was Capt. James Jabara of the 334th FIS, part of the 4th FIW. Jabara had already scored 3.5 kills, flying a P-51D against the Luftwaffe in the Second World War, and by May 1951 he had shot down 4 MiG-15s in a month in Korea. The 334th was rotated back to Japan on 7 May to be replaced by the 335th, but Jabara wanted a fifth victory – to become the first US jet ace. He badgered his superiors until they let him transfer to the 335th to stay in the battle. For most of the month he never saw a MiG, despite almost daily trips into MiG Alley, and he was in danger of completing his 100th mission after which he would automatically return to the USA.

On 20 May a flight of 12 Sabres was on an offensive sweep along the Yalu when they were attacked by a force of 50 MiGs; two flights of Sabres high above at 35,000 feet quickly joined the fight; Jabara was flying one of them. The whole flight jettisoned their long-range fuel tanks but one of Jabara's hung up and standing orders in that eventuality were to return to base. Jabara ignored the orders and joined the battle, flying his lopsided Sabre with rather stiff controls. He dived to 20,000 feet with his wingman, Lt Kemp, on his tail and just as they approached the dogfight a flight of six MiGs made a firing pass. Another pair of Sabres turned into the MiGs and broke them into two sections of three, going after one section themselves and leaving the other three to Jabara and Kemp. Jabara managed to get on the tail of one of them, just as another flight of MiGs attacked him. Jabara and Kemp then turned to face the new attack head-on and split the MiG flight into two and one. Jabara went after the lone MiG. The MiG pilot tried every trick in the fighter pilot's repertoire to shake him off, but at that altitude the advantage was with the Sabre, and slowly Jabara gained on him, Kemp covering his six o'clock. Jabara opened fire, at maximum range for his machine-guns, with three short bursts and saw tracer strikes along the fuselage and left wing. The MiG snap-rolled into a spin, trailing smoke. Jabara followed him down to 10,000 feet, coolly watching the MiG pilot eject, then he rolled his camera gun just as the MiG exploded, giving him the evidence of his fifth kill.

Instead of going home, the first USAF jet ace climbed to rejoin the fight, the faithful Kemp still watching his tail. They singled out another flight of six MiGs; Jabara picked one out, fired a single burst and the MiG caught fire immediately. Jabara pulled the throttle back and extended his air brakes to slow him down as he followed a second MiG down to 6,500 feet to film him crash and explode. Kemp, who should have been covering Jabara's tail, had broken off to engage two other MiGs on the way down, but as he did so Jabara came under attack from two more. Jabara was on his own, on Bingo fuel, against two MiGs. He opened the throttle again and popped in the speed brakes but the MiGs stuck with him. Seeing his predicament, Capt. Gene Holley and his wingman dived down. One of the MiGs broke off immediately, leaving the other exposed, and Holley got into his six o'clock and set him on fire. By then fuel was critical and all the Sabres headed back to Suwon.

Jabara was instantly given hero status, but he gave the credit to his aircraft, saying simply in a press interview back in the States what every fighter pilot wants to say and believe, 'The F-86 Sabre is the best jet fighter in the world and the MiG is second best.'

The only way to maintain superiority was for the Sabre pilots to keep going back, day after day. As they did, the Americans found that the CPAF pilots developed new tactics, looking for the Sabre's weak points. They knew that the Sabres only had a short time in MiG Alley before they had to return, and so tried to time their attacks as the Sabres were about to leave and low on fuel. The Sabres responded by splitting into flights of four or six aircraft so only the last flight would then not have support. The Sabre pilots also used ruses. They started arriving at ever closer intervals and on one occasion, on 22 May, when the MiGs expected only one wave and they sent up 36 MiGs against what they thought were 12 Sabres, they suddenly found themselves up against 24, losing four destroyed and four damaged for no loss to the Sabres.

By early June it was clear that the Chinese air offensive had failed. The CPAF commander got a lot of the blame, but he argued that he had not been given the time to rebuild his airfields in North Korea. As part of a new plan, he asked for experienced pilots from any communist country, an International Communist Volunteer Air Force, to help try and gain air superiority. In the meantime, the best he could do was fly nuisance raids by Il-10s and Po-2s at night, light bombing which had little effect except on one occasion hitting Suwon and destroying one Sabre and damaging eight others.

On 17 June the mood in MiG Alley, and the mathematics,

changed. Sabre pilots of the 4th Wing were patrolling along the Yalu as usual when they came under attack from 25 MiGs. The style of fighting was very different, more confident and aggressive, and when the Sabre pilots returned to base, having shot down one, there was a widely held view that they had been up against Russian or Eastern bloc fighter pilots for the first time. The following day they met the same, much more determined opposition and, although the Sabres managed to shoot down four MiGs, they lost a Sabre. Next day the MiGs brought down another Sabre and, although four of their number were damaged in the fight, all the MiGs returned to base. On 22 June 4th Wing Sabres were flying top cover for a force of F-80Cs attacking Sinuiju airfield again; the MiGs attacked and lost two of their number but one Sabre was lost.

The communist volunteer pilots experimented with tactics, one of which US pilots who had experienced Me 262 attacks in the Second World War recognised as a variation on the Luftwaffe's Roller Coaster attack, which they named the Yo-Yo. The MiGs would orbit, chasing each other's tails at high level, around 45,000 feet, where their performance was much better. When the Sabres arrived underneath one, or a pair of MiGs would swoop down at high speed, make a firing pass through the Sabres, then zoom climb back to the defensive circle high above.

The tactics and the maths changed a bit but the communist pilots could not break the UN air superiority. The fighting on the ground had reached a stalemate, too, and on 1 July 1951 discussions about an armistice began at Kaesong. The possibility of an end to the war restrained fighting on the ground, but in the air there was no let-up. Air superiority can never be permanently established, it has to be fought for on a daily basis, and the Sabres kept up the aggressive policy of leaning on the communist forces. July was a bad month for the communist air forces. On 8 July F-51s attacked Kangdong; when 20 MiGs attacked them, 35 Sabres arrived and shot down three MiGs; the following day the Chinese lost another two, and two days later they lost another three, all for no loss to the Americans.

The CPAF responded by challenging the obvious superiority of the UN with ever-greater numbers. The Antung base was enlarged and modernised, including a new operations centre and satellite airfields nearby, turning it into a fighter complex which could handle up to 450 MiGs at a time. It was manned by advisors and ground controllers from the Soviet Union and other communist countries who were there to help, but also there to give them first-hand experience of fighting against the Americans, their potential adversaries in the Cold War. The strength of the CPAF was built up to over 1,000 aircraft, of which 700 were kept at airfields in Manchuria, out of reach of either the Sabres or B-29s.

Against this, FEAF had a total of 89 F-86A Sabres, of which less than 50, normally around 44, were operational with the 4th FIW in Korea at any one time, the rest being in Japan undergoing maintenance. Gen. Otto P. Weyland, who had taken over command of FEAF on 10 June, sent an urgent request to the Pentagon for four more Sabre wings, and he also asked for the latest variant, the F-86E, which had 'flying tails', a modification in which both the elevator and the tailplane moved in a co-ordinated way, giving greater control at higher speeds – a direct result of the work done by Chuck Yeager on the X-1. But at the Pentagon the planners believed that the Chinese build-up was defensive, and the first examples of the F-86E went to Air Defense Command (ADC) in the USA because the biggest threat to the USA was still seen as a potential attack by Soviet bombers. The same policy applied to fighter bombers. The F-51s and F-80s, which had done very well in the first year of the war, were now suffering a high rate of attrition, and Weyland wanted the latest model F-84s, but they, too, were going to equip US-based squadrons and NATO allies confronting the Soviet Union in the Cold War. All Weyland got was one wing of F-84s, 75 aircraft, to be based in Japan.

After two months of talking it was clear that the armistice talks were stalled and the communists started a new air offensive on 1 September, making a concerted effort to take air superiority from the UN: 525 MiGs came over the Yalu in flights of 90 or more. On 2 September 22 Sabres took on 40 MiGs and a huge, swirling battle developed, spread over a hundred miles between Sinuiju and Pyongyang. It lasted over thirty minutes, a very long time for aerial combat, and it cost the communist forces four MiGs. On 9 September 1951 28 Sabres took on 70 MiGs and two more Sabre pilots, Capt. Richard Baker and Capt. Ralph Gibson, became aces. Among the Russian volunteers who were believed to be fighting at this time was Col. Evgeny Pepelyaev, a Second World War ace. The Sabre pilots called the communist volunteers 'honchos' and they did not need to see them to know they were up against men with far more of a grasp of aerial combat – they could feel it in the way they flew and manoeuvred.

In September the Sabres shot down 14 MiGs, but the numbers were beginning to have their effect. Three Sabres were lost and enough MiGs were getting through to take on the fighter bombers well south of MiG Alley. Three were lost: a Mustang, a Shooting Star and a Thunderjet. Once again Weyland asked for more Sabres and once again the Pentagon refused so he ordered the fighter bombers to stop attacking the airfields in the far northwest. It was just what the communists wanted, a lull in the constant pressure against them on the ground from the fighter bombers. They started to repair the North Korean airfields, planning to use them to make ground attacks further south, and by the end of October they had three airfields, Saamcham, Namsi and Taechon, all well to the south of the Yalu, operational again. They were also within forty-five miles of each other and so that fighters from one airfield could protect one another.

Instead of fighter bombers, FEAF used B-29s against these airfields, which led to some of the fiercest aerial fighting of the war. As a prelude, on 16 October the Sabres flew towards MiG Alley, drawing the MiGs into battle where they shot down nine, plus two probables, for no loss. On 18 October daylight bombing started again, with F-84s escorting the B-29s while Sabres provided top cover. The MiGs bounced the formation in huge numbers and shot down one B-29. On 23 October eight B-29s attacked Namsi airfield, escorted by 55 F-84s with 34 Sabres ahead and above. At 09.15 100 MiGs took on the Sabres, losing two in the dogfight which ensued, then another 50 MiGs arrived. First they tried to lure the F-84s away and failed so they cut through the F-84 screen and attacked the B-29s, losing four MiGs to the F-84s but shooting down 3 B-29s and one Thunderjet. Bomber killing was the kind of fighting for which the MiG-15 had been designed. It was the worst day of the war for the B-29s and, following such losses, heavy day bombing was stopped. The Americans were beginning to fight the air war on the enemy's terms.

The battle for air superiority went on for the rest of the month, big dogfights involving hundreds of MiGs and a smaller number of Sabres, and by the end of October 32 MiGs had been destroyed, 24 by Sabres, seven to B-29 gunners and one to an F-84. But seven Sabres, five B-29s, two F-84s and one F-80C were lost. The Sabre pilots held the line against overwhelming odds but they were hard-pressed and the Chinese were confident enough to move MiGs south of the Yalu to Uiju and ground attack aircraft to Sinuiju. The Sabres were winning the battle in the air, but by the sheer weight of numbers, and with massive help from the Soviet Union and other communist countries, China was slowly taking command of the sky over North Korea, with all the implications that had on the war on the ground.

Communist quantity was challenging UN quality, and the UN generals sent ever more urgent requests to the Pentagon for more and better Sabres. In late October the USAF Chief of Staff, General Vandenberg, visited FEAF in Japan to review the situation. He realised that the UN air force was in danger of being overwhelmed and went back to the USA with his mind changed. Just in case the point had not been made, on 1 October Col. Harrison 'Harry' Thyng, the new commander of the hard-pressed 4th FIW and a veteran of the Second World War, who started his career in Spitfires in North Africa and finished the war with eleven Germans to his credit, sent a signal to Vandenberg, bypassing all his immediate superiors with the simple message: 'I can no longer be responsible for air superiority in northwest Korea.'

The result of Vandenberg's visit was 75 more Sabres, including the latest F-86Es which were sent by sea, arriving on 9 November, a year and a day after Russell Brown's first victory.

So overwhelming were the numbers of MiGs at their disposal that the Chinese attempted to use what the UN pilots called 'train tactics'. Flights of up to 80 MiG-15s would form up in the safety of Chinese airspace, then come as far south as Pyongyang at 35,000 feet where they turned back. If Sabres or fighter bombers were spotted, a flight would detach itself, dive down, attack, then zoom back up again. The train then turned and headed back towards its base in the northwest and another would leave overhead Antung to repeat the process, covering the return of the previous train.

Under this massive fighter cover, small bombing raids could be mounted against UN troops and targets on the ground. On 30

November Col. Benjamin Preston was leading 31 Sabres on an offensive patrol along the Yalu. He saw a MiG train high overhead, flying south, while at the same time, 10,000 feet below, another Sabre flight led by Col. Thyng saw a slower, mixed flight crossing the Yalu at low level. Thyng went down to investigate and found a flight of 12 Tu-2 medium bombers escorted by 16 La-9 piston-engined fighters and 16 MiG-15s, heading south. Thyng called down first one squadron, then a second, and they made high-speed firing passes through the communist formation. In the ensuing battle eight Tu-2s, three La-9s and one MiG-15 were shot down, one of the best results in a day for the UN air forces. In the fight, two new aces made their fifth kills: Maj. George Davis, who shot down four; and Maj. Winton 'Bones' Marshall who shot down three.

No. 77 Sqn RAAF had been re-equipped with Meteors, and on 1 December the Australian pilots were on a sweep at 19,000 feet when they saw 50 MiGs high above. The MiGs came down in pairs and the Meteors turned to meet them, and in the dogfight which developed Flying Officer Bruce Gogerly managed to get off a three-second burst of 20 mm cannon fire into a MiG which exploded almost immediately. Several Meteor pilots fired into a single MiG, which also went down in flames, but three Meteors were lost. The Meteor was clearly not up to facing the MiG-15s in the same way as the Sabre and from that date it was relegated to airfield defence in South Korea. The Australian pilots found their new role very frustrating since it involved mainly sitting at base waiting for a Chinese attack which never materialised so they were transferred to ground attack and continued in that role until the end of the war. Where there is a huge disparity in the quality of the training of the pilots some technical deficiencies can be overcome, but having the best equipment is the only sure way to win.

On the same day that the Meteors were on the receiving end of a mauling by MiGs, the 51st FIW swapped its F-80Cs for the new F-86E Sabre. The CO was Col. Francis F. 'Gabby' Gabreski, a Second World War fighter pilot with twenty-eight victories in P-47s, who had already accounted for two MiGs. The new wing raised the number of Sabres in Korea to 127, with 40 more in reserve in Japan, evening up the numbers slightly, but giving the American pilots the best fighter available at the time.

The Chinese air offensive continued through December 1951

with 200 MiGs a day coming across, some of them high, others low, attacking fighter bombers. In the first week of December they got three, but in the same week the Sabres of the 4th and 51st FIWs shot down 10 MiGs. Two of those fell to Lt Col. George A. Davis, who had shot down seven Japanese aircraft in the Second World War, and in a huge battle with 150 MiGs on 13 December, in which 13 MiGs were shot down by pilots in the new Sabres, he shot down four more, making him the leading ace of the war at that time and a testimony to the superiority of the F-86E.

Over the winter of 1951–2, although the CPAF numbers continued as high as ever, the mood changed again and communist aggression declined. The MiGs stayed high, between 40,000 and 50,000 feet, and would not come down and fight, and the American pilots put it down to the departure of Russian instructors, pilots and controllers. The 4th FIW with its F-86As could not go that high, but the 51st with its F-86Es could, and its pilots shot down 25 MiG-15s in January 1952. It was not all one way. On 10 February George Davis was leading a flight of 18 Sabres which were escorting medium bombers on a mission near the Yalu. He saw a flight of 12 MiGs coming towards them and broke off with his wingman, leaving the rest of the Sabres to protect the bombers. With his uncanny skill, he shot down two of them and was attacking a third when a MiG got into his six o'clock and shot him down: his Sabre crashed into a mountainside and he did not eject. He was posthumously awarded the Congressional Medal of Honour, the only Sabre pilot to receive America's highest award for bravery.

The UN forces expected a spring offensive in 1952, but it never materialised, though the air battles went on. Between the beginning of March and the end of April the communists lost 83 MiGs for the loss of six Sabres, two Thunderjets and one Shooting Star. In May it was 27 MiGs and a Yak-9 shot down for five Sabres, three Thunderjets and 1 Mustang. Skill and determination continued to triumph over numbers, but the threat posed by the CPAF was still very real and the battle for air superiority had to be fought daily. The Sabres were winning the battle for air superiority, but air power could not win the war; the fighter bombers, while they prevented the Chinese from moving their air force south where it could be more effective, could not inflict enough damage on the ground to bring the communists to the conference table.

In an attempt to do so the UN decided on surprise attacks on four hydroelectric plants at Suiho, forty-five miles from the Chinese border, close to the Chinese airfields at Antung, Chosen, Fusen and Kyosen. Fighter bombers would attack during the day, followed by B-29s at night. The first attack was on the morning of 23 June and Sabres were on hand to deal with any interference from the MiGs. As the attacks started so there were the tell-tale puffs of dust from Antung as the MiGs took off. But instead of flying to meet the attack, the MiGs flew the other way, to airfields further into Manchuria, believing that Antung was about to be attacked. The idea was to reduce morale, and the electricity supplies were out for two days, but they had no effect on the armistice talks; two UN aircraft were lost.

The Cold War and the Korean War had combined to produce a policy of greater production of military aircraft, and the fruits of that policy started to be felt in the summer of 1952 as both sides built up their air forces. In June the 51st FIW was brought up to strength with a third squadron, the 39th FIS, which flew the F-86E. In July the first fighters flew across the Pacific direct from the USA to Japan, using in-flight refuelling; they were much-needed F-84 Thunderjet fighter bombers, and by September 1952 all the F-84 squadrons were up to full strength, with more in reserve in Japan. The Chinese had 1,800 aircraft, including 1,000 jets, 100 of them Russia's new Il-28 jet bombers stationed in Manchuria. Beyond the Russian border the Soviet Union had a further 5,200 aircraft, including radar-equipped MiG-15 interceptors.

The communists also improved their ground radar systems with twenty-five Early Warning stations and twelve Ground Controlled Interception (GCI) stations around the coast. The new complexes were protected from allied air attack by 2,000 anti-aircraft guns which ringed the most important sites, coupled with radar-guided searchlights against night attacks by B-29s. The heavy defences were a response to the relentless pressure which the Sabres had put the communists air forces under, turning MiG Alley into one of the most highly coordinated and well-defended areas of the world, but the whole posture was defensive, not offensive, and the communists still had the inestimable advantage of being immune to attack on its home bases.

The UN policy was to hold the line using air power while seeking a result at the armistice talks, but the talks remained stalled and the air battle had to go on. The tally continued to show the huge disparity in fighter pilot skills: on 4 July 1952 50 MiGs came up against 22 Sabres and lost 13 of their number for the loss of two Sabres; the total for July was 19 MiGs for four Sabres.

To put more pressure on the Chinese and North Koreans, the UN commanders conceived Operation Pressure Pump, the biggest strategic bombing offensive yet, designed to sap the morale of the North Korean population by bombing thirty targets around Pyongyang. It started on 11 July with leaflet raids, followed by 1,254 bombing sorties which killed or injured 7,000 people and flattened Radio Pyongyang which was silent for 48 hours. The process was repeated on 29 August, but it had no effect on the Chinese and North Koreans, any more than it had on the British or Germans during the Second World War, and the armistice talks continued to be stalled.

The communists also put on pressure by more aggressive tactics. On several occasions in August, flights of MiGs managed to escape from under the Sabre screen to penetrate south and attack fighter bombers, leading to a series of dogfights in which 35 MiGs were lost for two Sabres. One of those was the first MiG to fall to the guns of the Royal Navy. On 9 August a flight of the Fleet Air Arm's last propeller-driven fighter, the Sea Fury, led by Lt Peter 'Hoagy' Carmichael of 802 Squadron on HMS *Ocean*, intercepted one. He turned his flight into them, scoring hits on one MiG which started smoking, then Carmichael managed to get a long burst into another which crashed, the first jet to fall to a propeller fighter in the Korean War.

The more aggressive tactics continued in September, with the MiG pilots still trying to find a way of breaking UN air superiority. Huge battles developed: on 4 September, in seventeen separate dogfights spread over a huge area, 13 MiGs and two Sabres were shot down. As part of Operation Pressure Pump, on 9 September, when a large force of F-84s attacked the North Korean Military Academy at Sakchu, they were attacked by 175 MiGs; all the Thunderjets escaped. This spurt of activity in September was reflected in the monthly scores and the Chinese lost 63 MiGs for nine Sabres and, in the process, created the twentieth US jet ace, Capt. Robinson Risner, USAF, of the 4th FIW.

During September the first of the new F-86F Sabres arrived in Korea, really evening up the odds against the MiG-15. It was 20 m.p.h. faster than the MiG, capable of Mach 1.05 in a dive; it had 15% more power, which increased the rate of climb by 300 ft/min., and, though its service ceiling was still lower than the MiG's, a new wing made it more manoeuvrable and it could turn tighter than its predecessors at altitude where the MiG had always had the advantage. It also incorporated a new gunsight, the A-1CM, which was linked to a small radar in the nose so once the pilot had 'locked on' to his target the radar took over, adjusting for range and making the job a little easier. The younger fighter pilots took to the new technology eagerly, while the older men did not. Col. Gabreski became famous at this time by ignoring the high-technology gunsight, not even bothering with a gyro/optical sight; instead, he chewed gum and in a fight he used his instinct and experience to stick it on the front of his canopy, then used it to line up his shot. Gabreski finished the war an ace, with 6.5 MiGs to his credit.

In October 1952 the mood changed again, this time in the opposite direction. The experienced American fighter pilots felt the difference in their opponents' attitude in the air immediately: less bold, more hesitant about how to react and what to do once battle was joined. The communist pilots were 'greens': instead of coming down from their high-level eyries above 40,000 feet, as the 'honchos' had done, the 'greens' stayed high, where they were ineffective. Intelligence reports confirmed the UN fighter pilots' view that the communists were rotating batches of pilots through Antung, spreading the experience across their huge air forces, rather than concentrating on the small élite squadrons operated by the USAF. There was less fighting and the number of MiGs destroyed fell: for October it was 27 MiGs shot down for the loss of four Sabres; in November 1952 it was 28 for four and in December 28 for two.

On 4 December Robinson Risner was leading a flight of four Sabres who met up with four MiGs at 40,000 feet. Both sides dropped tanks and turned in to each other to fight. Risner opened fire, hitting a MiG's canopy. The communist pilot promptly dived for the deck with Risner in hot pursuit. They finished up with Risner chasing the MiG along a dry river bed, so low that the jet was sending up dirt. Risner managed to get in the odd burst of fire, causing more damage, and bits came off the MiG, but the pilot was heading for sanctuary across the Yalu. Risner's wingman, Lt Joe Logan, was still there behind his leader, guarding his tail. Risner flew up alongside several times and was greeted by the communist pilot with a shaking fist. The MiG pilot took them to an airfield inside China, probably one of the Antung satellites, where he flew between the hangars with Risner and Logan in pursuit, still firing. Eventually the MiG crash-landed alongside the runway at far too high a speed and flew apart.

As they exited the area all the anti-aircraft guns opened up on the two Sabres, and Logan was hit in a fuel tank. They climbed away but they were a long way from home and Logan's tanks were running dry. Risner spoke over the radio and when they were nearly dry he told his wingman to shut down his engine. Then he flew right up behind the stricken Sabre and put the top of his nosecone against the bottom of Logan's jet pipe and started pushing him. They crossed the coast and headed out into the Yellow Sea in this extraordinary feat of flying. About a hundred miles out, having alerted the rescue services which were there for the purpose – seaplanes and ships and helicopters – the two Sabre pilots parted company near Cho-do island and Risner headed home; Logan ejected but sadly drowned before he could be rescued.

It was the stuff of heroes: in 1953, to be a fighter pilot and to be in Korea was to be where it was at; to be in MiG Alley was to be in the only place where they could do what they had joined for, trained for, and aimed to be fighter pilots for. Many of those who fought over MiG Alley had to push their way through all kinds of bureaucratic barriers in the air force to get there. The lure of being an air superiority fighter pilot, and the possibility of becoming an ace as well, was huge, and there was fierce competition inside the USAF to be posted to outfits such as the 4th and 51st FIWs to fly Sabres at Kimpo and Suwon where there was daily contact with aerial combat; to be there, a pilot really had to want to.

The fighter bomber pilots did a hugely dangerous and important job but they never had the glamour of the air superiority pilots, and many aspired to become not only real fighter pilots but aces too. One such was Capt. Dolphin Overton, USAF, who had flown 100 missions in F-84 fighter bombers in Korea before transferring to air superiority Sabres for another 100 missions with the 16th FIS of 51st FIW. He had completed 197 missions before shooting down his first MiG and in his last four missions before being sent home he shot down his fifth to become the 24th ace of the war.

The 16th FIS was led by Lt Col. Edwin Heller, USAF, and he was one of those super-aggressive fighter squadron leaders, 'Heller Bust' painted across the front of his Sabre, taking everything to the limits. There had been border violations, Sabres being drawn over the North Korean border into China in a battle, but the suspicion arose in early 1953 in the higher echelons of the USAF that pilots of the 16th FIS were going over deliberately, hunting MiGs on the far side of the border to rack up their scores. Heller had been an ace from the Second World War with 5.5 kills, and on 25 January he went up to MiG Alley with his score at 3.5 MiGs, needing 1.5 to become a jet ace too, so the temptation to go and find MiGs in their sanctuary was huge. The day after Overton became an ace Heller became involved in a fierce dogfight which started at 40,000 feet over North Korea, moving northwest over the Yalu. He was badly wounded by gunfire and went into a long dive. He tried to eject but the same fire that had hit him had damaged his ejection seat, which was not functioning. He eventually managed to bale out at low level and landed 150 miles inside China, immediately being taken prisoner.

Another eager squadron in the 51st FIW wing was the 39th FIS. One of its fighter pilots was Capt. Harold Fischer who, like Overton, had already done 100 missions on fighter bombers before joining the air superiority Sabres; he became the 25th USAF ace on the same day.

Another was Capt. Joseph McConnell. McConnell had started his flying career as a bombardier on B-24 bombers in the Second World War when there had been a shortage of those skills and a surfeit of pilots. After the war he retrained as a pilot and started flying F-80 Shooting Stars in 1948. He was stationed in Alaska in 1952, still flying F-80s, having failed to get a transfer to Korea despite many pleas. Then he was posted to the 51st FIW, eager for combat. He shot down his first MiG on 14 January 1953; on 16 January he shot down his fifth but it took several days to confirm the kill and in the meantime another Sabre pilot, Capt. Manuel, J. 'Pete' Fernandez of the rival 4th FIW at Kimpo, shot down his fifth

MiG on 18 January to become the 26th ace of the war. McConnell became the 27th.

The third full year of the Korean War had started out with the inauguration of a new US President: General Eisenhower. He moved into the White House on 23 January 1953. Six weeks later, on 5 March, Josef Stalin died, distracting the communist world and briefly changing its priorities. The Americans made it clear through secret channels that unless the armistice talks produced some movement they could be prepared to extend the war into China, and there was always the implied threat that atomic weapons could be used as well. China had no atomic weapons and, though Russia did, the reckoning in China now was that Russia would not risk its own country for the sake of China, especially in the political turmoil.

The F-86F Sabre had the edge on the MiG-15 by this point in the war, but efforts to increase the Sabre's lethality continued. The 4th FIW carried out experiments with two devices designed to increase the Sabre's killing power. The first was to fit six F-86Fs with solid fuel rockets to the rear, which could be fired in combat, giving a burst of speed to catch up with a MiG. An existing ace, Capt. Clifford Jolley, flew one and shot down two MiGs using it, but his evaluation was that he might well have achieved the same result without them. Another experiment was to fit the Sabre with 20 mm cannon rather than machine-guns. Four pilots tried them out but though two of them shot down MiGs, the results overall did not have any impact and pilots stayed with what they knew and it, too, was abandoned. The Sabre was a thoroughbred fighter.

Throughout the war there was always a desire on the part of the Americans to capture a MiG-15 in flying condition to find out where its weaknesses were. On the day of Stalin's death a MiG-15 had been flown to Denmark and its pilot defected, but the aircraft was returned to Poland. In April 1953 Gen. Mark Clark authorised 'Project Moolah'. A million leaflets were dropped from a B-29 over the Yalu, stating that the USA would pay any MiG pilot $50,000 if he would bring over a MiG. On 21 September one turned up at Kimpo, flown by Lt Ro Kum Suk of the NKAF. He was granted political asylum and paid $100,000, though he claimed that he had come across without knowing about the bounty. To test it, Chuck Yeager, who had not been able to fly in combat in the Korean War because of the secrets to which he was privy about the X Program, went to Japan to test it.

In the closing months of the war the pressure on the Chinese in the air was stepped up and the competition between the 4th and 51st Fighter Wings with it. In March McConnell shot down two and Fernandez shot down four, bringing their respective scores to seven and nine. On 12 April McConnell was involved in a fierce fight, shooting down his eighth MiG, but his Sabre was badly damaged and could not possibly make it back to base. He managed to make it to the Yellow Sea where he ejected, landed in the water and was picked up by helicopter. The following day, 13 April, he was back in the fight and shot down his ninth, then on 24 April he shot down his tenth. But Fernandez shot down one more three days later on 27 April so was now on eleven, three behind the late George Davis and two behind the leading living ace, Lt Col. Royal N. Baker, commander of the 4th FIW, whose score was thirteen. The total for April was 27 MiGs for the loss of four Sabres. One of the Sabres lost was Capt. Fischer of 39th/51st who was on ten. He was over the Yalu when he became separated from his wingman and crossed the river into China – whether intentionally or by accident has never been clear – where he was shot down, ejected and became a POW.

The tide of the Korean air war was changing again – so was the mood. By May China and the Soviet Union had decided to get the best terms at the armistice talks and give up. The East European and Russian fighter pilots, the 'honchos', had gone home, leaving the Chinese and North Korean 'greens'. There were stories of very green MiG pilots over the Yalu not taking any evasive action when attacked, and US pilots reported some ducking beneath their canopies, relying on their armour plate to protect them while the MiG was shot to pieces, then they would eject.

The last months of war were characterised by extremely high scores by the Americans. It was a very attractive situation for the fighter aces on the UN side, but it brought out a dark, competitive streak in them – to be the top scorer of the war. The highest individual score at that time was still George Davis's 14. In the new situation, James Jabara wanted to beat it, and persuaded the USAF to send him back to Korea in May 1952. Before Jabara had time to score again, in early May Fernandez scored another two, to bring him equal with his boss at 13. Then, on 10 May, he shot down one more and shared credit for a second, taking him to 14.5, making him the leading ace of the war, 0.5 ahead of Davis. McConnell of the 51st shot down three more in early May, taking his score to 13, then he shot down two MiGs in a single morning on 18 May. The same afternoon he went back to MiG Alley and his flight was bounced from above by four MiGs. The communists played an old ruse: two of their number overshot the Sabres, appearing as easy targets ahead. McConnell and his flight were old hands and broke hard, to find many more MiGs behind. McConnell managed to get one in his sights and gave it a long burst. The MiG pilot ejected and the aircraft went down in flames, McConnell's sixteenth kill. McConnell and Fernandez both wanted to stay but the USAF sent them both back to the States, not wishing to lose their aces.

The total for May was 56 for the loss of one Sabre, two of them to James Jabara. On 26 May he was leading four Sabres over North Korea when they came across 16 MiGs; he shot one down and, in trying to manoeuvre to get behind the another, the MiG pilot took violent evasive action and went into an uncontrollable spin and crashed into the ground, Jabara's ninth kill.

In June the 4th and 51st FIWs scored a massive 77 MiGs plus 11 probables and 41 damaged, including 16 in one day. Jabara accounted for five of them, taking his score to 14. Among the new aces which the closing months of the war produced there were many from a younger generation, and the thirty-ninth and last ace scored his fifth kill on 30 June – Lt Henry Buttelman, aged twenty-three. The baton was being passed on.

In July another 32 MiGs went down, all for no loss to the Americans. Jabara shot down one more to take him to 15, one ahead of Fernandez and one behind McConnell. But it was all over. The armistice talks had finally produced a cease-fire and an agreement for the exchange of prisoners. On 22 July Lt Sam P. Young of 51st FIW was on patrol over the Yalu. He had not shot down a MiG when he saw a flight crossing the river below. He went down and shot one down. It was the 818th MiG destroyed in aerial combat by Sabres for the loss of 58 Sabres shot down in combat, a kill ratio in the air of 14 to 1. Five days later an armistice was agreed and fighting stopped at 10 p.m. on 27 July.

The communists had tried to wear the UN/USA down by fighting what Mao Tse-tung had defined as a 'protracted war', going on for long enough to make the enemy simply pack up and go home. By militarising the masses he hoped to make a victory for the Americans impossible. It didn't work, and the reason was air superiority. The brunt of the resistance to Mao's human waves was borne on the ground where a total of 3 million soldiers and 1.25 million civilians died over three and a half years. But the reason it did not work was because the one thing the communists could never achieve was control of the air over the Korean peninsula and, without it, the freedom to use those huge, expendable forces to any lasting effect.

Officially, the war is still going on nearly half a century later but, in the sense that South Korea was not occupied by the North and went on to become one of the 'tiger' capitalist economies of the Asian economic miracle, it was a victory for the UN, for the West and for America. Without air superiority even that victory would not have been possible. Without it, the UN would have lost the war early on. By sustaining it, against the odds, the US fighter pilots, and their fighter bomber cousins, enabled the armistice to be negotiated without the UN throwing in millions of men to take on the huge Chinese armies, something which was acknowledged by the Chinese in captured intelligence documents which said that but for air superiority they would have won in 1950.

Neither side ever had an overwhelming technical advantage in the air war. As the more advanced Sabres were sent to Korea so they gave the USAF pilots a more level playing field, but the MiG-15 was also improved as the war progressed. The difference was in the pilots. The younger American fighter pilots were eager for the fight and they had the advantage of being led by men with plenty of experience in fighting the hardest of opponents, the Luftwaffe, and that combination of youthful aggression and cool leadership was a crucial factor.

It was also a matter of doctrine. The small number of highly skilled fighter pilots on the communist side, almost exclusively Russian, could have been, individually, a match for the US pilots in combat, but they were operating under strict orders which came directly from Moscow to work as part of the larger, strictly controlled effort which was essentially defensive in nature; they were never let loose on the offensive, and even if they had been there were only a very few of them and they would have been outnumbered by their US counterparts. It was a battle between two ways of fighting: the US, or Western, way, having a relatively small number of highly capable aircraft with highly capable pilots, operating alone and deciding for themselves on the best way to fight and believing they were the best, an élite, superior in every way to their opponents; and the Soviet, or Eastern, view which relied on a more monolithic view of themselves as part of a huge army, on numbers and on strict control. There were occasions when communist numbers looked as if they might swing the balance against the UN, but relatively modest increases in the numbers of Sabres swung the situation back – aggression, individuality and competitiveness won.

The Korean War produced 39 USAF jet aces: 5% of the 800 US pilots who served in Korea accounted for 37% of all aerial kills, very close to the situation in the Second World War and the general experience in all air wars – that a tiny number of men excel and do a disproportionate amount of the damage. The Russian statistics were a closely guarded secret, but recent articles in the Russian aviation press suggest that the Russian experience was similar. According to those reports, 50 Soviet pilots scored over 5 aerial victories, accounting for 410 UN aircraft shot down between them. The highest scorer was Yevgeny Pepelyaev with 23 victories, followed by N. V. Sutyagin with 22, the only two to exceed Joe McConnell's 16. There were differences in the rules for claiming victories; in particular SAF pilots were credited with a kill if they believed that their target had been damaged beyond repair. On that basis they claimed a total of 1,300 UN aircraft shot down in aerial combat while USAF figures show a total of 971 aircraft lost in the Korean War in both aerial combat and to ground fire. The discrepancy is huge and is no doubt the result of overclaiming by Soviet pilots.

Long after the war the results of the US pilots were revisited by the USAF and the number of MiGs shot down was revised to a lower figure than was claimed at the time. The claims of the US fighter pilots were excessive, but the culture of the time – the few against the many – produced a climate of its own, a highly competitive climate in which too much benefit of the doubt may have been given to the claimant. No doubt the same was true of the SAF pilots, perhaps to an even greater extent.

The Korean War was an air superiority and fighter bomber war, not a bomber war. The use of strategic air power, bombing civilians and industry to reduce the morale of the North Korean people and destroy the economic base from which the war was being fought, was not decisive. There were not enough strategic targets in North Korea, and unless SAC had been unleashed against the source of supply, i.e., the Chinese economy and population centres, it could never be so. No overt threat of nuclear war was made against China, but the implication was made strongly and, so many commentators believe, it was that, and the fact that few believed that the Soviet Union would risk nuclear war for China, let alone Korea, which finally brought the Chinese to accept terms at the armistice talks.

Of 56 F-86 pilots known to have been shot down and whom those who saw them go down believed they had survived, only 15 were eventually repatriated by the Chinese and North Koreans. Most of those came home in October 1953; Heller and Fischer who had gone down well inside China had to wait two more years, but they did get back. In the bitter ideological Cold War, the communists were very hungry for F-86 pilots to learn about US capability. Many of those who came back had been tortured and brainwashed; nearly half a century later the others are still listed as Missing In Action.

CHAPTER FOUR
Cold War Warriors

The tensions of the Cold War, which had originated in the ruins of post-war Germany, lived on in a divided Europe. The Iron Curtain remained the focus of East–West confrontation, but from 1950 atomic bombs, long-range jet bombers, the Korean War and Soviet and Chinese support for other 'wars of liberation' around the world globalised the Cold War, institutionalised it and militarised it.

The US view of the Soviet Union was of a command economy geared first and foremost to arms production aimed at communist world domination, and the US response to that perceived threat was contained in NSC-68. That report had warned of the danger of regional wars in unstable, divided areas just three months before North Korea had invaded the South, costing America 54,246 lives. To prevent future such wars, NSC-68 recommended a US policy of containing communism and to do so, America entered into alliances with countries around the periphery of the Soviet Union, modelled on NATO. In 1954, following the collapse of French power in Indo-China, the South-East Asian Treaty Organisation (SEATO) was formed, with Britain, Australia, New Zealand, the Philippines, Pakistan and Thailand extending protection over South Vietnam, Laos and Cambodia; in 1958 the USA joined the Central Treaty Organisation (CENTO) with Britain, Turkey, Iran and Pakistan to confront Soviet expansion in the Middle East.

To make the policy work, without creating huge standing forces, America and its new allies needed the latest military equipment. Re-arming for a new military age was costly, and to soften the burden at home the huge increase in US military budgets was spread across the USA in a proliferation of defence contracts, providing many well-paid jobs both in the aerospace industry and at the many new military bases. The combination of jobs and prosperity at home, linked to security abroad, became a central plank of America's Cold War strategy.

The Soviet Union saw it differently. Containment was a threat to its empire and the consequences of NSC-68 little more than a capitalist conspiracy between vested interests: military officers who wanted bigger armed forces; politicians who wanted arms factories and military bases in their home states, and businessmen who profited by providing them. In the propaganda war they called the arrangement, in which the three categories of senior figures in US public life swapped influence and jobs to mutual advantage, the military/industrial complex.

The Cold War became the Arms Race as both power blocs increased military spending. America was richer and spent money to stay ahead, using technology to avoid having huge standing armed forces. The most immediate beneficiary of the increased spending was the USAF. In 1949 the entire US defence budget was $11 bn. Between 1950 and 1952 the USAF budget alone rose from $5.4 bn to $22.4 bn. Such lavish spending ushered in a decade of extraordinary aeronautical research and development, pushing back the frontiers of speed, altitude, range, electronic sophistication and the destructive potential of aircraft at a pace and to a degree never seen before. Nazi Germany's technical groundwork, with its erstwhile scientists now working alongside American and Soviet counterparts, wallowed in sufficient cash to make those ideas happen, and they went beyond aeronautical research into nuclear explosives, new forms of guided weapons, radar systems, electronic and optical sensing, ballistic missiles and strategic reconnaissance systems. The sky was not the limit since both sides made plans to take the Arms Race into space. In America the perception was that the Korean War had been fought by a small number of highly trained men, with high levels of advanced fire-power in the air, ultimately winning against massed communist manpower and the policy of spending on aircraft and systems and in fighter pilot circles, it was grafted on to the existing culture of technical and human excellence, the quest for the best.

The search for new ideas fostered a highly productive relationship between the aircraft companies and the government agencies which sponsored them – the Pentagon and the National Advisory Committee for Aeronautics (NACA), which became the National Aeronautics and Space Administration (NASA) in 1958 which together managed the X Program, at the heart of pure aeronautical research in America since Chuck Yeager's first supersonic flight in X-1 in 1947. Many other X projects, which had been initiated in the late 1940s, were given new impetus by NSC-68. In 1951 the X-3 reached Mach 2; by 1953 the X-1A-D series had reached Mach 2.4 at 75,000 feet; there were even experiments made to fit a machine-gun in the nose, turning it into an exotic interceptor. Between 1952 and 1956 the X-2 took the unofficial speed record to Mach 3.19, killing the test pilot, Mel Apt, in the process. The X-4 (based on the German Me-163 rocket-powered interceptor and the British de Havilland DH.108) and the X-5 (based on the Messerschmidt P.1101) explored the problems of tailless aircraft design and variable geometry in flight. The X-13 explored the concept of vertical jet flight. X-6 was a prototype bomber powered by engines based on nuclear reactors. The X-7 was a pilotless, ramjet test bed, the X-8 a rocket engine test bed, the X-9 a prototype air-launched missile, the X-10 an early cruise missile, the X-11 a ballistic missile and the X-17 a prototype Intercontinental Ballistic Missile (ICBM) which reached Mach 9.5 in tests. As the decade closed, on 8 June 1959, the hypersonic X-15 flew for the first time, a very-high-altitude, manned research aircraft which eventually reached Mach 6.7 at 250,000 feet on the verge of space; its later pilots were awarded the astronaut's flying badge. Gen. Arnold's predictions in 1945 of air power being transformed by technology seemed to be coming true.

Basic aeronautical research was fundamental to the future, but the essence of the Cold War in the 1950s was strategic air power. The USA had developed the huge, propeller-driven B-36 during the Second World War, a bomber to fly the Pacific and attack Japan from the US mainland. In 1950 the B-36 was still the only bomber with the range to reach across continents. The Soviet Union had its copy of B-29, the propeller-driven Tu-4 with only half the range. The first jet bomber was America's B-47 Stratojet, followed by Britain's superb medium jet bomber, the Canberra, which flew in May 1949 and went into service the following year, with the Soviet Union's medium range Il-28 'Beagle' coming into service just months later. None of this first generation of jet bombers had the range to match the B-36, but between 1951 and 1954 seven new high-altitude, high-speed intercontinental bombers made their first flights: Britain's Vickers Valiant on 18 May 1951, America's Boeing B-52 Stratofortress on 15 April 1952, the RAF's Avro Vulcan on 30 August 1952 and its Handley-Page Victor on 24 December 1952; the Soviet Union followed with the Tupolev Tu-16 'Badger', the M-4 Bison and the turboprop Tupolev Tu-95 Bear, all of which were revealed to the world on May Day 1954.

The same kind of progress was made in the destructive power of the atom bomb. The USA exploded the first thermonuclear device, the hydrogen bomb which had many times the destructive power of the atomic bomb, on 3 October 1952; in August 1953 the Soviet Union followed suit. In November 1955 the USSR moved ahead, becoming the first to drop an H-bomb from an aircraft. The USA followed with a much bigger bomb on 21 May 1956 and Britain joined the thermonuclear club by dropping its first H-bomb on 15 May 1957.

One of the new bombers, with just one bomb, could easily wipe out a whole city, and such huge destructive power carried in a single aircraft ended the need for the huge bomber streams of the Second World War. However, such was the impetus behind the Arms Race, with both sides fearing the worst, and with little in the way on intelligence as to what the opposition was doing, built many more bombers than it needed and the new bombers would need fighter protection. In the late 1940s plans were laid for long-range escorts like the F-101 Voodoo, but in the meantime experiments were carried out with tiny 'parasite' jet fighters such as the

XP-85 Goblin and later F-84 Thunderjets carried in the bomb bay of B-36s, to be released near the target to fight off attacking fighters. It was all part of the problem of the short range of jet aircraft at the time, and to give the USAF's Strategic Air Command (SAC) credibility it developed the in-flight refuelling techniques which had enabled jet fighters to cross the Pacific during the Korean War. As the SAC bomber fleet expanded in the 1950s so did its tanker fleet, based on the KC-135, a military version of the Boeing 707 airliner which gave almost unlimited range to bombers. In 1954 a B-47 crew stayed aloft for 47 hours 35 minutes flying between two SAC bases in Morocco and Britain, covering 21,000 miles.

In 1954 US Secretary of State John Foster Dulles announced that US policy in the Cold War would be 'massive retaliation' to any attack by the Warsaw Pact, and the strategic bomber force continued to build up. For NATO, the main instruments of that policy were the SAC and the RAF's V Force, air forces dedicated to operating independently of ground forces, by threatening a potential enemy's homeland with destruction – the air power theorists' dream for half a century. In 1950 SAC had 19 bomber wings; by 1957 it had grown to 51. In 1955 it had 3,000 aircraft – 1,309 bombers, 568 long-range F-84F escort fighters and 761 tankers. In 1957 the USAF believed the USSR would have twice as many bombers as the USA by 1959 and SAC strength peaked in 1959 at 1,854 bombers, all jets, the same year the last B-36 retired.

SAC's bombers were in the air all the time; Gen. Curtis LeMay used to boast that one was being refuelled in the air every six minutes round the clock. From 1950 to 1989, on virtually a daily basis somewhere round the world, bombers from both sides flew towards each other's airspace, providing tangible evidence of the threat they posed, but also probing each other's defences, eaves-dropping on radio communications, assessing alert times, provoking each other to send up fighters to intercept them in international airspace.

The other side of the air power equation was Air Defence which became a priority in the 1950s, aircraft and missiles dedicated to countering the manned strategic jet bomber which could fly fast enough and high enough, in all weathers, day and night, to intercept the bombers. From 1950 the idea of an integrated air defence system, the first glimmerings of which had been visible in the ruins of Nazi Germany, emerged as a reality: radar to see bombers, track them and guide missile-armed jet fighters to them; lightweight, single-seat day fighters without radar, and two-seat, night and all-weather fighters with on-board radar, plus a range of surface-to-air anti-aircraft missiles (SAMs), all linked by a communications system which could assess the threat and make an appropriate response.

As early as 1948 Stalin had seen that the Soviet Union, with its 50,000 miles of borders and huge areas of airspace, would take a lot of defending from air attack and he had laid down a plan for an integrated air defence force for the Soviet Union, PVO-Strany, Air Defence of the Homeland, a separate force which reached 550,000 men and women with its own selection process, training schools and academies, promotion policies and doctrine to protect the whole of the Soviet Union from air attack. In 1954 the commander of PVO-Strany was given the status of deputy Minister of Defence, the same status as the Chief of Staff of the Red Army. It had two arms: IA-PVO for the ground-controlled interceptor; and SR-PVO (Zenith Rockets) for surface-to-air missile, SAM, systems. With so much airspace to defend, and with the Soviet military doctrine of central control, missile systems were very attractive. Using the captured German technology as a starting point, the Soviet Union put a high priority on producing effective SAMs in large numbers. The two arms of PVO-Strany had to be very carefully co-ordinated to avoid mistakes, and missiles shooting down its own interceptors, and to do so it relied heavily on rigid drills and procedures in which there was little or no room for initiative on the part of the interceptor pilots.

NATO's policy of deterrence based on massive retaliation meant having a bomber force which was still credible in the event of a first strike by the enemy so Britain developed its integrated air defence system, based on a mixture of Hunter day fighters, Gloster Javelin all-weather interceptors and Bloodhound SAMs, but it was tasked with protecting US and RAF bomber bases in Britain and Germany so that they could retaliate, rather than defend those countries and their populations.

In the 1950s the needs of the Cold War moved fighter design in two very different directions – the tactical air superiority fighter and the pure interceptor. The priority in 1950 was the interceptor as a defence against the bomber, though the three traditional roles of the fighter – air superiority, escorting bombers and fighter bombers for ground attack – continued to be developed by both USAF Tactical Air Command (TAC) in the USA and its Soviet equivalent, Frontal Aviation.

Fighter design is a balance between looking back at the experience of the last conflict and looking forward to the future perceived threat, all complicated by the latest available technology, the budget available, the politics and the geography, and once the basic design had been set, the characteristics are fixed. The qualities for dogfighting are speed and energy from engine power with high manoeuvrability, especially the ability to get into a turn quickly. For escort the qualities are the same, the ability to fight and win over an attacker but at long range, and most good air superiority and escort fighters will, once they have become a bit long in the tooth, make good ground attack fighters, like the Mustang and Shooting Star. There is a great deal of commonality between the three types, but those qualities are inimical to the interceptor where virtually everything is sacrificed to high performance in top speed and rate of climb over short distances in a straight line, closer to a manned missile than a dogfighter.

In 1950 a bomber such as the B-47 Stratojet was nearly as fast as contemporary jet fighters. The problem of interception was the closing speed. A B-47 or B-52 flying at Mach 0.84 with a range of 2,000 miles approaching its target at 40,000 feet would be detected by the Early Warning Radar of the day at 100 miles, leaving fighters eleven minutes to get airborne, intercept it and shoot it down. So ever-faster interceptors were needed. That thought dominated the decision-makers, and high-speed, high-altitude interception became the priority for fighter design, fighter weapons system development and fighter pilot training.

America had not built interceptors before because until the 1950s it had been immune from air attack behind its vast oceanic moat. The USAF had no specialised command until 1951 when Air Defense Command (ADC) was formed. Like PVO-Strany, it was a combination of ground radar stations, SAMs and interceptors strung across the northern borders with bases in Canada and

Greenland since the perceived threat from the Soviet Union would come over the North Pole.

Its first interceptors, the F-94 Starfire and F-86D or 'Dogship' Sabres as they were known to their pilots, were variants of air superiority fighters, but only because they were all that was available at the time. They were dragooned into holding the line until 1954 when intelligence showed that the Soviet Union would have its intercontinental bomber force operational, and America's new generation of pure-bred interceptors, the F-102 and F-106 'Ultimate Interceptor', would be ready. To turn it into an interceptor, the Sabre was fitted with an afterburner, which did little for the top speed but its acceleration and rate of climb nearly doubled, at 11,100 feet per minute. The nose was completely different, representing two big changes – the guns had gone, and a bulbous extension above the air intake housed a Hughes E-4 interception radar and fire control system. The F-94 Starfire all-weather interceptor had a crew of two, but the F-86D had only one, the pilot. The E-4 could compute the target's position, guide the pilot to a beam attack position, then into a 'collision course' position from which, at 500 feet range, it automatically lowered a tray under the fuselage which contained twenty-four 2.75 in. Folding Fin Aircraft Rockets (FFAR) which it fired in salvoes at the bomber. They were unguided and operated on the same principle that the R4Ms had on the Me 262; later interceptor models of the Sabre were fitted with 20 mm cannon and Sidewinder air-to-air guided missiles.

Flying it was a world away from its dogfighting cousins, the F-86A, E and F variants. With a radar screen in front of him, the fighter pilot had his head in the cockpit most of the time during the attack phase of the mission, and to help with the workload he had a Lear F-5 autopilot. The last example of the interceptor Sabre, the F-86L, was fitted with a Ground Controlled Interception (GCI) system, much closer to the Soviet model in which the pilot increasingly became a systems operator rather than a fighter pilot.

The F-86D entered service in November 1953, six months late due to problems with all the electronics. The USAF bought 2,504 of them and by 1955, a year after the F-102 was supposed to be ready, they represented 73% of ADC's interceptors. The F-102 was a long way behind schedule. Its systems were very complicated, but its worst flaw was that even in early 1953, before it flew, it was clear from transonic wind tunnel tests that its performance would be disappointing. When flight testing started on 24 October that year, its maximum speed was only Mach .98 at 48,000 feet, virtually the same as the 'Dogship' Sabre it was supposed to replace. The problem lay in the aerodynamic drag produced by the delta wing. The solution was discovered by a NACA scientist, Dr Richard Whitcomb, who established what he called the Area Rule which related the ideal shape for a high-speed fuselage to the cross-sectional area at any given point of the wings and fuselage combined rather than simply the cross-section of the fuselage. He suggested changing the shape of the fuselage, pinching it in at the waist in a shapely curve rather than the straight sides of the original F-102 fuselage, prompting it to become popularly known as the 'ideal body theory' or the 'coke bottle' design. Whatever it was called, it worked, and the revised prototype F-102, nicknamed Hot Rod, reached Mach 1.22 at 53,000 feet a year later.

The delay and uncertainty led the USAF to order another interim interceptor from its inventory of straight-winged, two-seater fighters, the McDonnell F-89D Scorpion, which entered service in 1954. Though an ageing design, its introduction was a landmark in the development of aerial warfare – it was the first fighter to enter operational service with Anti-Aircraft Missiles (AAM) rather than machine-guns and cannon.

The USA, the Soviet Union, Britain and France all started developing guided missiles in the late 1940s, as a weapon against the bomber rather than a dogfighting weapon. They were based on radar guidance, but in the 1950s radar sets were sizeable and delicate pieces of equipment and the resulting missiles were complicated and heavy. To keep them to a realistic size, much of the radar system was housed in the fighter rather than the missile. America's first air-to-air guided missile to go into operational service was the Hughes GAR-1 Falcon, and the first one to be fired experimentally was launched from an F-89D in 1953. It was six feet long, powered by a solid fuel rocket motor which accelerated it away from the fighter at 50 g to a speed of Mach 3 in seconds. It had a range of about five miles. Hughes also built the F-89D's radar and fire control system, the E-9, which 'illuminated' the target for the pilot who then fired the missile. The fighter's radar stayed locked on to the target while the missile was guided by its Semi-

Active Radar Head (SARH) which used the reflections from the fighter's radar to home in on the target. The first tests threw up a lot of problems, but in 1955 the Falcon became the first AAM to shoot down an airborne target drone and it went into operational service on an F-89H in March 1956.

Another radar-guided missile whose career ran parallel to the Falcon and started at more or less the same time was the Raytheon AAM-N-2 Sparrow for the US Navy. The Navy started missile experiments with some urgency after the war as a defence against the prospect of jet-powered kamikaze attacks on aircraft carriers. It used a different form of radar guidance to start with, known as beam riding. The fighter crew aimed a narrow beam at its target, fired the missile into the beam which then picked up signals from the fighter and followed the beam to the target, which was fine as long as the beam was held on the target. The Sparrow I entered service in July 1956, but it was not particularly effective. Its successor, Sparrow II, had a fully active radar system on board but this was abandoned for Sparrow III which had a Semi-Active Radar Head (SARH) guidance system. Sparrow III, which could reach Mach 4 and had a range of twenty miles, was fired for the first time in 1958.

The main disadvantage of the radar-guided AAMs was that it took up to a minute to set up the SARH head for the shot, followed by a 30-second window in which to fire, then the Weapons System Officer in the back seat had to hold that lock on, which meant the pilot had to fly straight and level, until the missile hit. A missile which could be locked on, fired, then home in on the target on its own would be far more useful in aerial combat. A system to do that also came from the US Navy, this time from its own Weapons Centre at China Lake in 1949. It started life as XAAM-N-7, but became famous throughout the world as the Sidewinder. The breakthrough came from Dr William McLean of the US Navy's Ordnance Department who built an infrared (IR) homing device based on a photovoltaic cell which reacted to heat. Once locked on to the hot metal at the rear of a jet aircraft around the jet efflux, the IR homer sent messages direct to the on-board guidance system to keep it on target, 'passive homing' as it was called. Early experiments in 1953 used the bodies of 5 in. HVARs and the resulting missile was very slim compared with the Falcon and Sparrow. The Sidewinder was far simpler than its radar-guided cousins – 'fewer electronic components than the average radio' according to its original designers, and it had only twenty-four moving parts, including ingenious 'rollerons', little gyroscopes in the tail fins, driven by the high-speed airflow, which stabilised it in flight. They also help to explain the missile's name: when fired, the combination of the active guidance system and the stabilisers gave it a 'snaking' path to its target, very similar to the venomous Sidewinder.

Once fired, it accelerated to Mach 2.5 in just over two seconds, and with the IR detector locked on to the target the pilot could break off the engagement. One problem with all IR missiles was that they were not at all discriminating about the source of heat they homed on; they were fine in ideal conditions, at high levels in cold air away from the sun, but near the ground, in rain or cloud, where the contrasts between cloud and sun were greater, it could go awry. Another limitation was that it had to be fired from behind, the traditional position for attacking an enemy, but a head-on shot, with no heat to home on, was useless. With the limitations of both SARH and IR systems, the USAF doctrine was for fighters to carry both – the SARH for use at range, the IR for use close in.

The Sidewinder was supplied to America's allies and it was the first AAM to be used in aerial combat. One of the recipients was the Republic of China (Nationalist) Chinese Air Force (ROCAF) in Taiwan. Taiwan and Communist China disputed two islands in the Formosa Strait, Matsu and Qemoy, and ROCAF F-86 Sabres and CPAF MiG-17s regularly clashed in the disputed airspace above them. In the first encounter between the Sidewinder-equipped Sabres and the MiGs, the Nationalist pilots claimed 14 MiGs, but in close turning fights the limitations of the early Sidewinders were clear, and ROCAF fighter pilots continued to use guns more than missiles.

Undoubtedly the most powerful air-to-air missile ever produced was the MB-1 Genie air-to-air rocket which had a 1.5 kiloton nuclear warhead. With a lethal radius of 1,000 feet it could be unguided, and was designed to be fired at a bomber by a fire control system that tracked the target, told the pilot when to arm the missile, fired it, then whipped the fighter into a sharp turn to escape the detonation before triggering the warhead. It was fired for the first time experimentally on 19 July 1957, also from an F-89, and detonated 15,000 feet above the Nevada desert.

Guided missiles signalled a major change in air combat, but they had not grown out of the tradition of fast-moving, tight-turning, snap-shooting dogfights. They had been designed to hit bombers, and their limitations made them unsuitable for aerial combat between fighters. However, the view that the age of the dogfight was over had surfaced once again in the late 1940s as decision-makers faced a supersonic future. Part of the argument was that, to date, fighters had fought close to, at and occasionally beyond, their design top speeds, a maximum of around 500 m.p.h., and that as fighters went beyond the speed of sound, the idea of a turning battle was rapidly becoming a thing of the past. At Mach 2, where the turning circle would be vast and the g forces intolerable, fighter pilots would not be trying to get in each other's six o'clock. Instead, the theory was that they would make a single high-speed pass, with cannon or missiles, and that would be that. The bigger, long-range escort and penetration fighters would be too large to indulge in aerial combat, and with the advent of improved fighter radar and guided missiles, which would kill opposing fighters and bombers from a distance, the close, turning battle for air superiority was further discounted.

The close, turning battles for air superiority in the Korean War had disrupted that view and showed that the dogfight was still part of the air combat repertoire, and when American and Soviet designers went to Korea to talk to USAF TAC and Soviet Frontal Aviation fighter pilots, whose task was fighting for air superiority over the battlefield, they found they wanted the same thing: a highly manoeuvrable, lightweight fighter with as much power, energy, acceleration and speed as possible, all at the expense of additional equipment. Speed and power were important to get an advantage over the enemy by climbing quickly, getting above the enemy and then diving on him. The actual fighting would take place, not at the top speed of the aircraft but at around the same speed as before, 450–500 m.p.h. More engine power, speed and agility in the air were what they wanted – the hallmarks of the air superiority fighter down the ages.

The first genuine supersonic fighters were designed before the Korean War. The USAF's North American F-100 Super Sabre, as the name implied, had evolved from the F-86 Sabre as an air superiority fighter with a secondary capability as a fighter bomber to meet the tactical needs of US and NATO allies. Shortly after its first flight on 25 May 1953 it became the first aircraft in the world to fly supersonically in level flight. The MiG design bureau had built its reputation on swift results by building on, and extending, existing design and technology, and it had improved on the MiG-15 even before the Korean War with the MiG-17 Fresco which flew in 1949. Its top speed was not much higher than its predecessor but it was highly manoeuvrable, a natural dogfighter. The next in the MiG family was the MiG-19 Farmer which flew four months after the F-100 and, like the Super Sabre, could reach supersonic speed in level flight, but it was 42% lighter than its US rival, with a power to weight ratio greater than 1:1, and with its fuel tanks half full its rate of climb was far better. Both became operational in 1955.

The F-100 and the MiG-19 were the examples of the third, supersonic, generation of jet fighters, but even before they flew, plans were being made for their successors. On 12 December 1952 the USAF issued a requirement for a lightweight air superiority fighter to start replacing the F-100 in 1956. The aircraft chosen was the Lockheed F-104 Starfighter, designed after lengthy discussion between Lockheed's designer Clarence 'Kelly' Johnson and Korean War fighter pilots. The prototype flew for the first time on 28 February 1954 and in March 1955, still with an interim engine, it reached Mach 1.7 at 60,000 feet. The production model, fitted with the new General Electric J-79 engine, had a top speed of Mach 2 and a service ceiling of 53,000 feet. On 27 February 1956 it became the first aircraft in the world to reach Mach 2 in level flight, and it could reach Mach 1 in a climb. It had not been originally intended as an interceptor but, because of continued delays with the F-102, it first entered operational service in that role in January 1958, armed with a single gun, though later models had that removed and it flew with two Sidewinder missiles.

In the autumn of 1953 the SAF's Frontal Aviation asked the design bureaux for an agile, lightweight, single-seat fighter with guns and no radar other than for the gunsight, which could reach Mach 2 and 65,000 feet; it should have the capability to carry AAMs later. It was no surprise that Artem Mikoyan's MiG bureau was chosen to produce what became another classic fighter, the MiG-21. Mikoyan decided to compromise all design criteria to outright performance and it turned out to be an outstanding aircraft of its type.

The prototype, Ye.2, was flown for the first time by Georgii Mosolov on 14 February 1955. It was superb to fly, tough, simple and easy to build in large numbers, and easy to maintain in the harsh winters along the Soviet Union's Arctic coast. It was capable of Mach 2 with afterburner, but with only limited fuel its range at speed was very limited. It was armed with two 37 mm cannon, but with only enough ammunition for a two-second burst, calling for excellent shooting on the part of the pilot. Like its counterpart, the F-104, it was also dragooned into service as a day interceptor, relying heavily on ground control, and later models carried two AA-2 Atoll AAMs. NATO initially christened the MiG-21 the 'Super Farmer' but it later became known as the 'Fishbed' when it entered service with IA-PVO in 1959. Over ten thousand were eventually built, more than any other fighter since the Second World War, with two thousand more built under licence in China, and it was produced in a huge number of versions. In all it has served with 56 air forces worldwide and in 1997 it is still in service with some of them.

France's equivalent of Kelly Johnson and Artem Mikoyan was Marcel Dassault. His company had also produced a family of jet fighters, taking logical steps to improve them from the Ouragan in 1949, the Mystère in 1951, the Mystère IV in 1952 and the Super Mystère B2 in 1955. He responded to the need for a lightweight, highly capable fighter with a delta-winged design, the Mirage, which could be varied to carry out either tactical or interceptor roles. It flew for the first time in March 1956; it used a novel way of increasing its rate of climb by attaching rocket motors and came armed with two 30 mm cannon and Matra's R.530 AAM.

The F-104, MiG-21 and Mirage III were all highly capable Mach 2 fighters, owing their basic characteristics to the quest for performance as a fighting aircraft. They had different characteristics according to their national air force's needs, but all of them could be adapted to a variety of roles and all were exported to those countries' allies in large numbers. Among NATO countries, only America could afford the luxury of a range of tactical fighters tailored to different tasks and alongside the F-104, using two of the same J-79 engines, was the McDonnell F-101 Voodoo high-speed (Mach 1.85), long-range (1,000 miles with in-flight refuelling) penetration fighter to escort bombers and fight its way past enemy interceptors. It first flew on 29 September 1954 and, like the F-104, was first deployed as an interceptor, once again filling the gap while ADC waited for the F-102. Another example was the Republic F-105 Thunderchief, a fighter in the tradition of that company's P-47 and F-84, big, robust and suitable for penetration as a Mach 2 fighter bomber designed to carry a tactical nuclear bomb. It had a gun, and was designed to fight, but its huge reserves of power gave it fighting capability at low levels. It flew for the first time on 22 October 1955 and entered service in 1958.

The US Navy had not taken part in the great air battles over the Yalu in Korea because its first generation Panther jet fighters were no match for the MiG-15. Following the Korean War the Navy wanted a single-seat, supersonic dogfighter and chose the Mach 2 Chance-Vought F8U-1 Crusader, which flew for the first time on 25 March 1955; it retained guns but could also use AAMs. The Navy had replaced its propeller-driven attack aircraft with the single-seat Douglas A-4 Skyhawk, which flew for the first time in June 1954, and the Grumman A-6, a two-seater attack aircraft which flew in 1960. The Navy's next requirement was for a 'fleet air defence fighter', an aircraft with an endurance of up to three hours which could fly out 250 miles from the carrier group, loiter on combat patrol, fight if necessary and get back to the carrier. They wanted a long-range, all-weather interceptor and decided that it should dispense with the gun and rely on the Sparrow III AAM. As part of the earlier process of bidding for naval attack aircraft, McDonnell had designed the AH-1 but it never got past mock-up stage. The Navy showed interest in the McDonnell AH-1 if it could be reworked as a gunless fighter with a very advanced radar. McDonnell based it on two J-79s, like the Voodoo, put a second seat in, removed the 20 mm cannon and the result, when it flew for the first time on 27 May 1958, was the F-4H-1 Phantom which went into service with the Navy in February 1960. It was one of the most capable aircraft to come out of the hectic 1950s – twice the power of the F-104, a level flight capability of over Mach 2, a rate of climb of

45,000 ft/min., higher than the F-106 interceptor, and a comparable ceiling of 60,000 feet.

By the late 1950s designers had found the optimum performance for the third generation of jet fighters: speed between Mach 2 and Mach 2.5, an initial rate of climb of 40,000 ft/min. and a ceiling of 60,000 feet. While both sides in the Cold War struggled with the complexities of their pure interceptors, the F-102 and F-106 and their Soviet counterparts, the Yak-28 and Tu-28, the F-101 Voodoo, F-104 Starfighter, the MiG-17 Fresco, MiG-19 Farmer and MiG-21 Fishbed all filled the day interceptor role. As a result, they were also adapted to carry AAMs, not for dogfighting but against bombers.

In the same period, the US had managed to stay ahead of the Soviet Union in the all-weather interceptor role. The IA-PVO's equivalent to the F-89 Scorpion and F-86 'Dogship' Sabre all-weather interceptors was the Yak-25P Flashlight. In performance they were comparable, though the Sabre had a higher rate of climb and service ceiling than the Yak-25. But the Yak was armed with just two 37 mm cannon, no FFARs or AAMs, its radar was greatly inferior to the American interceptors and the Russian pilots were far more reliant on ground control to find their targets.

The Soviet Union had been developing AAMs since the early 1950s but, to catch up, from 1954 a far greater emphasis was put on airborne guided weapons, creating new, specialised design bureaus to develop the missiles and their fire control systems. The first designs were beam riding and SARH and the first Soviet AAM, K-5 (known to NATO as AA-1 Alkali) was fitted to IA-PVO MiG-17 and MiG-19 day interceptors, which became operational in 1958. The K-5 was used experimentally with the Yak-25P Flashlight and on the Yak-27, which was supposed to succeed it, but neither became operational. The MiG-21 day interceptor was equipped with a small radar when it was introduced as an interceptor in 1960, and the Mach 1.5 Yak-28P took over the all-weather role a year later; both carried the Soviet Union's latest AAM, the K-8, NATO reporting name AA-2 Atoll, which used IR homing and was believed to have been copied from the Sidewinder which the Soviet Union acquired in the late 1950s through espionage.

The first production models of America's first pure interceptor, the F-102A Delta Dagger, flew in 1955 and entered operational service in April 1956, two years late, and it was not until the end of

1958 that it had replaced the F-86D as the US primary interceptor, nearly five years later than anticipated. The 'Ultimate Interceptor', the F-106 Delta Dart, was flown for the first time on 26 December 1956. It was a true Mach 2 interceptor with a rate of climb of 39,800 ft/min. and a ceiling of 52,000 feet, and it went into operational service in May 1959, equipped with data links to a ground control system of radar and computers to guide it to the interception. The F-106 was built around Hughes electronic control systems which included the interception radar, fire control system, autopilot and missile-firing system. From the outset the whole concept was for a single, integrated 'weapons system' rather than a simple fighter, with the pilot becoming a 'systems manager' rather than a fighter pilot. The idea that fighter pilots and their dogfighting skills were becoming redundant, that fighters were simply missile-firing plat-forms – or even little more than manned missiles themselves – was taking hold. The F-106 had no gun and carried one Genie nuclear missile and four Falcons, all computer-launched.

In nine years the interceptor had more than doubled its speed, quadrupled its rate of climb, had swapped manoeuvrability for electronics and its killing power had gone from machine-guns to nuclear missiles. An entire mission was not expected to last more than ten minutes. The costs had the same multipliers: in 1953 an F-86D cost $343,839 from the factory and $187 per flying hour in maintenance costs; in 1959 an F-106 cost $4.9 million ex-factory, never mind the R&D costs, and $1,600 per flying hour in main-tenance. The fighter had become a manned missile itself.

In the late 1950s the Soviet Union was planning supersonic all-weather interceptors as well – the two-seat, radar-equipped, all-weather, Mach 2.75 Tu-28 Fiddler, which remains to this day the largest fighter ever built, twice the weight of the Voodoo, and beyond that there was the Soviet Union's Ultimate Interceptor, the Mach 3 MiG-25, which was already on Artem Mikoyan's drawing board. On Kelly Johnson's drawing board was America's Mach 3 interceptor, the YF-12.

Britain was also in the high-level interceptor business. The RAF's day interceptor was the Hawker Hunter and for all-weather inter-ception it relied on a two-seat version of the venerable Meteor, the NF.11, which was replaced by the purpose-built Gloster Javelin in 1956. The Javelin was a large, subsonic, delta-winged two-seater armed with two Aden 20 mm cannon and two Firestreak IR homing AAMs, or four Firestreaks without guns; the Firestreak became operational in 1958.

The British aircraft industry had been revitalised in the early 1950s as the Cold War got under way and, looking beyond the Javelin, it had four possibilities for interceptors to match the USA and Soviet Union. One was based on a pure research aircraft, the Fairey Delta 2, which caused a sensation on 10 March 1956 when it wrenched the official speed record from the USA; it qualified to hold the record because, unlike the faster X aircraft in the USA, it could take off and land like any aircraft, and Fairey's chief test pilot, Peter Twiss, reached 1,132 m.p.h. (Mach 1.76), increasing the record by a huge 30%. Fairey planned to build a two-seat, all-weather Mach 2 interceptor based on it with a ceiling of 60,000 feet, carrying Firestreak missiles to meet the RAF's stated requirement. Another pure research aircraft, the English Electric P.1, which had flown for the first time in 1954, had been designed to explore the possibility of sustained Mach 2 flight without afterburners; it, too, was being developed as an interceptor with a rate of climb of 50,000 ft/min., a ceiling of 60,000 feet and a speed of Mach 2.2. There were also plans for a supersonic version of the Javelin with a much thinner wing and Britain's ultimate interceptor, the Saunders-Roe SR.177, which had two power sources, rocket and jet, the rocket to get it to its operational height very quickly and the jet to take over once it was there.

The emphasis on high-altitude, high-speed interceptors was to counter the next generation of supersonic jet bombers which was already taking shape. The USA had started work on its first Mach 2 bomber, the Convair B-58 Hustler, which used four J-79 engines and was capable of sustained Mach 2 flight for over an hour; it had flown on 11 November 1956 and became operational in March 1960. In 1955 design contracts had been signed for the next leap forward in bombers, the Mach 3 North American XB-70 Valkyrie, capable of flying at 70,000 feet, faster and higher even than the planned interceptors. The Soviet Union was behind America in supersonic bombers, but the Tu-22 Blinder was first seen in 1961. It had a range of 2,000 miles and a top speed of Mach 1.4 and, beyond that, the variable geometry Tu-28 Backfire which flew at Mach 1.9.

It was like a dog chasing its tail – the dash for performance had turned full circle. It seemed that the next generation of bombers was just over the horizon, and that they would be able to fly as fast and as high as the current generation of fighters so interceptor designers looked for more speed and more altitude, and so the cycle continued into the future *ad infinitum*. Clearly something had to give, and one school of thought had it that, however fast, whatever their rate of climb and firepower, interceptors would be useless against Mach 3 bombers, and that the only answer to high-altitude bombers was surface-to-air missiles, SAMs. The extension of that argument was that if SAMs were the only way of dealing with new generations of bombers, they did away with the need for fighters as bomber killers, threatening the future of the fighter. The argument did not stop there: a little further over the horizon was the Intercontinental Ballistic Missile (ICBM), and once the two power blocs in the Cold War could threaten each other with rockets fired from their territory to the enemy's, the manned bomber, however fast and high it could fly, would be obsolete. Any defence against the ballistic ICBM, which would reach its target minutes after firing and operate on the fringe of space, would have to be other missiles, not manned aircraft.

The idea of rockets as weapons and space as their battlefield had taken hold by the end of the 1950s. The Soviet Union had taken the lead in rocketry and exploring space, putting the first satellite into orbit on 4 October 1957, thoroughly alarming the West; the first Soviet ICBM was launched on 26 August 1957 in great secrecy. The first US satellite, Explorer 1, was put into orbit on 31 January 1958. The Arms Race had become the Space Race, and the Soviet Union had moved ahead. Nikita Kruschev put great faith in long-range guided missiles as the Soviet Union's great leap forward; manned bombers had a place in the arsenal, but it was rockets that took centre stage, and Russian missiliers had a very high status, higher than that of the manned bomber force. The USA had also developed strategic nuclear missiles launched from submarines (SLBM) and they became operational on 15 January 1960 when America's first Polaris submarine, USS *George Washington*, took to sea with sixteen A-1 missiles. In 1962 the USA deployed its first land-based missiles, launched from underground silos.

Military aviation was at a crossroads again. Ahead lay a tantalising world of automated, strategic warfare waged by ballistic missiles, and both sides in the Cold War started work on the antidote to them: anti-ballistic missiles (ABM). Interceptors would not only be useless against ICBMs, they would be extraordinarily expensive compared with surface-to-air guided missiles (SAMs). The Soviet Union put huge effort into SAMs for many reasons, mainly because of the huge area they had to defend for which they represented the most cost-effective way ahead, especially on the northern borders, but they also fitted into Russian military doctrine of large forces controlled from the centre. Soviet interest in SAMs had started in 1954 with the SA-1 Grail system, followed by the SA-2 Guideline, which became operational in 1960, and the Soviet Union wove a web of interlocking SAM systems, creating boxes of airspace with an integrated defence with anti-aircraft guns and interceptors. This policy released fighters for tactical work over the battlefield, the traditional role of the SAF.

The Soviet Union saw SAMs as a means of general defence of the homeland, while the USA saw them more as a means of point defence of strategic targets, starting out in the same year as the Soviets with the Nike-Ajax system, followed by Hawk, then Nike-Hercules and Boeing Bomarc, a giant ramjet-powered nuclear-tipped radio-controlled, anti-aircraft missile with a terminal guidance system to bring it right on to its target. The British Bloodhound system was also used mainly for point defence, particularly of bomber bases, protecting the bombers which could deliver the massive retaliation which was NATO policy.

For Britain, the thinking that the future belonged to the missile and not the fighter was crystallised on 4 April 1957 when the British Minister of Defence, Duncan Sandys, stood up in the House of Commons to deliver the Defence White Paper. In part it was a recognition that Britain could no longer afford to match the expenditure of the USA and Soviet Union, but its conclusions were devastating for the RAF and its fighter pilots. The White Paper became known as the Sandys Storm, a vision of the future in which the fighter pilot played little or no role. In one part it said, 'Fighter aircraft will be progressively equipped with air-to-air guided missiles' but that 'in due course, [they] will be replaced by ground-to-air guided missile systems'.

The SR.177, ER.103 and the supersonic Javelin were all cancelled. The only one to survive was the English Electric P.1 which entered service as the Lightning in 1959; it had an initial rate of climb of 50,000 ft/min., the last of the British hot fighters. The SR.177 flew just six weeks after the announcement of its cancellation and proved very successful, but there was no reprieve. The cancellation of the SR.177 brought joy in the Soviet Union and some pleasure at Lockheed. Germany's reborn air force was going to buy it in October 1958, but it bought 300 Starfighters instead. It was the end of Britain's history of fighter development, a blow from which its industry emerged transformed, a partner in European projects rather than an originator of fighter designs.

The USA also cancelled some advanced interceptor projects: the Republic F-103, which started out in 1948 with a Mach 3 at 80,000 feet capability and cost $104 million in development over nine years; and North American's stainless-steel F-108 Rapier, known as the LRIX for Long Range Interceptor Experimental, which was projected to have the same Mach 3 at 70,000 feet with two nuclear-tipped Falcons and was designed to intercept bombers far away from their targets. It never flew, but it cost $141.9 million in R& D before it was cancelled in 1959. One high-speed, high-altitude project which survived in America was the Lockheed YF-12 – a month after the cancellation of the F-108, design of what started out as a Mach 3 plus interceptor which could fly above 80,000 feet, built out of titanium and embodying a whole range of new technologies. The prototype flew on 26 April 1962, not as an interceptor but as a top-secret project which eventually became the SR-71 Blackbird spy plane.

The SR-71 was the planned replacement for another spy plane which America had been keeping top secret since it was introduced in 1955: the U-2. As the new long-range bombers became operational, and as both sides started work on their ICBMs, one of the greatest problems they had was knowing what the other side was doing – hard information about the number of bombers and the sites of the ICBMs, which could not be provided by electronic eavesdropping. Ultimately, satellites would provide many of the answers, but in the mid-1950s President Eisenhower authorised the building of an aircraft which could overfly the Soviet Union so high that it would be out of reach of both interceptors and SAMs.

There were several submissions, but the contract was awarded to Lockheed's Skunk Works and Kelly Johnson.

To be sure of remaining out of reach of Soviet air defences at that time, it had to be able to fly at over 70,000 feet and have a huge range to penetrate deep inside the Soviet Union. It was a great challenge, but the Skunk Works came up with the answer: a glider-like design with long, straight wings built around a single jet engine which was specially adapted to run in the very thin air high in the stratosphere where, to survive, the pilot would have to wear a full pressure suit. One of the biggest dangers at that altitude was an engine 'flame out' which would require the pilot to descend to a much lower level where the U-2 would be in danger from interceptors and SAMs.

Kelly Johnson believed that the U-2 might be just beyond the reach of Soviet radar which meant that it could operate in complete secrecy. It was some comfort for the President since if the Soviet Union's air defences were able to see it, but were unable to shoot it down, they might think it was carrying a nuclear bomb rather than spying. In order to provide the thinnest of fig leaves for the operation, Eisenhower insisted that the U-2 was operated not by the USAF but by the Central Intelligence Agency (CIA). The pilots were drawn from the USAF but they had to have civilian status otherwise their flights might be regarded as acts of war. The cover story was that the U-2 was a weather research aircraft. Eisenhower also wanted the operation to be independent of the USAF which could have used the opportunity to maximise the number of Soviet bombers and missiles in order to procure ever-higher budgets for more advanced aircraft for the USAF.

The U-2 was ready in the spring of 1956, and to operate it a network of airfields in Britain, Germany, Japan, Turkey, Norway, Iran and Pakistan was established with small detachments of ground staff so that the U-2 could fly from one side of the Soviet Union to the other, maximising the value of each overflight. In case it was attacked, the U-2 was equipped with an explosive device which would destroy the aircraft and its sensitive cameras after a delay of seventy seconds after the pilot had thrown the switch, ensuring that little or nothing would fall into Soviet hands. Pilots were issued with poison pins with which to take their own lives and were expected, but not ordered, to use them; most viewed escaping from an aircraft at such altitudes as virtually certain to result in death in any case. Eisenhower weighed the advantages and disadvantages of the overflights carefully before authorising the first on Independence Day 1956, warning as he did so that one day a U-2 would be lost and the consequences would be dramatic.

The first flight was a short one, starting from Wiesbaden in Germany, across the Iron Curtain over Berlin, through Poland as far as Minsk in Byelorussia, then north to Leningrad and back to Wiesbaden over the Baltic States. It went as planned, except that it was very quickly picked up on Soviet radar and fighters were sent up to intercept it. Looking down through his drift sight, the pilot, Harvey Stockman, could see tiny, silver fighters far below, unable to reach him or fire up at him. NATO's electronic eavesdroppers heard the PVO communications network talking about it, too. The very next day another U-2 overflew Moscow, identifying several SA-1 and SA-2 missile sites defending the city, then took crisp, sharp photographs of the Kremlin which landed on Eisenhower's desk two days later. The Soviet Union protested loudly through diplomatic channels, and in public, that the USA was violating its airspace, but Eisenhower could respond that no US military aircraft had entered Soviet airspace. There was little the Soviet Union could do but watch the overflights and fume, except that as a matter of national pride they resolved to find a way of shooting one down and redoubled their efforts to do so.

U-2s continued to overfly the Soviet Union for the rest of the decade and they broadened their coverage to include the Middle East and Cuba once Fidel Castro came to power in 1958. U-2s were also flown by ROCAF pilots over Communist China, and the RAF supplied pilots for the programme as well. The intelligence provided was of great value, but it showed that the Soviet Union was not as well armed as some predictions indicated, and Eisenhower was able to resist some of the more extreme demands from the USAF for new weapons procurement.

By 1960 both sides were deploying ballistic missiles, and intelligence showed that the Soviet Union was about to build a site for its SS-6 Intermediate Range Ballistic Missile (IRBM) at Plesetsk to the southeast of Archangel, close to the USA over the North Pole. There were also the first glimmerings of a thaw in the Cold War, and a summit conference had been arranged in Paris for 16 May

1960 between the Soviet leader, Nikita Kruschev, the US President, Dwight Eisenhower, the British Prime Minister, Harold Macmillan, and the French President, Charles de Gaulle. The CIA was anxious to overfly Plesetsk and Eisenhower eventually agreed reluctantly because he knew it would upset the Russians ahead of the summit. He authorised the flight as long as it could take place before 1 May to give the dust time to settle. The weather was poor over Plesetsk for much of April, but on May Day, a national holiday in the Soviet Union, it cleared, and a nine-hour flight from Peshawar in Pakistan across Afghanistan into the Soviet Union covering a number of targets before Plesetsk, then landing at Bolo in northern Norway, was authorised. The pilot for the mission was Francis Gary Powers.

The flight went according to plan after take-off, then the U-2's autopilot started to malfunction. Powers took over manually and continued the journey, taking photographs of the Soviet space complex at Tyuratum, then heading for Sverdlovsk. The precise details of what happened over Sverdlovsk are still a matter of debate. According to the testimony of Col. Oleg Penkovsky of the GRU, who was supplying the West with secret intelligence in 1961, a salvo of fourteen SA-2 missiles was fired from directly underneath the U-2 at the same time that several IA-PVO interceptors were also trying to reach it. One of the SAMs shot down a MiG-19 Farmer by mistake, but another exploded sufficiently close to Powers's U-2 to bring it down. Powers later reported an explosion behind the aircraft and an orange flash which sent the U-2 into an uncontrollable spin; he tried to activate the destruct mechanism but was unable to reach the switches because of the high centrifugal forces exerted by the spin. He managed to escape from the cockpit at around 14,000 feet and deploy his parachute, landing on a state farm to be captured by farm workers and handed over to the army in Sverdlovsk.

The truth about what happened is still shrouded in mystery and secrecy. The single most important piece of information was the height at which Powers was flying when he was hit. He claimed that he told his interrogators that he was flying at 68,000 feet, lower than the true operational height of the U-2, in order to mislead them, but there was signals intelligence which indicated that the PVO controllers had found him at a much lower altitude. The U-2 engine was prone to flame-out and there is a distinct possibility that Powers was at a much lower altitude, well within the range of the SA-2, trying to relight it. Kelly Johnson, on examining what evidence there was from the pieces of the U-2 which were put on display, concluded that it was a near miss by a missile which had broken off the right tailplane, sending the aircraft into a spin, but at what height he could not say. Whatever the truth, the Soviet Union claimed it was an SA-2 Guideline missile which had shot the U-2 down, and USAF intelligence had been concerned at the growing capability of the missile. They believed it could reach 60,000 feet, still short of the U-2's true operational height, but that the ZR-PVO was having great difficulty in controlling it at that altitude because of the thinness of the air. Kruschev wanted the world to believe that the SA-2 could reach that altitude, making any aircraft that relied on altitude for safety vulnerable.

The precise truth hardly mattered. The shooting down of Gary Powers's U-2 proved one of two things, either that powerful radar and high-altitude guided missiles had shot him down or that, if not, they would soon be able to. Either way, the SAM had put paid to the prospects of high-altitude, Mach 3 bombers being a viable weapons system in the future so there was little point in having manned fighters or bombers at that altitude either. That conclusion was to have wide-ranging effects throughout military aviation.

The diplomatic fallout of the U-2 was considerable. Kruschev made a speech condemning the violation of Soviet airspace, especially on May Day, which was seen as a particular insult, and the incident wrecked the Paris summit. Eisenhower took responsibility, stressing that it was a civilian aircraft. Francis Gary 'Frank' Powers was interrogated by the KGB and sentenced to ten years for espionage but he was exchanged for the Soviet spy Rudolf Abel in 1962. The Cold War, far from thawing, took on an even colder aspect.

The U-2 overflights stopped, but the USAF continued to fly electronic eavesdropping aircraft to probe the edges of the Soviet Union in international airspace. Both sides had interceptors standing by on Quick Readiness Alert (QRA) to intercept them close to each other's borders. Most of the time the encounters between interceptors and their opponents were friendly. The bomber crews and fighter pilots would exchange waves and occasionally RAF fighter pilots held up copies of *Playboy* centrefolds inside their canopies, causing an animated response from Russian crews. Sometimes they were hostile. On 1 July 1960 a USAF RB-47, crammed with electronic listening devices and a crew of six, was flying at 30,000 feet over international waters in the Barents Sea off the northern coast of the Soviet Union. Capt. Vasily Polyakov of the Soviet Air Force, flying a MiG-21, attacked the bomber with cannon fire some fifty miles off the coast and shot it down. Four of the six crew died, but two managed to parachute into the sea where they were picked up by a Soviet ship. The Russians claimed that the RB-47 had violated their airspace and the Americans denied it. The two surviving members of the crew were returned seven months later.

After two terms in the White House Eisenhower left the field and John Kennedy was elected US President; there were hopes for change, but the Cold War stayed Cold. On 12 April 1961 the Soviet Union showed its lead in rocketry by putting the first man into orbit around the earth, an SAF fighter pilot, Yuri Gagarin; on 19 April the same year Cuban exiles invaded Cuba at the Bay of Pigs with CIA support and were repulsed; in May, the USA put its first man into space, but not into orbit, highlighting a Soviet lead; in August 1961 the East Germans built a wall right across Berlin; in May 1962 US Marines went to Thailand to counter Communist incursions from Laos; a U-2 flown by a ROCAF pilot over Communist China was shot down by an SA-2 missile, and both sides launched military reconnaissance satellites into orbit over each other's territory.

Then, on 28 August 1962, CIA U-2 flights over Cuba brought back indisputable photographic evidence of SA-2 Guideline SAM sites on America's doorstep; they were purely defensive, and could have been to counter the regular U-2 flights over the island, but further U-2 flights showed MiG-21 interceptors at Cuban air bases, too. Once again they were defensive, but the theory that the Soviet Union was about to move Medium Range Ballistic Missiles (MRBMs) into Cuba began to take hold in Washington, threatening the US mainland from only a short distance away, and far from the main US early warning and air defence network in the north. That view was strengthened when the pattern of the deployment of SA-2 sites was analysed, suggesting the type of arrangement normally associated with ballistic missile launch sites in the USSR.

Early in the morning of 14 October a U-2, flown by Maj. Steve Heyser, USAF, took off from Edwards AFB in California, flew over Cuba from southwest to the north, taking photographs all the way, then landed in Florida. The following morning another U-2, flown by Maj. Rudolph Anderson, USAF, made the same flight. The photographs showed clearly that the Soviet Union was installing SS-4 MRBMs at a site near San Cristobal in a pattern which was recognisable from U-2 overflights of the Soviet Union itself. Another twenty missions during the following week confirmed it and President Kennedy went public with the news backed up by the photographs, put the US Armed Forces on a war footing and announced a blockade of Cuba by the US Navy.

The following morning USAF RF-101 Voodoos and US Navy RF-8 Crusaders made high-speed reconnaissance flights over the missile sites at extremely low level, under the radar coverage of the air defence system and outside the capability of the SA-2 missiles, bringing back more evidence of the Soviet installations. The crisis deepened but, rather than have Russian ships heading for Cuba stopped and searched by the US Navy, Kruschev backed down, ordering them to turn around in mid-Atlantic. The U-2s kept up their surveillance and on 27 October Anderson was over the northern coast of Cuba again when an SA-2 missile exploded above his aircraft, sending shards of metal through the cockpit sides to puncture his pressure suit, and he died. The following day the Soviet technicians started dismantling the SS-4 sites and shipping them back to the Soviet Union. The U-2 flights continued, despite the danger, and photographed IL-28 medium bombers on Cuban airfields which were more than capable of reaching the USA with nuclear weapons. Kennedy insisted they be withdrawn, too, and eventually they were. Ten U-2 pilots were awarded the Distinguished Flying Cross for their part in the Cuban Missile Crisis and Maj. Anderson was posthumously awarded the Distinguished Service Medal, the highest US award in peacetime. It was the closest the world had been to nuclear war.

The shooting down of Gary Powers and the Cuban Missile Crisis, together with what both sides knew about their own technological advances, turned the world of military aviation upside down. The XB-70 high-altitude bomber, which was already flying in prototype form, was cancelled, and the USA, Britain and the Soviet Union developed strike aircraft capable of penetrating enemy defences at low level; meanwhile SAC and V Force bomber crews retrained to fly their giant machines at low level instead, under ground-based radar. A range of new technologies, doctrine and training was devised. The USAF converted Lockheed Super Constellation airliners, designated EC-121, equipped with radar that could look down on low-flying aircraft, and the SAF did the same using the Tu-126, creating the first generation of Airborne Early Warning and Control Aircraft (AWACS). To counter the new threat from the smaller, tactical strike aircraft, the F-111, the TSR-2 and the MiG-23 Flogger, which could penetrate defences at very low level and high speed, both sides started programmes to equip fighters with radar and air-to-air missiles which could 'look down' and 'shoot down'. Surface-to-air missiles had to change, too. Instead of hitting bombers in the stratosphere, their new targets were only a few hundred feet above the ground, and to counter them a new generation of radar and SAMs was needed which could engage low-level strike aircraft and penetration fighters in the horizontal rather than the vertical plane. To counter that new threat the US Navy started research on a completely new family of Anti-Radiation Missiles (ARM) which homed in on the emissions from SAM radar and blew them up.

Just fifteen years after the beginning of the jet age, and barely a decade since the Cold War had brought about huge changes in air warfare, it went through another revolution: the age of nuclear primacy was drawing to a close, and with it the ever faster, ever higher, missile-armed, gunless jet fighter mentality started giving way to a renaissance in tactical air forces. Up to the 1960s the superpowers confronted each other with nuclear arsenals based on high-altitude bombers and ICBMs, which could only be used to annihilate each other. To counter that threat both sides had developed air-to-air AAMs, including some with nuclear warheads, surface-to-air SAM missiles and Anti-Ballistic Missiles, ABMs, leaving little long-term future for the manned fighter. Such was the lure of offensive missiles and a missile-based air defence system that Kruschev even reduced the size of the Red Army because of the reliance he put on that nuclear strategy.

By the early 1960s it was clear to both sides in the Cold War that such a war could not be fought without committing national suicide. Kruschev was deposed in 1964, partly because that policy had been shown to be flawed. By 1967, as the Soviet Union, with its traditional reliance on numbers, was planning huge production runs of tactical fighters, NATO saw a new threat emerging, that the USSR might use its huge numerical superiority on the ground, with its new tactical air forces, to launch a conventional attack on Western Europe. NATO countered that threat with a new policy called 'Flexible Response', using conventional as well as nuclear forces, depending on the level of the threat. Underpinning the flexibility of that response was high-technology, tactical air power fighting a more traditional air war for superiority above and around the battlefield, giving it the ability to penetrate the front line and hit the enemy's rear echelons.

Even as the Cold War Warriors planned a new future based on new ideas and new technologies so the first American military advisors were getting involved in a war based on very old ideas, a very-low-technology war, a war in an ex-French colony in which aircraft played almost no role at all at first: Vietnam.

CHAPTER FIVE
Rolling Thunder

On 2 March 1965 a force of USAF F-105D Thunderchief fighter bombers and B-57 medium bombers, escorted by F-100D Super Sabre fighters, crossed into North Vietnam and blew up an ammunition dump at Xom Bong, thirty-five miles north of the De-Militarised Zone (DMZ), the border between North and South Vietnam. It was the first raid in Operation Rolling Thunder, an American bombing campaign against North Vietnam designed to put pressure on its communist government to stop supplying fellow communists, the Vietcong guerrillas, who were trying to bring down the US-backed government of South Vietnam. The raid did serious damage, but it was a pinprick and there was no political response from North Vietnam. Five USAF aircraft, three F-105s and two F-100s, were shot down by ground fire; four American pilots were dead and one was a prisoner of war. The losses sent a shock wave through the USAF, and through US public opinion. America was shocked that its large, high-tech, expensive air force, in combat for the first time since the Korean War, had been humbled by a third world country, a communist one at that.

Vietnam had been a French colony since the nineteenth century and, like Korea, it had been occupied by the Japanese during the Second World War. Vietnamese guerrillas, led by Ho Chi Minh, the head of the North Vietnamese government in 1965, and his Defence Minister, Gen. Giap, had fought the Japanese occupation with US assistance during the war and in 1945, when the French returned, they continued the fight for independence. That campaign culminated in the battle of Diem Bien Phu in 1954 when Giap defeated the French who left the country partitioned with a communist North and a capitalist South, separated by the DMZ which ran along the 17th Parallel. The parallels with Korea were obvious: Russia and China supported the North, and America stepped into the vacuum in the South, supporting a series of governments which were as undemocratic as they were corrupt. Ho Chi Minh was committed to reunifying the country under communism, but rather than invade he settled down for a 'long war', sending supplies to the Vietcong in the South along a route through the jungles of neighbouring Laos and Cambodia, known as the Ho Chi Minh Trail. The USA gave the South Vietnamese Army assistance with equipment and advisors to resist the Vietcong.

In November 1963 President Diem of South Vietnam was deposed in a military coup, throwing the country into confusion; three weeks later the USA was shaken by the assassination of President Kennedy. Vietcong terrorism went on, but it was an irritation rather than a huge threat to the South. The new US President, Lyndon Johnson, wanted to stop the infiltration of South Vietnam, but he was reluctant to commit US ground troops. Instead, the US Army and USAF continued to provide advisors for the South Vietnamese forces while the US Navy patrolled the coast.

On 2 August 1964 a US Navy intelligence-gathering destroyer, the USS *Maddox*, was attacked by North Vietnamese torpedo-boats. The *Maddox*, and aircraft from the USS *Ticonderoga*, returned fire and damaged two of them but in the confusion, followed by reports of attacks on another US destroyer, the *Turner Joy*, Johnson authorised the Navy to bomb the torpedo-boat base and oil installations at Quang Khe. Robert MacNamara, the US Secretary of Defense, announced the targets while the aircraft were still in the air so the defences were ready, and a Navy A-4 Skyhawk was shot down by ground fire. Two days later Congress passed the Gulf of Tonkin Resolution, authorising the President to act in support of South Vietnam. Such was the political support in America that it was passed almost unanimously and there was swift build-up of US forces in Vietnam, in the Gulf of Tonkin, where US carriers of Task Force 77 took up position on Yankee and Dixie Station, Dixie for operations against South Vietnam and Yankee Station for the North. The Air Force sent two wings of F-105 Thunderchief fighter bombers at bases in Thailand, the 355th and 388th at Korat and Tahkli, 80 aircraft in all and around 1,000 personnel, although it was not acknowledged at the time that they were operating from Thailand.

Far from deterring the North Vietnamese, the build-up of air forces and show of political and military muscle by the USA propelled them to escalate the confrontation themselves, and step up aid to the South. Pham Van Dong, the North Vietnamese Prime Minister, went to Russia to see Khrushchev's successor, Alexei Kosygin, to ask for increased military assistance, in particular air defence system: anti-aircraft guns, radar, SAMs and fighters. On 1 November 1964 a terrorist attack killed five US personnel and damaged or destroyed five B-57 bombers on the ground. On 7 February the Vietcong killed eight US personnel in an attack at Pleiku and then three days later they killed 23 more at Qui Non.

In response, Johnson and his advisors looked to the USAF to provide an answer to the stalemate on the ground, as Truman and Eisenhower had in Korea, though the situation was very different: US and South Vietnamese ground forces were not facing massed armies trying to invade from the North, but a small, invisible enemy inside South Vietnam. There was no need to establish air superiority over the South – they already had it – and the People's Army of North Vietnam Air Force (PANVAF) was not coming over the border to challenge it. The USAF had been transformed since the Korean War. It had been enlarged and reshaped for the needs of the Cold War and was led largely by bomber generals who believed in the independent effectiveness of air power to win wars by bombing the enemy's vital centres and disrupting their ability, and their will, to resist, something which had been impossible in Korea since it meant bombing China. They had spent the 1950s building

SAC with long-range bombers carrying nuclear weapons. Some wanted to 'bomb North Vietnam back into the Stone Age', but more limited bombing of a small country to stop it supplying guerrillas in another small country seemed feasible to some of them. The USAF identified 94 targets in North Vietnam, targets which they recommended hitting over two weeks, paralysing the North Vietnamese transport system and reducing its industry to rubble – a quick campaign with maximum shock effect. The White House simply wanted to send a message to the North Vietnamese: If you continue supplying the Vietcong, we will bomb you; if you stop, we will stop bombing you; if you do not stop, the bombing will escalate – hence the title, Rolling Thunder. The North Vietnamese saw no reason why they should be bombed in the first place, either gradually or all at once.

With no response to the first attacks, Rolling Thunder was stepped up. On 3 April 1965 two US raids were carried out against two important rail bridges in an attempt to bottle the North's railways in the capital, Hanoi. US Navy attack aircraft cut the Dong Phuong Thong bridge but in the course of the raid a US Navy F-8 Crusader from USS *Ranger* was bounced by three North Vietnamese MiG-17s and damaged, though the pilot managed to land safely on his carrier. It was the first aerial combat of the Vietnamese war.

On the same day a USAF 'strike package' of F-105s and F-100s attacked the Than Hoa road and rail bridge over the Song Chu River, a hundred miles south of Hanoi. One of the F-105 Thunderchief squadrons, the 67 TFS, was led by Lt Col. Robinson Risner, USAF, veteran and ace from the Korean War. To approach the bridge he had to lead his squadron through heavy anti-aircraft fire; they dropped 300 750 lb bombs on the bridge which was badly damaged, but the raid failed to bring it down. Risner's Thud was hit by 37 mm anti-aircraft fire on the bombing run and one of the F-100s was shot down, as was an RF-101 Voodoo sent to photograph the damage. Risner managed to fly his damaged aircraft to Da Nang air base just south of the DMZ from where he was flown back to his base at Tahkli in Thailand.

The following day a similar strike package went back to try and finish the job. It consisted of 79 aircraft: 46 F-105s, including Risner who was leading his squadron again, this time armed with 750 lb bombs and Bullpup air-to-ground guided missiles, four F-100C Super Sabres armed with 20 mm cannon and Sidewinder missiles for top cover, 17 other F-100s armed with 20 mm cannon and 2.75 in. HVARs to suppress anti-aircraft artillery (AAA) and to stand by to protect downed pilots if required, 10 KC-135 tankers to refuel the fighters and two RF-101 Voodoos to make bomb damage assessments (BDA). As protection against the MiGs, F-100Cs positioned themselves over the Gulf of Tonkin, some sixty miles north of the Song Chu estuary, on MiG Combat Air Patrol (MiGCAP), patrolling the shoreline as a shield across the most obvious route for any interception by North Vietnamese fighters. Several F-105s were orbiting just off the estuary, waiting their turn to go in and hit the bridge. Southeast of the estuary four more F-100Cs orbited in battle formation, two pairs in loose formation, waiting in case they were needed either for AAA suppression or pilot protection.

Suddenly they came under attack from dead ahead by two North Vietnamese MiG-17 Frescos who made a high-speed firing pass, then turned very tightly behind the Super Sabres, one of them getting behind each of the two pairs. The American pilots turned to meet them and a dogfight developed, with each side trying to get into a firing position. One of the Sabre pilots managed it, which prompted his opponent to go into a vertical dive. The American fired and saw flashes from his 20 mm cannon shells strike the tailplane of the MiG before he had to break off the fight, coming out of the dive just above the sea and overstressing his aircraft in the process.

The MiGCAP F-100s were flying south, towards the battle, when suddenly two more MiG-17s appeared to their left, from out to sea, heading for the F-105s. They flew straight across the path of the US fighters in tight formation, singling out a pair of F-105s. The Super Sabre pilots radioed warnings, but they were too late: the MiGs' pilots opened fire with heavy cannon and two of the bomb-laden F-105s were hit. One went down immediately; the pilot of the other managed to turn out to sea, nursing his burning aircraft. The F-100s closed on the MiGs but the American fighter pilots hesitated before using their Sidewinder missiles because of the danger of hitting the F-105s. At a thousand yards the leader saw a clear shot and fired a Sidewinder, but it passed harmlessly ten feet above one of the MiGs, alerting the North Vietnamese pilots to the

F-100's presence. The MiGs then went into a near-vertical climb with the F-100s after them, but the Russian aircraft were much more manoeuvrable and the North Vietnamese pilots skilfully avoided them and escaped. Forewarned by the raid the previous day, the North Vietnamese anti-aircraft gunners were ready at the Than Hoa bridge and AAA fire was heavy. One of Risner's aircraft was hit: the pilot, Capt. Carlyle 'Smitty' Harris, ejected low and was captured. The pilot of the F-105 struggling over the sea lost control and crashed; he was not rescued.

On 9 April 1965 Navy F-4 Phantoms patrolling off Hainan Island in the Gulf of Tonkin were engaged by Chinese MiG-17s. Lt Terence Murphy and Ensign Ronald Fegan apparently shot one down using an AIM-7 Sparrow missile, the first use of the missile in anger, but they were never seen again. All the evidence points to a fatal error by one of the other Phantom crews who, in the heat of battle, hit their squadron buddies by mistake with another Sparrow missile.

In a little over a month, in three raids, the USAF had lost 10 jet fighters, eight to ground fire and two in air-to-air combat, and the US Navy had lost one Phantom to friendly fire and an F-8 Crusader damaged in air-to-air combat. Of the 10 US aircrew involved, eight were dead and two were prisoners of war.

In private, American pilots were furious. It was not the nature of the task they were being asked to do – it was the way they were being asked to do it, which made a nonsense of the effective use of tactical air power. They had to fly under very tightly drawn Rules of Engagement (ROEs) with targets decided for them in Washington, and even the way they could attack them was heavily restricted by political considerations. A US fighter pilot's map of Vietnam was smothered in 'no go areas': no bombing within twenty-five miles of the Chinese border, within ten miles of Hanoi or four miles of North Vietnam's main port, Haiphong. In the air, enemy fighters had to be visually identified before they could be fired on. Since the American fighter pilot's missiles were designed to be fired from longer range than guns and were far less effective at very short range, this put them at a huge disadvantage from the start. The MiGs could not be attacked on North Vietnamese airfields, SAM sites could not be attacked, unless the missiliers fired first, for fear of killing Russian advisors. Even an elementary understanding of aerial warfare was lacking: by the time a SAM had been fired, it was a little late to be considering how to bomb it, and not being allowed to use surprise and knock the enemy out on the ground, to use maximum cunning, broke all the basic rules of air warfare. By forcing their pilots to behave predictably, the politicians were exposing them to dangers far greater than they needed to face, especially the reconnaissance flights after the raids, which the North Vietnamese expected and fired on with all they had. The North Vietnamese, very sensibly, sited their AAA on prohibited targets and the supplies the bombing was supposed to stop were simply stacked up in city streets, which were off limits, to await shipment at night.

The USAF's initial reaction to the setbacks was to strengthen the fighter protection for the F-105s. The F-100C Super Sabres were faster and more modern than the MiG-17s, but they were also far heavier and far less manoeuvrable, and they were immediately replaced by the 45th TFS which flew from its base in Florida straight to Ubon in Thailand. Their F-4C Phantoms were equipped with AIM-7 Sparrow and AIM-9 Sidewinder missiles, but no guns.

The American fighter pilots were happy, eager even, to go out and fight for air superiority; they regarded themselves as the best in the business, flying the best fighters in the world. But America's jet age Air Force and Navy had been built around strategic air power thinking, total, unrestricted war based on massive retaliation using nuclear bombers and defending the USA against similar attack. In Vietnam they were being asked to fight a limited war, a war for which neither their aircraft, weapons nor training were designed, and they were expected to do so under political constraints which made the effective use of their skills impossible.

The architect of Rolling Thunder was Robert MacNamara. Mac-Namara was a businessman who had made his name at the Ford Motor Company. He thought in terms of profit and loss and believed that if the cost for North Vietnam could be made too high, they would comply with America's wishes. The USAF wanted to carry out a massive and, they hoped, decisive attack. The politicians wanted a gradual approach: fearing, as they had in Korea, that anything too provocative might bring the Russians or Chinese, or both, into the conflict. The difference was that in 1950 neither communist country had had the ability to hit back at the USA. In 1965 Russia did. The policy tussle in Washington produced a 'politically correct' bombing campaign which was designed to achieve Johnson's limited political aims by the limited use of air power, hence the limitations imposed by the ROEs. Despite the misgivings of the Air Force generals, the idea of steadily increasing pressure on the North had carried high expectations for success, and its initial impotence, coupled with the losses in the first few weeks, sent a shock wave through the USA. Vietnam had been prepared, both militarily and psychologically, for the attacks. The government was willing to pay the price of being bombed for not giving in to the USA; Ho Chi Minh had planned for it, prepared the population and built up its air defences, which were much stronger than the Americans had expected.

On 5 April 1965 evidence that they were getting even stronger was brought back by an RF-8A from USS *Coral Sea*, the first photographs of SA-2 Guideline SAM sites, some fifteen miles southeast of Hanoi, although Hanoi and Haiphong were not on the list of targets. North Vietnam was building an integrated air defence system along Soviet lines, with Soviet equipment and advisors. It was based on anti-aircraft guns (AAA), SAMs and MiG-17 day fighters. In 1964 North Vietnam had 1,426, mainly lightweight, anti-aircraft guns effective up to 15,000 feet, 22 early warning radar sites, four fire control radars and 35 MiG-17 Frescos. By mid-1965 they had around 2,000 anti-aircraft guns, including some 85 mm which were effective up to 25,000 feet and 100 mm up to 40,000 feet with two height-finding radars to support them. They also had help from Chinese radar on the island of Hainan on the far side of the Gulf of Tonkin and from Russian ships in the Gulf, shadowing the US fleet. The number of MiG-17 fighters was doubled to 70. The air defences were operated on the Soviet principle of large numbers of radar sites covering interlocking areas, with SAMs and fighters under strict GCI. The SAM systems could be erected and operational in around four hours and the North Vietnamese built more SAM sites than it had systems, then moved them about to confuse the Americans.

One of North Vietnam's most important radar sites was on Bach Long island, seventy miles off the North Vietnamese coast from where it could watch every move of the US Navy's Task Force 77 off the Vietnamese coast, giving the air defences plenty of early warning as the American aircraft took off. North Vietnamese gunners were then waiting when the Navy aircraft crossed the coast, and every common-sense instinct indicated that it should be destroyed. Bach Long was off limits because of the possibility of hitting Russian technicians. The Task Force commander, Admiral Sharp, lobbied Washington hard and was eventually given permission to bomb nine radar sites, including Bach Long. It was very heavily defended and it took two waves of 70 aircraft to destroy it and there were more US losses.

On 17 April 1965 the Super Constellation-based AWACS, the EC-121Ds, were deployed to Saigon's Tan Son Nhut airport. They flew a long way off the coast but were able to give some warning of North Vietnamese fighters in the air. To provide radar jamming and voice jamming, specialised aircraft from all three services, USAF EB-66Cs, USN EA-1Fs, and US Marines EF-10Bs, were also brought into the battle.

Despite the reinforcements, Rolling Thunder was not working, and after a month, on 12 May, the bombing was halted. The North Vietnamese simply used the bombing halt to step up their activity, improve their defences and get more supplies through to the South. The USA tried to communicate with the North Vietnamese through the Russians, who refused to help, and when the US ambassador in Moscow wrote to his North Vietnamese counterpart, the letter was returned unopened so the bombing was resumed on 18 May and, to step it up, a month after that B-52s were brought in for the first time to bomb targets in South Vietnam. SAC's huge bombers were not used against the North because the loss of such a prestigious target to North Vietnamese air defences would have been too big a blow to the USAF, creating an ironic situation: strategic bombers being used for tactical operations in the South while an essentially tactical air force was being used strategically against the North.

When the strikes against the North resumed, American fighter pilots, both Navy and Air Force, wanted to avenge the first air-to-air kills of the war by the North Vietnamese. On 17 June the US Navy mounted another attack on the Than Hoa Bridge. A flight of F-4B Phantoms from the carrier USS *Midway* was flying Barrier Combat Air Patrol, BARCAP as the Navy called MiGCAP, when four MiG-17s flew towards the strike package. The Phantoms acquired them on radar, but under the ROEs they had to hold their fire until a visual identification had been made. They managed to do so and two of the Phantoms, flown by Cmdr Louis Page and Lt Jack Batson, fired their Sparrows, hitting two of the MiGs which exploded, the first air-to-air kills against the North Vietnamese.

The USAF was keen to open its score. Air Force fighter pilots had noticed that MiG-17s from the main North Vietnamese airfield at Phuc Yen avoided US fighters by waiting for the last wave in a flight of F-105 fighter bombers to attack when they would be low on fuel. The 45th TFS pilots decided to lay a trap for them, sending a flight of four Phantoms to appear as the last flight of the strike, flying in the same formation as the F-105s and at the same speed and altitude, so that the North Vietnamese radar operators would vector the MiGs on to them. The ruse worked: the ground controllers sent up two MiG-17s to attack them as they apparently waited for their turn to bomb. When the lead Phantom picked up the MiGs on radar at thirty-three miles he called for 'loose deuce' formation, signalling that the flight of four should split into two, widely-spaced pairs.

The plan was for the first pair to accelerate up to ten miles ahead of the second pair to make the visual identification required under the ROE, while the second pair would acquire the MiGs on radar. The first pair would then break off while the second pair fired their Sparrows from head-on. The problem was that by the time the Phantoms had the MiGs on radar, they were low on fuel and could not use afterburner to make the required separation, and only managed to get three miles ahead before making the identification, too close for a Sparrow attack. The two MiGs appeared slightly higher and to the left of the first pair who broke off and went high; the MiG pilots then made a high-speed turn to get behind the second pair of Phantoms, opening fire as soon as they came in behind. The second pair dropped their tanks, engaged afterburner and accelerated away from the tighter-turning MiGs, giving them some separation and room to manoeuvre for a counter-attack. The second pair of Phantoms then split, No. 3, Capt. Kenneth Holcombe with Capt. Arthur C. Clark in the back broke right, and No. 4, Capt. Thomas S. Roberts and Capt. Ronald Anderson, went left.

The idea was to give the two MiGs little option but to split themselves or risk being 'sandwiched' between the two Phantoms. The MiGs did split, one following each Phantom. Holcombe reversed the turn several times then went into a screaming dive, his speed reaching Mach 1.3, opening up a five-mile separation before turning for a head-on attack on his pursuer using a Sparrow, only to discover that his radar was out. The two fighters closed head to head, the MiG's nose sparkling as the pilot opened fire with cannon. How Holcombe must have longed for a gun during the seconds before the MiG passed very close overhead without scoring any hits. From the back seat Clark called, 'Go heat', meaning, get in the MiG's six o'clock for a Sidewinder heat-seeker shot instead. As the MiG turned and came back for another attack, Holcombe went into a steep dive, building up speed to Mach 1.3 again. From 800 yards the MiG opened fire as Holcombe pulled up into a high-g barrel roll which the MiG could not follow, forcing the North Vietnamese pilot to overshoot. Coming out of the manoeuvre behind the MiG, Holcombe acquired with a Sidewinder, heard the familiar growl in his headphones indicating that the Sidewinder had locked on, then fired all four of his Sidewinders in ten seconds: three missed, but the fourth exploded just behind the tailpipe as the MiG entered cloud, where it exploded in flames. Phantom No. 2 of the first pair saw the explosion from high above and confirmed the kill.

Meanwhile Roberts's radar was also out so he also elected for a high-energy manoeuvre to get behind the MiG for a Sidewinder shot. He nosed down, with afterburner, reaching Mach 1.4 and, staying well ahead of the MiG, then pulled up into a brutal, high-g zoom climb to 33,000 feet, where he pulled over the top and saw the MiG, which had followed him, 4,000 feet below, about to bank through ninety degrees and dive again. Roberts quickly closed the gap and fired two Sidewinders in rapid succession without waiting for a growl. Both missed, but the third, which had acquired, exploded just behind the MiG which started to belch out white smoke, then went into a high-speed dive to 6,000 feet with Roberts gaining on him relentlessly. Just as he was about to overshoot, Roberts acquired a growl and fired his last Sidewinder, then broke off quickly and started to jink to avoid ground fire which suddenly erupted. As he was leaving the area a large flight of MiGs approached; the Phantoms departed the area. Low on fuel, they formed up again and headed for Udorn, much closer than their base at Ubon. The MiGs were content to follow at ten miles without trying to engage the Americans, who would have been at a distinct disadvantage because they were low on fuel and had fired all their Sidewinders. The fuel warning lights in a Phantom come on at 2,000 lb, indicating just a few minutes' flying time, and they were blinking on all the Phantoms when they landed, their crews in very high spirits.

The age of aerial combat with missiles had arrived. The problem was that it was arriving in battle with air-to-air missiles designed for attacking bombers high in the stratosphere, not fighters at close quarters. The Phantom was a superb aircraft but not a natural, manoeuvrable dogfighter. The high-energy manoeuvres it could perform with its large power reserves gave its pilots the ability to turn the tables in a dogfight, but its reliance on AAMs meant that many opportunities which presented themselves could not be used because of the delay and restrictions which getting a radar lock-on imposed. In the USA plans were laid to give Phantom pilots a gun to back up their AAMs.

The age of the SAM in air warfare had been ushered in over Russia in 1960, but SAMs such as the SA-2 Guideline had been designed to attack high-flying bombers, not low flying fighters, though they were still lethal at medium level. The American pilots and their commanders knew that the first thing they should have been doing was establishing air superiority over their target areas by attacking North Vietnamese airfields, radar sites and the SAM missile sites; the best way to counter SAMs was to bomb the sites before they became operational, using aggressive tactics against ground defences as well as in the air. Permission to attack the SAM sites was repeatedly sought from Washington, but it was equally consistently refused at first because of the possibility of killing Russians. One US fighter pilot, returning from a mission in the North, came across a missile site under construction, protected by anti-aircraft guns. In breach of the ROEs he shot it up with 20 mm cannon fire and set the missiles on fire. When he returned to base he reported the action and went out on another mission. While he was airborne, orders came through that he was to be grounded and court-martialled; he was killed on the second mission.

On 27 July 1965 Capt. Richard Keirn, a veteran of the Second World War, who had been a POW in Germany, was flying one of four F-4Cs of 47th TFW on MiGCAP for F-105s attacking targets northwest of Hanoi. They were above dense cloud, looking for fighters, when an SA-2 came through the clouds and exploded nearby, wrecking Keirn's Phantom and damaging the other three; Kiern ejected and became a prisoner of war again.

It was the first kill of the war by a SAM but there was still point-blank refusal from Washington for permission to attack the missile sites or their radar. On the night of 11–12 August a Navy A-4 Skyhawk, flown by Lt Donald H. Brown, was shot down by another SAM. The protests from the USAF and Navy were repeated, and permission was finally granted. Not waiting for it to be subsequently cancelled, later the same day, the Navy launched 124 aircraft from the carriers *Coral Sea* and *Midway* to attack missile sites. In two days no active sites could be found and no missiles were destroyed, though five US aircraft were shot down by anti-aircraft guns and seven more were damaged in the attempt.

To meet the threat posed by the SAMs and their radar, the USAF and the US Navy developed Electronic Countermeasures (ECM) pods, to warn pilots of SAM activity and to jam their radar. They also worked on providing specialised fighters to seek out and destroy the missile sites. Their missions were given the codename 'Iron Hand' and the Air Force began experimenting at Elgin AFB in Florida using the F-100F, the two-seater training version of the Super Sabre. The flying controls in the rear cockpit were taken out and replaced by radar displays and a position for an Electronic Warfare Officer (EWO) who operated the Radar Homing and Warning System (RHAWS) which locked on to the enemy radar once it started transmitting, then guided the crew to the site. The idea was for four aircraft to operate as a team, two with Bullpup air-to-ground missiles and two with cluster bombs to hit the site once it had been found. The new anti-SAM aircraft were given the name Wild Weasels and they deployed to Vietnam on 26 November 1965 to start their 'hard kill' electronic warfare missions.

It was a very hazardous mission, calling for a high degree of not only courage but coolness on the part of the crew, and within a month the unit had its first casualty. Capt. John Pitchford, with Capt. Robert Trier, in the back seat, was escorting a flight of Thuds when they detected 'Fansong' radar normally associated with SA-2 missiles. Pitchford turned towards the site and as he approached his F-100 was hit in the rear by a 37 mm cannon shell and the engine started to overheat. He managed to fire off a number of rockets to mark the position of the SAM site, which the Thuds then attacked with bombs, but the F-100 was badly damaged. Although he nursed it towards the sea it was clearly doomed, and he and Trier ejected just before it exploded in mid-air. Trier was listed as missing in action and Pitchford was captured.

Iron Hand and Wild Weasel missions pitched human ingenuity and courage against electronic fortifications, and to be effective called for a high degree of coolness on the part of the US fighter pilots. The only way that the radar operators could escape detection was to switch off their sets, in which case the mission was successful because it allowed the attacking aircraft to proceed to the target without being attacked. The Navy used A-6 Intruders for the same mission using its anti-radiation missile, the AGM-45 Shrike, developed after the Cuba crisis to home in on radar emissions. The next stage in suppressing the ground defences would be for F-105s, using the same flight profile, to attack the other installations on the missile site with 'pickled fruit', bombs which burst open to spray a variety of sub-munitions over the area, or 'daisy cutters', 3,000 lb iron bombs with a long spike on the front which hit first and detonated it three feet above the ground to create a huge blast effect over the whole site.

Despite permission to attack the missile sites, and the dedication of the Wild Weasel crews, North Vietnam's air defence system continued to increase in size, complexity and effectiveness, partly because of the ROEs, which meant that pilots had to use particular routes in and out of North Vietnam, making them predictable and therefore vulnerable. The enemy concentrated its AAA on those routes, creating areas of dense fire which the pilots had to fly through while denying them two of air power's most precious and effective ingredients – surprise and flexibility. At very low level they flew into a wall of deadly small arms fire; up to 5,000 feet, light AAA, heavy machine-guns and cannon were equally deadly; from 5,000 to 25,000 feet and above, the heavy calibre AAA took over, coupled with SA-2. The number of radar sites increased from 22 to 47 by the end of 1965, concentrated at three major centres which were immune from attack, the airfields at Phuc Yen, Bac Mai and Kep.

The growing electronic threat forced the Americans to develop both electronic countermeasures (ECM) and new tactics to over-come them. They carried RHAWS to warn them when they had been picked up on enemy radar and, to confuse the radar operators, they carried a radar decoy system of Second World War vintage, chaff, thousands of strips of thin metal foil which, when discharged into the air, gave the radar a huge reflective target which caused the whole screen to light up, obscuring the target aircraft. Under their wings the US fighters started to carry increasingly soph-isticated ECM pods housing a whole variety of 'black boxes' which jammed the enemy radar frequencies, radio control signals and communications. When the American fighter pilots were about to enter North Vietnamese airspace, they checked around the cockpit to make sure that all systems were operational, switching weapons systems from safe to ready and getting the green lights to show they were armed, then switched on their ECM as a last act before facing the defences, a ritual they called: 'Clean up, green up and turn on the music.'

The lower they flew the more difficult it was for radar to pick them up. Thud pilots used the flight profile devised to deliver nuclear bombs in Europe, starting very low, 'in the weeds', then, on approaching the target, they would pop up to medium altitude, identify the target, dive, bomb it and return to low level to clear the area. The problem was that flying like that put the aircraft into the dense small-arms and light AAA fire. To avoid it, as more effective ECM pods became available, they moved back up to 6,000 feet, relying on electronic defences, but when all else failed the pilots finished up actually dodging the missiles, outwitting the ground controllers in the air. Outflying a SAM missile is the ultimate test of man versus machine. Those who had put their faith in automation and unmanned systems to draw down the curtain on aerial combat were surprised. It called for extremely cool thinking but, as many American pilots showed, it could be done. The key, if possible, was to see the launch, the tell-tale puffs of smoke and dust from the initial thrust of its motor. An SA-2 is the size of a large telegraph pole and the pilot had to keep it in vision all the time, turning towards it, then flying straight at it, getting as close as possible, head-on, then turning violently at the last second, forcing the missile, which was doing Mach 2 or faster, into a turn the controllers could not sustain and maintain the lock-on. An SA-2 could sustain around 8 g but, given the speed, that meant a huge turning circle, which, by the time it had turned through half a circle or more, gave the fighter time to escape; sometimes the SA-2 simply ran out of fuel looking for their hard-manoeuvring target.

American fighter pilots had been trained to fight a different kind of war, one which did not include dogfighting, especially with guided missiles. The USAF, born to fight the Cold War on a massive scale, suddenly found itself fighting a small, intimate, close-up, counter-insurgency war with the wrong equipment and the wrong training, and being expected to do it under severe political constraints. The F-100s lacked the manoeuvrability of the MiG-17, making them highly vulnerable in aerial combat, and were withdrawn from operations over the North, though they stayed on in the South as fighter bombers. The B-57 medium bomber, based on the British Canberra, was designed for medium- or high-level bombing long before the SAM made such missions suicidal. The F-102 Delta Dagger interceptors, which were deployed in South Vietnam against the remote possibility of air attack by North Vietnam, were wonderful interceptors designed to fly against bombers approaching the USA from over the North Pole at high altitude. How they would have fared at low level against tight-turning MiG-17s was never put to the test, though their IR sensors, built in to detect bombers high in the stratosphere, were used at night in the jungle to detect the heat from Vietcong trucks and fires, which would then be attacked using 2.75 in. rockets.

The F-105 Thunderchief, a huge penetration fighter designed to carry a nuclear bomb at high speed deep into Soviet territory in Europe where the enemy air defences would have been a legitimate target, was being used to drop 'iron bombs' on bridges and supply routes in the jungle, a job for which it could not use its main advantage, which was very high speed at low level, and the pilots did so without being able to take out the air defences first. Flying the Thud over North Vietnam was not the job it was designed for but, in the right hands, it was good at the job, which job called for great skill and nerve. On 2 October 1965 24 Thuds flew north of Hanoi to attack a bridge. They approached in six waves of four aircraft at 600 m.p.h., flying between 200 and 300 feet above the ground, dropped their external fuel tanks before reaching the IP, the pull-up point, then, three miles short of the target, pulled up into a hail of anti-aircraft and small-arms fire, dived on the bridge, dropped their two 3,000 lb bombs each and hit the deck again to clear the area. Of the 24 aircraft only three returned to their original base in Thailand after the raid: three were lost, their pilots ejecting over the North and the others, too badly damaged to make it back to Thailand, landed in the South.

The F-4 Phantom reinforced the value of the capable, powerful, versatile, fighting aircraft. It was a better interceptor than the Super Sabre or the F-106, a better fighter bomber than the F-100 or the F-105 and a better fleet defence fighter than the F-8, and once the RF-4C was introduced in October 1965 it came to be regarded as a better reconnaissance fighter than its McDonnell stablemate, the RF-101 Voodoo. The Phantom had its own radar, giving it an advantage over the MiG-17 at range, and if it could get the missile shot in it was deadly, but it had no gun for the really close-in 'knife fight'. It could hold its own in a dogfight, especially once its pilots found out how to use its power to create 'energy manoeuvrability', and in its first six months in Vietnam F-4s accounted for 13 MiGs, due as much to the aggression of its pilots as to anything else.

The F-4 Phantom and the F-105 Thunderchief were the mainstays of Rolling Thunder. They carried the fight to the enemy, and the Phantom was the more influential of the two: it was the rapier, while the Thud was the blunt instrument. Thud pilots named a geographical feature of North Vietnam after it – Thud Ridge, a line of jungle-clad mountains which ran northwest from Hanoi towards China. Its slopes were too steep for AAA emplacements and for Thud drivers it became a friendly, green-tinged signpost, pointing to Hanoi, which they used as a navigational aid. At the end of it was the enemy fighter base at Phuc Yen. The Thud had an integral gun and its pilots would take on the MiGs when not bombing. One of the great Thud pilots was Col. Jack Broughton, a former Blue Angels aerobatic team leader. Broughton and Risner were inspirational squadron leaders who built up strong teams of pilots with superb morale which spilled over into extra fighting effectiveness in the tradition of Boelke, Richthofen, Mannock, Bader and Galland. That effectiveness in battle could not be used to get results for Rolling Thunder, which was flawed as a concept. A strategic bombing campaign, which is what the Thuds were being asked to wage, needed targets to destroy, and one of the problems was that North Vietnam did not have a sophisticated economy with large industrial areas dependent on a complex transport system. The will of the people would not break either; they had been prepared by their leaders to expect worse, they even became blasé about going into air-raid shelters.

Despite the efforts of the pilots, Rolling Thunder was a costly campaign for the USAF. By the end of 1965 there were 18 squadrons in the theatre, 661 aircraft and 181,000 men on the ground, with US losses running at one a week. MacNamara's policy of making it unprofitable for the North to continue was turning out to be very expensive. To even up the balance sheet, on 22 December 1965 Washington briefly escalated Rolling Thunder by authorising the bombing of the Uong Bi power station, one of the few industrial targets of strategic value since it provided 25 per cent of all North Vietnam's electricity. It was destroyed, but it showed the flawed thinking from Washington. Putting out the lights in Hanoi was supposed to be the stick, to be followed three days later by the carrot in the form of a Christmas bombing halt to try and get the North Vietnamese government to the conference table. The truce lasted thirty-seven days, but North Vietnam did not see it as a concession and simply used the time to step up supplies to the South and went on improving their air defence system. When bombing resumed on 31 January 1966 the pilots' work was even harder.

The idea of achieving air superiority was even more elusive, and a year into Rolling Thunder there was little to show except a steadily escalating commitment on the ground, precisely what it had been designed to prevent. By March 1966 there were 215,000 US troops on the ground and the size and commitment of the air campaign was so large that from 1 April the air forces operating in Vietnam, which had been part of the 13th Air Force based in Okinawa, became the 7th Air Force, with its own HQ at Tan Son Nhut near Saigon, its commander reporting directly to Pacific HQ (PACAF) in Hawaii. The only aircraft which were not part of the 7th AF were the B-52 bombers which were still controlled by SAC via a planning cell at Tan Son Nhut. The Navy also had a separate command structure, and the fragmented control reflected the tensions within the USAF between bomber men and fighter men, between the USAF and USN and between all the aviators and the politicians.

The bomber men of SAC wanted to take part in the war, but the problem was twofold – heavy bombing of the North would have presented an image of overwhelming might being used against the North Vietnamese, and the air defences around Hanoi were now the heaviest in history and the huge, high-flying bombers would be perfect targets for MiG-21 interceptors, which the Russians were now also supplying to the North Vietnamese, and for their SAMs. Losing a B-52 to a Russian system would have been a huge political defeat for SAC. On 11 April 1966 30 B-52s from Guam dropped 600 tons of bombs on the Mu Gia Pass, one of the main crossing points between North Vietnam and Laos at the start of the Ho Chi Minh Trail. The cost of the raid was put at $21 million and the pass was open again two days later.

Rolling Thunder continued as a fighter bomber and fighter war, and as the coverage, sophistication and lethality of North Vietnam's air defences increased so the number of US aircraft needed to support each raid increased. The 'strike packages' put together for each raid frequently consisted of two and three times as many aircraft in supporting roles as were actually attacking the targets. A large part of that extra effort was in providing electronic counter-measures. Two EB-66C Destroyers (converted bombers packed with jamming equipment) normally operated as a team, orbiting at 25,000 feet some 30–35 miles from the target area, protected by fighters. One of their jobs was to jam the Fansong radar, making the SAMs impotent long enough for a strike package to get through to its target. At that height the EB-66 was very vulnerable to fighters and SAMs unless its jamming was extremely effective. On 25 February 1966 that effectiveness lapsed and an SA-2 hit an EB-66, and they had to be pulled further back from the target area, making them less effective.

The anti-radar and anti-missile war received a boost in the spring of 1966 when the USAF Wild Weasels were equipped with the US Navy's AGM-45 Shrike missile to use against the SAM guidance radar sites. A fundamental rule for Wild Weasels was that the attacking aircraft had to be positioned so that the time of flight of the Shrike was less than the flight time of the SAM. The Weasel pilot flew towards the target radar at around 20,000 feet, provoking the radar operators to switch on, relying on RHAWS to tell him when the enemy radar had locked on. Once he had been observed he switched on the homer in the Shrike, then, with the call 'take it down', followed by a power dive to around 500 feet, continued towards the radar. The Weasel stayed low and, with Shrike locked on to the emissions from the SAM or GCI radar, the pilot climbed again to a height appropriate for firing the missile. It was a race against time, firing the Shrike before the enemy could get off a SAM. The Shrike could be lofted from fifteen miles away on a ballistic flight path and when the motor cut off the guidance system would move the four fins, like the tail of a dart, to home it in on the radar; it could also be fired from two miles away. If the enemy radar was switched off the Shrike 'went ballistic' and maintained its flight path, less accurate than if the target radar was still on but still capable of hitting the target. Either way, it had achieved its objective because if the radar was switched off they could not control the MiGs or launch SAMs.

The air war hotted up in the spring of 1966. On 23 April Phantoms of the 555th TFS/8th TFW shot down two MiG-17s, the first air-to-air kills for nine months. The first ace of the war, not claimed publicly by the North Vietnamese, was a MiG pilot, Capt. Nguyen Van Bay, who shot down his fifth US aircraft in May 1966. In addition to radar and SAMs, the North Vietnamese deployed their MiG-21s, the Soviet Union's latest fighter, and it was not long before both sides' newest fighters met in aerial combat. On 26 April 1966 Maj. Paul Gilmore was flying a Phantom as cover for EB-66Cs jamming for a strike package on its way North; his EWO was Lt William Smith. They were bounced from above by a flight of MiG-21s which made a high-speed firing pass. The Phantoms turned to fight while the EB-66s made their getaway. After the pass the MiG pilots engaged afterburner, then climbed steeply back to their high altitude perch; in the climb, one of them was making gentle turns to check his six o'clock. Gilmore selected him as the slowest and followed him into the climb. When the MiG reached 30,000 feet, against a clear blue sky, Gilmore fired a Sidewinder which hit. The MiG pilot ejected, but Gilmore did not see him and fired two more, one of them going right into the MiG's tailpipe.

The two fighters were very different – the Phantom a two-seat, twin-engined, long-range, heavyweight, all-weather fighter with radar and missiles, while the MiG-21 was a single-seat, single-engine, short-range, nimble day fighter. The Phantom, though technically of the same vintage as the MiG-21, was a generation ahead in its electronics. The MiG-21 nearly matched the Phantom's top speed but the Phantom had greater power and could use 'high energy manoeuvres', against which the MiGs had higher manoeuvrability, especially in instantaneous rate of turn which, if applied at the right moment, could be used to escape the Phantom. High manoeuvrability was at such a premium against the Phantom that many of the best North Vietnamese pilots preferred the more manoeuvrable MiG-17 to the MiG-21. Both MiGs were small and not easy to pick out at a distance, while the Phantom was not only big but had notoriously smoky engines, making it even easier to see first.

The Phantom had been designed to fight at long range, using its on-board radar to acquire a target, its Sparrow missiles first, with their 28-mile range, the idea being to hit the enemy at Beyond Visual Range (BVR), and, if that failed, its Sidewinders at closer range. The ROEs, with their requirement that American pilots made a visual identification, robbed the Phantom pilots of their main advantage, forcing the pilot and his EWO to wait for the close-quarter battle when the MiG was highly likely to be inside the minimum range for the Sparrow. Once they were in a violent close battle and the Phantom pilot was engaged in evasive manoeuvres, which produced high g loadings, the EWO was unable to find the thirty seconds to a minute of stable flight to get a lock-on. In the close fight they had to fight on the enemy's terms, breaking one of the cardinal rules of air combat: first seek some advantage over the enemy. Close in, what was needed was a gun, and the Phantom had no gun. Each pilot had a different agenda, looking for the best conditions for his aircraft and armament. The Phantom pilot's repertoire included breaking away to put some distance between it and the MiG, then turning back into the fight with missiles ready. It could not match the MiG's turning ability so getting in its six o'clock was difficult, but by rolling away from the MiG's turn and pulling above it, keeping an eye on it all the time, then pulling through off the top of the roll, it could get on the MiG's tail for a Sidewinder shot. To develop these tactics, to find the secret little weaknesses in the enemy's performance envelope, Cambodian Air Force MiG-17s were used in mock combat over the South.

The task of the North Vietnamese fighters was not to engage in aerial combat with US fighters but to disrupt the American bombers by intercepting them, forcing them to jettison their bombs early in order to defend themselves or to alter course into the path of the SAMs or AAA. ECM was succeeding in blunting the effectiveness of the SAMs so the North Vietnamese simply fired them in salvoes. The defences were getting more effective and losses to all three systems, AAA, SAMs and fighters, frequently rose to two a day during 1966. On 21 September the first F-4C Phantom was lost in air-to-air combat in a dogfight with three MiG-17s; on 9 October the first MiG-21 shot down by a US Navy pilot fell to Cmdr Richard Bellinger flying an F-8 Crusader. The worst day of the war for the US aviators came on 2 December. USAF strike packages made up mainly of Phantoms and Thuds from South Vietnam and Thailand, and Navy strikes from five carriers on Yankee Station, combined to strike at the North Vietnamese fuel and oil supplies. The Navy lost two A-4C Skyhawks and an F-4B Phantom, all to small-arms fire or AAA, and the USAF lost three F-4Cs and an F-105 to SAMs, and an RF-4C to AAA; 13 men were missing, either dead or POWs. To add to the gloom among American pilots, on 14 December a MiG-21 attacked a flight of F-105Ds near Hanoi using the Soviet equivalent of the Sidewinder, the AA-2 Atoll heat-seeking AAM, the first time that a US aircraft had fallen to an air-to-air missile.

By the end of the year the air war had been reduced to an expensive, and unacceptably bloody, stalemate. The cost of Rolling Thunder was 451 US aircraft lost, including 126 F-105s, 111 of them over the North, and the 79,000 sorties which US crews had flown, dropping 100,000 tons of bombs, had only increased the North Vietnamese will to resist. The worst aspect of it for pilots remained the knowledge that what they were doing was ineffective, even in the limited goals set for Rolling Thunder, for all their efforts had not stopped increased US commitment to the ground war and by the beginning of 1967 there were 380,000 US troops in Vietnam. MacNamara's measure of success was based on sortie rates and it seemed to the pilots in Vietnam that the outcome of a sortie was less important than the fact that it had been flown. What pilots saw as his obsession with statistics led to pilots' lives being risked during a bomb shortage when, simply to keep the sortie rate up, F-100 fighter bombers took off on ground attack missions in the South with a concrete block on one side to balance the only bomb available which was on the other side.

It was very hard for pilots to accept the loss of comrades to air defence systems, large parts of which were immune from attack, and it took a particular kind of professional courage to continue. In the autumn of 1941, before the introduction of the heavy bombers, RAF crews went on flying against impenetrable defences, taking heavy losses in the knowledge that what they were doing was ineffective; they were amongst the most courageous of all, and so it was in Vietnam. There was a yawning gulf between those who were fighting the war and those who were directing it from thousands of miles away.

At the end of 1966 a committee of scientists from the Institute of Defense Analysis in Washington published the *Jason Report*, the result of months of work on the effectiveness of Rolling Thunder. It concluded what had been true of most previous strategic bombing campaigns, that there was not much chance of changing a government's mind by bombing its people. Indeed, it usually only hardened opinion against those doing the bombing. It said it had 'no measurable effect on Hanoi's ability to mount and support military operations in the South at the current level ... and the damage to facilities and equipment in North Vietnam has been more than offset by the increased flow of military and economic aid, largely from the USSR and Communist China'.

In the middle of the gloom among aviators the 8th TFW, the Wolfpack, produced a morale-boosting success. It had arrived in September 1966, equipped with F-4C Phantoms, and was based at Ubon in Thailand, commanded by Col. Robin Olds. Olds was forty-four, and he had been flying fighters for twenty-five years. His first encounter with a jet aircraft had been in the air on 7 November 1944, flying a P-51D, when he was credited with a 'probable' Me 262 of JG7; he finished the Second World War as an ace with 24.5 victories in P-38s and P-51Ds. Olds was a fighter pilot of the old school, a leader in the traditional mould of Western fighter leaders, a man who could transform a squadron into a highly effective weapon by a mixture of personal toughness, aggression and skill, leading from the front, hard-drinking, with a charisma that infected the entire wing with confidence. Morale was high when they arrived in Thailand, and once in the operational area pilots thought of little else but getting at the enemy.

They all knew, as did everybody in the Air Force, that the way to get at the enemy was to bomb his airfields, but that was not allowed. So they came up with something else. Capt. John Stone, one of the Phantom pilots, came up with a ruse out of the history books. The North Vietnamese MiGs were avoiding combat with American fighters so the plan was to simulate an attack on Hanoi by the much more vulnerable F-105s while, in fact, they would be Phantoms, armed and equipped for aerial fighting. It was on the model of Hinton's first foray over MiG Alley in 1951, flying his F-86 Sabre like the much less threatening F-80 Shooting Star. It was a classic case of planning to go MiG-killing in the air. There was great professional confidence in planning the mission, but no complacency; Robin Olds had a very healthy respect for the North Vietnamese fighter pilots, both in terms of aggression and skill, believing that they were better than the Germans he had fought towards the end of the Second World War, but he also believed that in the F-4 Phantom, in the hands of pilots whom he trained relentlessly in air combat tactics and close formation flying, he had the answer to them.

The idea was given the codename Operation Bolo and set for 2 January 1967. It was planned by Stone and other junior officers at Ubon with input from Olds. It involved 56 Phantoms, seven flights of four aircraft each from two wings, the 8th and 366th, in two waves, the 8th taking off first. The 8th was in turn split into two waves, three flights, then four flights, which took off thirty minutes apart, with the Phantom pilots using the same ECM pods as the F-105s. In all, 100 aircraft were involved, including 24 F-105D Wild Weasels to suppress ground defences, 4 EB-66s, an RC-121 radar surveillance aircraft, their radar probing the NV fighter stations, all protected by more Phantoms. Another 100 aircraft were to stage diversionary attacks to confuse the North Vietnamese fighter controllers and their Russian advisors.

The flights were given call signs based on the US automobile industry, and in a piece of bravado Olds led the first flight to reach the target area with the call sign 'Olds Zero One'. Such apparent breaches of security are odd, but have a great morale-boosting effect. The second flight, Ford, was led by Col. Daniel 'Chappie' James, a black American. James was deputy commander of the 8th TFW and he and Olds were inseparable, known as 'Blackman and Robin'. John Stone led the third flight with the call sign 'Rambler Zero One'. The 12 Phantoms comprising the first wave took off from Ubon at 12.25 local time and headed along Route Pack Six, skirting the airfields at Phuc Yen and Gia Lum, then towards Hanoi. Over the radio came a warning from an RC-121 that MiGs were taking off from both and heading in the direction of the first wave.

After refuelling, the Phantoms arrived in the target area at 15.00 local time and went into an orbit as if preparing for a bombing run. The Phantom pilots could not see the MiGs because they were under the cloud, but they picked them up on radar on a reciprocal course so Olds led the entire first wave through a 180 degree turn so they were flying in the same direction, timing it so that as the first MiG came up through the cloud it was immediately behind Olds Flight and in front of Ford. Olds then broke right with his wingman, with a MiG one and half miles away in his eleven o'clock, also in a left-hand turn. Olds 04, on the outside of the turn, went high, looking for a position from which to attack the MiG in the rear and clear his leader's six o'clock.

Olds ignored the danger from behind and went for the MiGs in front, getting a lock-on and firing two Sparrows at close range. They lost the lock-on because they were so close, and the MiG went back into the cloud, so he fired a Sidewinder after it for good measure. The fight had taken them down to about 9,000 feet where the Phantom had a manoeuvring and power advantage over the MiG. As one MiG disappeared into cloud so another came out, also in a left-hand turn, across Olds's path. Instead of trying to get on his tail at short range, Olds rolled to the right, away from his adversary, engaged afterburner and pulled up into a barrel roll to the left. Upside down, as Olds went over the top of the roll, he looked down and saw that the MiG was still in the left-hand turn. He sensed that the North Vietnamese had not seen him so he waited, judging his roll out to bring him below the MiG and about a mile behind, just gaining on him with about 1.5 g on. The MiG was against blue sky, a perfect Sidewinder shot, and as soon as he heard the growl in his headphones Olds fired two. The first tracked straight to the MiG, hit the left wing, which came off, and the MiG went down in a flat spin.

As Olds's missile hit, his wingman, Lt Ralph Wetterman, who was now about 4,000 feet above, saw another MiG come out of the cloud and managed to get a lock-on with his radar at one and half miles and fired two Sparrows. He held the lock-on and the missile hit the MiG just in front of its tailfin and it exploded seconds later. Olds 04, Capt. Walter Radeker, had meanwhile turned in behind the first MiG which had come into view and he fired a Sidewinder which hit in the tailpipe and the MiG exploded. MiG-21s continued to pop up through the cloud in front of Ford Flight which was suddenly confronted by seven of them. Where Olds Flight had fought a series of separate engagements, Ford Flight went into a whirling dogfight to avoid several MiGs attempting to get on their tails. The MiG-21s had no head-on capable missiles like the Sparrow, but they did have cannon. The Americans fired four Sidewinders and two Sparrows and Ford 02, Capt. Everett T. Raspberry, hit one MiG with a Sidewinder which went down, tumbling end over end, then into a spin.

Between them, the eight Phantoms had shot down four MiGs for certain, without loss, and they left the area. As they did, Rambler Flight came into the area at 15,000 feet, with John Stone leading. He orbited the flight and saw two MiGs below, getting off two Sparrows, one of which hit one of the MiGs which went straight down. Just as that happened, two more MiGs came at them head-on, cannon firing, and one of them passed between Stone and his wingman, Lt Lawrence Glynn. Stone and Glynn engaged afterburner, broke upwards, then rolled to the left and down, building up speed to 600 knots, coming out inside the MiGs, who were turning away. Glynn fired two Sparrows – the second one hit the MiG which had earlier passed between the two Phantoms and the pilot ejected.

Rambler 04, Maj. Phillip Combies, got a lock on another MiG below and fired two Sparrows. One disappeared and the other did not track to its target so Combies fired four Sidewinders at once. The first two detonated either side of the tailpipe but before anybody could see if the other two hit they had to break hard right as they came under attack from more MiGs. As they cleared the area they saw a parachute floating down so Combies was credited with a kill. By the time the second wave arrived the MiGs had disappeared. The three flights fired 28 missiles; 16 missed, but Operation Bolo had achieved 7 kills plus one probable for no loss.

It was a major aerial victory but the problem was that, though the sweep had been a huge success, it was not the way to get air superiority – that would have to be done by attacking the aircraft on the ground as it had been in the Battle of Britain and Germany, and as Korea had shown. Over the following twelve months 36 MiGs were shot down in aerial combat, 23 of them by crews from Robin Olds's 'Wolfpack', and Olds himself finished the war with 4 MiGs. For this Bob Hope described him as 'the largest distributor of MiG parts in South East Asia'.

Four days later, on 6 January 1967, the 555th 'Triple Nickel' TFS shot down two more MiGs. The losses had a salutary effect on the PANVAF and they went into a period of avoiding combat altogether. When they did start emerging again it was not *en masse* but in pairs, under strict GCI which positioned them very high above their targets and some way away, from which perch, well beyond visual and Phantom radar range, they would swoop down in a high-speed dive, fire off two Atoll heat-seekers, then zoom climb to safety again.

In early 1967 the President released new categories of targets which could be attacked. They included the Thai Nguyen steel plant forty miles from Hanoi which produced many of the steel spans for bridges used to replace those bombed by the Americans, and was protected by AAA, SAMs and fighters. The first raid was on 10 March and it was the F-105s that did the work: five minutes before the attacking F-105s went in, an Iron Hand mission arrived to suppress the missile sites. No. 3 in one flight of four F-105 Wild Weasels from 355th TFW was Capt. Merlyn H. Dethlefsen. The leader was shot down by anti-aircraft fire. MiG-21s made repeated firing passes, trying to get the Wild Weasels to dump their ordnance, but Dethlefsen pressed home his attack, destroying the SAM site. All three remaining aircraft were damaged but made it back to base. Dethlefsen was awarded the Congressional Medal of Honor for the action; he was shot down and killed on a subsequent sortie.

One of the attacking F-105s was flown by Capt. Max Brestel who finished his bombing run then turned south, following his leader, and was just setting up to go back to base in Thailand when they saw two flights of four MiG-17s slightly below and heading north. They had not seen the American fighters, or saw them as no threat, but the F-105 pilots were eager for a fight and turned in behind them. Brestel managed to shoot two of them down with 20 mm cannon fire, becoming the first US pilot to shoot down two in a single sortie.

On 12 March the USN started to use the Walleye glide bomb which could be released outside the range of defences and glide to its target on stubby wings, a TV camera in the nose guided to the target by the EWO. Cmdr T. Walker put one through the window of an army barracks; on the same day, they were used against the Than Hoa Bridge and scored hits but were not powerful enough to bring it down.

This was the start of a period of very tough fighting. Industrial targets in the Hanoi and Haiphong area were released and the NVAF was forced to fight to protect them. In the battle for air superiority, the Wild Weasel's battle against the SAMs was every bit as important and demanding as the idea of aerial combat in the sky. On 19 April 1967 Maj. Leo K. Thorsness was leading a four-ship F-105 Wild Weasel mission in support of a raid on the North Vietnamese Army barracks at Xuan Mai, 37 miles southwest of Hanoi. Thorsness was a veteran of 90 missions over North Vietnam, 53 of them Wild Weasel sorties in six months. His backseat operator was Maj. Harold Johnson; his wingman was Maj. Tom Madison whose backseater was Capt. Tom Sterling. They refuelled over Laos, then flew into North Vietnam to arrive some five minutes before the strike aircraft at a height at which the Fansong radar could acquire them but low enough so that they could hit the deck quickly. A hundred miles from the target they heard the crackling sound in the headphones that indicated that they had been acquired by radar. The SAMs had an 18 mile range. The site came up on the radar screen in front of Thorsness, growing bigger as they got closer. He turned towards it and at seven miles fired an AGM-45 Shrike missile which would home in on the radar van at the centre of the site. Seconds later the radar blip disappeared. Other blips then began to appear as other radar sites lit up and the crackling in the headphones intensified as the blips multiplied, 'growing hair' as the pilots and their EWOs called it. They found another SAM site which Thorsness attacked with cluster bombs, then they flew into furious anti-aircraft fire at the same time as there were signals that SAMs had been fired.

'Take it down,' ordered Thorsness, the signal to go on to the deck where the SAMs could not get them, but as he said it Madison was hit by gunfire and his engine instruments showed that he was overheating quickly. Thorsness switched to guard channel on the radio and as he did so he picked up the sound of Madison's emergency bleeper which indicated he had bailed out. Seconds later he heard Sterling's bleeper, too. He could also hear that his Nos 3 and 4 were having a dogfight with MiGs, and No. 3 could not get his afterburner to light up, leaving him with only manoeuvre to escape. They managed it by flying skill alone against the more manoeuvrable MiGs. In the middle of this battle Thorsness and Johnson managed to acquire a second SAM radar and fire off another Shrike and destroy it. Then they flew to the position where Madison and Sterling had bailed out and saw two parachutes floating down. Johnson got a fix and started to transmit details of their position and the weather to a HC-130 Crown aircraft, which would then co-ordinate a helicopter rescue. As he did so, two more MiG-17s appeared, low at nine o'clock. Fearing that they might attack his colleagues on their parachutes, Thorsness dived behind the MiGs and opened up with his 20 mm cannon fire from about 1,000 yards, missing with his first burst but hitting one MiG with a longer burst, sending it down in flames. At that moment Johnson called that they were coming under attack from two more MiGs. Thorsness engaged afterburner and sped away as his two squadron colleagues landed in the jungle, then set course for a tanker over Laos to take on fuel.

Over the radio Thorsness and Johnson heard the HC-130 bringing two A-1E fighter bombers and a helicopter to the rescue. He knew what they were headed for, and as soon as he had refuelled he headed back to provide protection for the rescue operation. As he approached the area he saw MiGs at eleven o'clock and three o'clock but they had not spotted him. He flew towards one flight and hit one, seeing pieces flying off it and using his last 500 rounds of ammunition in the process. The other flight of MiGs was quickly on his tail so once again Thorsness hit the afterburner and went for the deck, weaving through the valleys to escape. But instead of

Major Walter Nowotny, the leading German fighter ace, who assumed command of the first operational detachment of jet fighters, the Luftwaffe's Me262, in July 1944.

© Archiv Werner Held, Ransbach-Baumbach

A Me262 pursues a USAAF P-51D Mustang in a gun-camera photograph taken from a second P-51D, which then shot down the German fighter.

© USAF

To give the Me262 greater firepower against allied bombers the Luftwaffe experimented with giving it a 50mm Rheinmetall BK5 cannon. © Philip Jarrett Collection/APL

The USAF's Lockheed F-80C Shooting Star which made history by winning the first ever jet-to-jet air combat. © Lockheed/APL

Lockheed's chief designer, Kelly Johnson, responsible for the Shooting Star and the F104 Starfighter, seen here with a Lockheed YF-12A, one of America's most exotic fighter prototypes. © Lockheed/Hugh Cowin/APL

An F-86E Sabre undergoes maintenance, Suwon, Korea. © USAF/Hugh Cowin/APL

An F-86 Sabre drops its wing tanks as it prepares to go into action against Russian MiG-15s, 1952. © USAF/TRH/APL

A MiG-15 pilot ejects from his aircraft seconds after it was hit by gunfire from an F-86 during a May 1953 dogfight. The pilot of the US F-86 Sabre, whose gun camera recorded this sequence, was Lieutenant Edwin E. Aldrin Jr., who would walk on the moon 16 years later as an Apollo 11 astronaut. © USAF/Aerospace/APL

Ezer Weitzmann, the father of the Israeli Airforce.

© Camera Press Ltd

An Israeli photograph showing the damage done to Egyptian MiG-21s after one of the raids that destroyed the Egyptian Air Force on the ground in 1967.

© Israeli Airforce/TRH/APL

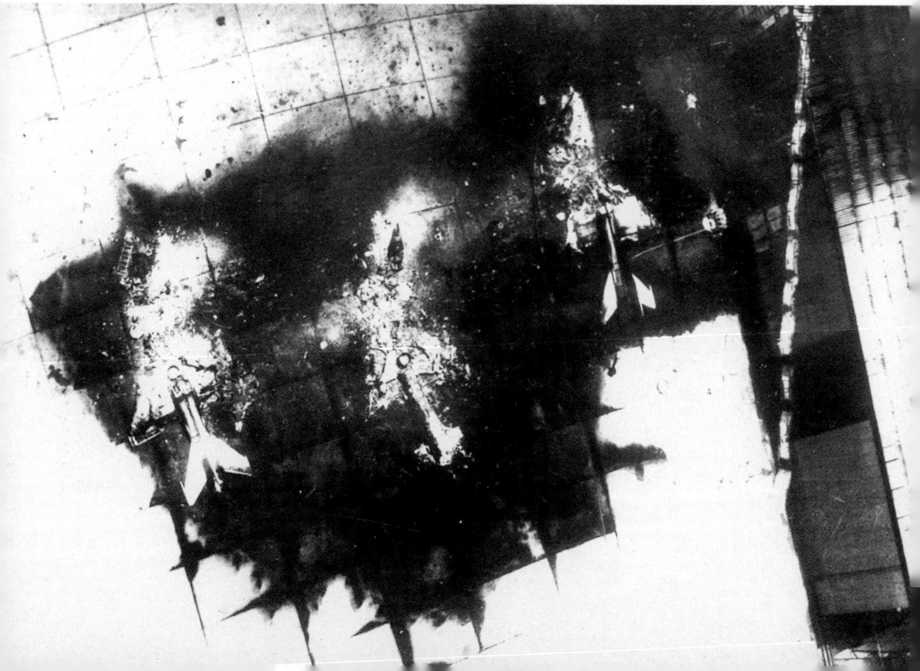

The backbone of NATO airforces; the F16 Fighting Falcon, has been produced in greater numbers [t]han any Western fighter since the Electronic revolution of the 1970s. via LMTAS

Lieutenant Randall Cunningham, USN, safely back on board the aircraft carrier USS Constellation[,] describes how he downed three MiG-17s during a single mission to enthusiastic squadron colleagu[es.] © USN/Robert Dorr/APL

A radar-equipped EB-66 Destroyer provides electronic assistance to USAF F-105D Thunderchiefs as they bomb a military target through low cloud over the southern panhandle of North Vietnam. © USAF/Aerospace/APL

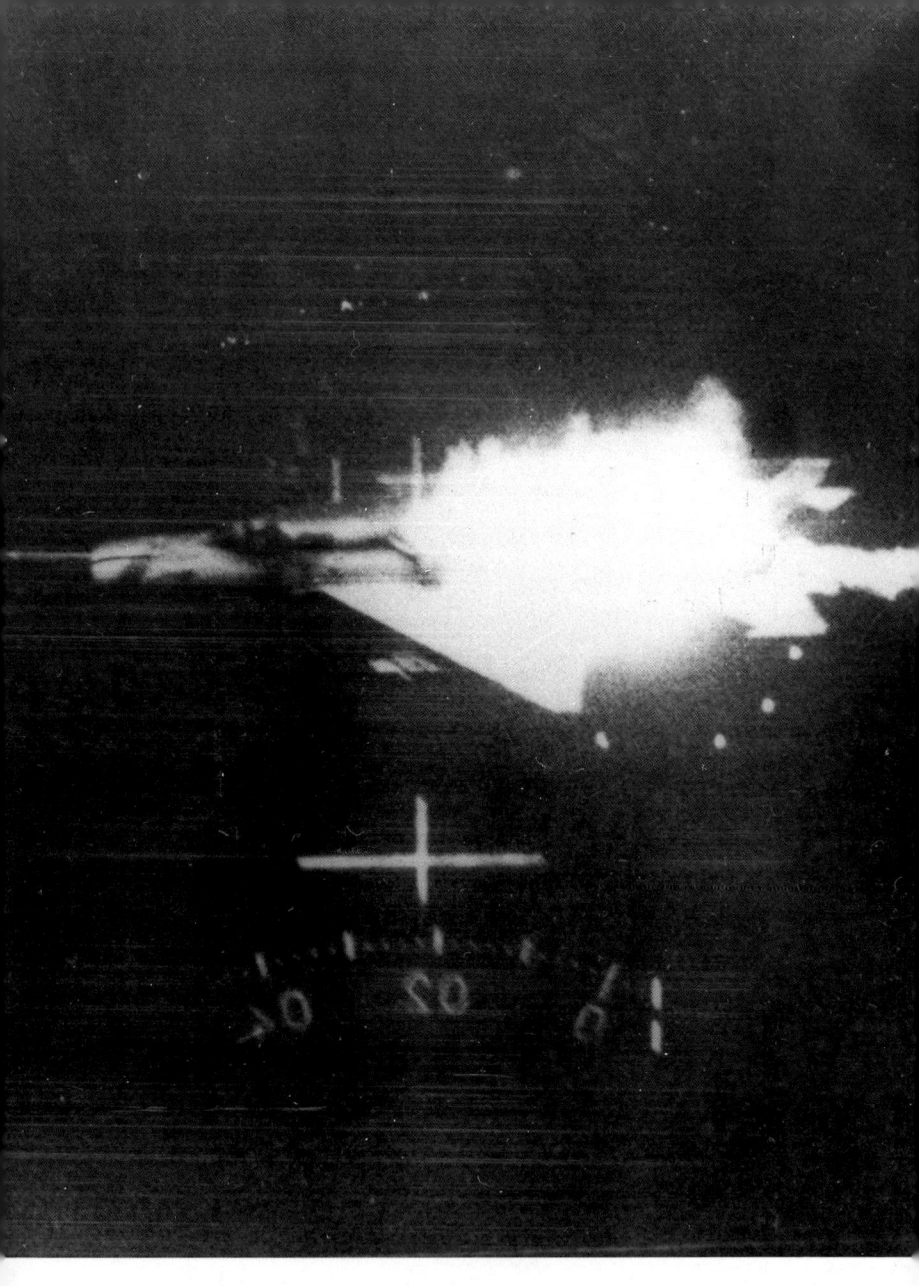

The gun camera aboard an Israeli F-4 Phantom II shows an Arab MiG-21 hit during the Yom Kippur War. The fuel tank behind the pilot has exploded. © USN/TRH/APL

Captain Richard S. Ritchie and
Captain Charles Debellevue sit
in the cockpit of their F-4E prior
to a mission; the stars denote kills
Ritchie was the first USAF ace.

© USAF/TRH/APL

Colonel Jack Broughton (left)
congratulates Captain Max Brestel
on completion of the latter's
100th combat mission over North
Vietnam. Brestel was the first
American pilot to shoot down
two North Vietnamese MiGs
in a single air action.

© USAF/Robert Dorr/APL

USAF heat-seeking Sidewinder missile.

© Peter Newark's Military Pictures

An AIM-9L, the first 'all aspect' Sidewinder, intercepts a target drone at the Naval Weapons Centre, China Lake, California.

© USN/TRH/APL

The jet fighter's greatest enemy in Vietnam; the launch of an SA-2 SAM missile captured on film by a USAF RF-101 reconnaissance pilot on July 5, 1966, northwest of Hanoi.

© USAF/TRH/APL

F4G Phantom II 'Wild Weasel' carrying AGM-88 Harm (port outer), AGM-65 Maverick (port inner), AGM-78 Standard ARM (starboard inner), AGM-45 Shrike (starboard outer) and ALQ-101ECM pod (forward port sparrow bay).

The Russians learn their lessons: the impressive MiG-29A Fulcrum, the first Soviet fighter to really match highly capable Western fast jets. via DJM/JD

Royal Navy Sea Harrier FRS1, of 800 Squadron, operating from HMS *Hermes* in the Falklands, Spring 1982. © Royal Navy/Hugh Cowin/APL

McDonnell F-15C Eagle launching a Hughes AIM-120 AMRAAM.
via Hugh Cowin/APL

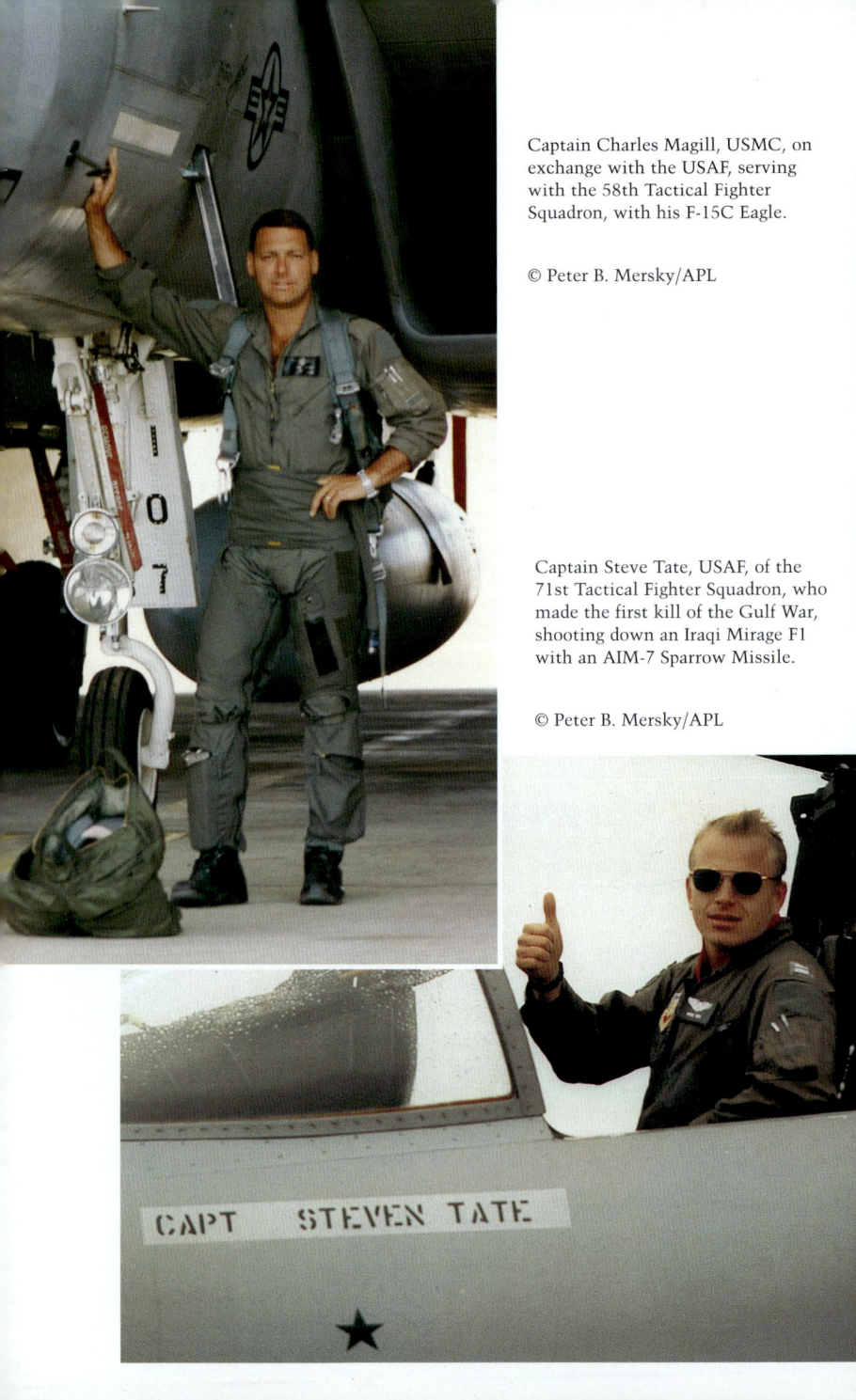

Captain Charles Magill, USMC, on exchange with the USAF, serving with the 58th Tactical Fighter Squadron, with his F-15C Eagle.

© Peter B. Mersky/APL

Captain Steve Tate, USAF, of the 71st Tactical Fighter Squadron, who made the first kill of the Gulf War, shooting down an Iraqi Mirage F1 with an AIM-7 Sparrow Missile.

© Peter B. Mersky/APL

CAPT STEVEN TATE

Outside and inside the USAF E-8C J-STARS (Joint
SurveillanceTarget Attack Radar System) which
provides real-time battle management information.
© Northrop Grumman Corp/APL

A still from the J-STARS moving target indicator map showing
the Basra Road out of Kuwait City during the final stages of the
Gulf War in 1991. © Aerospace/Robert F. Dorr/APL

leaving he heard one of the A-1E pilots report that the other had been hit and was about to crash so back he went to the rescue area, unarmed but trying to attract the MiGs on to him rather than the A-1, which was trying to protect the men on the ground while they waited for the helicopter. As he did so, a flight of four more F-105s arrived on the scene to help with the MiGs and Thorsness, once again low on fuel, headed back to the tanker over Laos. The F-105s accounted for three more MiG probables, but the rescue had to be aborted and Madison and Sterling were captured. Bitterly disappointed, Thorsness landed with dry tanks at Ubon before going back to base at Tahkli. For his persistent bravery, Thorsness was awarded the Congressional Medal of Honor.

On 30 April Thorsness and Johnson flew their 93rd mission, another Wild Weasel sortie ahead of a strike force. Just as they entered North Vietnam he heard a warning that he had been acquired by an air-to-air missile but did not take evasive action because he was sure it was a 'friendly' lock-on by mistake from one of the US fighters. In fact, there was a faulty emergency bleeper on one of the Wild Weasels, which had been picked up by the North Vietnamese, and MiGs were already in their six o'clock below; seconds later an Atoll hit the F-105 and another hit Thorsness's wingman, Abbott. He knew from the impact and from the sudden sloppiness of the controls that the aircraft was doomed and called for Harry Johnson to bail out, following him seconds later. Thorsness was severely injured by the blast of the ejection. A huge rescue operation was mounted for both men, and Abbott, but they were captured and spent over six years as POWs.

The war against the ground defences was a new dimension in the battle for air superiority, calling for the fighter pilot's aggression, exceptional flying skill, coolness and courage, and Wild Weasel operations brought out extraordinary qualities in fighter pilots. Another posthumous Congressional Medal of Honor was awarded to Lt Cmdr Michael J. Estocin, USN, from the USS *Ticonderoga*, flying an A-4E on a Shrike mission against SAM sites and pressing home his attack against a missile site on 20 April in the face of murderous fire; he was shot down and killed on a similar mission six days later.

Overcoming ground defences by jamming and confusing them if possible, but by smashing them on the ground too, was established as central to any battle for air superiority by the experience of Vietnam. Electronic warfare had started in the First World War, it had played a hugely important part in the Second World War and the Cold War was waged through radar stations strung across continents and miniaturised electronics for guidance systems, automation and rapid data transmission. In Vietnam electronic superiority was brought into the rugged business of imposing air superiority on the enemy and on the battlefield from the air.

In April 1967 a total of 11 MiGs were shot down in aerial combat, nine by the USAF and two by the USN, in 50 air-to-air engagements, and the taboo on attacking North Vietnamese airfields was partially lifted. Phuc Yen, the main MiG base, was still off limits, but on 24 April eight F-105s attacked Hoa Lac airfield thirty-four miles from Hanoi, destroying 14 MiGs on the ground, while the US Navy attacked Kep, damaging several aircraft on the ground and shooting down two MiGs as they took off.

The increased activity in the air was partly a direct consequence of lifting the immunity of the airfields. Each individual attack on an airfield had to be authorised from the White House, but when a strike package was detected on its way in, the North Vietnamese did not know whether their airfields were targets or not and the MiGs were forced into the air and into combat with US fighters. The fighting intensified further in May with a total of 72 engagements, the highest number of the Rolling Thunder campaign, 20 of them to the Air Force, including seven to the 8th TFW Wolfpack, of which three were to Robin Olds personally, and six to the Navy.

In May 1967 the Phantom got a gun, not as an integral part of the aircraft – that would take longer – but in another of the growing number of different pods which could be slung under the wings or along the fuselage centreline. It was a device designated SUU-16/A, Suspended Underwing Unit in the alpha-numeric jargon of the flight line, an M61A1 Vulcan 20 mm cannon, capable of firing 6,000 rounds a minute. On 14 May Phantoms with SUU-16s were flying as MiGCAP for F-105s attacking a North Vietnamese Army base at Ha Dong when MiG-17s came up in two flights, one of 10 and one of 16, to protect it. Maj. James Hargrove had used up all his missiles without scoring when another MiG presented itself in a long descending right-hand turn. He closed first to 700 yards and started firing, closing right up to 100 yards before the MiG burst into flames. In the same battle Capt. James Craig also missed with two Sparrows, but hit with a two and a half second burst of cannon fire. On 20 May Col. Robert F. Titus of 389th TFS based at Da Nang in South Vietnam shot down three MiG-21s in a single sortie, one with a Sparrow, one with a Sidewinder and one with his SUU-16, the first three kills in one sortie victory of the war.

Spring 1967 was a better time for the American pilots. In the two months of more intense fighting the North Vietnamese Air Force lost 37 aircraft in air-to-air combat, 15 in two days, and many more on the ground. But the Rules of Engagement were a constant source of frustration amongst pilots. On 2 June a flight of F-105s was returning to their base in Thailand from a raid on the Bac Giang railyards. As they flew over the port at Cam Pha, anti-aircraft guns on the shore and on a ship fired on them. The Thunderchiefs turned and fired back, hitting gun emplacements on the land and on a ship. This was strictly forbidden under the ROEs and in this case the problem was that the ship was the Soviet freighter *Turkestan*. When the aircraft returned to their base the Deputy Wing Commander, Col. Jack Broughton, destroyed the camera gun footage. The USA denied the attack, but the Russians produced American 20 mm shells which they claimed had been recovered from the *Turkestan* and an investigation followed. Broughton and two pilots were court-martialled; the president of the panel was Col. Charles E. 'Chuck' Yeager, commander of the 405th TFW in Okinawa, who had managed to fly 127 combat missions over the Ho Chi Minh Trail in B-57s. The court established that the pilots had responded to ground fire and the two pilots were acquitted. Broughton, who had tried to protect them with a cover-up, was fined $100 a month for six months and admonished for destroying government property, a derisory fine but one which finished his Air Force career. He did it as an act of leadership among men who had to do the fighting and who could not understand how they were supposed to operate under such ludicrous conditions.

Rolling Thunder reached its climax in the summer of 1967. On 11 August F-105s protected by Robin Olds's Wolfpack brought down the Paul Doumer Bridge, a road and rail bridge across the Red River near Hanoi. To do so, fighters took on the MiGs, the Wild Weasels took on the SAMs and the F-105s continued to bomb.

Permission to attack Phuc Yen airfield was finally given on 24 October 1967 and, eager to do as much damage as possible before the order could be changed, Gen. Momyer cancelled all other bombing that day. The Navy and the Air Force kept up attacks over three days and 20 MiGs were destroyed on the ground. Phuc Yen and another MiG airfield, Cat Bi, were put out of action and many of the remaining MiG-21s were redeployed to airfields in southern China.

The intensification of the bombing and the greater success in the air only increased North Vietnamese support to the Vietcong, including supplying regular troops to take part in the war in the South. Rolling Thunder was not working, but its continuance had now become a political battle in Washington. On one side were the air power generals who had support from the more hawkish members of Congress who wanted to be able to make much more effective use of air power to bomb the North, while against them was Robert MacNamara, the architect of the original gradualist policy, who was nevertheless becoming disillusioned with it because it was not working. The Air Force commanders were worried that if the bombing was scaled down it would be seen as a failure of air power in general, with implications for a scaled-down air force in the future; they counselled escalation. President Johnson had lost faith in MacNamara so, under pressure from the Senate Armed Services Committee, he backed a policy of escalating the bombing, and though new targets were permitted and some restrictions were lifted there was still tight political control.

On the night of 30 October 1967 a single Navy A-6 Intruder was sent to attack the slipway for a ferry which had been brought into service following the downing of the Paul Doumer bridge. Its crew, Lt Cmdr Charles B. Hunter and Lt Lyle F. Bull, dodged eighteen SAM missiles, without jettisoning their bombs, and attacked the slipway, putting it out of action – a demonstration of skill, courage and determination while operating under severe restrictions, which was not unusual among US aircrews. In November MacNamara, according to some reports on the verge of a nervous breakdown, resigned as Secretary of State for Defense to take up a job as President of the World Bank. The gulf between the men who made the policy and those who had to carry it out was a wide one.

Christmas and Tet, the Bhuddist New Year at the end of January, had traditionally been times of truce in the air war. In 1968 that changed. On 30 January 1968, the eve of the Tet holiday, the North Vietnamese launched a massive offensive with 80,000 troops, mainly North Vietnamese regulars, against provincial capitals in the south. Their mistake was to come out into the open, and the attack was repulsed, largely by US air power. The North Vietnamese objective was to spark off a general uprising in the South and take control of areas of South Vietnam. They lost 39,000 killed, against 318 Americans so, in any practical sense, the USA came out on top, but in the USA the success on the ground was obscured by a sense that it was not leading to victory in the war. The American people saw callous violence on the part of South Vietnamese Army and questioned why American lives were being lost supporting such a dubious cause. The North Vietnamese, and the remains of the Vietcong, went back to terrorist action, but to Americans the Tet Offensive looked like a defeat.

Tet also showed that Rolling Thunder had failed – in fact, it had managed to achieve precisely the opposite of what had first been intended, namely that North Vietnam was now fully engaged in the South and there were half a million US troops on the ground in Vietnam. The gradualist approach had played into the hands of the Vietnamese who had always prepared for a long war. Rolling Thunder was wrong in the first place. For bombing to have any hope of working it should have been as the air force generals wanted it: short, sharp, total and unrestricted. For the USA, Vietnam had started as a limited war; for the North Vietnamese and their communist allies it was always a total war. The North Vietnamese population had settled in for the long haul – the USA had not. Like the French after Dien Bien Phu, the USA lost the will to fight any longer, especially with a conscript army and a troubled population at home which could see that the war was not making any progress. On 31 March 1968 Johnson said he would not seek re-election. On 1 April, after three years, the bombing was halted for a month. After that occasional raids were made, but they had frittered away by 1 October when they stopped altogether. Rolling Thunder was formally ended on 1 November, in time for the US Presidential election.

It had been a wasteful and ineffective campaign. Up to that point in the war, Rolling Thunder had involved 300,000 aircraft sorties to drop 600,000 tons of bombs at a cost of 382 aircrew known to have been killed and another 702 'missing in action'. The USA lost 392 aircraft in 1968, 257 to ground fire, at a cost of $450 million in that year alone. The total number of combat aircraft lost was 900. In aerial combat between 2 August 1964 and 1 October 1968, 118 MiGs were shot down in aerial combat for 56 US losses, a kill to loss ratio of 2:1. In the first battles using AAMs the results had been poor: the AIM-7 Sparrow made one kill for every 10 fired and AIM-9 Sidewinder was not much better. The comparison with Korea has been made many times but, like many comparisons, it is misleading: there were never hundreds of targets in the air as there had been over the Yalu; secondly, the ROEs made it very difficult, specially those restricting the proper use of AAMs. What was true though was that dogfighting skills had not been taken seriously enough during the 1950s and they had to be put back into the fighter pilot training curriculum.

In 1968 the US Navy commissioned a report on the problem from a seasoned US Navy fighter pilot, Captain Frank Ault. It was to address three matters: how to improve Air Combat Manoeuvring (ACM) capabilities; how to improve the use of AAMs and the missiles themselves; and how to provide a cadre of seasoned air combat specialists as instructors to teach future generations of fighter pilots. His main conclusions were that the ROEs gave almost limitless advantages to the enemy, but that while missiles could mean fighting at longer range the days of close dogfighting were not over, that fighter pilots had been trained to rely too much on missiles rather than fighting skills and the missiles were wrong for the job, and that ACM should be an important part of training and it should be taught using dissimilar aircraft, as close in their performance to the enemy's as possible.

The result was the US Navy's 'Post-graduate Course in Fighter Weapons, Tactics and Doctrine' at Miramar Naval Air Station in California, better known today as 'Top Gun', which opened for business in March 1969. Top Gun got under way as the Vietnamese War was winding down and on the first class was a young Navy pilot called Lt Randall 'Randy' or 'Duke' Cunningham of VF-96, the 'Fighting Falcons', which flew the latest Navy version of the Phantom, the F-4J.

Richard Nixon was elected President in 1968 with a pledge to start bringing US ground troops home, the beginning of the end of direct US involvement in the Vietnam War. The policy was to 'Vietnamise' the war, making the South Vietnamese Army (ARVN) take over the fighting. The one area that could not be Vietnamised was the air war: without US air power to support ground operations in the South, the ARVN would have crumbled. Peace talks started in January 1969 and they dragged on for two years, and while there was no peace the American airmen who were POWs stayed in prison in the North.

The USAF and USN retired a lot of the aircraft which had been there at the start of the war: the venerable B-57s, F-100 Super Sabres and RF-101 Voodoos were all retired back to the USA as the Phantom became the workhorse of the Vietnamised war, which was waged entirely in the South. The Phantoms flown by both the USAF and the USN were new, the Navy's F-4J still had no integral gun, though one could be mounted on a pod, while the Air Force did go back to basics and ordered the F-4E Phantom which did have a gun and was introduced on 26 November 1968. The F-105s went back to the USA.

The first four years of the Vietnam War had also given a great boost to new, precision, tactical, air-to-ground guided weapons, AGMs, designed to do a variety of specific jobs with great accuracy – from attacking missiles sites, radar sites, bridges and airfields to ships at sea and tanks on the battlefield, launched or dropped from a variety of aircraft. They came in several families, some of which had started their lives in the post-Second World War era using radio and radar control, others of which relied on more recent technologies such as infrared, laser beams, television cameras and high-speed data links. Many of them started their operational lives in the Vietnam era and by 1968 the early examples were into their second generation and new systems were in an advanced state of testing.

The AGM-12B Bullpup, essentially a radio-controlled, rocket-powered missile, which relied on somebody in the launching aircraft using a little joystick to guide it to the target, was used extensively in Vietnam, but radio control gave way to TV with the AGM-62 Walleye glide bomb and the AGM-65 Maverick, a TV-guided missile with a true 'fire-and-forget' system which took over as soon as the pilot had locked it on to the target and fired it. The anti-radiation family of missiles, which started with AGM-45A Shrike, grew in Vietnam with the AGM-75 Standard ARM missile which still homed in on the enemy's radar but had longer range and a larger warhead. Another family which was to grow prodigiously was the Paveway Laser Guided Bombs (LGBs) which were free-fall bombs with controllable fins, operated by messages relayed from a laser beam which the aircraft fixed on the target so that the bomb could follow it down. Its successor was the GBU system which used TV and IR systems in the same way. The lessons of Vietnam were put into new weapons systems and into new countermeasures against the missiles, particularly against SAMs. The AN/ALQ-119 ECM pod gave a much wider range of radar-jamming than its predecessors.

Between 1968 and late 1971 there was very little in the way of aerial combat and no bombing of the North, which replenished its losses. There were reconnaissance flights at very high altitude by U-2s and SR-71s and at low level by Navy RA-5C Vigilantes, and it was one of those flights that ended the long spell in which there had been no aerial combat. On 19 January 1972 an RA-5C was tasked with photographing a new North Vietnamese airfield. Flying on an AAA suppression mission in support of the Vigilante was a flight of Navy F-4J Phantoms from the USS *Constellation* on Yankee Station; it was led by Lt Randall 'Duke' Cunningham and his Radar Intercept Officer, Lt William Patrick 'Willie' Driscoll, among the earliest graduates of Top Gun. Cunningham deliberately placed his flight between the new airfield and one known to operate MiG-21 interceptors, and in doing so put his flight within range of several SAM-2 missile sites. The first part of the sortie was spent looking for the puffs of smoke on the ground as the missiles were launched. Two SAMs were launched and Cunningham dodged both of them. His flight successfully avoided a total of 18, then came under attack by MiG-21s.

Cunningham saw a pair of MiGs-21s flying well below with afterburners in. He dived to attack while Driscoll locked a Sparrow on to one of them and prepared to launch. But Cunningham did not trust the Sparrow and he had no gun so he manoeuvred behind the MiGs and switched to Sidewinders. Almost immediately he heard the low growl in his headphones which told him that his missiles had locked on to their target. In turn, the MiG's systems detected the Sidewinder and transmitted a high-pitched noise to the pilot, indicating that a missile had locked on to him. Cunningham fired and the North Vietnamese pilot broke hard right, still in afterburner, and just managed to turn tightly enough to shake off the Sidewinder.

From his Top Gun training Cunningham knew that the MiG-21 could out-turn the Phantom so, instead of following the North Vietnamese fighter and trying to get on his tail, he turned left, away from the MiG, and down to treetop height at 600 knots, opening up some distance between him and his quarry, looking for a better position for a second Sidewinder. The MiG wingman broke off the fight, but the leader had come out of his turn and was looking for Cunningham but he could not see him lurking below. He banked left just as Cunningham pulled the Phantom's nose up, locked on at 1,000 yards – a perfect range for the Sidewinder – and fired, all in one single, flowing movement. The Sidewinder hit the MiG in the tail. It was the Navy's first victory in aerial combat for nearly two years, and there was much celebration on board the *Constellation*, not only in the kill but because it was clear that the intensive training in air fighting had paid off.

On 30 March 1972 120,000 North Vietnamese soldiers invaded the South across the DMZ in a Spring Offensive, including tanks, with which they intended to annex the South. They came south without air cover, bringing the new shoulder-launched SA-7 SAM as a defence against tactical air power such as helicopters. The Americans had only small numbers of combat aircraft in Vietnam but these were soon beefed up from the USA with F-105s going back to Thailand, B-52s put at readiness on Guam and the carrier USS *Kitty Hawk*, sent to Yankee Station.

On 6 April the North captured Quang Tri, a provincial capital in the north of South Vietnam. President Nixon decided that the US answer to the invasion would be through air power, and on 15 April he ordered air strikes against the North to resume under the codename 'Freedom Train'. He also lifted many of the restrictions which had been imposed on pilots during Rolling Thunder, including the use of B-52s against the North. In the two years of respite from bombing North Vietnam's air defences had been improved and enlarged: out of a total of 8,000 anti-aircraft guns, 1,500 were radar-directed, there were 300 SA-2 sites with new updated versions of the missile and 250 interceptors, a third of them MiG-21s and including the MiG-19, Russia's first supersonic fighter.

The new US weapons and ECM systems also paid off: on 16 April USAF pilots shot down three MiGs in a day and on 6 May Navy pilots did the same. Over 200 SA-2s were fired at the high flying B-52s, but their ECM systems jammed them very effectively and only one was damaged. On 8 May Nixon authorised the mining of Haiphong harbour. The job was carried out by Navy A-6 Intruders; 'Duke' Cunningham flew as an escort and got his second kill.

Two days later, on 10 May, American air power was used to demonstrate what it could do. Freedom Train became Linebacker, a major raid against five bridges and the main railyards between Hanoi and Haiphong, through which much of the aid from other communist countries was flowing, in a major effort to create havoc in North Vietnam's transport system and make North Vietnam withdraw from the South. The first raids were a concerted attack on the air defence system. The day opened with two Navy F-4J Phantoms hurtling across Kep airfield at near supersonic speed. Two MiG-21s were about to take off as they did so, and once they were airborne a dogfight developed over the airfield in which one MiG-21 was shot down.

The main target for the Air Force was the Paul Doumer road and rail bridge, using Paveway LGBs for the first time. The attack started from 14,000 feet with the lead Phantom aiming the laser designator at the bridge, creating a cone with its point on the bridge. The bombing aircraft then dropped their bombs at the base of the cone and the laser beam guided them on to the target. They all missed, but other conventional bombs were dropped by Phantoms and damaged it badly. An RF-4C then photographed it, showing that it was still standing but unusable.

A flight of 555th TFS Phantoms, led by Maj. Robert Lodge, was heading for Yen Bai airfield northwest of Hanoi; his EWO was Capt. Roger Locher. Over the RT he heard from an EC-121, 150 miles away, that MiGs were to the north, and though he could not see them he knew there were no friendly aircraft to the north. There were rules about positive identification to protect pilots from shooting down their comrades, but they got a lock-on at long range and through Combat Tree, a system for identifying hostile and friendly aircraft, fired a Sparrow head-on at the MiG-21s, long before they came within range of the MiG-21s' guns and outside the capability of their Atoll heat-seeking missiles. Lodge's first missed, but his second scored a kill. Two more of Lodge's flight scored kills with Sparrows, Lt John Markle and Capt. Steve Ritchie, then, while Lodge was lining up for a second shot, a pair of MiG-19s dropped down on to his tail. Markle shouted warnings over the RT, but Lodge stuck with his target and the two MiGs hit him with heavy cannon fire from behind. Locher ejected, but Lodge, one of the Air Force's best fighter leaders at the time, died in the aircraft. Locher evaded capture inside North Vietnam for an epic twenty-three days before being picked up by a rescue helicopter.

Cunningham and Driscoll were taking part in bombing raids on railyards alongside Haiphong harbour, where ground fire was the greatest threat. Approaching the target, they spent much of their time looking for muzzle flashes on the ground, with Driscoll keeping a lookout behind while Cunningham dropped the bombs on a warehouse. As he was climbing away Cunningham saw another Phantom hit by ground fire and erupt in a sickly orange and black ball of fire, just as Driscoll reported a MiG-17 at 'seven o'clock low'. Cunningham looked back: it was one and a half miles away and climbing. Seconds later Driscoll reported four more MiGs in echelon formation just as they split into two pairs for combat, one pair turning left towards Cunningham, trying to get into a firing position, the other pair disappearing behind. Cunningham was still concentrating on the first MiG-17 which was still in a right-hand turn, going east. He tried to draw the MiG into the line of fire of his wingman, but he was now under fire from the second pair of MiG-17s.

In the same second Cunningham came under cannon fire from the leader of the first pair, still in their turn below but closing fast. Instead of turning away, Cunningham turned even tighter to the left, into the first MiG's path. The MiG's controls, as he knew from Top Gun lectures, were slow to respond at high speed. As he expected, his target could not match the speed with which he tightened the turn and so lost its firing position and shot past underneath the Phantom. Cunningham then violently reversed his turn, breaking hard right, pulling 5–6 g, and there, as he expected, was the first MiG dead ahead, higher and slightly to the right. He was now in a perfect firing position and the MiG pilot knew it for he put on full afterburner to try and outrun the Phantom. Cunningham had no gun and he was inside the minimum range for the Sidewinder, but the MiG was opening up some distance between them so he selected one, heard the growl and fired. The missile streaked towards the MiG which was distancing itself fast, but thereby put itself just within the limits of the Sidewinder's capability. It hit and the MiG exploded.

Cunningham put on full power and climbed to 15,000 feet, then turned and looked back at the dogfight which had developed. The Americans were outnumbered: he counted a total of seven MiGs in a turning battle with three Phantoms, each MiG covering another's tail. Suddenly one of the Phantoms broke away quickly followed by three MiGs, a pair in formation and a single aircraft. They were underneath him so he pulled up into a hard left-hand climbing turn, then dived down behind the four aircraft, lining up on one of the MiGs for a Sidewinder shot. The Sidewinder locks on to the hot spot around the jet efflux and cannot discriminate between friendly and enemy aircraft so there was a danger that he had locked on to the Phantom. Cunningham spoke over the radio:

'Showtime, break right, break right.'

Nothing happened.

'Showtime, reverse starboard.'

There was no reaction.

'If you don't, you're dead.'

That did it: the Phantom broke right. The Sidewinder was still growling in Cunningham's headphones, then it stopped, then it started again, and there were only MiGs ahead. Cunningham never gave it a chance to stop growling again and fired, hitting one of the MiGs.

To clear his six o'clock Cunningham then rolled through 360 degrees so that Driscoll could check behind and below. It was not clear – there was a MiG-17 on their tail, lining up to shoot. Cunningham snap-rolled in the opposite direction and put on full power, then reversed the roll again. The MiG pilot tried to match the manoeuvres, but lacked the power and manoeuvrability, and when Driscoll reported the MiG at 1,500 metres, falling behind, they decided it no longer represented a threat.

Cunningham was heading for the coast and the *Constellation* when he saw a MiG-17 right on the nose, coming straight for them. He was planning a very close pass, something else he had learned at Top Gun: in a head-on position, pass as close as possible, leaving your opponent less room to manoeuvre into a firing position after the pass. He banked slightly, preparing for the pass, then suddenly he saw flashes coming from the MiG's cannon. He brutally reversed the turn to put himself out of the line of fire, then, just as suddenly, pulled up into the vertical, expecting the MiG to head for home. But the North Vietnamese pilot was made of sterner stuff and pulled up, too, right alongside the Phantom, canopy to canopy, then started falling back slowly to get into a firing position behind Cunningham. Climbing vertically, the Phantom was getting dangerously slow so Cunningham pulled over the top into a dive, just as the Vietnamese tracer started passing him. He rolled, trying to make the MiG overshoot, but the Vietnamese pilot rolled through the manoeuvre with him.

They disengaged and then came back to the fight, Cunningham trying a vertical roll without success, the MiG pilot staying with him all the way. Cunningham tried again but the MiG stayed with him, then Cunningham suddenly throttled right back and extended his speed brakes and the MiG shot ahead. To avoid putting himself in a dangerous position in front of the Phantom, the Vietnamese pilot pulled through into a near-vertical dive, with Cunningham on his tail but a long way behind. Unhopeful, because the Sidewinder's infrared homer could be confused by ground heat sources, Cunningham fired a missile. But luck was with him: it locked on and went straight for the MiG which exploded on contact. There was no sign of the pilot ejecting.

That last dogfight had been 'ace' against 'ace'. Intelligence reports from intercepted signals traffic later that day confirmed that the North Vietnamese pilot was Col. Toom, their leading fighter pilot, who had already shot down 13 US aircraft. Unlike other aces, Col. Toom had never been identified by the North Vietnamese, and there was a lot of speculation that it was because he was not in fact Vietnamese, but Russian.

Three kills in a single sortie, but Cunningham's and Driscoll's day was still not over. As they headed for the coast again a SAM-2 missile, which had not shown up on any of their warning systems, exploded nearby, showering the Phantom with shrapnel and puncturing the hydraulics. The controls became steadily stiffer, but the two men stayed with the aircraft until they were well out to sea. Cunningham radioed their plight to the *Constellation*, which launched a rescue helicopter. When the Phantom was no longer flyable he gave the helicopter their position and they ejected, landed in the water and were picked up within twenty minutes. In just a few months, with five aerial victories, 'Duke' Cunningham and 'Willie' Driscoll had become aces, the first of the Vietnam War and the first aces to achieve that status exclusively with missiles: both were awarded the Navy Star.

That day saw by far the fiercest aerial battle of the Vietnam War, and between them the USAF and the USN shot down 11 MiGs, plus one damaged. In exchange, they lost two Phantoms in aerial combat, one to ground fire, one to a SAM and one more damaged. The North Vietnamese fired 93 SAMs and claimed to have shot down 18 US aircraft without revealing any losses.

Of the four bridges attacked by the Navy, three were brought down. The Paul Doumer bridge was unusable, and the next day USAF Phantoms returned and brought one of the spans down with Paveway LGBs. Three days after that the Than Hoa bridge, which had resisted all attempts to destroy it during Rolling Thunder, was brought down by LGBs.

The Navy had produced the first ace of the war after nearly seven years of fighting, a result that the USAF was eager to match. On 31 May Steve Ritchie was leading a flight of Phantoms as MiGCAP for another strike over the North when they came under attack by MiG-21s. The American pilots split, Ritchie pulling up, forcing one of the MiGs which was following to overshoot, then diving on to his tail. He fired two Sparrows but the first went awry and the second exploded well short of the target so he fired two more, one of which exploded short, but the fourth hit home and the MiG blew up.

On 8 July Ritchie was back over the North on MiGCAP near Hanoi when an EC-121 picked up MiGs forty miles to the south-west. Ritchie led his flight towards them, and as the two blips on the Red Crown radar screen merged he saw a MiG-21 two miles to the north of his position, in his 10 o'clock. Ritchie turned hard left and engaged afterburner while the MiG did the same, and the two passed close to each other with neither of them in a firing position.

Ritchie then nosed down into a dive from 5,000 feet and waited; he was sure that there was a second MiG behind the first and, sure enough, there was, about two miles behind the first. The second pilot did not see Ritchie, who was lower and camouflaged against the green jungle, so Ritchie went into a maximum rate turn to the left. He saw the MiG above, turning right, so he barrel rolled and came out just over a mile behind and below, a perfect Sparrow shot. With the MiG right in his sights, he pressed the auto-acquisition button on the throttle and was immediately rewarded with a lock-on. He then had to wait four seconds before firing, hoping that the MiG would not see them and turn sharply, breaking the lock. As he fired two Sparrows the MiG went into a turn and Ritchie had to pull 4 g to maintain it while the second missile launched. The first hit the MiG squarely in the wing root and the second passed straight through the debris, part of which collided with Ritchie's left wing.

Even with all the manoeuvring, Ritchie had kept his awareness of the first MiG, which was now on the tail of the No. 4 in the flight. Ritchie came out of the turn, dived again in afterburner to gain energy, then pulled hard right behind the MiG. This time the MiG went straight into a hard left turn, trying to avoid the lock-on. Ritchie got a lock-on and waited the four seconds, in which time the MiG managed to pull them into a 5 g turn, putting him 60 degrees off the nose. Ritchie was unable to reach the master switch to turn on the guns because of the high g load, but the missile suddenly launched, well outside normal limits, and hit the MiG. Ritchie had raised his score to four, equalling that of Robin Olds, the last two in under ninety seconds. On 28 August he scored a fifth, another MiG-21I, making him the Air Force's first ace.

Under US rules, EWOs were given equal credit for kills so Cunningham, Driscoll, Ritchie and Feinstein were now aces. De-Bellevue was not because he had flown with another pilot and had only been with Ritchie for four of his victories. Later in the war, with another pilot, he scored two more, bringing his total to six, making an EWO the fifth ace of the war and the highest-scoring. He later retrained as a pilot and served as a fighter pilot and staff officer until he retired. Cunningham stayed in the Navy after the war and one of his first jobs was to return to Miramar to become a Top Gun instructor, passing on the secrets of his success to a new generation of fighter pilots. After several other postings he was back again, this time to lead the 'aggressor squadron', A-4 and F-5s which were flown as near as possible to Soviet tactics to give some experience of fighting against dissimilar aircraft.

Linebacker had little effect on bringing the North Vietnamese to negotiate a cease-fire at the Paris peace talks, and on 13 December 1972 they walked out of the talks. All the USA wanted to do was to get out of the war, but the North Vietnamese would not let them disengage on terms acceptable to the USA. President Nixon decided to use air power once again to bring them back. He authorised Linebacker II, what air force generals had wanted to do way back in 1965 – unrestricted bombing of military targets in the North using heavy bombers. Starting on 15 December, B-52s rained bombs on military targets in Hanoi and Haiphong in a way which would have been unthinkable when the war started in 1965. They kept it up for eleven days, destroying 10 airfields, numerous SAM sites, reducing military targets inside Hanoi to rubble and completely wrecking the rail transport system. The North Vietnamese fired SAMs in salvoes, up to 10 missiles aimed at individual aircraft, and 15 B-52s were lost, but the bombing went on around the clock until 29 December when the North Vietnamese returned to the conference table. Even then it was only reduced in scale and kept going until 15 January 1973 when the North Vietnamese agreed to terms. On 23 January a cease-fire was signed, officially ending US involvement in the war, which had started on 5 August 1964. Two months later, on 28 March, a USAF C-141 cargo aircraft landed at Hanoi's international airport to collect American POWs.

The air war in South Vietnam, Rolling Thunder, Freedom Train and Linebackers I and II resulted in three times as many bombs being dropped on Vietnam than were dropped on Germany and Japan in the Second World War. The USAF lost 2,118 aircrew killed and 599 were listed as still Missing in Action; the US Navy lost 317 aircrew. America lost 2,257 aircraft on operations, including 445 Phantoms, 397 F-105 Thunderchiefs and 243 F-100s. The total cost of the aircraft lost was put by the Pentagon at $3.1 billion.

The moral and political cost to America was much larger, a price paid in international relations and in social disruption at home. America had won the air war: the unrestricted use of air power had made North Vietnam sign a cease-fire and South Vietnam was left intact. Linebacker achieved what Rolling Thunder had tried to do, influence the North Vietnamese government's thinking and behaviour, but it was a bitter victory because all it achieved was to make the Vietnamese agree terms so that America could pull out.

America lost the Vietnam War. Two years later in 1975, the North Vietnamese invaded the South again and, shorn of US air support, the ARVN and the State crumbled within four weeks. North Vietnam had won its twenty-one year struggle for unification. The Vietnamese had won, and in the process they had taught the West an important lesson: when you fight a war you have to fight to win. Whatever weapons are used, there is no room for using them delicately. With Rolling Thunder, each time it started to hurt the pressure was relaxed, and many airmen still believe that the bombing could have achieved its aim if it had been applied in a conventional way.

In winning and losing the Vietnam War, the USAF, USN and PAVNAF had rediscovered the importance of air superiority over the battlefield on the ground and in the air, and redefined it, bringing home the new reality that aerial combat was an electronically driven battle, not just between fighters but between fighters and guided missiles. The enduring legacy of the Vietnam War was the realisation that air superiority still had to be fought for, not only in the air, and by destroying the enemy air force on the ground, but in the electronic spectrum, too, that winning meant having the best missiles with the most advanced systems, whether AAMs or SAMs, as well as the best fighter pilots and fighters. It showed that ground-based defences, far from making the manned fighter redundant, simply required more of the man and of his aircraft.

Chapter Six

Six Days in June

Dawn came peacefully to the Middle East on 5 June 1967. Political tension was high, as it had been for several weeks, and Israel and her Arab neighbours, Egypt, Jordan, Iraq and Syria, had been on a war footing for weeks, but a diplomatic process was going on and there was no immediate sign that it was about to end. The dawn patrols of the Israeli and Egyptian air forces, which had taken the same form for as long as anybody could remember, passed off as usual with both sides keeping a wary eye on each other. Israeli Mirages patrolled off the coast of the Sinai at 20,000 feet in international airspace over the sea, while Egyptian MiG-21s patrolled to the south, over the desert. As dawn came up both sides behaved as normal and returned to their bases, landing with the sun well up. The radar screens on both sides showed nothing unusual. The conventional time for a pre-emptive air strike had passed.

The tranquillity was illusory. Not long after the EAF fighters had returned to base, far out to sea, northeast of the Nile estuary, a group of Egyptian fishermen gazed in amazement as three Mystère fighter bombers shot past just a few feet above the sea, so low that they left a foam-flecked wake on the surface of the water. Leading the flight was Avihu Bin-Non of the Israeli Air Force. There should have been four aircraft but one of his pilots had turned back with a technical fault. Their target was Fayid airfield, home to Egyptian Air Force (EAF) Su-7, MiG-19 and MiG-21 fighters; their objective was to destroy the fighters on the ground before they could scramble and intercept the other attacking Israeli aircraft, Vautors, Mystères, Super Mystères and Ouragan fighter/bombers and Mirage fighters equipped with bombs and guns. Virtually the entire operational strength of the Israeli Air Force, 196 combat aircraft, was airborne that sunny morning, heading for 10 Egyptian airfields in the Nile delta to carry out a pre-emptive strike in complete surprise.

Ahead of Bin-Non's Mystères was a flight of four Mirage IIICs, flying in a fighter/bomber role, led by Odd Marom, deputy commander of the squadron. They were heading for Cairo-West airfield. Behind Bin-Non, in the elaborate choreography, was a flight of four Vautor fighter bombers heading for Beni-Souef airfield in the southern Nile delta. Cairo-West and Beni-Souef were priority targets early in the attack because they were home to Egypt's force of thirty Soviet-built Tu-16 jet bombers. Once airborne, the Tu-16 could reach Israel's centres of population in thirty minutes. Only 12 Mirages were left in Israel to guard against Egyptian counterattack.

Egypt was covered with low stratus cloud so the Israeli pilots flew under it, out of sight of the radar and under the operational envelope of the Egypt's SA-2 missiles. As they crossed the Suez Canal the cloud began to break up and the sun illuminated patches of bright green Nile farmland, but they stayed low. The plan was to attack nine airfields simultaneously, and one slightly later. Each airfield would be hit by flights of four who would have ten minutes over their targets before the next wave came in behind them. The Israelis flew in complete radio silence. The whole plan depended on complete surprise and the first attacks happening at precisely 07.45, shortly after the Egyptian fighters had landed, to be followed at very precise intervals by successive four-ship flights arriving over the airfields on a rota that would give the Egyptians no respite. Among the leading flights was one of four Mirages led by Ran

Pecker, flying over the sea at 420 knots, faster than the planned 360 knots, to make up time lost on take-off. His target was Inshas airfield near Cairo, the home of forty EAF MiG-21 interceptors. As he crossed the edge of the Bardavil Lagoon, where the Nile runs into the sea, he had cut the initial deficit of five minutes to just two, and as they crossed the Suez Canal at Qantara his calculations showed that with the increased speed they would arrive precisely on time.

Pecker saw the airfield dead ahead at precisely 07.45; he pulled up and the other three in the flight followed his every move. They rolled inverted to see Inshas spread out below them, the MiG-21 pilots in their cockpits. Their first target was the main runway. At around 6,000 feet they rolled over again and set up for a shallow diving pass over it, dropping their bombs at one-third and two-thirds of its length. Lighter and more manoeuvrable without their bombs, the Mirage pilots turned outside the airfield perimeter and came back to make the first of five low strafing passes, firing 20 mm cannon at the parked MiG-21s, aiming at the small high-octane fuel tanks centrally positioned in the fuselages. The idea was to set them alight and the fires would spread quickly to the rest of the aircraft. Pecker and his men went on firing until they heard the commander of the next flight on the radio announcing their arrival.

Major Aharon 'Yalo' Shavit and his flight of Super Mystères carried 'dibber' bombs which had a small rocket in the tail which shot them at high speed into the reinforced concrete of the runway, penetrating several feet, where a time fuse started ticking, causing explosions several minutes later, or much longer, to deter removal and runway reparations. They then made three cannon-firing passes and on the last one Shavit's aircraft was hit by heavy machine-gun fire which caused his speed brake to deploy and lock open.

Bin-Non arrived at Fayid airfield on time to see a flight of MiGs about to take off. He led his flight straight down the runway and dropped bombs on them as they were lining up to take off. At the other end of the runway he was suddenly confronted with an Antonov An-12 transport about to land. He pressed his trigger, but his guns had jammed and the Antonov pilot managed to land. He then turned and came back to strafe aircraft on the ground, and by the time the three Mystères left, a total of sixteen aircraft were burning on the ground.

Marom's flight of Mirages hit Cairo-West on time to see great pillars of smoke rising above the airfield from previous bombing runs; he pulled his flight up to 9,000 feet, rolled over, then dived for a bombing run on the runways, at the same time picking out undamaged aircraft for attention on the strafing runs to follow; his flight destroyed five Tu-16s.

Shavit nursed his aircraft back to base only to find that his undercarriage would not come down. Ignoring orders from the ground to bail out, with a superb piece of flying he lined up for touchdown well down the runway, belly-landed and skidded off, preserving the aircraft largely intact and clearing the runway for those who were following.

At IAF headquarters the reports began to come in, showing that the first strikes had accounted for 32 fighters and all the Tu-16 bombers on the ground. As the later flights reported back the number quickly passed the hundred mark and there was some concern that the pilots were exaggerating the damage done. One of the 12 pilots left behind to guard Israeli skies against the Tu-16s was twenty-two-year-old Lt Giora Rom. He and his colleagues were eager to join the fight, and with the immediate danger of the bombers neutralised he took off with a flight of four Mirages for Abu Suweir airfield near Ismailia, home to MiGs and Il-28 bombers. They took off at 9.00 and found the airfield wreathed in smoke from burning aircraft. The main runway was unusable, but Rom saw a MiG-21 lining up on a small parallel runway, about to take off. He dropped down from the formation into a firing position behind the MiG to attack, but his flight commander was there first and ordered him to break off, then riddled the MiG with cannon fire just as it was getting airborne. Suddenly the air was full of MiGs, two of them dropping right in front of Rom on the tail of the Mirages ahead. He engaged afterburner and closed quickly to 200 metres, opened fire and missed. He kept the burner in and closed up to 150 metres, and this time his cannon fire hit home and the MiG exploded in the air. He turned tightly, headed back over the airfield and was immediately on the tail of another MiG. He opened fire and it went down in flames on to the airfield. He fired at a third, but saw no hits, then had to return to Israel because he was low on fuel. His flight leader had to bail out because he had run out of fuel.

No sooner had the pilots arrived back at base than the aircraft were refuelled and re-armed in ten to thirty minutes, and they were back in the air heading for new targets. The very swift turnaround times meant that the sortie rate reported to the Egyptian High Command appeared to them to suggest that the Israelis had far more aircraft than they had and at one point there were protests to the Americans and British that they were helping the Israelis.

The attacks on the EAF lasted around three hours and by mid-morning the largest air force in the Middle East had virtually ceased to exist. By noon Egypt had lost the use of 13 airfields and 250 aircraft, including 75% of the MiG-21s, had been destroyed. The Egyptian ground-based SA-2 SAM system was not effective below 2,000 feet and failed to acquire a single Israeli aircraft, though anti-aircraft guns hit a number of Israeli fighters. The second part of the attack included plenty of air-to-air combat where the Israelis triumphed. They knew a great deal about the capabilities of the MiG-21 following the defection of an Iraqi pilot with a MiG-21 in 1966. The IAF had flown hours of mock combat between the Mirage and MiG-21 and had found its Achilles heel at low level, where the Israeli Mirage pilots always had a real advantage in manoeuvring. When a combined flight of 20 MiG-19s and -21s ventured into the Sinai they were bounced by Mirages and all were shot down or crashed, having run out of fuel after the dogfights. Another flight of 20 MiG-21s, sent up to replace the losses in the north from Hurgheda airfield in the southwest, near Sharm El Sheik, arrived over the battle near Cairo, and all of them were either shot down in aerial combat or ran out of fuel while looking for an airfield with an undamaged runway to land on. Some landed at Cairo International Airport, and though there was no plan to attack civilian airports they were destroyed on the ground when they did.

Most Israeli pilots flew four or five missions on the first day, and some of them flew eight, which Arab commanders refused to believe. With Egypt's air power neutralised, in the afternoon the IAF turned its attention to Syria, Jordan and Iraq. Giora Rom flew with Eitan Carni, Asher Snir and Eliezer Prigat to an airfield in Syria known simply as H-4. When they arrived there were MiGs on guard over their base and the Israeli pilots went straight into the attack, dropping their bombs on the runways before the Iraqis really knew they were under attack. Snir was the first to get amongst the MiGs while the other three strafed the airfield with cannon fire. Coming out of a strafing run behind Prigat, Rom saw a MiG drop on to Prigat's tail. He shouted a warning over the radio, then dropped his tanks and turned towards the MiG. As he did so, a second wave of Mirages joined the fight and one got in ahead of him and opened fire, only to suffer a compressor stall, slowed and suddenly became a target. Another MiG fired two missiles at him, which missed, just as Rom's cannon fire hit the MiG and it caught fire to crash on to the airfield, his third that day on two fronts.

Ran Pecker was also on a second mission, leading a four-ship flight of Mirages across the Sinai at 30,000 feet. At the Red Sea coast they dropped to the deck to cross the sea at 500 knots just above the surface of the water, popping up over the Hurgheda airfield on the Egyptian side. The defenders were ready and the bombing run was made in the face of heavy anti-aircraft fire. They hit the runway, then turned to strafe as Pecker heard his wingman call 'break' as a MiG-19 suddenly appeared on his tail. Pecker let the attacker pass him, then turned on to his tail and shot him down over the airfield. There were four MiGs and his wingman was now sandwiched between two more. Pecker went for the one on his tail while the wingman shot down the one in front. Another member of the flight was on the tail of the fourth MiG when its pilot decided to land, lining up on the runway at landing speed with the Israeli struggling to stay airborne at such a slow speed behind him. The MiG landed, then promptly crashed into one of the bomb craters.

Yalo Shavit and his flight were sent to Syria in the afternoon to carry out a second attack on Saygal airfield on the Syrian–Iraqi border. It was a difficult target, involving a long flight over the desert, but their navigation was spot on. On the final run in they were guided by huge palls of smoke rising from previous attacks. It was the same technique practised by all the Israeli pilots – they pulled up to 6,000 feet, rolled inverted, then dived to bomb the runways. As Shavit pulled his flight out of the dive, two MiG-21s, which had been patrolling above the airfield, dropped on to their tail. At high altitude the MiG would have been at an advantage in manoeuvring, but on the deck much of that advantage was lost.

Shavit ordered one of his pilots, who had flown the entire mission with a slow fuel leak, to break off the fight, then managed to turn tightly and get on the tail of one of the MiGs. The MiG had a huge advantage in power and the Syrian pilot made full use of it by engaging afterburner and climbing steeply away from the fight. Shavit then tried a ruse. He broke off and rolled over, showing his belly to the MiG, now high above. The Syrian pilot thought Shavit was making a getaway and dived to attack. As the MiG came down, Shavit turned back level and dived too, then forced an overshoot to get behind the MiG. Both Shavit and the Syrian pilot turned tightly, each trying to get into a firing position, and both lost height in the process, until they were turning right above the hangars. Shavit could not get into a firing position in the tight turn the MiG was leading him into so again he tried a feint instead, reversing the turn suddenly. The MiG pilot followed suit and turned too, whereupon Shavit turned yet again, bringing him head-on to the MiG, and his first cannon shots hit the MiG which exploded immediately and crashed into a hangar. Shavit's wingman had shot down the second MiG and after several strafing passes over the airfield to use up their remaining cannon ammunition, the two men joined up with the other two Mirages and flew home. Later in the day Shavit flew to Amman in Jordan and destroyed three Hawker Hunters parked in a neat row on the airfield.

The IAF had established air superiority in a little over ten hours, turning itself into an instant legend, especially in America which was mired down in Vietnam and getting nowhere. The Israelis had shown how air power should be used: decisively, ruthlessly, flexibly, with maximum surprise and minimum operational restriction. The pilots were clearly products of the tradition of individual excellence, and the disproportionate level of the victories spoke for itself: 393 Arab aircraft destroyed, 58 of them in air-to-air combat, for the loss of 26 Israeli aircraft, mostly to anti-aircraft fire. The result not only inspired confidence in the rest of the Israeli armed forces but, literally overnight, Israel looked like a local superpower.

The basic plan of a swift pre-emptive strike against all her neighbouring Arab air forces was something the Israelis had planned for years, and planned meticulously under the codename Operation Focus. The pilots had trained hard for it throughout their careers in the air and on the ground. Complete individual Egyptian airfields were marked out in the Negev Desert with 4 ft × 4 ft targets to represent aircraft. Pilots attacked them again and again, and it was not good enough simply to hit the target with cannon fire at high speed and low level – they had to hit it in the middle.

Israel's Air Force, the Chel H'Avir, was born out of the struggle for an independent Jewish state which culminated in the War of Independence in 1948. Nobody was prepared to sell Israel modern arms, and its first aircraft were a motley collection of pre-war biplanes, a single B-17, a DC-3 and some Harvard trainers, acquired covertly. Its first real fighters were ten Avia S. 199s, Czech copies of the Messerschmidt Bf 109s, and its first pilots were drawn from the Israeli irregular army, the Palmach, and from Jewish and non-Jewish volunteers who had learned their trade in the RAF and USAAF during the war. It was shaped by Israel's political and geographical vulnerability: isolated from the international community with tightly drawn national borders which were difficult to defend against large Arab land armies. The Arabs had never made any secret of their wish to strangle Israel at birth before it could arm itself with modern weapons, including a fully fledged air force. After the 1948 war Israel remained engaged in a state of simmering war for its national survival, and having a highly effective air force was its counter to the numerical superiority of the Arabs.

The IAF's most influential commander was General Dan Tolkovsky, a South African, who believed in the idea that a small, highly trained and highly skilled air force could beat a numerically larger one. He had served as a fighter pilot in the RAF in the Second World War and took command in 1953, the same year that Britain agreed to supply Israel with Meteors, its first jet fighter, and with advanced pilot and flying instructor training. Tolkovsky shaped the IAF from its mercurial and haphazard origins into an élite fighting force.

He paid great attention to the human factor, only taking candidates for training as pilots who fitted into, and would sustain, the tradition of personal aggression, discipline and skill, a pure fighting élite. With limited numbers of aircraft, only the very best trainees made it through the system to fly, and the best of them became fighter pilots, creating a cohesive body of men, most of whom knew each other personally because their numbers were so small, which combined competitiveness, informality and subdued pride. This ethos was true not only of pilots but also of the ground crews, controllers and other IAF support services. Through this process, and the strict anonymity of the pilots for security reasons, the IAF became detached to some extent from Israel's huge, reservist-based army which was culturally and naturally egalitarian, a citizens' army.

Tolkovsky also recognised the need for highly capable aircraft which could be used for different missions and kept his pilots current on several different types of fighter at once, maximising their flexibility. This was also partly because the IAF could not afford specialist aircraft, but it was also because, with limited and uncertain resources, he wanted a force which could be used according to changing military and political circumstances. Israel is such a small country that using its air force as a first line of defence meant having a policy of going on to the offensive and fighting its wars over other people's territory, and it was in Tolkovsky's time that the basic idea of hitting Arab air forces on the ground in a maximum effort, pre-emptive strike to gain air superiority, then converting swiftly to support of the army on the ground, was first developed.

That policy was followed through by the IAF's next commander, another inspirational leader and ex-RAF fighter pilot, Ezer Weizman, who was born in Haifa. He took over in 1958 and went on to become Israeli President. He was followed in 1966 by Mordechai Hod, commander during the Six Day War, who also received his flying training in Britain, passing out top of his course in 1953. By cultural background, geographical size, population, economic position and because they knew it was the most effective way, the Israelis modelled their air force on the ideas of individual excellence of the West European and American traditions.

The rise of Arab nationalism following the coming to power of Col. Gamal Abdul Nasser in Egypt in 1954 gave Israel a much more belligerent southern neighbour. The Egyptian Air Force (EAF) also had its origins in the traditions of the RAF. As the ex-colonial power, Britain trained EAF pilots when it supplied Spitfires, Meteors and Vampires in 1949, but in 1954, with the rise of Nasser, Britain stopped. Nasser turned initially to Czechoslovakia, purchasing Il-28 medium jet bombers and MiG-15 fighters, then turned to the Soviet Union for training and equipment. Their new Warsaw

Pact mentors organised their air defences along Soviet lines, with larger numbers, more ground defences and heavy ground control of its fighters, and the same broad policy was adopted by Egypt's Arab nationalist allies, Syria and Iraq.

The first ever jet-to-jet combat between Arab and Israeli fighters was between IAF Meteors and EAF Vampires on 1 September. Two Vampires made a reconnaissance flight into Israeli airspace north of Gaza. Col. Aharon Yoeli and his wingman, Maj. Yehoash Chatto, were on standby at Hatzor airbase just south of Tel Aviv when the call to scramble and intercept them came, but such was their personal eagerness for combat, and such was the individual *modus operandi* of the IAF, that since they made it to the fighters before the pilots on alert they took off on the mission. The Vampire was slower than the Meteor but more manoeuvrable. Once airborne and on the tail of the Vampires, Yoeli found that his gunsight had been set up for night interception at 150 yards but still managed to shoot both Vampires down, landing back at Hatzor twenty minutes after he had taken off. He was awarded Israel's second highest award for bravery.

The IAF's first advanced jets came in November 1955. France was fighting Arab nationalists in Algeria and Egypt was supplying them with arms so, to give Nasser something to think about, the French government agreed to sell Israel 60 Mystère IVA swept-wing fighters, 75 Ouragon fighter bombers and Vautor light jet bombers and Magister ground-attack and training aircraft.

The first Mystères arrived in time for Israel to support Britain and France in their abortive attempt to prevent Col. Nasser from nationalising the Suez Canal in 1956. By then the Egyptians had MiG-17s, too, but in the hands of the Israelis, the Mystères proved more than a match for them, shooting down one MiG-17, three MiG-15s and four Vampires in air-to-air combat, for no loss. As a result of the 1956 war, Israel occupied the Sinai Desert. Up to 1954 the Sinai had been an empty desert, but from the middle 1950s Nasser began to build roads, airfields and military barracks, clearly in long-term preparation for military operations against Israel. By occupying it, Israel prevented that, while providing itself with a huge land buffer between its true borders and its principal adversary, but following the Suez War Israel was forced to give Sinai up by the UN.

Shorn of its buffer zone, which was soon militarised, Israel's leaders realised even more clearly that air superiority would count for a great deal in any future war, and from then on the IAF was given increasing priority in budgets and human resources. It swiftly developed into a strategic force, based on fighters, dedicated to striking against its clearest potential enemies, its Arab neighbours.

A regional arms race developed between Israel and the Arabs. With French help, Israel began a top-secret nuclear programme which had the potential to make an atomic bomb. The USA was so concerned that it made U-2 flights over Israel to confirm the potential of the Dimona reactor. Also with French help, the IAF kept abreast of the latest fighter technology. In 1959 it received the Super Mystère B2s to match the MiG-19s which the Soviet Union had supplied to the EAF, and when the Soviet Union supplied Nasser with MiG-21s in 1962, Israel bought 72 of the latest in the Dassault family, the superb Mirage IIICJs, armed with a DEFA 30 mm cannon, which could also carry two French Matra 530s or two US AIM-9 Sidewinder air-to-air missiles. Having the flexibility of both was Ezer Weizman's idea so that they could be used not only for dogfighting and air superiority work but because they were also perfect for ground strafing and so fitted into the plan for pre-emptive strikes. The IAF had around 300 combat aircraft, but it was superbly organised and trained, with an instinctive understanding of air power and how to use it. An offensive culture, instilled by Tolkovsky and nurtured by Weizman and Hod, permeated Chel H'Avir, summed up by Weizman in the simple line: 'Israel's best defence is in the skies over Cairo.'

By 1965 Egypt had by far the largest air force in the Middle East: over 600 aircraft, including around 100 MiG-21s, 60 MiG-19s and 40 Su-7 fighter bombers and a bomber force of Il-28 and 30 Tu-16 twin jet bombers capable of striking at Israel. It also had the beginnings of a Soviet-style interlocking air defence system of SAMs and radar and the doctrine in air fighting to go with it.

Tension between Israel and her Arab neighbours rose during the 1960s. In 1964 the Palestinian Liberation Organisation (PLO) was formed, an underground organisation backed financially by Arab countries, which used guerrilla warfare, terror bombings and such imaginative devices as diverting the Jordan River to deny Israel water, in order to attack Israel. The PLO had the support of the

Syrian government and operated from Syrian territory, and the Syrian army on the Golan Heights regularly bombarded villages inside Israel with artillery in support of the PLO. Israel responded to the attacks with air strikes against Syrian gun emplacements or PLO bases. On 14 July 1966 a flight of Mystère IVAs was carrying out a punitive strike against Syrian artillery with Mirages flying CAP. Capt. Yoram Agmon was the first to spot two Syrian MiG-21s, even lower, heading for the Mystères, and turned in behind them. The Syrians saw him coming and made a very sharp and tight turn to the left. Agmon followed, managing to stay on the tail of the leader, closed to 350 yards, fired his cannon without result so moved in closer to 250 yards, took careful aim and fired into the wing root. The wing came off the MiG as it exploded and spun down, the pilot just managed to eject despite the low level.

In 1965 an Iraqi pilot had defected to Israel in a MiG-17; in August 1966 another followed with the real prize, a MiG-21. IAF pilots flew the MiGs in mock combat, searching out the weak spots in its repertoire but also gaining experience in fighting against a very different aircraft. The MiG and the Mirage were both Mach 2 fighters whose origins lay in the search for new air superiority fighters following the Korean War. The MiG was underpowered compared with the Mirage, though its acceleration was good, largely because it was very light; the MiG-21 was more manoeuvrable than the Mirage, but the dissimilar combat training left the Israeli pilots knowing just where the Mirage had the advantage in combat manoeuvring. After gaining their experience, the Israelis almost certainly passed the MiG-21 on to the USAF for similar exercises.

On 28 November two Mirages were flying CAP for a Piper Cub reconnaissance aircraft which was flying along the Israeli border with the Egyptian Sinai when the tiny aircraft came under attack from two MiG-19s. The Mirage pilots managed to get within missile range of the MiGs without being seen, and one of the Mirage pilots managed to get a good lock-on with his radar and fired a Matra R.530 which hit one of the EAF fighters, the first aerial victory by the IAF using an AAM; the other Mirage pilot shot down the Egyptian wingman seconds later with cannon fire.

On 7 April 1967 Israel turned to its air force once again to attack Syrian artillery on the Golan Heights, and when 12 Syrian

MiG-21s intervened the Israelis shot down six of them for no loss. A week later, on 15 May, Nasser started moving troops into the Sinai Desert between Israel and Egypt and on 18 May he ordered UN observers out and started moving his armies in. By 20 May there were 100,000 soldiers with 1,000 tanks in the Sinai. On the surface the Israelis responded by continuing to seek a diplomatic solution, but behind the scenes the leaders knew that the threat of invasion was real and unlikely to be avoided by any more talks. Moshe Dayan, one of Israel's most accomplished generals, was secretly moved into the position of Defence Minister to start planning for war – a war of survival, a war in which a pre-emptive, counter air strike by the IAF had long been accepted as the first move. Israel mobilised its huge reserves, but released soldiers to splash around in the sea, as if on holiday, giving the impression that the emphasis was on diplomacy even while they were planning one of the most audacious and clearly thought through uses of air power in history. By committing virtually its whole air force to a series of pre-emptive strikes against Arab air forces on the ground, Israel had set its own agenda to win the war.

After the stunning success of the first day the attacks continued, and by the end of the second day all Arab airfields within 400 miles of Israel had been neutralised save one, which the Israelis needed for the evacuation of casualties and bringing in supplies to its armies as they moved into the Sinai. With complete air superiority, the IAF quickly converted to the ground-support role, using fighter bombers to attack Egyptian ground forces. In the four days that followed, the Egyptian armies were caught in the open and hammered from the air, and by Israeli armour. One of the main roads through Sinai goes through the Mitla Pass; Israeli tanks blocked the pass so that the Egyptian army retreating through it had no escape and became sitting targets. In scenes reminiscent of the roads in South Korea in 1950, and those which would be repeated on the road out of Kuwait City in 1991, what followed was what happened to large armies caught in the open without air cover – carnage. The IAF turned the roadside into a graveyard for Egyptian armour, transport and soldiers. Egypt lost 700 tanks, 520 artillery pieces, over 12,000 trucks and between 10,000 and 12,000 men killed and another 5,500 taken prisoner. With great courage, knowing what they faced, Egyptian Su-7 fighter bomber pilots flew into Sinai to try to support their army, and they did inflict casualties, but they were no match for the IAF in air combat and continued to suffer a high level of attrition in combat with the IAF Mirages. The final tally was 469 Arab aircraft destroyed for the loss of 46 Israeli aircraft, with 24 IAF pilots killed in action.

By the sixth day the Israeli army had taken back most of Sinai, the Egyptians were retreating across the Suez Canal and the UN brokered a cease-fire. It was a textbook lesson in how to use air power – the value of surprise, of going on to the offensive, how to use aircraft flexibly and, above all, of the value of individual excellence versus numbers. The Arab pilots, particularly the Egyptians, fought bravely, but they had been beaten comprehensively on all fronts by forces smaller than theirs but much better equipped, trained and motivated. Israel controlled an area two and a half times its own size and it had Sinai, its strategic buffer, back. The Suez Canal was closed to all shipping and the Israeli Army commander, General Haim Bar Lev, swiftly fortified the eastern bank with high sand fortifications and a string of forts which became known as the Bar-Lev Line. Egypt dug in on the far side and for a time the two sides stared at each other across the canal.

The success of the IAF pre-emptive strike sent ripples though air forces round the world, especially in Vietnam, where American pilots, subject to ROEs which left them semi-impotent, could only dream of being allowed to do in North Vietnam what the Israelis had done in the Middle East. It concentrated minds in air forces on a problem which had been growing some time: air power was very flexible, but it was tied to airfields which were, as the IAF pre-emptive strike had shown graphically, also highly vulnerable. In Israel there was an understanding that they would never be able to get away with the same plan twice. The secret was out and in any future war they could expect to have the same tactic used against them. In preparation for that day, the IAF started building airfields, workshops, hangars and readiness hardstandings, almost entirely underground, the aircraft coming up from behind blast doors on to huge runways and away. On existing airfields most air forces started building hardened shelters for individual aircraft, capable of withstanding anything but a direct hit. Britain's vertical-take-off Harrier, the so-called jump jet, which had been in development for some time, was nearing operational service in the RAF and later in the US Marines, and the Sea Harrier which was being planned for the Royal Navy suddenly seemed very practical because it did not need an airfield.

The Mirage IIIC immediately became one of the most famous fighters in the world, and much in demand, but almost immediately following the Six Day War France stopped supplying Israel with high-performance jets. The IAF had worked with Dassault to produce the Mach 2.2, multi-role Mirage 5J, a smaller French equivalent to the F-4 Phantom, and had fifty on order and paid for. They were never delivered: President de Gaulle, his war in Algeria over, had seen the way the diplomatic winds were blowing, and the power of the oil weapon, and switched arms sales to the Arabs, supplying versions of the Mirage 5J to Egypt and Libya. For the Israelis, the sudden end to their way of keeping pace with the Arab air forces heightened awareness of their dependence on the major powers for fighters and, with air power as their first and most important line of defence, they developed two long-term overt strategies – turn to the Americans, who built the best in the world, and learn to build them in Israel. They also established a covert relationship with a strange partner, racist South Africa, which had many of the same problems in buying arms. France had also supplied the Mirage III to South Africa before further supplies had been embargoed by the UN. Israel obtained the plans of the Mirage 5 by espionage in Switzerland and France, and started a joint programme to build it for the Chel H'Avir.

Russia swiftly resupplied Egypt with replacement fighters and bombers, but it also vastly improved the Egyptian ground-based air defence system with more SA-2 Guidelines and, having experienced low-level attack, the SA-3 'Goa' which was effective down to 350 feet. Egyptian Army units were equipped with the SA-7 'Grail', a small, shoulder-fired heat-seeking missile, and one of the most deadly systems, the ZSU-23, 23 mm anti-aircraft guns. The aim was to create a dense, integrated, interlocking system on the lines of that which protected the Soviet Union and was being built in Vietnam. Like Vietnam, much of the system was operated by Russian technicians. By mid-1968 the EAF was back to its pre-Six Day War strength, its airfields repaired with hardened shelters for its fighters. There were artillery and SAM sites along the full length of the Suez Canal and both were ringed with anti-aircraft missiles and guns, making air attack difficult and dangerous.

The speed and extent with which the Soviet Union resupplied Egypt and its other Arab client states had prompted the US government to change its policy and supply Israel. Confronted by much the same problem as the USAF had in North Vietnam, what the IAF needed was a similar solution: a highly capable fighter, one which could give a good account of itself in combat against MiG-17s and MiG-21s in aerial battles for air superiority, and which could also carry out attack missions, especially against a sophisticated air defence system – a fighter like the F-4E Phantom which had evolved for precisely that job in Vietnam. F-4Es would take some time so the first American fighters to be sold to the IAF were 48 Douglas A-4 Skyhawks, which started arriving in late 1967 and were in service a year later. Israel eventually bought 300 A-4s and found them, as the US Navy did, a very robust attack aircraft.

In September 1968 Egyptian artillery started shelling the Bar-Lev Line to begin what became known as the War of Attrition. Nasser put his faith in a combination of artillery bombardment of the Bar-Lev line and PLO guerrilla attacks inside Israel's borders to destroy Israel's will to resist. Israel responded with its own artillery bombardments and commando raids, but relied on its air force for its main response. The IAF fought the War of Attrition as an aggressive battle for air superiority over the Suez Canal, waged between Israeli fighters and the Egyptian air defence system. The A-4 became the workhorse of the attacks, not only on Egyptian artillery and SAMs but also against PLO bases in Lebanon, Syria and Jordan.

In aerial combat the IAF remained supreme. When Syrian MiG-21s intervened during an attack on a PLO camp near Damascus on 25 February 1969, the escorting IAF Mirages shot three down for no loss. When EAF MiG-21s made an incursion over the Great Bitter Lake on the Suez Canal, IAF Mirages intercepted and shot one MiG down. Arab artillery barrages and commando raids continued. On 17 June two IAF Mirages penetrated the Egyptian defences and flew supersonically at treetop height over President Nasser's home in Heliopolis, breaking windows for miles around. It was a warning, and it cost the commander of the EAF and the general in charge of air defence their jobs. The IAF was back on the offensive, and in response to each shelling the IAF attacked;

the air battles reached a crescendo in July 1969 with a massive series of IAF air strikes across the Canal against Egyptian positions. The IAF's first Phantoms arrived in September that year and they came with the AGM-45 Shrike anti-radiation missile which had made its reputation as a SAM-buster over North Vietnam. Israel had wanted Lance surface-to-surface missiles so that it could attack the SAM sites across the Canal without endangering the lives of its pilots, but the USA said no because the Lance could be used with a nuclear warhead. The A-4 Skyhawks continued to strike just across the Canal at the artillery, but when the Phantoms became operational in January 1970 Israel used them to raise the stakes by striking deeper into Egypt, attacking supply depots and successfully hitting the SAM batteries and their radar. As a consequence, the artillery and their protective air defence shield were gradually pulled back from the Canal Zone.

President Nasser eventually had to acknowledge that the IAF had air superiority over the Canal and could do what it wanted there, but he found such superiority – what he characterised as Israel's 'arrogance of power' – intolerable, and turned to Russia for more help. The stakes were raised following an exchange of letters between the Soviet Prime Minister, Alexei Kosygin, and the US President, Richard Nixon, supporting their respective clients. Nixon would not undertake to try and restrain Israel so a massive Soviet airlift of new air defence equipment started, including Soviet technicians to operate them. On 18 March 1970 it was revealed that Soviet help included five squadrons of the latest MiG-21MF fighters flown by 150 volunteer Soviet pilots, the cream of the Red Air Force's fighter pilots. President Nixon responded by letting the Soviet Union know that the USA was supplying Israel with 25 more Phantoms and 80 more Skyhawks.

Israel continued to attack targets in central Egypt, including the air defence system, but it ended the deep penetration raids into Egypt and took care not to provoke the Russians, by avoiding targets where they knew Russians were based and where their fighters patrolled. An unspoken agreement emerged – that the Russians would not come to within thirty kilometres of the Canal if the Israelis would not attack them directly.

On Israel's northern front the stakes were raised, but not in the same way. Once again the problem was artillery. The Syrians continued to shell Israeli positions and the Israelis responded from the air. When the Syrians replied by sending up fighters they invariably came off worst. In retaliation, a Syrian MiG-21 flew supersonically over Haifa, shattering acres of glass. The same afternoon the IAF retaliated with similar flights over Damascus and other Syrian cities.

With Soviet pilots patrolling over Egypt, tacitly immune from attack by the IAF, in April the EAF carried out air raids against Israeli positions in the Sinai, penetrating as far as El Arish at one point. By early May Soviet and Egyptian technicians had managed to install new SAM sites along the Canal and the EAF raids continued. It seemed that the Egyptians, backed by the Russians, were gaining the initiative. Egyptian commando raids continued and an Israeli patrol boat, the *Orit*, was sunk by a surface-to-surface missile. On 16 May Yalo Shavit led a flight of eight Phantoms on the longest fighter/bomber raid to date, across Sinai and the Red Sea to Ras Banas, the Egyptian port where the Egyptian Navy destroyer which had launched the attack on the *Orit* was based. The Egyptians had thought it was beyond the range of the IAF but they were wrong: Shavit and his colleagues sank it in port with iron bombs.

In the Canal Zone the air defences were getting the upper hand. In June the Egyptians and Soviets started moving the SAM sites closer to the Canal, providing local air cover for air attacks and commando raids on the far bank. Israel began to lose Phantoms in a deadly, hard battle between aircraft and missiles for control of the skies over the Canal, and the only way for the Israelis to fight it was to go on to the offensive.

So started what became known as the Electronic Summer, a confrontation between the IAF Phantom pilots with the latest American electronic countermeasures and the Russian and Egyptian radar operators and missiliers. Avihu Bin-Nun, now a colonel and commander of an IAF Phantom squadron, was tasked with attacking the SAM sites on 30 June. He led an attack against three sites and destroyed them, using 850 lb iron bombs. As his flight was leaving the area one of the Phantoms pulled up from the deck in an uncharacteristic mistake and was instantly hit by missiles from a fourth site, so close and interlocking were the batteries. On 5 July two more Phantoms were lost, attacking SAM sites between

Cairo and the Canal, but in one of the attacks a Russian major general was killed. Most of the IAF pilots and navigators ejected and parachuted to safety to become POWs.

On 18 July the IAF Phantoms attacked SAM sites, using the latest ECM pods recently supplied by the USA to jam the radars, and the raid was successful, but an SA-3 hit the Phantom flown by the commander of Israel's first Phantom squadron, Lt Col. Schmuel Hetz; Hetz was killed and his navigator was captured. Hundreds of sorties were flown against the air defences, but they could not be swept away. For the Israeli pilots there was a falseness about the situation because they were not permitted to carry the fight deeper for fear of involving the Soviets. However, the Russians started to get more confident, and on 25 July they broke the unwritten rule that they would not penetrate to the Canal Zone by shooting down an IAF A-4 Skyhawk over the Canal from a MiG-21, using an Atoll heat-seeking missile.

The gloves came off: IAF pilots were eager to have a go at the Russians by setting a trap, and the Israeli government agonised for a week before finally approving a plan to teach the Russians a lesson. On 30 July a flight of four Mirages headed for the Canal at 30,000 feet as if on a reconnaissance flight. The Russians responded by scrambling 20 MiG-21s in five flights of four from three airfields in their sector. Waiting for them were two flights of four Phantoms, one led by Avihu Bin-Nun, the other by Ehud Henkin. Between them, the pilots in the 12 Israeli aircraft, eight Phantoms and four Mirages, had a wealth of successful aerial combat experience, with 60 aerial victories to their credit. As the MiGs attacked the Mirages the Israelis turned into the attack immediately, and Asher Snir opened the score for the IAF by shooting one down immediately, his target exploding but not before the pilot could eject. Sadly, either through malfunction or because the pilot made a mistake, his parachute opened immediately at 30,000 feet in the freezing cold, and he floated down in the middle of the battle. Some of the Israeli pilots even used his position as a fixed point in the battle, giving their positions in relation to the frozen Russian pilot.

It was the largest aerial battle since the Six Day War and the Israeli pilots, though outnumbered, quickly got the feel of the mettle of the Russians whose inexperience showed immediately: they fell for the Israeli ruses and fired off Atoll missiles indiscriminately. One of the problems for the Israelis was that the MiGs, with their greater number, could protect each other, and each time an IAF pilot got on the tail of an opponent a MiG appeared on his tail, forcing him to break off. Israeli Sparrows broke up the tight formations of Russians, wrecking their mutual support, and in the turning battles that followed Sella, Bin-Nun's No. 2, managed to get on the tail of a lone MiG who tried to evade by very tight turns, then diving. The duel gradually got lower and lower, each one turning and reversing the turn to find some advantage, when finally, at 2,000 feet, Sella managed to get a Sidewinder lock-on and sent the Russian spinning into the ground. The fight had separated Sella from Bin-Nun who had managed to get on the tail of a second MiG which went into a high-speed dive to 7,000 feet, giving Bin-Nun time to get a lock-on with his radar and launch a Sparrow which hit, but the MiG flew on. Bin-Nun fired another but, before it hit, the MiG disintegrated from the impact of the first missile. The Israelis shot down five Russians without loss to themselves, three with Sidewinders, two fired by Phantoms and one by a Mirage, one with a Sparrow, and one to cannon fire. Three of the Russian pilots were killed in the battle and one died in hospital later.

Publicly, the Israeli government made little comment, not wishing to provoke the Russians by rubbing their noses in their inability to win air superiority. However, the message to the Russians was clear – they were not up to the rigours of fighting the IAF in the air. In private, the Israeli pilots were jubilant, a joy which, ironically, they shared to some extent with their Egyptian counterparts who had suffered from a certain arrogance on the part of the Russian pilots to that date. The Russians had never believed the Egyptian stories of how good the Israelis were, but the Soviet mauling proved it, and the aura of invincibility which the IAF projected increased, having its own effect: Egyptian pilots went into a fight expecting to be shot down, putting the IAF pilots at an advantage from the start.

The confrontation between the IAF and the Russians, and its conclusive result, had an immediate effect on the course of the war. Neither superpower could let their client state lose, and neither side wanted to be drawn into a wider conflict. On 7 August 1970 the United States and the Soviet Union brokered a cease-fire and the Electronic Summer, and the War of Attrition, came to an end. It was not the kind of war to which Israel was used – no swift movement of troops and armour on the ground, no exchange of territory, just artillery bombardment and casualties. In the 1,141 days since the Six Day War, the IAF had shot down 113 aircraft and a further 25 to ground fire and Hawk anti-aircraft missiles, all for the loss of 2 in air-to-air combat and 13 to ground fire. The highly capable Phantom had proved its value as a counter to the dense ground defences. Five were lost in the war, but it had shown that the latest ECM pods did jam and confuse and, ultimately, even the densest ground-based systems could be penetrated by manned aircraft.

As Vietnam and the War of Attrition had shown, in the twenty-five years since the end of the Second World War the guided missile had changed aerial warfare by adding the electronic spectrum as a battleground, just as General Arnold had predicted in 1945. But it had not done so by bringing an end to the use of manned aircraft – on the contrary, it had simply demanded more of the men in the aircraft. The Wild Weasel concept had established itself as being of as much importance, if not more, than the pure fighter in the battle for air superiority. Just as with other technical developments throughout history, it took time, and the experience of fighting real wars, for the thinking and the tactics to catch up.

In three years fighter pilots had changed the political and military landscape of the Middle East. It was changed again in 1970 with the death of President Nasser on 28 September from a heart attack, bringing a specific era in Israeli–Arab relations to end. He was replaced by a long-time colleague, General Anwar Sadat, who scaled down both the rhetoric and the aggression on the ground, starting a period of relative peace. But behind the peaceful mask there was a huge build-up of arms. The Russians continued to supply Egypt, Syria and Iraq with their latest weapons systems. The EAF received 210 MiG-21s, 100 MiG-17s, 80 Su-7 fighter bombers and 16 Tu-16 bombers. The Syrians received 200 MiG-21s, 120 MiG-17s and 45 Su-7s, plus some Hunters and MiG-21s on loan from Iraq. Egypt also received the latest mobile version of the SA-6 'Gainful' SAM, which was mounted on an armoured car so that it could move forward with the army. Its radar could detect hostile aircraft at twenty-five miles and fire a radar-guided missile with a heat-seeking head which took over close in – during the radar-guided phase, if the enemy started jamming. The SA-6 could switch to a completely different frequency and continue. The ZSU-23 anti-aircraft gun became a mobile flak battery mounted on a tracked vehicle to become the ZSU-23–4. The air defences along the Canal were built up yet again to the point where it was said they surpassed even those around Moscow, both in depth and density. With missiles along the whole Canal and close to it, Egypt had air cover over a substantial part of Israeli-occupied Sinai. By 1973 the EAF was back up to 650 aircraft with more anti-air systems; Syria had a 360-aircraft air force including the MiG-21. The balance between Israel and her main potential Arab adversaries was around 2:1.

There was practical help from the Russians, too: from 1971 the latest, Mach 3, Soviet MiG-25 Foxbats were flown over the Sinai by Soviet pilots at 70,000 feet to gather intelligence. In November of that year they overflew Israel. The IAF tried an interception, using a Phantom to fire a Sparrow missile in a high-angle climb from about 45,000 feet, but the Foxbat was too high and too fast for it to manoeuvre close enough to damage the MiG.

The IAF grew, too, and was better equipped. Within a year of the end of the War of Attrition, Israel's aerospace industry had produced its own fighter, the 'Nesher', or Eagle in Hebrew. It was clearly a derivative of the Mirage V, and to help pay for it the Nesher became available for export as the Dagger – one customer was Argentina. By 1973 Israel Aircraft Industries (IAI) had produced the prototype of an even more advanced and highly capable fighter, the Kfir or Lion Cub, which first flew in that year. It was an air superiority fighter capable of carrying out ground attack, loosely based on the Mirage but built around a single General Electric J79 engine which also powered the Phantom. Israel had also started to build its own air-to-air missile, the Shafrir, as early as 1961. It was based on the Sidewinder, a simple but highly accurate heat-seeker. The home-produced fighters were good but lightweight, and Israel continued to rely on America for its big, state-of-the-art fighters, which now numbered 120 Phantoms, including six very expensive RF-4Es for reconnaissance, and 160 A-4 Skyhawks. These were supported by 70 Mirages and Neshers and 16 Super Mystères. Israel also built its own Remotely Piloted Vehicles (RPVs) for reconnaissance over Egypt and Syria during peacetime. America continued to supply its Hawk SAMs and 300 anti-aircraft guns, but the IAF's policy of relying on manned aircraft as its main weapon, against both other aircraft and missiles, remained. The IAF was well equipped and experienced, but a new danger lurked beneath its invincible image: it had grown complacent; it had come to believe it really was invincible.

Underneath the peaceful image President Sadat was preparing for war, preparing to take the offensive. He had learned the value of surprise from the Israelis and the preparations went on in great secret, despite the signs of tension. On 13 September 1973 IAF Mirages and Phantoms patrolling off the Syrian Coast were engaged by a large force of Syrian MiG-21s: 13 MiGs were shot down for the loss of one Mirage, adding to the aura of IAF invincibility. On Friday 5 October there were more warning signals when Egypt and Syria moved troops into forward areas. The IAF had plans for a pre-emptive strike, similar to that which had been successful in 1967. The IAF was put on alert and Israel's army was mobilised, but the Prime Minister, Mrs Golda Meir, would not authorise a strike because she did not want to start a war.

Saturday, 6 October 1973 was the Day of Atonement, one of the holiest days in the Jewish religious calendar, Yom Kippur, and the streets of Israel were all but empty. At 2 p.m. that afternoon the Egyptians and Syrians launched simultaneous attacks over the Suez Canal and on the Golan Heights. Surprise was on the side of the Arabs. For the first time the Israelis did not hold the initiative – they were on the back foot, in the middle of a religious festival, with a war on two fronts. Egyptian commandos crossed the Canal with high-pressure water hoses which they directed at the sand fortifications of the Bar-Lev Line, washing away the sand walls to create breaches in the fortifications through which the advance troops poured to attack the Israeli forts, occupied by around 450 Israeli soldiers each. The Israelis were quickly overwhelmed and once the Egyptians were in control of both banks they put pontoon bridges over the Canal, allowing hundreds of vehicles and thousands of soldiers to cross. An army of 70,000 men, supported by tanks and very tightly interlocking air defence systems, crossed the Canal, advanced just a few miles into Sinai, then dug in. The army was supported by 200 fighter bomber sorties flown against Israeli targets in Sinai, including attacks by Tu-16 bombers using

Soviet Kelt long-range, air-to-ground missiles against Israeli HQs and airfields in Sinai. The Israeli airfield at Refidim, in central Sinai, was attacked by successive waves of Su-7 fighter bombers and put out of action.

On the Golan, Syrian fighter bombers carried out similar attacks, hitting Israeli armour and troop positions, causing a great deal of damage and losing just one fighter in the process. With surprise on their side, Syrian helicopters lifted commandos on to Mount Hermon and they took the Heights where the IDF had an important observation post. The air attacks were followed by an attack by five Syrian divisions, 70,000 men and over 1,000 tanks, which began to overwhelm the 8,000 Israeli defenders. The Syrians were protected by SA-2, SA-3 and SA-6 SAMs, ZSU-23–4 radar-guided guns and SA-7 shoulder-launched heat-seeking missiles.

The Israelis were caught unprepared, and with attacks on two fronts Israeli Army commanders on both of them started calling for air support. The IAF could not concentrate its forces. It was at its best fighting in the air, but the Egyptian plan was not based on taking the IAF on in the air – it was based on Soviet doctrine. The Egyptian army was shielded, not by fighters, which remained to the rear, but by mobile AAA guns, mobile SA-6 SAMs, which had a range of seventeen miles and were virtually immune from Israeli and US ECM, and SA-7 shoulder-launched, heat-seeking missiles, which were more of a threat to slower aircraft such as helicopters. The plan was to hold its ground and make the Israeli pilots attack them, then hit them with missiles, wearing them down, exhausting them, impaling them on a thicket of SAMs, then moving forward under its mobile air defence umbrella.

The IAF commanders would have preferred to establish air superiority first, then use aircraft to support troops on the ground but, shorn of their advantage of a pre-emptive strike, they had to fight for air superiority in air-to-air combat over the battlefield while also flying into the battlefield areas to support ground troops where the electronic shield was very effective. The mobile missile threat was particularly deadly: Israeli pilots had to fly in the battle area always on the lookout for the threat, not being able to choose their targets and how best to approach them. In the first thirty minutes of the IAF attacks on the Egyptian army, they lost five Skyhawks and five Phantoms. In the first few hours of the war, the

Arabs fired 1,500 SAM missiles and achieved a hit rate of about 1.5%, but most of the losses were to the ZSU-23-4s. The IAF lost 25 Skyhawks and five Phantoms on the Golan – 40 aircraft, over 10% of its air force, and many good pilots, with 60 more aircraft damaged. Israel was not prepared for the effectiveness of the air defences and the IAF could not sustain the level of losses; the IAF was ordered not to venture within ten miles from the Canal.

The situation on the Golan was worse, where Syrian tanks had advanced across the buffer zone which had been established in 1967, so the Israelis decided to hold the line against the Egyptians in Sinai, while repulsing the Syrians on the Golan. IAF Phantoms and Skyhawks were thrown into the battle as fighter bombers while the Mirages and Neshers took on any MiG-21s which ventured above the battle area, but by the second day the Syrians had virtually destroyed the Israeli armoured brigade on the Heights and was still advancing. The main enemy was the SA-6 with its ability to change its radar frequencies, but a fortunate attack destroyed the computer which controlled the interweaving network of air defences, creating a gap which the IAF managed to fly through to attack Syrian armour and the air defences further back, while deepening and widening the gap.

At dawn on the second day on the Egyptian front, while EAF fighter bombers attacked the Israelis on the ground, the IAF concentrated on breaching the air defences around the Canal so they could mount strikes against seven Egyptian airfields. It was not like 1967: the Egyptian fighters were housed in shelters and runway damage repair teams were more efficient but a large number of Egyptian aircraft were shot down and destroyed. They also attacked Egyptian bridges over the Canal but suffered more losses, including five more Phantoms.

The hard battle for control of the airspace above the Golan continued. The Israeli Army used RPVs over the Golan, both for reconnaissance and as decoys, leading the Syrian ground-based radar to believe that attacks were imminent, making them switch on their radar and give away their positions, then IAF fighters were ready to pounce with Shrikes. To avoid the SA-7, the IAF pilots innovated: in addition to using the standard decoy flares to distract heat-seeking missiles, IAF pilots developed weaving manoeuvres in which each pair crossed each other's jet wash, creating hot spots in the sky which also attracted heat-seekers. IAF losses in hitting the launchers and radar sites were higher than they should have been because of the urgency, but it was the only way to get at the Syrians. By the end of the second day the IAF had cleared a way through the air defences for the Skyhawk and Phantom pilots to get at the hundreds of tanks which were by far the largest threat to Israel. Once they had destroyed the tanks, they probed deeper into Syria, where the SAMs were still a threat, but the air defence system was far less dense and eventually they cleared a way through to Damascus to attack supplies and reinforcements moving up from the rear. After three days the IAF had the measure of the air defences and in dogfights the IAF remained supreme, shooting down 32 Syrian aircraft in the two days. In the same period the Israelis lost 22 more fighters and on the third day it lost another four Phantoms.

On the fourth day, 9 October, the Israelis began to push the Syrians back on the ground and the Syrians pleaded with the Egyptians to take the pressure off by starting their offensive in Sinai. The Egyptians did, mounting an armoured breakout from their position on the Canal, but Israeli armour, supported by IAF fighter bombers, counter-attacked and halted it.

The IAF had lost over 50 aircraft in the first three days of the war, but it stabilised the situation. Both sides had used up huge amounts of equipment and both sides turned to their respective superpowers for resupply, the Arabs for more missiles, the Israelis for more Phantoms, Skyhawks, more advanced ECM and more Shrike anti-radiation missiles.

The Israelis struck deeper into Syria against armour, supply depots and oil and petrol supplies, including the huge Homs oil depot. This had the effect of making the Syrians pull back more of the mobile air defence from forward positions to the rear areas, weakening the defences over the battlefield, giving more access to IAF, and forcing them to use fighters for protection, an area where the Israelis knew they excelled. In the dogfights the loss ratio was about 25:1 in Israel's favour. Morale in the IAF stayed high and they planned ahead for taking air superiority. There was very high pressure on the men, both pilots and ground staff. In the course of the whole war 236 IAF aircraft returned to base damaged and 215 of them were repaired and flew again. One Mirage came back from a sortie covered in sticky black soot, having flown through the debris from an exploding MiG; it was back in combat before being fully cleaned.

On 12 October four Skyhawks, led by N. Merchavi, were sent right up into the Damascus area to attack the fixed SA-2 sites near the city. He made the first attack, leaving his Nos 3 and 4 three miles behind him to warn him of any missile attack. He identified a site and prepared to attack it just as he himself came under attack from about 20 SA-6 missiles. He and his wingman dropped their bombs and went very low, twisting and turning violently to lose them. One of the SA-6s passed between Merchavi and his wingman and exploded on its proximity fuse, but damage was slight and they all made it back to base.

On the same day an Iraqi armoured brigade was sent to help the hard-pressed Syrian forces. As it rolled along the Baghdad–Damascus road IAF reconnaissance aircraft photographed it. That night Israeli commandos were landed in the area by helicopter, where they blew up a bridge and mined the road ahead of the convoy. When the lead vehicles hit the mines the Israeli commandos withdrew to be picked up by helicopter while IAF Phantoms attacked the stationary column and destroyed it. Supplies from the Soviet Union started arriving at Damascus airport on 11 October, and on 14 October IAF Phantoms finally broke through the SAM barrier to bomb the airport where the Russian transports were unloading, in a clear demonstration that command of the skies had been won.

The same day the Egyptian army mounted a huge armoured thrust along the roads to the Gidi and Mitla passes. To soften up the Israeli defences waves of Arab fighter bombers attacked the Israeli defensive positions, but when the Egyptian tanks started to roll, the Israeli tanks came out, supported by IAF fighter bombers, to fight the largest tank battle since the Second World War. The Egyptians lost over 200 tanks and the Arab air forces lost 10 aircraft for no Israeli loss.

On 15 October the USA publicly acknowledged that it was resupplying the Israelis, not only with an airlift of supplies but with Phantoms and Skyhawks flown direct to Israel from USAF, USN and USMC squadrons by American pilots. On the night of 16–17 October General Ariel Sharon counter-attacked across the

Canal at a point near the Great Bitter Lake which was also the junction between the Egyptian 3rd and 4th Armies. By morning he had established a bridgehead on the far side and had started moving into the hinterland, destroying SAM sites to open up a gap in the defences which IAF Phantoms could fly though to targets in the Egyptian rear. IAF fighters patrolled overhead and fell on the EAF fighter bombers which tried to attack the Israeli crossing-point. It was the same as on the Golan front: shorn of part of its missile defences, the Egyptians were forced to put fighters into the gap, and once again in the air the IAF fighter pilots were on top immediately. They had stabilised the situation and were dictating some of the terms now, and after the initial phase of containment, then supporting the counter attacks, they went for air superiority.

Under protection from air attack, on 17 October Sharon put a pontoon bridge across the Canal and started pouring 10,000 men into Egypt with 300 tanks. On the same day senior officers, including General Benny Peled, the commander of the IAF, gathered for a meeting to plan a surprise raid to widen the gap in the air defences by hitting a large complex of SA-2, SA-3 and SA-6 missile defences near El Qantara on the Sinai side of the Canal. The plan was to fly out to sea, then back across the Nile delta towards the Canal, south along the Egyptian side of the Canal, then left to attack El Qantara from behind. The whole mission was to be carried out at extreme low level, which was a defence against all but the SA-6.

Col. G., the commander of the Phantom squadron which would carry out the raid, picked his eight most experienced crews, especially those with experience which went back to the War of Attrition and the Electronic Summer of 1970. They took off and set out over the sea, just above the flat calm surface, the rest of the raid forming up behind him. His navigator was responsible for landfall at a place called Danietta Gulf on the edge of a small lagoon on the Nile delta. They made a perfect landfall, then turned back low over the muddy waters, which gradually turned into a shoreline and then into sand. As they approached the Canal, warning lights started to show that radar had seen them and were locking on. The pilots had dodged missiles before, but each knew that once they reached the Initial Point (IP), where they had to pull up to start the bombing dive, they would not be able to take violent evasive action because they would be lining up for attack and at that moment they would be flying a steady course, perfect for the missiliers.

Suddenly, over the headphones, G. heard that one of the Phantoms had been hit, then he saw a missile coming low towards his aircraft. He flew lower, and in an attempt to get even lower the missile flew into the ground where it exploded harmlessly. A second did the same thing moments later. Close to the IP another Phantom was hit, this time Guri Palter and his navigator, Yitzhak Baram. Approaching the IP, G. put the throttle fully forward into afterburner, building up to maximum power and speed, then he pulled up brutally, almost vertically, for a few seconds then rolled over, looking for the target, an SA-3 battery. He had to move the nose slightly to bring the sights on to it and started the dive, squeezed the trigger and suddenly the bombs were gone. He was free to weave and turn to avoid missiles but as he did so he heard that another Phantom had been hit, Doron Shalev and his navigator, Lev-Ari. Of the three hit, R. made it to Refidim for an emergency landing. The other four Israelis all ejected: Shalev landed between the Egyptian and Israeli forces and Phantoms circled overhead, trying to get a helicopter to the site, but the Egyptians got there first and he was captured. The missile site was completely destroyed.

By 19 October Sharon's army had overrun 40 SAM launchers, opening up the gap, and the missile defences were frayed at the edges, making the overlapping network ineffective. The Phantoms went through the gap and started hitting targets deep inside Egypt, threatening Cairo. To keep Sharon's lines of communication open, his bridges over the Canal had to be protected from the air, and on the morning of 19 October Lt Col. G., flying a Mirage from Refidim in central Sinai, was patrolling over the Canal and saw two Su-7 fighter bombers and shot them both down. In the afternoon he was doing the same and shot down two more, while his wingman accounted for a MiG-21 which had latched on to the tail of a Phantom.

The next day, at 4.30 in the afternoon, he was leading a flight of four and came across two MiG-2 is at 10,000 feet. He dropped tanks, got on their tail and shot one down using a Shafrir heat-seeking missile. But it was a trap, and soon 10 separate pairs of MiGs had pounced on him. What followed was a hectic dogfight in which he shot down three more MiGs, two of them after the rest of his flight and 10 of the MiGs had either been shot down or left the battle. The fight got lower and lower until – as his target pulled out of his dive – his jet efflux blew a wake in the sand, but he held on and got him. Lt Col. G. shot down another three over the Canal when he went to join a fight which he had been ordered to leave when he heard others being vectored to it by a controller. When he arrived he immediately locked a Shafrir on to a MiG and fired and it hit, but all that happened was that the MiG developed a fuel leak. He started to move in closer, to use his guns, when the pilot ejected anyway. He shot down two more, one with his second Shafrir, the other with guns, making his total 11, the highest-scoring fighter pilot of the war. He was the epitome of the Israeli fighter pilot and the tradition of aggressive excellence, happy to take on 10 MiGs alone, finding his way to three and four kills in a single dogfight – a natural, an ace.

The IAF had air superiority on both fronts and could have threatened to move on Cairo. On 22 October the Golani Brigade took back the summit of Mount Hermon on the Golan Heights, from which it could dominate the surrounding area. The air attacks and Sharon's tanks started to have an effect on the supply situation for Egypt's 3rd Army – the Israelis were so confident of their position in the air that Fayid airfield on the Egyptian side of the Canal was opened up for transports to supply Sharon's army. Egypt's 3rd Army was encircled and Israel could have massacred it from the air or forced it to surrender. To the south of Cairo, US satellites photographed Soviet Scud missiles, capable of carrying nuclear warheads, which could be fired into Israel. It was an open secret that Israel had a nuclear capability.

The United Nations passed a Resolution calling on the warring parties to stop fighting. Neither superpower was prepared to let its client state be crushed, but neither could insist on a cease-fire. Anwar Sadat indicated he would settle for a cease-fire and the Syrian President, Hafiz al-Assad, under Soviet pressure, did the same. The USA leaned on Israel to do the same, but Israel was very reluctant to move back to the suggested cease-fire line of 22 September, determined to secure an ability to bargain its position on the west bank of the Suez Canal for the gains which the Egyptians had made on the eastern bank in Sinai, and fighting continued.

Sadat called for the stationing of US and Soviet troops to secure the cease-fire, and the Soviet Union moved troops to airfields in

Yugoslavia. Among other sources, the RAF shadowed the Soviet fleet in the Mediterranean as it built to 70 ships. The Soviet Union seemed prepared to commit troops, and there was plenty of intelligence which showed that the Soviets were not bluffing. President Nixon, who was at the height of the Watergate scandal, was very reluctant to commit troops but responded to the Soviet move on 25 October by placing all US forces, worldwide, at DEFCON 3, the first condition above normal peacetime condition with all leaves cancelled and units awaiting orders. The Soviet Union hesitated, more pressure was applied to Israel and two days later a cease-fire came into force.

Israel had turned the tables on Egypt and Syria and it was the flexibility of the IAF, with its ability to fight on both fronts while helping the hard-pressed ground forces and fighting to establish air superiority, which had ensured success. It was a battle of doctrines: small numbers of Israeli fighter pilots went on the offensive and drove a wedge into the massed, defensive SAM missiles and AAA guns and, with the help of ground troops, gradually widened and deepened the gap until the Soviet-style, ground-based air defence system had lost its integrity. After that, the Arab fighters were not a huge problem for the IAF: Israel claimed 334 air-to-air kills, 60 to cannon fire and the rest to Shafrir AAMs; they also claimed a further 180 to ground fire, including US Hawk SAMs. The Arabs admitted to 440 losses. Recovering from the initial surprise attacks had made the IAF pay a high price for its success: Israel lost 103 combat aircraft, 20% of its air force, over half of them Skyhawks. They were lost almost entirely to ground systems, 40 to SA-2 and SA-3, 40 to ZSU-23, 10 to SA-6 and 4 to SA-7; the IAF say 3 were lost in air-to-air combat against Arab claims of 20.

Years of air supremacy based on air combat skills, particularly in the Six Day War and the War of Attrition, had led the Israelis to overrate the performance of even their superb pilots against the threat posed by electronic warfare. Israel had placed too much emphasis on pilots and aircraft and not enough on ECM, and the decisive factor was ECM. Once the Israelis had the latest black boxes from America they learned quickly how to overcome the Soviet systems effectively. Israel's victory in the Six Day War in 1967 had been based on surprise and the supremacy of its air force. Six years later, in the Yom Kippur War, when it was Israel which had been surprised, when it had not taken pre-emptive action and had then came up against effective ground-based defence systems, it had come perilously close to defeat. It was a lesson that could not be ignored and the analysis started even before the Yom Kippur War was over.

CHAPTER SEVEN
Flying Computers

The use of US air power against the communist insurgency in Vietnam in 1965 had started with high expectations which dwindled into frustration and shame. In seven years, at a huge cost in blood, treasure and credibility, America managed to bomb North Vietnam to the conference table in Paris, only to expose the reality that America had lost the Vietnam War. It was the first time in its history that the USA had lost a war. Worse, as a superpower, America had been humbled by a guerrilla army and a small third world country, and the whole country was traumatised by a sense of national failure which permeated the USAF and US Navy pilots who had actually fought the air war with great courage and skill. For many Americans, the failure of Rolling Thunder contrasted starkly with the brilliant success of the Israeli pre-emptive strike which achieved total air superiority in a few hours on 6 June 1967.

The lessons of Vietnam, the Six Day War, the War of Attrition, Linebacker and the Yom Kippur War were many and complex. They made clear the inherently offensive nature of air power: it remained a brutal weapon to be used ruthlessly or not at all. It could not be used piecemeal under heavy political restrictions; any advantage over the enemy had to be exploited to the full, making maximum use of its greatest asset – surprise. They showed that technology had changed air warfare, but the basic rules re-emerged: the need for air superiority was paramount and to achieve it required excellence in aircraft and pilots. The experience of real aerial combat in several fierce, regional wars between 1964 and 1973 saw air power re-emerge fundamentally changed by the electronic revolution while remaining what it had always been, a very politically incorrect way of waging war.

The Cold War also changed its character in the 1960s. Tension between the superpowers and their alliances decreased following the Cuban Crisis, and fears of a Third World War, actually fought with massive nuclear exchanges, declined. The ICBMs with their multiple nuclear warheads offering Mutual Assured Destruction (MAD) remained; the B-52s continued to fly, and one supersonic bomber project, the low-level Rockwell B-1, remained in development and went into service in the 1980s, but most of the new, supersonic, US strategic bomber programme was cancelled, and during the early 1970s the USAF dismantled large parts of its strategic air defence system, including long-range SAMs such as BOMARC, and the RAF scrapped the Bloodhound system. US and British pure-bred interceptors, the F-106 and the Lightning, remained in service well into the 1980s, regularly intercepting Soviet reconnaissance bombers probing NATO's defences, but NATO never had any plans to replace them; that era was over.

Soviet policy was different. Rather than start with something new, the highly ordered Soviet military culture, with its huge manpower and its continent-wide history, was much slower to respond to change, and it retained the IA-PVO and ZR-PVO homeland air defence system with MiG-21 interceptors and SAMs and even introduced a new generation of interceptors: the huge, two-seater Tu-28 Fiddler, the single-seat MiG-25 Foxbat and Su-15 Flagon. It also continued with its supersonic nuclear bombers, the Tu-22 Blinder and Tu-26 Backfire, ultimately followed by the Tu-160 Blackjack, broadly equivalent to America's B-1.

The pendulum had clearly swung away from air defence to

tactical air forces, or Frontal Aviation as the Soviet Union called them, air forces to fight for air superiority over the battlefield, even a battlefield the size of Europe. Warsaw Pact military planners believed it was possible to invade Western Europe with an armoured offensive based on its massively larger conventional forces moving fast enough during an initial, nuclear-free period to beat NATO, and for this plan the Soviet Union revitalised its tradition of strong tactical air power supporting large land armies dating back to the Second World War. At the heart of creating that offensive capability was the multi-role MiG-23 Flogger which was produced in huge numbers and first deployed in Europe in 1972, but the tactical fighters had to fit in with the Soviet Union's heavy emphasis on missiles as part of its offensive, tactical plans as well as its defence doctrine. Mobile SAM and radar-controlled anti-aircraft guns were deployed in Eastern Europe to provide the same interlocking air cover for armoured operations as had been carried out by the Egyptians in the early stages of the Yom Kippur War, and operating ground attack fighters as part of that offensive capability called for a very high degree of co-ordination and control of both missile systems and fighters.

It was to counter this Soviet offensive capability, and give the West a middle route between surrender and global annihilation by going nuclear immediately, that NATO developed its doctrine of Flexible Response, a graduated reaction to specific threats which depended on the nature of that threat, up to the use of theatre nuclear weapons if required. Fighting a conventional war in Europe against a numerically superior enemy would mean fighting for air superiority, and Flexible Response relied heavily on the traditional Western view of how to use tactical air power: state-of-the-art fighters with pilots who could get the best out of them. To penetrate the interlocking, multi-layered battlefield air defence system, NATO developed a multi-layered attacking force, a variation on the 'strike package' which had evolved in Vietnam, but with even greater emphasis on both offensive and defensive electronics and computers.

It was a costly business. A strike by 32 F-4D/E Phantom fighter/bombers had to be supported by well over 40 other aircraft: U-2 or SR-71 strategic reconnaissance aircraft first, followed by two RF-4Cs to gather last-minute intelligence at low level and check the weather over the target area, then two more RF-4Cs to take photographs of the target; they were followed by eight F-4Es to saturate a wide area around the target with chaff, four F-105D Thunderchief or F-4 Phantom Wild Weasels with anti-radiation missiles and cluster bombs to clear a path through the defences, and three or four radar-jamming EB-66C Destroyers with ECM and radar which could spot fighters taking off and SAMs being launched and warn the attacking force. Flying close to the attacking force were another eight F-4Es, with guns, to provide close escort, while the whole package operated under a MiGCAP umbrella provided by 16 F-4Ds with AIM-7 Sparrow and AIM-9 Sidewinder missiles and four more F-4Es with guns.

All the fighters would be in touch with an EC-121 Warning Star with airborne radar to search for enemy fighters and vector the MiGCAP fighters to them, and on the way in and out KC-135 tankers would be on hand to refuel the attacking force, and both the tankers and the EC-121s were protected by more fighters. After the strike, two more RF-4C flew photographic Bomb Damage Assessment (BDA) missions. The whole ethos of the strike package was offensive, its job to tear open the enemy's air defences at the Forward Line of Troops (FLOT) by battering the electronic systems, opening the way for more packages to follow, with heavier attack aircraft, to strike at the front-line armour, at supply and logistics targets further to the rear, and at the second echelon of Soviet forces following through.

The early strike packages were based on aircraft designed in the 1950s – the F-100, F-101, F-104, F-105, A-4, A-6, RF-5 and FU-8 – but the most influential fighter which, more than any other, had shown the way forward was the F-4 Phantom which had come through the Vietnam and Middle East wars with its reputation greatly enhanced, a true multi-role fighter and a flexible weapons system. The Phantom was built around the new technologies, a big radar, the ability to carry a wide variety of ordnance and ECM pods and the full range of guided missiles, and while fighter pilots had found the AAM frustrating in combat at first during their baptism in Vietnam, by the early 1970s they had become much more reliable. If Vietnam was the baptism of the Phantom and guided missile in its many forms, then the combination came of age in the War of Attrition and the Yom Kippur War. Yom Kippur was a watershed in the dialectic between gun and missile in aerial combat: in 1967 all Israel's 60 air-to-air victories were with cannon; between 1967 and 1973 the split was 70/30 between cannon and missile, but in the Yom Kippur War the split was reversed 30/70 in favour of the missile. The guided missile also came of age in ground and sea warfare in October 1973, particularly against armour, yet more evidence of the inexorable march of new technologies in warfare, and in the plethora of analysis which followed the Yom Kippur War there were commentators who believed they saw in the effectiveness of the guided missile not only the end of the manned fighter again but the end of tanks and surface warships, too.

Such ideas did not prevail in the 1970s and, in addition to improving the breed and extending the range of anti-aircraft missiles, the search also went on for two new capabilities, in particular a 'shoot down' AAM which could be used by fighters against low-flying attack aircraft and an 'all-aspect', close-range missile for dog-fighting to overcome the restriction on the current Sidewinder and Atoll IR AAMs which still had to be fired from the traditional six o'clock position.

For fighter pilots, the best defence against the ground-launched missile was low flying, and the new generation of tactical fighters and strike aircraft were designed to go very low, requiring ever higher levels of pilot skill. The first USAF low-level strike aircraft was the General Dynamics Tactical Fighter Experimental (TFX), which started life in 1960 as a high-speed, Mach 1.2 at sea level, long-range penetration fighter to replace the F-105 Thunderchief. At the same time, the US Navy was looking for a long-term replacement for the F-4 Phantom, with even longer range and an even more capable radar and missile system which could look down and shoot down over ranges of up to 150 miles.

When Secretary of Defense Robert McNamara took up his post in 1960, one of his first decisions was to combine these two requirements in the name of commonality between the services and cost effectiveness for the taxpayer. To meet the stringent requirements, the F-111 was designed from the outset as a two-seater, side by side, with variable geometry wings which could be swept back for high-speed flight and straightened for landing and take-off. There were continuous arguments between the USAF and the USN as to whose performance criteria would predominate, and its development was beset with many problems before the prototype flew in 1964.

The Navy was not happy with the final result and, after evaluation, turned it down, though it quietly continued work on the AWG-9 radar and the AIM-54 Phoenix long-range missile which they had planned for it.

The USAF did order the F-111, the world's first supersonic, multi-role, all-weather fighter bomber, a high-technology fighter with a highly capable radar, built-in electronic countermeasures and the first Terrain Following Radar (TFR), giving it the ability to fly at night, in all weathers, just fifty feet above the ground at, or near, the speed of sound, all with a range of 3,000 miles. The F-111 could operate without Wild Weasels, without EC-121 airborne radar, without fighter protection and without refuelling, and in March 1968 the USAF deployed six to Tahkli in Thailand for service over North Vietnam, just as Rolling Thunder was winding down. They carried out several raids in the North, but three were lost due, it was decided, to failures in the TFR system, and the others were brought back to the USA, though they were deployed in Europe as part of Flexible Response. The early problems had been ironed out, and in 1972 they were redeployed to Vietnam for the Linebacker operations, flying 4,000 combat missions, without support aircraft, in weather which kept all other aircraft grounded; seven were lost.

The RAF, which had seen its equivalent, the TSR-2, fly and then be cancelled by the Labour government in 1966, ordered F-111s instead, then saw that order cancelled too.

The Soviet Union followed the MiG-23 Flogger with the variable geometry Su-24 Fencer, which had broadly the same role as the F-111, but which was smaller, lighter and without the same degree of electronic sophistication. It was first introduced in 1974 but only operated inside the Soviet Union until 1982 when it was first deployed in Eastern Europe.

Once the US Navy had abandoned the F-111, and the USAF had turned it into a high-technology strike aircraft, the two services went their separate ways in replacing the Phantom – the Navy with the F-14 and the Air Force with the F-15, the first of a new generation of jet fighters which embodied both the new thinking in air warfare and the new technologies. The first was the Grumman F-14 Tomcat, which was rolled out in 1970 and flew for the first time on 21 December. By comparison to its predecessor, the Phantom, it was a monster: 40 per cent larger with close to twice the engine power and, compared to any previous fighter, it was a flying computer. It was a masterful compromise between the conflicting requirements of economic cruising speeds for range, supersonic flight in short bursts for manoeuvrability and combat, all combined with the low landing speed and high degree of control required for deck landings at sea. This was achieved using infinitely variable wings linked to a computer which gave the best angle of sweep for the speed and altitude.

After some debate it was decided to continue in the tradition of the Phantom with a two-man crew. In Vietnam, 40 per cent of visual sightings were made by the backseater in the Phantom even though he had very poor visibility. The back seat and canopy arrangement of the F-14 was designed to give the backseater far better visibility. A second pair of eyes and hands were also needed to manage the weapons system which had taken a quantum leap forward. The F-14 was a long-range interceptor, the idea being to patrol at a distance from the carrier group and detect the enemy well away from the warships, before it became a threat, and then engage enemy aircraft with long-range missiles without getting into close combat unless absolutely necessary. Just in case, the missiles were backed up by a single M61 20 mm Vulcan cannon. The F-14 was built around the AN/AWG-9, pulse-Doppler radar combined with the AIM-54 Phoenix AAM originally developed for the F-111, the first weapons system to have a real 'look down, shoot down' capability. It could sweep an area the size of England and Wales, identify low-level threats at up to 195 nautical miles and shoot them down at up to 90 nautical miles. To put that in perspective: a Tomcat flying over London would be able to detect an enemy aircraft over Newcastle, track it and shoot it down over Northampton.

The radar was backed up by on-board computers which could be updated through data links to other Tomcats, to Hawkeye AEW aircraft, the carrier and to satellites, extending the range of coverage even further and giving the crew a quantum leap in situational awareness. The AWG-9 had the computing power to track 24 targets separately, decide which six posed the greatest threat, display them on the Tactical Information Display (TDI) while still monitoring the others, then fire from its range of four AIM-7 Sparrow, four AIM-9 Sidewinder and up to six AIM-54 Phoenix AAMs which could either share the radar's lock-on and be fired in salvoes or be used to engage six targets at once; the downside was that each Phoenix cost $500,000. Nothing had been spared in building the F-14. At £17 million a copy, it was also the most expensive fighter ever built, a huge cost compared with $2 million for the Phantom, but on top of all the capability which was built into it, it was also 'a pilot's aeroplane', one which handled well in all configurations, one with few vices – true testimony to the philosophy that nothing but the best would do.

The USAF had a different problem from the US Navy. In April 1965 the Soviet Union claimed a world speed record of 1,144 m.p.h. for the Ye-266, in fact the prototype of a new fighter, the MiG-25 Foxbat, which was the Soviet Union's answer to the North American B-70 Valkyrie high-altitude, Mach 3 bomber. The B-70 had been cancelled, but the Soviet Union continued with the MiG-25, and it first appeared in public on Aviation Day 1967. The Pentagon believed it was an advanced air superiority fighter in the tradition of the MiG-21, a fighter which could be used as an interceptor but which could also dogfight, and that if so – and it was capable of Mach 3, as the US knew from its work on the SR-71 – then the Soviet Union must have made great strides, particularly in materials, to build it. This caused great concern in the USAF which immediately sought funds to build a Mach 3 fighter to counter it. At the same time, the new threat posed by the Warsaw Pact's huge increase in tactical aviation in Europe, and NATO's Flexible Response, needed a replacement for the Phantom.

The result was the specification for the F-15, a large, very capable, air superiority fighter, tailored to USAF requirements, with a top speed of over Mach 2.5, not enough to catch the MiG-25 but the best compromise with its role as a dogfighter and, as the saying went, 'not a pound for air to ground'. McDonnell-Douglas was awarded the contract to build an initial batch of 20 in 1969. The key characteristic of the F-15 was huge reserves of power from two F100-PW-100 engines specially developed for it. They operated at a far higher temperature than previous jet engines, using fewer compressor stages, making it much more efficient. The F-15 was built out of titanium which was lighter and stronger than steel and aluminium, making it light for its size, and parts of it were made from epoxy resins, further reducing its weight. The combination of engine power and lightness gave the F-15 a power to weight ratio greater than 1:1, giving it very high acceleration and an initial vertical rate of climb of 29,000 feet, the height of Everest, *per minute* to a ceiling of 65,000 feet.

The main difference between the F-15 Eagle, as it was named when it flew for the first time in June 1972, and its naval cousin, the F-14 Tomcat, was that it was a single-seater with the pilot having to do all the battle management tasks as well fly the aircraft and fight. The main similarity between the two aircraft was their new electronics and computers to help him do the job: seven per cent, 2,000 lb, of the empty weight of an F-15 was miniaturised electronics. The Eagle's APG-63 radar lacked the range of the Tomcat's AWG-9, the maximum detection range being 85 nautical miles, but range had deliberately been sacrificed for greater detail in the information it gave the pilot on the height, range and speed of targets. It was armed with four AIM-7 and four AIM-9 and a 20 mm M61 Vulcan cannon.

To assist the pilot with his workload, McDonnell-Douglas combined two new ideas known by the acronyms HUD and HOTAS. HUD stood for Head Up Display, a system that projected flight, navigation and target information on to the canopy in front of him, which meant he need not constantly be looking inside the cockpit to check instruments – all he had to do was focus at the distance of the canopy and green and red lights gave him all the information he needed. HOTAS stood for Hands On Throttle and Stick. A fighter pilot flies with his left hand on the throttle and his right hand on the control column, or stick. By placing many of the most important flight controls and switches either on the throttle or stick, especially those needed in combat, including those to select what information to display on the HUD, the pilot could fly without looking down into the cockpit or taking his hands off the main controls.

These two ideas, straight from the information age, and impossible without the revolution in miniaturised electronics, harked back to the timeless need for the fighter pilot to feel part of his machine, the small switches under his thumbs and fingers making him ever more an extension of that machine, or the machine an extension of him. He could change the information displays, change the range or elevation of the radar, fire the gun, select and fire the missiles, deploy flares and chaff against hostile missiles and radar, adjust the gunsight, make a radio transmission, interrogate a target using IFF, deploy the speed brake or trim the aircraft, without taking either hand off the controls and keeping his eyes outside the cockpit looking for the enemy. The information flow enabled him to make decisions and implement them in an uncomplicated, fluid way which men like Boelke had identified as crucial to the art and science of aerial combat in 1915. In another testimony to those early basic lessons, the F-15 still had simple mirrors, three of them, alongside the HUD to look backwards to check the six o'clock.

In the months following its first flight the F-15 broke a whole clutch of world performance records, just as its nemesis, the Foxbat, had done in 1965, taking eight new time to height records from the Soviet fighter. It was another pilot's aeroplane, and it was expensive: F-15s cost $6.5 million each, required around forty hours of maintenance for every flight, and one of its many thousand components would fail for every twenty minutes of flight time. Like the F-14, nothing had been spared to make it the best machine for the job, and it was an instant hit with pilots when it started arriving on USAF squadrons, mainly replacing Phantoms, in 1974.

Two years later, on 6 September 1976, Lt Viktor Balenko of the Soviet Air Force's IA-PVO was flying an MiG-25 Foxbat on a training exercise from his base at Sakharovka near Vladivostok in the Russian Far East. He suddenly broke off the mission and headed out into the Sea of Japan, activating an emergency bleeper which indicated to the Soviet controllers that he was about to crash, then switching it off to convince them that he had. He flew just above the waves, occasionally having to avoid fishing boats, but had to climb to 20,000 feet to save enough fuel to make it to his intended destination: Japan. Soviet and Japanese radar had both picked him up and sent fighters to intercept him but the weather was so bad they missed him. When he broke out of cloud at 1,800 feet over Japan he expected Japanese Phantoms to find him and guide him to a military airfield, but when fuel became critical he landed at a civil airport in the north of Japan.

Viktor Balenko had defected, and the Russians put enormous pressure on Japan to return both the pilot and his MiG-25 immediately, arresting and imprisoning Japanese fishermen without grounds as a demonstration of their firmness. They also flew fighter sorties right up to Japanese airspace to intimidate the Japanese, but they held firm and Balenko was handed over to the US military and granted political asylum in the USA in exchange for a lengthy and informative debriefing. His MiG-25 was taken to a military airfield near Tokyo where it was stripped down and examined in minute detail by US and Japanese experts, the first time the West had managed to get really close to one, and what they found was both surprising and reassuring. Rather than representing the breakthrough in metallurgy and aerodynamics that the USA had feared, the MiG-25 was shown to be a pure interceptor, a massive, manned missile of an aircraft which could not possibly dogfight. The MiG design bureau had stretched existing technologies to their limits. It was made of steel alloys and aluminium, making it very heavy to start with; it carried four of the largest air-to-air missiles in the world, the AA-6 Acrid, over twenty feet long and weighing three-quarters of a ton each, the equivalent of the AIM-54 Phoenix but with only a quarter of the range for a little under twice the size. Instead of microelectronics, it had vacuum valves and its huge radar was so powerful that it was reputed to kill rabbits on the calibration ranges at 1,000 metres by microwaving them in the open. The radar had been optimised for unjammability rather than range, and while it was virtually unjammable its range was under fifty miles. It had been produced quickly, purely to counter the threat posed by the B-70, but when that was cancelled the SAF had not abandoned the MiG-25 because they believed the B-70 could have been reinstituted at short notice. The MiG-25 was the culmination of the Soviet tradition of ground-controlled interceptors. Its systems were computerised, but instead of using the new technology to give the pilot more flexibility a computer allowed the ground controller to fly the aircraft to its target via a data link and the pilot, stripped of the ability to plan the battle himself, only took over when the target was visual to fire the missiles.

The speed and altitude records which the Foxbat had broken, and which had caused so much alarm in the West in 1965, had been achieved using highly specialised versions and at the expense of wrecking the engines. It could reach Mach 3.2, but above Mach 2.8 the engines ran out of control, leaving it with a real operational top speed similar to the F-15. It was a straight line speed too, and to achieve it the design parameters left it with very poor man-oeuvrability. In an ironic twist of fate, the perceived threat which the MiG-25 posed, and which had prompted the F-14 and F-15, even at the enormous cost they represented, left them without peers once the truth about the Foxbat was known. Its main effect was to stimulate the USA into perfecting the new generation of jet fighters, with the emphasis on microelectronics and computing power, areas in which the Soviet Union already lagged behind.

The F-14 and F-15 were expressions of the quality over quantity philosophy, of the highly skilled high-technology few against the less well-equipped many, but one of the problems with that phil-osophy was that it produced almost unaffordable aircraft. The F-14 in particular was so costly that it was nearly cancelled and had to be cut back in numbers, and the Navy ultimately bought 557 Tomcats instead of earlier plans for 750. Meanwhile, the Soviet Union was producing the MiG-23 Flogger and a ground attack version, the MiG-27, in thousands, and the Warsaw Pact would have a more than two to one advantage over NATO in combat aircraft in Western Europe. The USAF had planned to have around 800 F-15s, putting the emphasis on countering the MiG-25, but by the time the F-15 was flying in 1972 another strand of thinking was developing at NATO and in the Pentagon – that quantity had a quality all of its own.

As the Luftwaffe had found, the Me 262's performance advantage was no use against the huge numerical superiority of the Allies in the closing months of the Second World War, and when the MiG-15s had come across the Yalu in hundreds at a time the USAF fighters had had to fall back. They argued for a lightweight, multi-role fighter and announced a competition to build one in January 1972. It had to be highly manoeuvrable with plenty of power and good acceleration for close combat, be relatively small with a smokeless engine for low observability and simple to maintain, giving it a high sortie rate. Two companies, General Dynamics and Northrop, were chosen to build demonstrators: the YF-16 and YF-17.

The F-16 was built around just one of the F-15's F100 engines and was very light, giving a power to weight ratio better than 1:1 so there was plenty of extra power for climbing and accelerating, but the key characteristic, which gave it very high manoeuvrability, came from being inherently unstable. The balance between stability and instability had been a prime concern of fighter designers ever since the First World War. In a stable aircraft the centres of lift and gravity are close together. Move the centre of lift to the rear and the aircraft can change direction far more quickly, giving it an advantage in combat over a more stable aircraft but making it much more difficult, if not impossible, to fly. To overcome that problem, instead of movements of the control column being transmitted to the moving surfaces through power controls, they were transmitted by a computerised 'fly-by-wire system', the problems of instability being reconciled through four computers before the right message went down the wires. Once the computerised control system had overcome the instability problems, there were other aerodynamic advantages, for example, the tailplane could be used to generate lift, keeping the size of the wings down and adding to its lightness. It had a small nose with a small radar and a single M61 20 mm cannon with two Sidewinders, one on each wingtip. It also had a simple bubble canopy, with no metal struts to impair vision.

The YF-17 was twin-engined and the engines were not fully developed; it was 25% heavier than the YF-16, and while the F-16 could go into production as built the YF-17 still needed more development. The F-16 was the most manoeuvrable fighter in the world and there was export interest from Holland, Belgium, Denmark and Norway, who wanted a multi-role version, and General Dynamics won the contest.

The F-16 became the backbone of NATO tactical air forces and it ranks as one of the most successful US export fighters: of the 3,835 built by 1994, the USAF bought 2,203 and the US Navy 26, the balance of 1,570 going to Turkey (240), Holland (213), Israel (210), Egypt (174), Belgium (160), South Korea (160), Pakistan (111), Denmark (70), Greece (80), Norway (74), Thailand (36), Portugal (20), Bahrain and Indonesia (12), and Singapore (10), making it the most successful export fighter in the West since the F-4 Phantom.

Northrop teamed up with McDonnell-Douglas which, with its experience of building carrier-based aircraft, turned the YF-17 into a contender for the US Navy's requirement for a new carrier-borne attack aircraft, the F/A-18 Hornet, which flew for the first time in November 1978. The F/A-18 was a single-seater with a fighter and attack role, and to ease the pilot workload it made full use of the electronic revolution: it took HUD and HOTAS from the F-15 and in the fighter role, in addition to the single M61 Vulcan cannon, it carried two AIM-7 Sparrows which could be replaced by a Forward-Looking Infra-Red (FLIR) pod and a laser tracking pod and the AGM-65 Maverick laser-guided missile in the attack role, so it could switch between its two roles very quickly. The US Navy initially ordered some 800 Hornets but by 1994 total production stood at 1,366 of which 948 were for the USA, the remainder going to Canada, Australia, Finland, Switzerland, Kuwait and Spain.

The F-14, F-15, F-16 and F/A-18 were the fruits of an electronic revolution which they in turn had helped to drive. The F-14 and F-15 were very expensive: by the early 1980s the cost of a new F-14 had risen to $30 million and an F-15 to $20 million, but they were the best fighters in the world. The F-16 and F/A-18 were relatively simple fighters which could be used very flexibly in the battlefield, but even they had substantial amounts of computing power. Computers were at the heart of the new generation of fighters: the airframes were expected to last thirty years or more, but the electronics could be updated constantly as new threats developed and new weapons systems were devised to counter those threats, adapting to different missions using the astonishing range of new smart weapons which were different fruits of the same computer-driven revolution. By detaching one set of missiles, ECM pods, low-level navigation pods, laser trackers, laser-guided bombs and imaging systems, they could perform a wide variety of roles – anything for which the pilot was trained. To remind them that they were still fighters, they all carried a single M61 Vulcan cannon for last-ditch dogfighting.

The same revolution was driving new variants of the AAMs with three new capabilities: range in general, and beyond visual range (BVR) in particular, 'look down, shoot down' for low-flying targets, both reliant on the fighter's radar and on the missile's own radar guidance, and a short-range missile with an 'all-aspect' capability. The Sidewinder had been through many modifications to improve its performance, including a variety of ways of cooling the seeker head before use to make it more sensitive to heat, more precise guidance systems once it was in flight and more power in the rocket motor to produce higher acceleration to hit ever-faster targets, but the breakthrough came in 1976 when, after long development, the first Alasca (All-Aspect Capability) Sidewinder, the AIM-9L, went into production. The breakthrough came in the sensitivity of the IR seeker which could detect the heat generated by the friction between the target aircraft and the air.

During the 1970s the Israelis also updated the Shafrir IR close-range missile, which was itself a copy of the Sidewinder, into the all-aspect Python III which emerged in 1981 for export sales. In Europe, British Aerospace (BAe) developed the SRAAM (Short Range Advanced Anti-Aircraft Missile) as a potential successor to the Sidewinder. It was very successful in tests, but when the all-aspect AIM-9L Sidewinder became available in 1977 the RAF bought the latter instead. Although SRAAM continued in development, it was at a very low level of activity.

The AIM-7 Sparrow continued to be upgraded, as did its British equivalent, the Sky Flash, but both were regarded as requiring a completely new replacement. Britain opted for Sky Flash 2, while the USA went for the Advanced Medium-Range Anti-Aircraft Missile, AIM-120 AMRAAM, a fire-and-forget, radar-guided, BVR missile, which started out as a US Navy/USAF joint venture aimed at replacing the Sparrow in the 1990s.

In 1978, with European and American aerospace companies both developing competing advanced short and medium range AAMs, the cost of development for the West grew unnecessarily and an agreement was made that the USA would concentrate on AMRAAM, while the British work on SRAAM was combined with a German partner, Bodenseewerk Geratetechnik (BGT), who had also been working on a short-range AAM, to produce the Advanced Short-Range Anti-Aircraft Missile (ASRAAM) which became AIM-132, designed to replace the Sidewinder in the 1990s.

In Europe, the Warsaw Pact continued to rely heavily on ground-based defences with around 12,000 SA-2 Guideline and SA-3 Goa SAMs at over 1,200 fixed sites, with mobile SA-6 and a new, low-level mobile system, the SA-8 Gecko, coupled with shoulder-launched SA-7. To counter the SAMs, and as the F-15 replaced the Phantom, so NATO used the Phantom in the Suppression of Air

Defences (SEAD) role, replacing the F-105 Wild Weasels of Vietnam vintage. Their job remained what it had been in Vietnam: 'first in, first out', to take on the SAMs. Just as the capability of the AAM had increased, so the SEAD missiles had also been improved. The AGM-45 Shrike was still in service, but in 1972 the US Navy started development of a new anti-radiation missile, the AGM-88 High-Speed Anti-Radiation Missile (HARM), which could be fired from twelve miles, reaching a speed of Mach 2 and shortening the time available to the SAM radar sites to fire before being hit. Another feature was that it could be fired with only the minimal information from radar contacts which were too weak for a lock-on, its own radar continuing the search after launch, and it could be pre-programmed from other electronic intelligence sources and fired blind in the direction of known radar, and if one switched on, it immediately homed in on it. HARM entered NATO service in 1983.

The computer found its way into many aspects of air warfare in the 1970s, but nowhere was the impact felt more widely than in the processing of information about the aerial battlefield and disseminating it to fighters. In the Vietnam era, the piston-engined, USAF Super Constellation-based EC-121 Warning Stars and Navy E-2A Hawkeyes had provided airborne radar and some control, but both services needed a new and much faster system. The US Navy upgraded the Hawkeye in 1971 with a new radar with a range of 300 miles; the early models simply sent data back to the carrier, from which it was then passed on to the fighters by sea-borne controllers, but with the new E-2C Hawkeye, the controllers were on board the aircraft, increasing not only the amount of information available but the speed with which it reached the fighter pilots.

On 26 January 1973 the USAF gave the go-ahead for the development of a replacement for the EC-121, and two years later Congress approved funding for a completely new AWACS, the Boeing E-3 Sentry, based on the 707–320 airliner, with a huge, rotating radar antenna on its back. Inside were fourteen stations for operators to marshal the information from the AN/APY-1 Overland Downlook Radar (ODR) and other radar, then process all the data with the assistance of three on-board IBM CC-2E computers which could store well over a million words and process 740,000 separate operations per second to detect and identify every aircraft which came within range, then store that information in a rapidly changing situation. The precise details of its full capability are a closely guarded secret, but at altitude it can look up into the stratosphere or down to the ground from the middle of a cylinder of airspace at least 500 miles across so if it was over the middle of the North Sea it could probably cover the whole sea from coast to coast. All the information could then be passed through the Joint Tactical Information Distribution System (J-TIDS) straight to fighters' own visual displays in what is called a 'picture call', a view of the complete battle area, making the individual fighter pilot aware of the whole position in a snapshot, increasing his situational awareness and his ability to make decisions.

In addition to the 34 AWACS aircraft, the first of which went into service in 1978 with the USAF, NATO bought another 18 for delivery from 1982. They cost slightly over $110 million each, slightly more than the total cost of R&D and purchase of the first batch of 554 F-86A Sabres just twenty-five years earlier.

By the mid-1970s the cost of developing and building state-of-the-art fighters was beyond the pocket of any single country except the two superpowers. France continued to build lightweight fighters such as the Mirage 2000. Its attempt to build a F-15 equivalent, the Super Mirage 4000 which flew for the first time in 1979, was abandoned in the mid-1980s. Britain joined forces with Germany and Italy to build the Tornado multi-role combat aircraft, which developed into a penetration fighter to match the F-111. One of its specialities was the destruction of enemy airfields, which became a priority, and special runway destruction bombs, JP-233, were developed for the Tornado; later versions, with Foxhunter radar, were turned into air defence fighters. Another British answer to the airfield problem was to dispense with the airfield altogether, making fighters which could operate from anywhere. That was the thinking behind the British Vertical/Short Take Off and Landing (VSTOL) fighter. All the major aircraft-building countries tried to build such a fighter, but the only successful example was the BAe Harrier. Its main task was ground attack in support of troops in the battlefield, operating from fields and small hard areas, and it adapted for the Royal Navy as the FRS.1 Sea Harrier to operate from the smaller British aircraft carriers.

After the Yom Kippur War in 1973 both the Israelis and the Arabs conducted full-scale enquiries into what had gone wrong. After four wars in which it had come off worst in the air, Egypt turned away from the Soviet Union as its supplier of aircraft, pilot training and doctrine, but, perversely, it was the comparative success of the Arabs in 1973 which made the Israelis rigorous in examining their own failures. The Yom Kippur War had lasted three times as long as the Six Day War and IAF losses had been two and a half times as heavy. The Israeli aura of invincibility had been seriously dented, if not punctured. They had relied on their intelligence services giving them adequate warning if war was imminent, and that a combination of their secret but, in reality, well-known nuclear capability, the IAF's prowess and the quality of their army would deter Arab attacks. The Arabs judged that if Israel proper was not attacked then the war would not go nuclear so Egypt limited its attacks to the Sinai and liberating its own territory. Israel had delayed mobilisation, believing they could hold initial attacks more easily than turned out to be the case, and this thinking helped to cause the initial setbacks, making it more difficult to recover. In the final analysis, the Israelis had to admit to themselves that in 1973 they had suffered from simple overconfidence.

On the battlefield, and in the air, the clear lesson was that aircraft, tanks and ships were increasingly vulnerable to ever more accurate and deadly missiles. It also showed that the rate at which modern munitions were used was much higher than expected, that much higher stockpiles had to be held and that modern warfare was very expensive, but the biggest lessons were in communications, command and co-ordination and it was here that the electronic revolution could be applied to improve effectiveness. With war on two fronts, Israel had lacked proper central HQs to co-ordinate both its air force and the support for ground forces, and it had been a scramble to sort out the priorities in the first few hours: poor co-ordination between air force and army had denied the army the support on which it relied. The early air battles developed as the opposing forces met up rather than being planned; there was no central management of the air-to-air battles. Caught by surprise, aerial reconnaissance was slow and inefficient with no real-time intelligence. Once the battle had been joined there was a clear lack of the latest ECM systems to counter the SAM systems and they had to be shipped from the USA as a matter of urgency. The Israeli pilots learnt very quickly how to put them into effective use, but overcoming the missile threat had taken longer than it should have.

Israel's armed forces were reorganised, re-equipped and expanded as a result, based on a more integrated approach, using new weapons from the USA and from its own arms industry, which received a huge boost after 1973, especially in electronics and high technology. Gen. Benny Peled, the IAF commander during the Yom Kippur War, was in charge of air force re-organisation, and he put a large part of the effort into airborne intelligence-gathering, especially tiny Remotely Piloted Vehicles (RPVs), such as the Scout and Mastiff which were home-produced and could loiter over enemy-held territory for hours, gathering electronic or photographic intelligence. In 1978 the IAF received the first of four E-2C Hawkeyes, to which IAI added their own upgraded radar and electronic systems.

The IAF mission priorities were being able to fight for and gain air superiority; be capable of more strategic actions if required, including deep penetration and interdiction while being able to continue to provide ground forces with close support, though this was relegated because Gen. Peled, like many others, felt that the increased cost of fighters made using them for close support too expensive. He had to have a bigger air force to do the job. On the eve of the Yom Kippur War the IAF had 340 combat aircraft, fighters and fighter bombers; by the end of 1973 it was back to that strength and by 1980 it had grown to 650, and they were all of higher quality than those possessed by the Arabs.

Within eighteen months of the end of the Yom Kippur War Israel had built its own supersonic fighter, the Kfir, a derivative of the Mirage fuselage around a single J-79 engine which also powered the Phantom. It was a good lightweight fighter built around a home-produced radar, designed to replace the Skyhawks in attack role but able to dogfight. For air superiority, Israel wanted the best, and it went for the F-15, the first of which arrived exactly three years after the Yom Kippur War on 10 October 1976, the first foreign country to receive the new top of the range US fighter. Later the same year the first of Israel's F-16s arrived. These purchases were also part of retaining air superiority as the main function but moving from close air support of the army to breaking down the enemy's ground-based air defences, longer range strike and interdiction.

Throughout the IAF expansion and its adoption of the computer revolution, Peled never took his gaze far from having the best, and that included the best people – the most important factor for any IAF commander. When Gen. David Ivry replaced Peled as commander of the IAF in 1977, it was a much larger and more effective fighting force, reliant on a much higher degree of high technology, much of it home-produced, but in human terms little had changed since the traditions of the IAF had been laid down by Dan Tolkovsky – that only the best would succeed in becoming fighterpilots.

Microelectronics had widened the technological gap between the two sides in the Cold War. The microprocessor revolution in the USA and the West generally had become part of Western popular culture, finding its way into the Walkman mini-cassette recorders, fax machines, washing machines and photocopiers, while in the Soviet Union it was largely secret and unavailable outside military applications. Consequently, computers were not part of Soviet everyday life and they were more expensive to develop and produce. America has often been accused of waging the Cold War with dollars rather than weapons, that the USA, because it was richer and could afford to produce ever more costly weapons systems, forced the poorer Soviet Union to overspend on defence. That may be true, but with its huge economy the USA could afford the best and its whole tradition was to have the best. The difference was that the USA put its resources into expensive technology to give its fighter pilots the best that money could buy, which was a costly policy, and the Soviet Union put its resources into maintaining very large air forces with a lower level of individual capability.

Both sides in the Cold War had learned lessons from the Vietnam and Middle East wars. America's response had been to put even greater faith in the traditional policy of excellence, and introduced specialist air combat training schools, like Top Gun, and ordered two new high-technology fighters, the F-14 and F-15, but the Soviet Union was smarting from the drubbing inflicted on their Arab client states by the Israelis and by the quality of US air power as demonstrated in the final year of the Vietnam War, especially the determination of US fighter pilots in penetrating the combination of SAMs and ground-controlled fighters. It, too, was forced to examine its doctrine, equipment and training and undertook a fundamental re-evaluation in the 1970s. One of its first responses was to issue specifications to the MiG and Sukhoi design bureaux for a new, highly manoeuvrable, high-technology fighter to take on the NATO strike packages. At the same time, the SAF was determined to sustain and improve PVO-Strany's SAMs and interceptors and build up Frontal Aviation's offensive capability, and the combination of these two policies, while also seeking to match the US superfighters, virtually from scratch, put a huge strain on the resources of the SAF and on the Soviet economy.

By the early 1970s senior commanders in the SAF had become acutely aware that the changing world of military aviation would also require a re-evaluation of pilot training, and at the heart of any change in thinking would be the question of increased fighter pilot autonomy. Soviet doctrine had been based heavily on the GCI system for decades, and the MiG-25 had been designed around the principle that the pilot had little or no room for autonomous action. This 'passive' approach permeated Soviet flying training and fighter pilot mentality. Training still relied heavily on repeating drills and procedures rather than the individual flair and aggressive spirit required for the new air defence and tactical environment in which combat would be at lower levels, at higher speeds, with long-range AAMs. On top of that, the microprocessor had ushered in the age of the electronic battlefield, and far from requiring less from the pilot it required more: specialist electronic warfare aircraft, such as the EB-66, Shrike-equipped Wild Weasels, and the ECM pods carried by all fighters, had given pilots the ability to jam and destroy the radar and radio communications on which Soviet GCI systems depended.

Soviet doctrine in both air defence and tactical aviation relied on a mixture of fighters and SAMs operating in the same piece of airspace, which called for a high degree of control to avoid fatal accidents between the two. The dangers had been illustrated in the shooting down of Gary Powers which cost PVO-Strany at least one of its own fighters to a 'friendly' SA-2. To provide air cover for an armoured offensive in Western Europe, and to counter the strike packages, Frontal Aviation used a mobile version of the integrated system of SAMs and tactical fighters, moving forward under strict control from the ground. It was a difficult task at the best of times, with one SAM unit covering another while it moved, requiring a huge effort to provide the tight control needed to manage the airspace over the battle area. That control in turn relied on communications which NATO would be jamming and bombing, further reducing the effectiveness of fighter pilots used to operating under tight control while also leaving them more vulnerable to friendly fire. Either way, the implications were that the greater the autonomy of the fighter pilot – the greater freedom he had to search for and identify targets and act on his own initiative – the more effective he would be. Soviet commanders knew they had to change.

The need for change in pilot selection and training was evident as the first examples of the fourth generation of Soviet fighters, the MiG-29, took shape. Work started in 1972 and its first flight was on 6 October 1977 at the Ramenskoye flight test centre where it was first observed and photographed by US satellites and dubbed Fulcrum by NATO. The MiG-29 was lightweight, compared with the F-15S, closer in size to the F/A-18, but with two engines it was a single seater with HUD, armed with a 30 mm cannon and six AA-10 Alamo SARH missiles linked to a pulse-Doppler radar, giving the pilot a good look down/shoot down capability against low-flying targets, AA-11 Archer close-range IR AAMs linked to a helmet sight, leaving the Soviet fighter pilot free to search for and identify targets for himself and fight his own battles largely free of tight GCI control, able to use his own equipment and his own initiative. It was a huge step forward for the SAF, but it was 1985 before the MiG-29 went into operational service.

Development of the Soviet Union's second new fighter, the Sukhoi Su-27, had started in 1969 but it did not fly until May 1977. Two test pilots were known to have lost their lives in testing and it went through a complete redesign before going into production in 1979 with the first flight of a production aircraft in 1981. It was an air superiority fighter capable of converting to a ground attack role and was first officially referred to in 1982; given the NATO name Flanker, it entered service in 1984. To support the new generation of fighters with airborne radar, the Soviet Union also updated its AEW&C aircraft from the Tu-126 Moss to the Il-76

Mainstay, which also started development in the early 1970s, and there were four in service by 1984.

The Soviet Union was a decade behind the West in introducing the new generation of fighters, partly because there was a great deal of catching up to do in developing the technologies, but it was also because the two new fighters had far-reaching implications for SAF organisation and training, both on the ground and in the air. Soviet fighters had traditionally been relatively simple to produce and maintain; they were very robust, able to operate from relatively primitive airfields in very harsh weather conditions. The SAF had a core of career technical officers and warrant officers with good training and skills, but most of the technicians who maintained the aircraft were conscripts doing three years' service, making it difficult and expensive to train them to the standard needed for the existing inventory, let alone more complicated aircraft such as the MiG-29 and Su-27. High serviceability and quick turnaround between sorties is crucial to an air force in war, especially with lower numbers of highly capable aircraft, as in the West, but a large, low-technology air force like the SAF swiftly becomes a small, low-technology air force if a large proportion of its aircraft cannot fly because of serviceability problems, and the sheer size of SAF and the nature of many of its technical crews made absorbing such advanced fighters difficult.

The standard of Soviet fighter pilots varied considerably. The best pilots in the best air regiments were on a par with those in the West, but standards were not uniform either in regiments or between regiments, all suffering from a general lowering of standards to that of the least able, and that was inherent in the Soviet system of selection and training pilots, which was large, bureaucratic, inflexible, ideologically driven and open to abuse. The status of SAF pilots in the Soviet Union was very high, their salaries three times that of a doctor, for example, a highly privileged group in Soviet society, with far better housing, food and travel than almost any other group. That status meant that there was a strong desire to become a pilot, and competition to get in was high. One of the consequences was that the SAF was disproportionately Slav and Russian, both in pilots and in career technical staff. Academic achievement in the Russian language was part of the entry qualification, as was study of the history and literature of the USSR, the training manuals were in Russian and conscripts from the ethnic minorities were used largely for menial duties. The selection system was tough, based on physical and psychological soundness as well as high academic achievement, but it also took into account political activity and influence from the Party was always helpful, and conformity outweighed that spark of special, individual talent and aptitude for the job.

The approach to combat training was completely different from that in the West: after four years of training as an officer and basic flying training, a new pilot was sent straight to an SAF regiment as a lieutenant where he received his combat training. If the senior pilots were good pilots and good instructors, the newcomers were well trained and if not then standards fell. Western air forces standardise such training in specialist flying schools at which standards are checked and the weaker pupils weeded out.

Victor Balenko, who was an instructor before flying the MiG-25, was among the best in the SAF. His account of the Soviet training process was of an unwieldy system which, once a trainee pilot was in, was supposed to turn him into a pilot, come what may, unless he showed a monumental lack of aptitude. On one occasion he reported to his seniors that one of his pupils was a danger both to himself and to the unit in the air, but he found it almost impossible to have him taken off flying duties because he had been selected by the system – because the flying school had targets to meet and it would reflect badly on the flying school, and the system, if it failed to turn him into a pilot.

He also told his USAF debriefers of flying exercises being faked when the weather was too bad to fly so that the record showed that it had taken place when, in fact, they had just flown round the airfield, dumping tons of surplus fuel over the countryside to make the record show that it had been used. On another unit two pilots were grounded when they conspired to make it appear that one had intercepted the other when actually the target aircraft had made it deliberately easy; they were only caught because the exercise had been monitored on radar.

Soviet pilot training relied heavily on a great deal of theoretical work before combat flying training, and that training relied heavily on performing drills, on having a response to every conceivable tactical situation, rather than encouraging individual personal initiative and the ability to cope with the unexpected. While the more enlightened SAF commanders exhorted their unit commanders to instil greater 'creativity' in their fighter pilots, it was difficult to encourage initiative and self-reliance in a very ordered society in which rigidity of ideas and conformity of thinking are considered virtues and the means of advancement. In Soviet military culture it was very difficult to make the U-turn in basic attitudes which was needed to operate the new fighters, and the problem had started to manifest itself even before the MiG-29 and Su-27 came into service. As early as 1972, the SAF recognised that many of the new pilots arriving at MiG-25 interceptor regiments were not up to the job. The Foxbat, straight line interceptor though it was, was a quantum leap in terms of performance and complexity compared with its predecessors and many of them found the stress of operating it at the limit, which is what they would have to do in war, too much to handle. The initial response of the Soviet training system was greater emphasis on its traditional methods and trying to level out the skills in units, and between units, rather than making harsher judgements on individuals, concentrating on the best and creating more uniform standards by selection and a centralised system of air combat training.

The recognition that the level of competence differed widely was allowed for in the regulations that governed flight safety in training, which were set to allow for the lowest standard, a levelling down, which meant that some of the more difficult forms of flying training, low-level combat for example, were restricted in their scope, making it more difficult for those with real talent to practise their skills in a realistic environment.

The new high-technology age had rediscovered the age-old importance of manoeuvring to advantage in air combat, of individual prowess and the need for an offensive spirit in fighter pilots. Largely behind closed doors, a debate took place in the SAF between the competing needs of modern air combat, which required greater autonomy on the part of pilots, and the need for strict control for both military and doctrinal reasons. The debate covered both offensive tactical operations and air defence, and it was between the traditionalists who wanted to maintain a system based on strict discipline and order in the air and those who favoured a more freelance culture.

In the Soviet Union of the 1970s, the Communist Party also played a part in the debate through the political officers in each regiment. Senior SAF officers did recognise, and argued strongly, that advanced flying schools with plenty of realistic training in ACM, combined with more emphasis on pilot initiative and purposefulness, was the key to getting the best out of the new fighters. Slowly the system started to change. In 1984, Marshal of Aviation Golubev, a Second World War fighter pilot and Hero of the Soviet Union, was quoted in an article advocating greater autonomy in fighter operations as recognising that such autonomy was only possible given particular qualities on the part of the individual, the qualities of a 'hunter' as he put it.

Sources published since the collapse of the Soviet Union show that while the regiment remained the basis of combat training the SAF did start to centralise and standardise aspects of it, and in 1974 a regiment of specialist instructors was established at Kara-Kum in Turkmenistan, which enjoyed good weather all the year round, flying the latest MiG-21s to develop realistic air combat training along Top Gun lines. Whole regiments would visit the base and engage in exercises with the staff which then assessed their effectiveness. Therein lay their difference to the West: at Top Gun and similar combat training schools, Western pilots go as, and are assessed as, individuals.

Senior NATO commanders have never been in any doubt that the best fighter pilots in the SAF were a match for the best in Western air forces, even if their aircraft still lagged behind the West, especially in microelectronics and computers, but that, equally, the quality of pilots was very variable. They were also aware that the technology gap was narrowing, as demonstrated by the MiG-29 and Su-27, and that Soviet commanders were aware of the deficiencies in their system and were making efforts to correct them, too.

The doctrine of Flexible Response to a Soviet armoured thrust through Western Europe relied heavily on the flexibility and effectiveness of the NATO air forces facing it, and that effectiveness was dependent not only on the latest technology but, above all, on the priceless asset of the skill and determination of their pilots. For NATO, continuing to enhance both was the best way to stay ahead of the Soviet Union. Part of the advanced training of US fighter pilots at Top Gun and at USAF fighter pilot competitions such as

William Tell, which were inaugurated in the early 1970s, involved using Pilotless Target Aircraft (PAS) for practise with AAMs. One such was the BQM-34A Firebee I, a variation of the unmanned reconnaissance aircraft which had been used in Vietnam.

In 1971 the use of unmanned aircraft in training was taken a stage further: a Firebee was adapted for simulated combat between manned and unmanned aircraft using MASTACS (Manoeuvrability Augmentation System for Tactical Air Combat Simulation), which enabled the Firebee to be flown by a pilot on the ground. On 10 May the CO of Top Gun, Cdr John C. Smith, flew in the back seat of one of three Phantoms which took part in the experiment; he was in overall control of the manned aircraft. In charge of the unmanned Firebee was a senior instructor from Top Gun, Cdr John Pitzen, with a 'pilot', Alan Donaldson, from the Firebee's manufacturers beside him on the ground. Donaldson sat in a simulated cockpit with a display in front of him showing the view from a television camera in the nose of the Firebee and surrounded by flight instruments fed by a data link. Without a pilot, the Firebee could pull much tighter turns at much higher g loadings than the Phantoms, making a 180 degree turn in just twelve seconds to get into the six o'clock of the top men at Top Gun; had the Firebee been armed, it could have shot them down. The prospect of unmanned fighters loomed, but the technology of the day left the Firebees with only very short range, they had to be dropped from a parent aircraft and, with most of their computer power on the ground and being transmitted by data links, they would be vulnerable to jamming. They continued to form part of the training regime of the USAF and US Navy, both as targets and also in air combat manoeuvring, but while the fighter pilot fraternity looked askance at any idea that they might one day be used to replace manned fighters in combat they had been given a tantalising glimpse of the future and of debates to come.

In 1979 NASA built two unmanned, High Manoeuvrability Aircraft Technology Aircraft (HiMAT) to explore the aerodynamics of transonic flight, the speed at which much combat took place. They, too, were dropped from a parent aircraft, a B-52 bomber, from 45,000 feet, were very short range and, like the Firebee, much of their computing power was on the ground, but in twenty-six test flights they showed that they would have been impossible to shoot down by manned fighters in a dogfight. What the unmanned experimental aircraft did emphasise was that the best defence of the manned fighter against an unmanned, highly manoeuvrable aircraft with the potential to fight back was the ability to engage them at long range with missiles, shooting them down at twenty to thirty miles before they got into a turning fight at close quarters where they would have the advantage, and the Navy's Phoenix missile showed it was capable of engaging them at that range.

As the computer revolution of the 1970s moved into the 1980s, greater computing power in the West was used to improve fighter pilot training by building ever more realistic simulators, where pilots could become more intimate with the nuances of their fighters and more familiar with those of potential enemies in a realistic, but much less costly way than mock combat with real aircraft. Fighting imaginary battles against computers, programmed to mimic the performance of enemy aircraft by projecting images of those aircraft on to huge screens around the simulator, was a way of honing skills, but simulation, however realistic, is no replacement for the real thing. From Vietnam onwards real, hard, mock combat had become a priority, 'turning and burning' against dissimilar fighters whose performance was as near as possible to that of the enemy, flown by instructor pilots who were versed in the latest Soviet tactics, the philosophy of 'fight like you train'.

The air battles for superiority in the skies over Europe have been rehearsed many times above huge tracts of the unpopulated parts of the USA, but in the 1980s even these exercises were subjected to computerisation through the Tactical Aircrew Combat Training System (TACTS) and Air Crew Manoeuvring Instrumented (ACMI) systems. Fighters taking part were fitted with pods that monitored every move the pilot made in relation to his adversary – every twitch of the stick, every simulated weapon firing – then the data was transmitted back to the training centre to be analysed by yet more computers. After the exercise, every move of every pilot in the exercise could be replayed in a debriefing suite the size of a cinema, every mistake analysed, showing each pilot and his colleagues how he might have fought the battle to greater advantage. The first such systems were installed at Nellis AFB, the USAF's equivalent to the Navy's Top Gun, and NATO has joined in since with more electronic combat training centres in Sardinia, at Cold Lake, Canada and at Chung-Chu in South Korea. Apart from training in procedures, it also encourages the competitive streak in fighter pilots by pinpointing with great accuracy any mistakes, making them ever more determined to be top of the pile after the exercise and not to have to answer for any basic mistakes when they were replayed to them after the flight.

Even as the first fruits of the computer revolution were transforming air warfare in the 1980s, the seeds of the next phase were being sown. Less than a decade after the first flight of the F-15, in 1981, the USAF started work on planning its replacement, the Advanced Tactical Fighter (ATF), a high-technology fighter which would take the manned fighter into the twenty-first century. The United States also used the electronic revolution to go down the unmanned route, developing a whole range of intelligence-gathering UAVs, or RPVs. Since 1973 Lockheed's famous Skunk Works in Los Angeles have pursued a top-secret, or black, project to produce a fighter invisible to radar. Air warfare had been increasingly reliant on radar since the Battle of Britain in 1940, and any country which possessed an aircraft that was undetectable by radar, a stealth aircraft, would have a considerable advantage. The original concept for stealth was contained in a Russian academic paper on microwave radiation in 1962, but the engineers at Lockheed who read the paper used it to offer the USAF an invisible aeroplane. They used two techniques – deflecting radar impulses at an angle which made them difficult for the receiver to pick them up again, and Radar Absorbent Material (RAM) which weakened the signal that went back to the receiver.

Much of the early work was used in the SR-71 reconnaissance aircraft, but by 1974 they had an order for three proof of concept aircraft. It was tested in great secrecy at Groom Lake, Nevada in 1977. The F-117A Nighthawk, as it was christened, was subsonic, a very draggy aircraft, not really a fighter at all. Relying completely on stealth to escape detection, its curious shape made it quite difficult to fly, causing its pilots to give it the unofficial name, Wobblin Goblin. Manoeuvrability was very low on the list of priorities and it would come off very badly in a dogfight, but its mission was night penetration and precision attack, and it could only fly at night otherwise it was visible to the naked eye which would defeat the object. The F-117A, what many people saw as heralding a new age in air warfare, entered operational service in great secrecy in 1983.

The technical advances in jet fighters and their weaponry between the 1970s and early 1980s were as great, if not greater, than those of the 1950s. They were also infinitely more expensive and one of the main results of that was that as the aircraft and the pilots became more capable so they were required in fewer numbers, concentrating ever more capability in a single pair of hands. The difference from the 1950s was that, even with the huge emphasis on new technologies, the basic offensive nature of air power was always recognised – that attack was the best policy, even in the face of all the deadly wizardry of SAMs, and that the pilot was the key element in finding a way through by individual skill and courage.

CHAPTER EIGHT

The Uneasy Peace

President Anwar Sadat's strategic objective in the Yom Kippur War had been to destabilise Israel, to cause serious casualties in a country with a small population and reduce its willingness to wage war in the future. From that position he hoped to reclaim Sinai and create a new political climate in which he could negotiate with Israel. He also wanted to dent Israel's image of invincibility, particularly that of its air force. By crossing the Suez Canal, he established an honourable position for Egypt by the performance of its armed forces, even though in the end Israel had them at its mercy. Sadat had seen that America held the key to negotiating with Israel, and in the closing stages of the war he saw that engaging with America was the way ahead. In November 1977 he made a speech to Israel's parliament, the Knesset, a landmark in the process which led to a peace treaty signed on 18 September 1978: Egypt recognised Israel diplomatically and the Sinai desert, Israel's great buffer zone, went back to Egypt.

Anwar Sadat had seen his country defeated three times by Israel, and the IAF had been the key to victory each time. Israeli pilots, flying largely American aircraft, and using American technology, had overcome the air defence system provided by the Russians, and given the Israeli army the upper hand. As Sadat engaged with the Americans so he turned his back on the Soviet Union, whose aircraft, weapons systems, doctrine and training had been shown to be inferior to those of the West. America responded positively and gained influence with Egypt by agreeing to equip its air force. In June 1978 the US Congress ratified the sale of arms to Arab countries – 35 Phantoms and 40 F-16s to Egypt and F-15s and AWACS to Saudi Arabia – once a peace treaty with Israel was signed. It has never been confirmed, but there have been reports that Egypt supplied the USAF with MiG-23 Floggers which were then used in dissimilar air combat training at Nellis AFB in Nevada. The USA also supplied Israel with 75 F-16s, but the prize came after a lot of negotiation and heart-searching by the USA, and by the IAF when in 1976 it became the first export customer to be allowed to buy 25 F-15As for a reported $24 million each. They were everything the IAF wanted, and they wanted 26 more which arrived two years later, the F-15C model, with four E-2C Hawkeye AEW aircraft to act as airborne warning and control for them.

The peace treaty between Israel and Egypt angered much of the rest of the Arab world, and Syria would have no part in the peace deal, remaining firmly in the Soviet sphere of influence, as did Iraq. The PLO not only rejected the idea of a peace deal with Israel but established bases in Lebanon and continued their struggle from across Israel's northern border. In 1974, in the worst of many incidents, they took children hostage in their school in the Israeli village of Maalot, all of whom were killed when Israeli commandos attacked the building and killed all twelve terrorists. On another occasion terrorists arrived by sea from Lebanon and took over a Tel Aviv hotel. In retaliation for these terrorist acts, IAF fighters bombed PLO bases in Lebanon.

Lebanon had always been well governed by a delicate balance struck between its Muslim and Christian populations, but the attacks by Israel upset that balance and polarised the Lebanese, and in early 1975 a smouldering civil war, between the Muslims and the PLO, backed by Syria, and the Christian, supported by Israel, dragged the country into long-term turmoil. On 15 March 1976 the Israeli Army, covered from the air by the IAF, invaded southern Lebanon to attack the PLO bases. The IAF's job was to keep the Syrian air force out of the battle. To monitor the progress of the army and identify targets, the Israelis used home-produced RPVs extensively over the battlefield. The UN brokered a cease-fire, leaving Israel occupying most of southern Lebanon, and the attacks subsided for a time, then started up again from bases further north, including some in areas controlled by the Syrians. The IAF retaliated with attacks on ammunition dumps, HQs and training areas, but there was an unspoken arrangement between Syria and Israel that there would be no direct confrontation between them. Israel was free to operate against the PLO as long as it did not attack the Syrians, but the Syrians could never rely on that arrangement and in 1976 they started introducing air defence systems into the Bekaa Valley northeast of Beirut just in case. In an uneasy time the civil war continued to smoulder, the IAF had control of the skies over southern Lebanon and the Syrians glowered from behind their SAM defences in the north.

This arrangement broke down on 27 June 1979. A flight of IAF F-4 Phantoms was attacking targets near Sidon on the south Lebanese coast; fighter cover was provided at 20,000 feet by a mixed force of F-15s and Kfirs. The Phantoms finished their strikes and climbed away from the area so that a flight of A-4 Skyhawks could follow them in to the target. Standing some way off the coast was an Israeli E-2C Hawkeye, its powerful radar covering Lebanon and part of Syria. As the last Phantom climbed away, the Hawkeye crew sent a warning that two flights of MiG-21s were heading towards them from under the SAM umbrella to the north, a lower flight ready to attack covered by a second flight above. The F-15 pilots turned their radar northwards and quickly picked up the MiGs 5,000 feet below about ten miles away. The Israelis put their noses down, in afterburner, leaving the Kfirs well behind, each F-15 pilot selecting a target and locking on an all-aspect AIM-9L Sidewinder.

The leader, Col. M, locked on to one of a pair of MiGs in a wide turn, going across his path, and when the Syrian pilots saw him they reversed their turn, just as he fired. His target broke in two as soon as his Sidewinder hit, the first aerial victory for the F-15. It was followed swiftly by three more F-15 kills, and by the time the Kfirs arrived the MiGs had broken in all directions, two of them hit by Shafrirs fired by Kfirs, one of which went down, the other leaving the battle damaged as the Syrians escaped into cloud, the first aerial victory for Israel's home-produced fighter, too. The Syrians lost 5 MiG-21s without inflicting any damage on the Israelis. More importantly, none of the MiGs had broken through the fighter shield, and underneath the dogfight the Skyhawks continued to attack their targets unmolested. That night the IAF squadron drank five bottles of champagne in the mess, one for each Syrian shot down; a sixth was kept on ice pending intelligence reports on the damaged MiG which had been claimed as a probable, but Israeli intelligence called to say that it had been seen landing at its base, probably by an RPV flying over Syria.

Leaving aside the difference in the pilots, the aircraft were a whole generation apart: the MiG-21s a lightweight legacy from the 1960s, the F-15 and the Kfir both part of the 1970s electronic revolution. The engagement showed graphically how that revolution had given the edge to those skilled in using it. The initial warning of the threat from the E-2C, the ability of the F-15s to pick it up on their radar and immediately plan how to position themselves to the best advantage, and especially their ability to make a head-on shot with AIM-9L, then follow up with intelligence which put no life or expensive aircraft at risk, all held together with maximum situational awareness, thanks to the ability to process information quickly.

Three months later, on 19 September, a flight of four F-15s was flying top cover for a lone RF-4E Phantom on reconnaissance over Lebanon when it was bounced by a flight of Syrian Air Force MiG-23 Floggers, a more modern adversary than the MiG-21. The Flogger pilots fired several AA-8 Aphid AAMs which all missed and the Phantom escaped. The F-15s had locked on to the MiG-23s but they were swiftly beyond the range of the Israelis' missiles as the F-15s could not leave the Phantom unprotected.

The F-15's radar suddenly showed another flight coming towards them at the same level – four MiG-21Js, flying in pairs in loose battle formation. Once again the F-15s were at a huge advantage, having locked their radar on to the MiGs at a distance, and positioned themselves, one pair meeting them head-on while the other made a wide turn to get behind them. The leader of the first pair fired a Shafrir, hitting a MiG which blew up when it was hit in the tailpipe, and the pilot ejected. The F-15 wingman then dived low at full power and came up behind a second MiG which had dived away from the battle, using the speed from the dive to close in quickly and shoot him down with a burst of cannon fire. The remainder of the MiG flight turned east, towards Syria, exactly as the Israelis had expected, and both pairs of F-15s gave chase and fired more missiles, hitting two MiGs which crashed into a forest. In a little over a minute the F-15s had doubled their score to eight MiGs confirmed and no loss. The F-15 had put the IAF back on top and that night there were four more bottles of champagne for the Israeli pilots.

The smouldering war between Israel and the PLO continued in Lebanon through 1980–81 and the Syrians continued to be bested in the air superiority battle, losing a further four aircraft for no Israeli loss. On 13 February 1981 an RF-4 reconnaissance Phantom was on a high-altitude reconnaissance mission over Lebanon, escorted by F-15s, and the Syrians sent up a pair of MiG-25 Foxbats, the fighter the F-15 had originally been built to counter. The two fighters, designed for NATO and the Warsaw Pact to challenge each other over northern Europe and the Arctic, finally met in combat in the Middle East. The Israeli pilots used their ECM systems to the full and turned before the MiGs had come into lethal range, then started dispensing large quantities of chaff and flares, preventing the Foxbat's powerful radar from getting a lock-on, but while the Syrian pilots went on trying, the covering F-15s were brought into a firing position by an E-2C Hawkeye off shore and fired a salvo of AIM-7 Sparrows at the MiGs, downing one.

There were lulls and periods of more intense activity but there were no more dogfights until 21 April 1981, when Syrians lost two more MiG-23s, and a month later, on 26 May, they lost two more MiG-21s to F-16s. Both sides raised the stakes that summer: unable to wrest control in the air, the Syrians put even more effort into ground-based air defences to give the PLO air cover by moving the latest Soviet SA-6 SAM systems into the Bekaa. Under that umbrella, on 28 April, Syrian Mi-8 helicopters had been used to transport PLO troops inside northern Lebanon and a flight of Israeli F-16s shot two of them down. They also increased the number of

Scout and Mastiff RPV flights over the Bekaa, probing the defences, getting the SA-6 battery commanders to switch on their radar to reveal valuable information about their radar frequencies, which could be stored away and used in the development and preparation of ECM. If they did not switch on then they were blind, and the RPV could gather intelligence with TV cameras and other sensors.

This provoked Syria into moving even more SA-6 batteries into the Bekaa, to which Israel responded by protesting and saying that it would attack the sites unless they were withdrawn. They were not withdrawn, and the Israelis did not attack, one reason being the same as it had been in the Electronic Summer of 1970 in the War of Attrition – that many of the technicians who operated the batteries had been identified as Russians and the Israeli government, possibly under pressure from the USA, did not want to provoke the Soviet Union by killing Russians.

While all eyes were on South Lebanon in the summer of 1981, on 7 June, in the middle of dealing with the PLO and Syria, the IAF carried out one of the most powerful demonstrations of how Israel's new air force had developed the capability for deeper strikes and how its new aircraft had extended its reach in the Middle East.

Behind the visible wars that had erupted between Israel and her Arab neighbours there was always the unspoken threat that such wars could go nuclear. Developing nuclear weapons first became an issue in the Middle East in the late 1950s when David Ben-Gurion, the Israeli Prime Minister, started to build a nuclear reactor at Dimona in the Negev Desert, with secret help from France.

The prospect of nuclear war in the Middle East was no less devastating than in any other part of the world: a single nuclear bomb in the right place in the Nile delta would probably wipe out Egypt as a country, relying as it does so heavily on the agriculture of the banks of the Nile. Col. Nasser wanted Egypt to have a nuclear capability, too, to deter Israel or to attack it. He tried to buy nuclear bombs off the shelf from the Soviet Union, and later from China, and he also tried to build jet fighters and ballistic rockets using German scientists and aircraft designers, including Willi Messerschmidt, to deliver them over Tel Aviv; one plan was to use radioactive material, rather than a bomb, carried to Tel Aviv in an Egyptian-built rocket.

Few doubt today that Israel has nuclear bombs and Western

intelligence believed that it had thirteen actual bombs in 1973, but the first real evidence came during the later stages of the Yom Kippur War. There were reports that General Moshe Dayan, the Defence Minister, put IAF Phantoms, Kfirs and the aptly named Jericho missiles on alert, visible to Soviet and US satellites, a warning to the superpowers that the war was a matter of national survival and Israel would use them if pushed too far. The Soviet Union had given Egypt a nuclear guarantee rather than supply it with weapons, and US satellites were shown the evidence that it was being put into effect when Soviet ships in Alexandria unloaded what were believed to be nuclear bombs and transported them inland to an Egyptian air base. The stakes were very high in that war, and both superpowers worked hard to avoid the Middle East going nuclear, putting Egypt and Israel under strong pressure not to do so while supplying all the conventional weapons their client states needed.

Egypt was not the only Arab country which had tried to build its own nuclear bomb. Through the 1970s and 1980s Col. Ghaddafi of Libya had funded Pakistan to build an Islamic bomb. Ironically it was France which had once supplied Israel with nuclear technology, and Italy which began to supply nuclear technology to one of Israel's most implacable enemies – Iraq. Iraq has no border with Israel, but had supplied soldiers and equipment to the Arab cause in all its wars with Israel and had never agreed a peace. After President Nasser's death, President Saddam Hussein of Iraq steadily took on the mantle of leader of the Arab nations against Israel. He wanted Iraq to be the dominant Arab country, the country which carried out the long-stated extreme Arab aim of destroying Israel. Iraq's nuclear reactor was at Osirak, twenty miles from Baghdad, and there was no doubt that it was capable of producing weapons-grade plutonium. Israel tried to stop it by diplomatic means and failed, and there is little doubt that intelligence operations were carried out to stop the reactor cores leaving France: one shipment was blown up in the warehouse near Toulon while awaiting shipment to Iraq.

By 1980 the Osirak reactor was well advanced and Middle Eastern nations had to contemplate the real prospect of Saddam Hussein having a nuclear bomb. Nervousness at the development went wider than Israel to include some of Iraq's Arab neighbours who were uneasy about his expansionist policies, his claims over Kuwait and his threats to Iran and Saudi Arabia. That instability turned to war on 21 September 1980 when Iraq went to war with Iran. On 30 September two Iranian Air Force Phantoms attacked the reactor, causing only minimal damage, but the attack alerted the Iraqis to its vulnerability to air attack and the site was immediately surrounded by SAM missiles, making any repeat attack much more difficult. French technicians left the reactor as soon as the war started, but once they were convinced it was safe they trickled back and other French technicians arrived to help improve the air defence system around it.

France was due to supply Iraq with uranium to fuel the reactor in 1981, but with the Iran–Iraq war already destabilising the Middle East international diplomatic pressure was put on France to withhold the supplies. France offered Iraq an alternative fuel which could not be used for weapons, but Iraq turned the offer down flat and, fearful of losing important contracts, France gave in and started shipping the uranium. By early 1981 Mossad, the external Israeli intelligence agency, was sure that Iraq had at least 12 lb of uranium. The Israeli government was determined to neutralise the possibility of an Iraqi bomb and it had a contingency plan, codenamed Operation Babylon, for a swift strike against the reactor before it went active, since any attack once it was in operation would have released radioactivity over a wide area. For Israel it was a matter of national survival once again, and the country turned to its air force for a solution. There was a split in the government about whether to bomb or not, and behind closed doors, in great secret, there was a fierce debate. The hawks won the argument and the decision to bomb Osirak was taken on 7 May 1981.

The IAF started an intensive period of meticulous planning for Operation Babylon in three separate phases: approach, execution and withdrawal. The strike force consisted of a combination of Israel's latest America fighters: eight F-16s to carry out the attack with eight F-15s providing fighter cover. Using single-seat fighters put fewer aircrew at risk and fewer people needed to know about the operation. The pilots were hand-picked for the job and the IAF Chief of Staff, General David Ivry, took a keen personal interest, flying on some of the training missions. The F-15s carried ARM-45 Shrike anti-radiation missiles as well as AIM-7 and AIM-9 anti-aircraft missiles so they could take on both the air-to-air and ground-based threats. The F-16s would carry the bombs and both types would carry ECM pods to jam the Iraqi SA-6 and SA-9 SAM systems surrounding the reactor.

Secrecy was paramount, and it was most difficult in the approach phase. The Middle East is covered by military and civil radar sites, which are on a high state of alert most of the time, and the superpowers' satellites overfly the area regularly. Iraq itself had a forward-based air defence system which followed the Soviet doctrine with radar, SAMs and AAA guns along its borders. The most direct route to Osirak, and the most obvious, was the northerly route, straight across Jordan and Syria, an area of many interlocking borders where radar sites were thick on the ground and very active. The alternative was the southerly route, over northern Saudi Arabi then up through southern Iraq. The USAF and the Royal Saudi Air Force both had E-3 AWACS aircraft in northern Saudi Arabia, flying round the clock monitoring the Iran–Iraq war, so they were positioned to look northeast, away from Israel, but their radar had a very long range. The southerly route, between the two areas of high radar coverage, was chosen and the aircraft were gathered at the IAF base at Etzion, near Eilat, right in the south of Israel, one of the most modern in the IAF with huge underground hangars and very little above ground. Being underground also kept the preparations away from the prying eyes of US and Soviet satellite – the strike package could come out at the last minute, up a ramp, straight on to the runway and take off immediately.

To avoid the ground-based radar the Israeli pilots had to fly very low, between thirty and sixty feet, the most inefficient height for fuel consumption, and, since any in-flight refuelling would draw attention to the force, bomb loads were light. To familiarise the pilots with the appearance of the reactor as they made their final approach there were photographs of the reactor pinned to the wall of the operations room at Etzion; they had been supplied by Iranian intelligence which, despite being an enemy of Israel, was an even more implacable enemy of Iraq. The walls of the reactor were eleven feet thick and there was quite a debate as to whether to use smart bombs or the standard US Mk 84 iron bomb, which would rely heavily on the pilots' skill in placing the bombs accurately.

The Mk 84 was a well-proven weapon, with far less to go wrong than the smart weapons, and the final decision to use it followed the KISS principle, one of the basic principles of the IAF: Keep It Simple, Stupid.

The Israeli pilots were all geared up for the raid on 7 May, but it was cancelled at the last minute because of the political division in the government. Training missions continued, maintaining peak readiness of the crews but also to make everybody around Etzion believe, including a lot of tourists at Eilat resorts, that such intensive flying was normal. On 7 June orders for the raid came through again and this time they were not cancelled. It was a Sunday, the Christian Sabbath, and the expectation was that French technicians would not be working.

The pilots were given their final briefing by an IAF colonel in the presence of Israeli Defence Forces Commander-in-Chief, General Raphael Eitan, and the IAF commander, General David Ivry. At 3 p.m. the 16 aircraft came out of their underground hangars and took off; so tight was the fuel condition that they rolled down the runway without afterburner until they reached 80 knots, then engaged it and were off in seconds, going straight into ultra-low-level flight and crossing into Saudi Arabia in loose battle formation at high subsonic speed less than fifty feet above the ground.

That is how they continued for two and a half hours, low and fast, in complete radio silence, keeping alert for mile after mile over featureless desert with very few visual references to help navigation. As they approached Baghdad the pilots began picking up the roads and railway lines that would lead them to the reactor. Three minutes before they arrived over the target the F-16s changed formation from loose spread into long line astern, some fifteen seconds apart. At the IP the leader lifted his nose, going up to just a few hundred feet, then started a gentle, sloping bombing run towards the target. The other seven F-16 pilots followed his every move. There was no reaction from the defences, no fighters and no anti-aircraft fire; the Israelis had the advantage of complete surprise. At the same time, the leader of the F-15s saw the dome of the reactor in the distance and took the fighters up to 2,000 feet, covering the leader of the F-16s as he lined up and released the first two bombs which were direct hits, blowing a huge hole in the concrete. Fifteen seconds later the second pilot released two more bombs, which went straight through the hole opened by the leader and exploded inside. The job was done, but the six other F-16 pilots put all the bombs on target and the whole dome collapsed; one French technician who was working on the Sabbath died.

As the last F-16s were attacking several anti-aircraft guns opened up but long before there could be any co-ordinated defence; the bombing itself had taken exactly two minutes. The F-16s joined up with the F-15s and the whole force headed west, climbing to altitude to save fuel on the return journey high above Syria and Jordan. There were no fighters, no Syrian MiG-25s, to challenge them and all 16 aircraft returned safely to Israel. US satellites had picked up the Israeli aircraft as they crossed the desert and they had photographed the attack itself. The first US intelligence reports said that Israel had used smart bombs in the belief that such accuracy could not be achieved with free-fall iron bombs. It was a flawless operation by the IAF, adding to its reputation for almost sublime levels of skill. Israeli intelligence had reports that every officer above the rank of captain in the Iraqi Air Defence Command squadron which was supposed to defend the reactor was summarily executed on the orders of President Saddam Hussein.

World leaders expressed outrage at Israel's action. No country had ever before taken such drastic action in peacetime to stop a neighbour becoming a nuclear power. It is impossible to say how the history of the Middle East might have been had Saddam Hussein built a nuclear weapon in the 1980s, but, judging by what he did in 1990, most of his neighbours, and most of the rest of the world, must have been relieved that the Israelis had had both the will and the skill in its air force to take such action, even if they choose not to express it publicly.

In June and July 1981 the state of near-war on the Israeli–Lebanese border went on unabated and Israel was forced to abandon some of its most northern settlements in the face of PLO artillery bombardment. On 17 July the IAF lashed out at the PLO by bombing its headquarters in Beirut, killing hundreds of people, following which the USA brokered a peace, and on 24 July the guns and the reprisal air attacks stopped, though Israel retained the right to fly reconnaissance missions over Lebanon and the Syrians retained the right to challenge them. On 29 July another Syrian MiG-25 was sent to intercept an RF-4E Phantom and was shot down by the escorting F-15s.

In the spring of 1982 the peace broke down completely. The PLO started shelling Israel and the IAF retaliated with air raids, but this time Israel decided to take more decisive action, 'Operation Peace for Galilee', a well-prepared plan for the Israeli army to invade South Lebanon and sweep the PLO out of Lebanon for good. Before the army crossed into Lebanon the Syrian air defences in the Bekaa had to be neutralised. Intelligence-gathering by Israeli RPVs on 8 June showed that there were 15 mobile SA-6 missile batteries in the Bekaa, some of them only recently moved in to back up the fixed SA-2 and two SA-3 sites which between them had around 200 missiles. The missiles sites were surrounded by approximately 400 anti-aircraft guns including radar-guided ZSU-23-4s; just over the border was the Syrian air force with Soviet interceptors. Much of the interlocking system was manned by Soviet technicians. To prepare the way, the IAF would first have to batter down a concentrated and technically advanced ground- and air-based system, the best the Soviet Union could supply.

The coming battle would be a direct clash between an essentially defensive electronic shield and an offensive, electronically guided sword. Surprise was impossible. The Russians and Syrians already knew broadly what was being planned and would be ready, but against that the IAF was well prepared and RPVs had pinpointed every missile battery.

Phase One of the air battle started on 9 June with RPVs crisscrossing the Bekaa gathering real-time intelligence with TV cameras and other sensors, but also acting as decoys, mimicking a flight of fighters, forcing the SAM commanders to choose between the rock of staying silent and the hard place of switching on their radar, tracking and engaging the RPVs but giving away vital information about frequencies and their positions if they did. Some did light up their radar and the E-2C Hawkeyes patrolling off the coast, protected by F-15s, instantly sucked up valuable information. Those that did switch on were then subjected to what David Ivry later called 'superior electronic devices', which included the latest Israeli-produced ECM systems based on years of watching and listening to the Syrian defences, but also included blasts of propaganda and rock music from other Israeli aircraft broadcasting on the control frequencies. Even if the Syrians did shoot down an RPV, there would have been another one along in a minute.

Phase Two was a long-range Israeli artillery barrage, including surface-to-surface rockets which hit known PLO and Syrian HQs, damaging their ability to command and control the defences. Phase Three was direct attacks on the SAM sites themselves from the air by F-4, A-4, F-16 and Kfirs from medium altitude, using anti-radiation missiles and iron bombs and defending themselves against those missiles which were launched with chaff, flares and ECM. The newly arrived mobile SA-6 batteries were not dug in and so were easier to spot, and once they were pinpointed IAF Phantoms went in very low, using an improved Israeli version of the ARM-45 Shrike missile. The Syrians released a huge smoke screen to try and hide the batteries, but with only limited success. The concerted attack on the air defences lasted about two hours and 10 of the missile batteries were put out of action in the first strike. Israel had learned many lessons in the nine years since the Yom Kippur War: the Russian/Syrian/PLO ground-based air defence network in the Bekaa largely crumbled on the first day under the combined effect of the three phases, and by the end of the day seventeen out of the nineteen sites had been destroyed.

The Syrians responded to the loss of their ground-based system by launching MiG-21 and MiG-23 fighters to take on the Israelis, a step back in history and a complete reversal of the logic of modern air combat – using aircraft to defend SAM sites. It was an absurd response, an act of desperation, something like the Charge of the Light Brigade, which called on huge courage from the pilots but was, in fact, futile. David Ivry called it a reaction of impulse rather than consideration. RPVs were airborne over the Syrian bases as the fighters scrambled and Israeli operators watched the fighters take off in real time on TV, then reported their exact time and initial course to the Hawkeyes whose own radar looked deep into Syria and could monitor them after take-off and jam their GCI control frequencies and data links, denying the pilots the information on which the Soviet doctrine and tactics depended. The E-2Cs then vectored the F-15 and F-16s into the best positions to attack each wave of Syrian fighters, and when the Syrian pilots reached the battle area the IAF fighters were waiting for them.

What followed was one of the most intense air battles of the jet age, the largest confrontation between opposing fighters since the Second World War, with up to 90 Israeli and 60 Syrian fighters in the same airspace at the same time, fighting for control. The Israelis had better pilots, better aircraft, better electronics and better weapons and, despite great courage, the Syrians lost 22 fighters on the first day. It is easy to get the false impression in reporting Israeli victories that it was easy, which was not true – it was a hard-fought battle.

Major R was leading a flight of F-15s on the evening of the first day. He was in touch with an E-2C Hawkeye which reported two Syrian fighters approaching from the west, coming out of the setting sun and making it difficult to identify them visually. They were MiG-21s and Major R's wingman shot one of them down immediately. The other turned north to escape towards Syria, followed by Major R. At this point the F-15s came under fire from the ground, but he held his aim and closed to about 200 yards range when the Syrian pilot started a very tight turn to try to get behind the F-15. Major R followed him into the turn and stayed on his tail but the range increased to about 800 yards and the chase went lower and lower into a valley. Major R fired an IR missile but it missed; his second shot found its mark in the tailpipe of the MiG which then crashed into a field. The Israeli pilot was mesmerised by the sight of his victim crashing, but was brought out of it by a sharp word in his headphones when a colleague told him to break hard as there was a missile heading his way. It was too late. It hit Major R's right jetpipe seconds later. He cut the engine, but there were flames already pouring out of it. The rest of the flight deployed around him for protection as he climbed slowly on one engine, just clearing the mountains at the side of the valley. He contemplated flying west towards the sea and ejecting close to Israeli ships, but decided instead to try and get the F-15 home. He nursed it carefully back to Ramat David where later examination showed 400 hits by AAA fire in addition to the missile damage, providing the best testimony yet to the robustness of the F-15 and its ability to go on flying even with heavy battle damage.

With air superiority established, the Israeli army headed north towards Beirut the following day while the Syrians moved more missile batteries into the Bekaa. The IAF reacted swiftly, hitting the new batteries hard as their arrival was monitored by RPVs, just as the two remaining SAM sites were also destroyed. Syrian Air Force fighters continued to try and protect the PLO but on the second day they lost another 25 fighters in aerial combat for no Israeli loss, the majority of kills falling to all-aspect AIM-9L Sidewinders and their Israeli equivalents, while the Syrians only had AA-2 Atoll and AA-8 Aphids which had to be fired from behind their target. By the beginning of the third day 50 of the Syrian Air Force's 200 fighters had been lost and the Israelis had lost one to ground fire. The Soviet Union sent a high-level team to investigate the failure of their systems.

With complete air superiority and no deep interdiction targets to attack, the IAF started flying close support missions for the Israeli Army. Cease-fire negotiations started before the Israelis had reached Beirut and the Army made a dash for the city to secure ground before it came into effect. In doing so they threatened to cut the road from Beirut to the Bekaa, and in an attempt to stop the Israeli advance the Syrians lost a further 18 fighters in aerial combat. By the end of the third day the Syrian Air Force had lost 40% of its fighters and at least 20 SAM batteries and all but gave up. A cease-fire was in place but it broke down two days later and fighting continued for a month during which Syria made more attempts to put SAMs into the Bekaa. On the night of 24 June they started to move in four of the latest Soviet mobile low-level SAM systems, the SA-8 'Gecko', but they were spotted by Israeli RPVs and IAF fighters destroyed three of the four batteries in the first strike; the remaining battery managed to shoot down one of the attacking Phantoms and two RPVs.

Israel had the freedom of the skies over Lebanon as far north as Beirut and, working under a tight air superiority umbrella, the Israelis laid siege to the city. On 1 July IAF fighters started flying over Beirut supersonically, producing a shock wave that shattered windows. They also made mock bombing runs to put psychological pressure on the PLO fighters who had gathered in the city. The siege worked, and by the end of August the PLO had moved out of Beirut to Tripoli in Tunisia. Israel's objective had been achieved, and by 1 September a formal cease-fire had been agreed.

The IAF had flown 2,000 sorties in the fight for air superiority and the IAF doctrine had worked – and worked well. The IAF claimed 85 aerial victories, a figure the Syrians have not disputed:

40 to F-15s; 44 to F-16s, and 1 to an F-4 Phantom. The battles were so large and close and in such crowded skies that it was rarely possible to use the AIM-7F Sparrow radar-guided missiles, and most of the victories were to short-range, 'all aspect', 'heaters', the Sidewinder AIM-9L, Israeli Shafrir and Python III. The AAM had become both more reliable, 'all aspect' and more accurate, realising the idea of the guided missile as the primary weapon in aerial combat thirty years after it had been first mooted: 93% of all the aerial victories were to AAMs with 7% to cannon fire. The idea of missile-based air warfare had been right, but the technology to achieve it had taken far longer to develop than had been anticipated, not to mention the experience of many engagements in several wars to reach that position. The new missiles, the result of the electronic revolution of the 1970s, meant that a fighter pilot could get into position more quickly, cutting out a great deal of the hard manoeuvring for cannon fire, and fire from longer range, reducing risk, and, though few fighter pilots would be without one, the gun was going out of fashion.

The lessons of the war were absorbed around the world: the value of closely integrated communications systems disseminating real-time intelligence from the battlefield, that relatively small numbers of well-led, well-trained fighter pilots with a strong offensive spirit and the latest equipment could overcome even the most sophisticated air defence system. The Soviet Air Force analyst, Col. Vasily Dubrov, in his report on the combat to the Soviet Defence Ministry, predicted that the all-aspect missile would profoundly affect the future of the dogfight, and he described the E-2C Hawkeye and the electronic countermeasures used by the Israelis as 'the wave of the future'.

In January 1983 RPV intelligence showed that Syria had deployed long-range SA-5 SAMs which could reach into northern Israel, threatening IAF operations over Lebanon. The PLO had gone, and as long as they were not used the IAF did not attack them. On 1 October 1985 IAF made a long-range strike against PLO HQ in Tunisia, a round trip of five hours using 707 tankers, E-2Cs and F-15s as back-up and as fighter cover for the force.

The air battles over Lebanon in 1982 were a victory by offensive air operations over a defensive doctrine, but when the Soviet Union replaced Syrian losses it did so on the same basis, though it did supply Su-22G Fitters for offensive ground attack roles, too. In subsequent skirmishes the IAF came off best and several more Syrian fighters were lost over Lebanon in the 1980s.

As IAF goes into its sixth decade it continues to grow. It has bought another 75 F-16s, but while the size increases so there is a continuing emphasis on quality rather than quantity in meeting its role as Israel's first line of defence. The number of active Israeli fighter pilots at any one time is around 600, and in the past it has been smaller, but of them it can be truly said that they have made Israel the arbiter of events in the Middle East, always able to provide an option for governments, either in war or the uneasy peace which has been the history of the Middle East for centuries. Alongside the politicians and the generals, a few hundred highly committed and skilful men, the products of a competitive system of selection and training, with the best aircraft money can buy, have been central to shaping the history of the region over the last fifty years.

CHAPTER NINE

'I counted them all out and I counted them all back.'

F ew people in Britain watching the BBC Television News on 1 May 1982 will forget the phrase coined by Brian Hanrahan as he watched Royal Navy Sea Harriers land back on their aircraft-carriers, HMS *Invincible* and *Hermes*. They had just carried out the first attack on the airfields at Port Stanley and Goose Green in the Falklands, and Hanrahan coined the phrase to tell millions of viewers that while he could not say how many Harriers were involved, for security reasons, they were all safely back. The actual number was 12, over half the total of 19 fighters available to the Task Force commander, a tiny number to provide both air cover for his ships and to attack targets on the Falkland Islands.

On 2 April 1982 the Falkland Islands, a small British dependency off the Argentinian coast in the South Atlantic, was invaded by Argentina. The islanders were of British stock and wanted to stay British, and the British Government had supported that stand, despite Argentina's long-standing claim to sovereignty. The

Argentinian government, a military dictatorship with a failing economy, social unrest and much innocent blood on its hands, used a popular foreign adventure to distract attention from problems at home. They planned the invasion in great secrecy, and when it came the British were unprepared. There was small detachment of Royal Marines on the islands, and they put up fierce resistance against overwhelmingly superior forces until the British government ordered them to surrender. Next day the Argentinians invaded another small British dependency, South Georgia, a small island 900 miles southeast of the Falklands.

Argentina did not expect a military response from Britain, 8,000 miles away and without, or so they thought, either the resources or the will to attempt to take them back. It was a not unreasonable expectation. Any re-invasion would involve mounting an amphibious landing which would be opposed by superior Argentinian forces, and a prerequisite to that would be air superiority. The RAF had no bases anywhere near, the nearest being Ascension Island, a tiny island over 4,000 miles to the north, and Britain no longer operated large, self-sufficient aircraft-carriers capable of projecting power round the world. The Royal Navy had only two 'through deck cruisers' equipped with 28 Vertical Take Off FRS.1 Sea Harriers, naval air superiority fighters based on the RAFs GR.3 ground attack fighter, to provide air defence of the fleet. The future of RN fixed-wing aircraft was doubtful: one of the through deck cruisers, HMS *Invincible*, had already been earmarked for sale to Australia, and HMS *Hermes*, a commando carrier which could also operate Harriers, had already been sold to the Indian Navy.

The day following the invasion, a Saturday, the House of Commons held an emergency debate on the invasion. The Prime Minister, Mrs Thatcher, announced that a Task Force would sail the following Monday to repossess the islands unless Argentina withdrew first through diplomatic efforts. Britain was not prepared for the conflict, but after a weekend of frenzied activity the Task Force did sail from Portsmouth on Monday, 5 May, to an emotional farewell from thousands of well-wishers who lined the banks of the Solent. On board the *Invincible* and *Hermes* were 800 and 801 Squadrons, Fleet Air Arm, a total of 20 Sea Harriers.

The biggest hole in the Task Force's air defences was the lack of any airborne radar. In the North Atlantic, where the Royal Navy normally deployed its carriers, it relied on the US Navy, NATO AWACS or RAF Nimrod AEW aircraft to provide warning of any threat, especially low-flying fighters with anti-ship missiles, which could then be engaged by the Sea Harriers or shipboard anti-aircraft missile systems. The Sea Harrier carried 30 mm cannon and Sidewinder AIM-9L missiles, but its radar had nothing like the range of the F-14 Tomcat and had to fight close in. It was not equipped to attack enemy ships or ground targets, nor were the pilots trained for it, so to give the Task Force an attack capability the RAF was tasked with adapting its GR.3 Harriers to operate from the carriers. The GR.3 Harrier was a ground attack fighter and its pilots were neither trained nor equipped for aerial combat, but the RAF hurriedly adapted six Harriers of No. 1 Squadron, fitting them with AIM-9L Sidewinders and training the pilots to operate from the ski-jump launching system on the *Invincible* and *Hermes*, and they joined the Task Force when it stopped at Ascension Island to reorganise and prepare for the final sailing south.

Argentina had not planned for this type of response and had no way of providing adequate air defence of the Falklands. The Islands' main airfield just outside the capital, Port Stanley, only had short, grass runways, far too short and rough for Fuerza Aerea Argentina's (FAA) and Commando Aviacion Naval Argentina's (CANA) fighters. Argentina's air forces were of 1960s vintage under the command of General Lami Dozo, who stated after the war that he had 82 fighters, though British intelligence put the figure at around 100 fast jet combat aircraft: 11 Mirage IIIAs with Matra R.530 SARH and R.550 IR Magic AAMs for air defence, backed up by 33 Israeli Daggers (export Neshers) with Shafrir AAMs, 32 A-4 Skyhawk attack aircraft and 6 very old Canberra bombers. They did not have the range to operate over the islands for more than minutes at a time from their bases in Argentina. They had no in-flight refuelling capability and no night-fighting ability. They had some elderly SAM systems: British Tigercat; German/French/US Roland, and Soviet SA-7 Strela and ageing British Blowpipe shoulder-launched missiles. The Argentinian Navy had one aircraft-carrier, the very old, ex-US *25 de Mayo*, which had another 11 A-4 Skyhawks, but it would be very vulnerable to submarine attack, and Britain was one of the world's leading nations in submarine warfare. The Navy had Argentina's only really modern weapons system, four French Super Etendard naval attack aircraft equipped with Exocet, sea-skimming, anti-ship missiles. The French had only delivered five Exocets when the invasion took place, and training was still incomplete. Once hostilities started, France cut off supplies and other forms of support.

The Argentinians tried unsuccessfully to install arrester hooks at Port Stanley airfield so that the naval Skyhawks could be used from it, and Army engineers did lengthen the runway to take a mixture of 34 light attack aircraft, MBB-339 jets and home-produced Pucara, a twin-turboprop counter-insurgency aircraft which could bomb and strafe with cannon, machine-guns, rockets and air-to-surface missiles, and could be used against amphibious landings. The light aircraft on the Falklands included two Shorts Skyvans transports and some 25 helicopters, bringing the total number of aircraft on the Falklands to around 60, dispersed around the islands at rough and ready strips at Pebble Island and Goose Green.

Britain and Argentina both spent April preparing for war. Argentina had the numbers, Britain had more modern aircraft, but however the arithmetic was done the Argentinians outnumbered the Harriers by around 4 to 1. Both half expected diplomacy to work, with the other side backing down, but as the weeks went by and the forces built up, neither side backed down and it became increasingly clear that there was likely to be fighting. It came as a shock to the Argentinian government that they would have to fight a war, including a sea and air war, for which they were not prepared or equipped. Britain declared a 200-mile Maritime Exclusion Zone around the Falklands, banning the use of surface vessels and threatening submarine attack. This kept Argentinian cargo vessels in port, forcing the FAA to fly supplies to Stanley from the mainland in C-130 Hercules, Lockheed Electras and Fokker Friendships, and in April they flew in 9,000 people and 500 tons of supplies. The cargo included three long-range AN/TPS-43F surveillance radar, two of which were put close to houses in Stanley and one was installed on Canopus Hill to the west of Stanley airfield. To protect the airfield, 35 mm and 20 mm anti-aircraft guns were deployed with some obsolescent Tigercat and Blowpipe shoulder-launched SAMs.

Without fighters in Stanley, the FAA had no real plans to

establish air superiority over the islands, and attacks on the British Task Force would have to be carried out from the mainland, with fighters escorting the attack aircraft over 450 miles of sea. Most of the fighters were moved to Rio Grande, Rio Gallegos and Santa Cruz air bases in the extreme south of Argentina, leaving some of the Mirage IIIAs in the north in case Britain attacked the Argentinian mainland.

Such a possibility did exist. Britain had moved much of what remained of the RAF's 1950s strategic bomber force – Handley Page Victors, which had been converted to tankers, and Avro Vulcans – to Ascension Island, and with in-flight refuelling they could have bombed Buenos Aires. The Task Force sailed from Ascension for the South Atlantic on 19 April and the following day the RAF carried out a hugely complicated, long-range reconnaissance patrol from Ascension: four Victors refuelled each other so that just one of them could make a fourteen-hour round trip to South Georgia to carry out a radar search for the Argentinian Navy. There were no Argentinian ships and the next day the first British troops were landed on South Georgia by helicopter to prepare to retake it.

The FAA also used an unorthodox method to search for the British Task Force, converting a 707 to search the mid-Atlantic. To counter just such a threat, Harriers flew patrols ahead of its position, and on 21 April Lt Simon Hargreaves picked up the 707 on radar 150 miles south of the Task Force. While diplomatic efforts continued, the Harrier pilots kept watch on the 707, flying right up to it and photographing it. As diplomacy failed and conflict seemed inevitable so the 707 became a threat, and a message was sent to Buenos Aires that if it persisted it would be shot down: the flights stopped. On 30 April Britain declared a Total Exclusion Zone around the Falklands. Argentina did the same. The USA, having done what it could to stay neutral and act as a diplomatic go-between, came down firmly on Britain's side.

The next day, 1 May 1982, the fighting started. The first move was a show of force by the British in a classic, if somewhat unusual, strike against the enemy's air power while it was still on the ground: a single Vulcan carrying out the longest bombing mission ever, 3,900 miles from Ascension Island to Stanley and back, to drop a stick of 21 bombs across the main runway in pitch darkness at 4.46 in the morning. The Task Force commander, Rear Admiral John

Woodward, moved to within 100 miles of the Falklands, then used his air power to follow up the raid at dawn. With no airborne radar, he kept six Sea Harriers to fly CAP over the Task Force to provide top cover for the attacking force. Nine Sea Harriers were tasked with attacking Stanley airfield, the first four going for the anti-aircraft defences, using radar-fused, air-burst, 1,000 lb bombs against the anti-aircraft gun positions, the other five hitting the hangars and other buildings with cluster bombs. Three more Sea Harriers were tasked with attacking the tiny airfield at Goose Green.

All 12 Sea Harriers took off at 07.50. The Stanley force reached their target ten minutes later, just as it was getting light. The four defence suppression aircraft, led by Lt Cmdr Tony Ogilvy, attacked the gun positions first, then broke off while the five attacking Sea Harriers came in seconds later at very low level, led by Lt Cmdr Andrew Auld, the CO of 801 Sqn, pulling up to 170 feet to release their cluster bombs into a hail of ground fire, much of it small-arms fire. In their brief time over the target the Argentinians fired several Tigercat SAMs, one of them hitting a small hill then veering off into the sky, while the radar locked on to the last of the attack Harriers, flown by Flt Lt David Morgan. Just as his radar warning device told him of the threat he was hit by small-arms fire so he dispensed chaff, broke hard left and followed the others straight back down to the deck, and the warning stopped. All nine Sea Harriers landed back on *Hermes* ten minutes later. The Goose Green raid was a complete surprise: just as the Harriers came in, they saw a Pucara getting ready for a flight with its engines running; seconds later, it was destroyed by cluster bombs, killing the ground crew and the pilot.

The FAA did not put in an appearance in the air, and all the attacking Sea Harriers returned to the carriers covered by the six CAPPERS which also landed back on *Hermes* shortly afterwards. David Morgan's Harrier had a single hole through its fin, which was swiftly repaired. These were the aircraft which Brian Hanrahan counted out and back.

Having been provoked, the Argentinians had to retaliate. Later that morning the *Invincible*'s radar picked up two contacts approaching the Task Force at high speed at 120 miles. Without radar, during daylight hours there were always two Sea Harriers on

CAP at 15,000 feet over the Task Force, and on that occasion they were Flt Lt Paul Barton and Lt Cmdr John Eaton-Jones of *Invincible*'s 801 Squadron. The radar operator then reported a second pair of contacts, then another: six fighters against two Sea Harriers. The radar contacts were FAA Mirage IIIs flying at 35,000 feet, and the pilots were keen to stay high where their turning circle was better and their limited fuel would last longer. For the same reason, Barton and Eaton-Jones wanted to stay low where they could dictate the terms of the fight to a greater extent, and since the FAA fighters represented no threat to the Task Force at 35,000 feet the Sea Harriers stayed 20,000 feet below, inviting the Argentinian pilots to come down and fight or stay where they were. The Argentinians stayed where they were so there was no fight.

Later that morning HMS *Glamorgan*, *Alacrity* and *Arrow* went inshore to bombard Stanley airfield from the sea. Three MBB-339A Mentors took off to attack them with bombs but the two CAP Harriers, flown by Lt Cmdr Nigel 'Sharkey' Ward, the CO of 801 Sqn, and his wingman, Lt Mike Watson, intercepted them in layered cloud, going straight into a firing pass. To avoid a fight the Mentors went into cloud and the Harriers followed, then they came out underneath, the FAA pilots jettisoned their bombs and headed back to Stanley.

Ward and Watson continued their patrol as another flight of Mirages approached from the mainland, flying high again. The Sea Harriers maintained their altitude but turned towards them in a classic dogfight manoeuvre, though they were still separated by 20,000 feet. The Mirages turned away. To draw them into a fight, Ward then turned and flew north. The Mirages followed, closing in from behind but maintaining their height, largely out of prudence considering the huge difference in the performance of their missiles. Ward, equipped with all-aspect AIM-9Ls, then suddenly turned through 180 degrees to face them and lock on his radar, but as the two RN pilots looked up they saw what at first appeared to be condensation trails but they soon realised were smoke trails from Magic missiles fired from hopelessly outside range. If there had been a lock-on, the turn had broken it and both Magics fell harmlessly into the sea.

In the late afternoon the Argentinians became more aggressive. A forty-strong, mixed force of Daggers, Skyhawks and the

Canberras was sent to attack the Task Force, protected by Mirages. Paul Barton was flying CAP again with Lt Steve Thomas when a pair of Mirages, ahead of the main force, were detected at medium level flying about a mile apart in echelon formation, a very inflexible formation which meant they could not protect each other's tail if attacked. The leader was Capt. Garcia Cuerva, with Lt Carlos Perona as his wingman. Thomas stayed facing the Mirages, searching for a lock-on to make a head-on shot, while Barton pulled away to the right at full power to put himself in a position to come in behind the Mirages once they had made their pass. The Harriers made visual contact at about eight miles. At five miles the Mirage pilots fired their missiles from a head-on position: one misfired and tumbled into the sea, while the other failed to lock on and flew aimlessly away. Thomas failed to get a lock-on from head-on and held his fire, climbing away to his right as the Mirages shot past 100 feet below. They had not seen Barton who was already coming in behind them and locking on a 'winder. The growling noise confirmed the lock-on and he eased down just enough to put the Mirage against cold blue sky, then fired. Neither Mirage pilot reacted and the Sidewinder hit Perona's Mirage, which immediately broke in two. He ejected and landed by parachute close to a beach on West Falkland and walked ashore.

Meanwhile, Thomas had turned on to Cuerva's tail who, realising the danger he was in, headed for cloud just as Thomas heard the growl and fired. Cuerva made it to the cloud just as the missile closed on him and was detonated by the proximity fuse, showering the Mirage with shrapnel and puncturing the fuel tanks. Realising that he would never make it back to the mainland, Cuerva headed for Stanley to try and make an emergency landing, but as he approached the airfield the anti-aircraft gunners mistook him for a hostile fighter and opened up on him, hitting his damaged fighter several times. It crashed into the ground and Cuerva was killed.

At the same time, the attacking force was approaching the Stanley area over West Falkland at 300 feet. The leading Daggers caught HMS *Glamorgan*, *Arrow* and *Alacrity* in the open, heading away from the coast, having just bombarded the airfield. The British ships had no warning against aircraft flying at that level because there was no airborne radar, and the Dagger pilots dropped bombs and raked the ships with cannon fire, causing some damage.

Two Sea Harriers, flown by Flt Lt Tony Penfold and Lt Martin Hale, were flying CAP at 20,000 feet when they came under attack from above by Daggers with Shafrir missiles. The Harriers were flying in a defensive spread about a mile apart when they saw the Daggers eight miles ahead at 35,000 feet. When he saw the smoke trails from their missiles Hale went into a vertical dive, dispensing chaff to confuse the missile, but looking back he could see the Shafrir still following him. At 5,000 feet he turned sharply towards some cloud and saw the missile start to track erratically, then fall away – it had been fired from too long a range. Hale then started to climb back up to the fight, just in time to see Penfold shoot down the Dagger which had fired the Sidewinder at him.

The Canberras were attacked by Lt Cmdr Mike Broadwater and Lt Al Curtis of 801 Sqn, and Curtis shot one down with a Sidewinder. Argentina had lost four aircraft on the first day, for no British losses. Both sides took stock. It had been a good first day for the Sea Harrier pilots who had come through their baptism of fire intact, managing to get the FAA to fight at its level or make them fire from too far away, while making best use of the all-aspect abilities of the latest Sidewinders which also intimidated the Argentinian fighter pilots into keeping their distance.

The RN pilots were astonished by the lack of aggression of the FAA pilots, and at their lack of tactical awareness. They flew in tight formation and fired from far too far away to be effective and from head-on, from which position it was not really feasible to make a kill with a Magic, which should be fired from behind. But, with the numerical odds so much against them, the RN pilots knew that at some point one of the Magics would find its target and they could ill afford any losses.

The Argentinians had a report of a Harrier being shot down by ground fire, which gave them some cheer that evening. They imagined that they had weakened the Task Force's air power, but the report was of Cuerva's Mirage and not a Harrier. They could not escape the conclusion that in aerial combat the Harriers had shown that they had the upper hand, and that realisation came as a shock. None was anxious to face the Sea Harriers, not through any lack of courage but because they realised that in equipment and training they were outclassed, adding a psychological victory to the physical one scored by the British pilots.

The Vulcan raid, which had dropped only 21 bombs, alerted the defences, did little damage which had been quickly repaired, and was regarded in some quarters as disproportionate in cost to the damage it caused, but the psychological effect was also disproportionate: the Vulcan's attack did cause confusion and it had shown the capability, as well as the will, to carry out strategic attacks, and the Argentinian commanders could not rule out attacks on their mainland airfields. On the evening of the first day some of the Mirage IIIAs were redeployed to the north to strengthen the air defences in case of attack from Ascension.

Each side had launched an attack, the British inflicting more damage, both physical and psychological, but that night the Task Force remained at risk of an attack from the sea. The British commanders knew from intelligence that the Argentinian Navy's capital ships, the cruiser *Belgrano* and the aircraft-carrier *25 de Mayo*, were at sea, but they lacked the airborne early warning radar to detect them at range so Sea Harriers had to patrol through the night. One of the pilots, Ian Mortimer, went to investigate radar signals which had been detected from a position northwest of the Task Force. As he approached the source of the emissions his radar warning receiver told him that he was being tracked by radar from the British-made Sea Dart ship missile system which had been supplied to the Argentine Navy. He broke off and left the area to break the lock-on, then turned back and used his Blue Fox radar in a passive mode to establish that there were six ships 200 miles northwest of the Task Force. It was the *25 de Mayo* with her guard ships and she could have carried out a night attack, but it was a virtually windless night and the Skyhawks needed a wind blowing across its decks for its aged catapults to launch them fully loaded. During the night the Argentine Navy also launched two of its Super Etendards with Exocet missiles from the mainland. They lacked the range to reach the British Task Force so they tried an improvised refuelling system, using a C-130 Hercules, but the refuelling went wrong in the dark and the attack had to be abandoned.

That night the Argentine cruiser *Belgrano* was patrolling outside the exclusion zone to the southwest of the Falklands. It represented no immediate threat to the Task Force but the decision to sink it was taken, and the British submarine *Conqueror* torpedoed it, with the loss of 362 lives. The psychological impact was huge and, fearing a similar attack, the 25 de Mayo returned to port at daybreak and the Argentine Navy's ships took little further part in the conflict.

After the first day the FAA avoided any more massed attacks. The Sea Harriers kept up the pressure on the ground attack aircraft on the Falklands, and on the morning of 4 May three of them from 800 Sqn, flown by Lt Nick Taylor and Flt Lt Ted Ball and led by Lt Cmdr Gordon Batt, attacked the Pucaras at Goose Green again. As they ran in over the airfield from different directions, Taylor's Harrier was hit by anti-aircraft fire and exploded immediately, killing Taylor, Britain's first loss in the air.

The same morning an ageing FAA Neptune maritime patrol aircraft made a long-range reconnaissance flight south of the Falklands where it detected four British warships some ninety miles south of Port Stanley. It was the RN destroyer HMS *Sheffield* with three frigates on radar piquet duty some twenty miles west of the carriers and the main body of the Task Force. The Neptune crew went to within sixty miles of *Sheffield* and alerted its base of the position. At 09.45 two Super Etendards armed with Exocets took off from Rio Grande and this time, in daylight, they managed to refuel from the C-130 tanker, then dropped down and headed for the *Sheffield* fifty feet above the sea. It was precisely the kind of attack that RAF Nimrod AEW airborne radar was supposed to detect at long range, then vector the Sea Harriers to attack, but the two Super Etendards approached in total radio silence, getting a last-minute update from the Neptune which climbed to 3,000 feet to transmit. At twenty miles range, still undetected, they popped up to 120 feet, switched on their radar, acquired a target, fired, then went back down to fifty feet and turned for home. The radar emissions should have been picked up by the *Sheffield* in time for the crew to launch a cloud of chaff to confuse the Exocet's homing radar, but at that moment they were masked by transmissions from her satellite communications equipment; operators briefly saw two blips on their screens as the Super Etendards rose to 120 feet, then they disappeared again. Two minutes later officers on the bridge of *Sheffield* saw a smoke trail from an Exocet as it skimmed the sea at Mach .9 and seconds later it hit the *Sheffield* amidships. The warhead failed to explode, but the missile embedded itself in the ship where its rocket motor continued to burn, setting the ship on fire. Twenty-one crew members were killed and many more wounded. The crew fought the fire and more fire-fighting teams were flown in by helicopters, which took off the wounded, but they were unable to contain it and after several hours *Sheffield* was abandoned to burn herself out.

The loss of a warship was a sobering moment for Britain, just as the loss of the *Belgrano* had been for the Argentinians, the more so because it was a loss which should never have happened and might have been avoided with airborne radar. The second missile missed, but had the Neptune found the main Task Force it could have been one of the carriers which was hit. The attack had shown how vulnerable the Task Force was to a modern system such as Super Etendard/Exocet, and it was moved further east, over the radar horizon from Stanley around 200 miles from the Falklands and out of range of the Super Etendards. The Harriers would have to operate from greater range for the rest of the conflict.

The weather closed in and hampered further operations. Following the loss of one Harrier on 6 May, two more Sea Harriers flying CAP were lost in very bad weather, presumably in a collision, bringing losses to three. There were replacements on their way from Ascension Island but they would take time to arrive, and in the meantime the fighters were down to 17.

Both sides were preparing for the day when the amphibious landings would take place: the British continued to attack the FAA on the ground while the Argentinians continued to try and hit the British ships. On 12 May four Skyhawks went for HMS *Brilliant* and *Glasgow*, which engaged them with Sea Wolf missiles and shot down two while a third crashed into the sea trying to avoid a missile. Another flight of A-4s came in just as Sea Wolf had a technical failure, and one bomb went straight through *Glasgow*'s superstructure, out the other side and exploded in the sea beyond; another bounced off the sea right over *Brilliant*; *Glasgow* had to withdraw to carry out repairs while the A-4s headed home via Goose Green where the anti-aircraft gunners mistook them for Sea Harriers and shot one of them down. Out of eight aircraft in two attacks, four had been lost, one had battle damage, and when the survivors were coming in to land another ran off the runway, its pilot virtually blinded by the build-up of salt deposits on his windscreen. The FAA had a problem with the fusing of their 1,000 lb bombs which, ironically, were British-made. They were not made for low-level attack, and had they been dropped from a higher level they could have been fused to explode immediately. At low level they were fused to delay exploding until the attacking aircraft, and any others in the flight, would be clear of the explosion. Had they flown higher, they would have been vulnerable to the ship's anti-aircraft missiles.

The Harriers destroyed much of the FAA's ground attack capability on the Falklands, but the weather had made operations even more difficult so to speed matters up and deal with the Pucaras and Mentors at Pebble Island off West Falkland, the nearest airfield to the proposed landing site, an SAS raid was launched on the evening of the 14 May which destroyed a further six Pucaras, four Mentors and one Skyvan, around a third of all the aircraft left on the Falklands.

The preparations for the landings continued. On 12 May the British government had made it plain that any Argentinian ship more than twelve miles off the coast would be attacked. With the Task Force over the horizon to the east, the FAA continued to fly supplies into Stanley using C-130s, mainly at night. On 15 May a Nimrod maritime reconnaissance aircraft made a record-breaking nineteen-hour flight from Ascension Island right down to the southern tip of Argentina, then right up the full length of the Argentine coast about 400 miles offshore, in broad daylight between 7,000 and 12,000 feet, using its Searchwater radar to make sure the Argentinian Navy was not at sea. Submarines were then positioned offshore, effectively blockading the Argentine Navy in port.

On 18 May eight Sea Harriers, made into 809 Sqn for the duration, and the six RAF GR.3s of No. 1 Sqn took off from the *Atlantic Conveyor*, a container ship which had been converted into an improvised aircraft-carrier for the purpose, and landed on HMS *Hermes* and *Invincible*. On 19 May *Hermes* sailed to the west of the Falklands, between the islands and the mainland, close enough to launch a Sea King helicopter on a one-way mission to the mainland, which is still a secret but was probably used to drop off SAS troops in Argentinian territory where they could observe the movements of aircraft leaving their bases. The Sea King was burned out on Chilean territory and the crew gave themselves up to the

Chileans. Two days later, by way of a baptism of fire, literally, for the GR.3 Harrier pilots, they attacked a fuel dump at Fox Bay, destroying huge amounts of fuel.

The Task Force Commander did not have air superiority in anything like the sense in which the words are normally used, but by a mixture of intimidation of the FAA fighters and high attrition among the attack aircraft sent from the mainland, and by destroying most of the Argentinian aircraft actually on the ground in the Falklands and capable of attacking soldiers as they were landing, Admiral Woodward judged that he had sufficient advantage to go for the landings on 21 May. He had little option because the soldiers were at sea, the weather was getting worse and success depended on getting as many troops on to dry land as quickly as possible without too much further damage to their morale by remaining at sea. To make a final check on the Argentine Navy, a second very long range flight was made by an RAF Nimrod from Ascension, this time going to within sixty miles of the Argentine coast; the Searchwater radar showed that the Argentina's Navy was still in port.

Under cover of darkness, when the threat of air attack was at its lowest, and with a diversionary attack by the SAS on Goose Green which went on all night, the troopships moved into Falkland Sound between the two main islands and headed for the landing site in San Carlos Water on East Falkland. British troops went ashore unopposed and spread out, taking all the high ground around San Carlos and putting Rapier SAM systems on high points to protect the stationary ships from air attack. One Pucara took off from Goose Green but was shot down by an SAS patrol with a shoulder-launched Stinger missile. To try to create a layered defence, the Sea Harriers started flying CAP over the area as dawn broke.

The carriers had to stay 200 miles away from San Carlos, away from the Super Etendard threat, so the Harriers had to transit at 25,000 feet to save fuel, making them highly visible to the Argentinian radars at Port Stanley. Once in the area they flew standing patrols in pairs, flying a race-track pattern over West Falkland, well to the west of San Carlos, creating a first line of defence across the most likely route from the Argentine mainland to the landing area. It was a low-level operation: the FAA Mirages and Skyhawks would have to fly low to get under the Rapier's radar above San Carlos Water so the Sea Harrier pilots had to patrol low too, around 200–250 feet above the ground. Once they had finished their patrol, they climbed back up to 25,000 feet, dropping down to low level again for the last fifty miles on their return so that they would not give away the position of the carriers to the radars at Port Stanley. Even transiting at high level, each flight of Harriers only had ten minutes over the landing area, and with this arrangement there were two Harriers on patrol over the landings for twenty minutes out of each hour. The air defences were meagre, and had the FAA made a maximum effort from the start they could have been swamped. Instead, a single Pucara on a dawn patrol spotted the landings and reported back.

Just as dawn was breaking two RAF GR.3 Harriers, flown by Sqn Ldr Jerry Pook and Flt Lt Mark Hare, arrived in support of the landings and were controlled to Mount Kent where there were Argentine helicopters which could be used to move troops: two Pumas, one Chinook and a single UH-1, dispersed on the ground. The Harriers made a single firing pass, but missed; on the second pass Hare set the Chinook on fire and on the third between them they managed to set the two Pumas on fire.

The next pair of GR.3s to take off were Wing Cmdr Peter Squire with Flt Lt Jeff Glover as wingman. Squire's undercarriage failed to retract after take-off so he had to return and Glover went on alone. Over the target area he was asked by the controller to attack and then photograph Port Howard. He made a high-speed pass and was hit by heavy AAA which broke off one wing and the Harrier started to revolve. He waited until the aircraft was the right way up again and ejected. He was knocked out by the blast of the air which also ripped off his face mask and helmet, and he came to in the water. He was later picked up by an Argentine army doctor in a rowing boat who treated him for a broken collar-bone.

At 10 a.m. a single MBB.339 arrived from Port Stanley to find San Carlos Water full of ships. Had he been part of a heavyweight attacking force, they would have been sitting ducks, but he was alone and fired his 30 mm cannon and loosed off his 5 in. rockets at HMS *Argonaut* in a determined attack which did little damage. The first attacks from mainland-based aircraft came at 10.30 a.m. Six Daggers came round the north of West Falkland, skirting the Sea Harrier CAPs. HMS *Broadsword*, *Argonaut* and *Antrim* were at the head of San Carlos Water to protect the entrance. The Daggers went for them with 1,000 lb bombs, putting one through the side of HMS *Antrim* which failed to explode. *Antrim*'s anti-aircraft missiles locked on to the flight and a Sea Cat missile hit one of the Daggers.

At 12.00 two Pucaras took off from Goose Green, but as they came into San Carlos Water they came under attack from HMS *Ardent* and they were spotted by a CAP of three Sea Harriers, led by Sharkey Ward with Lt Cmdr Al Craig and Lt Cmdr Steve Thomas, who dived to attack them. Craig and Thomas made the first pass but closed too fast and both missed. Ward then managed to get on the tail of one of the Pucaras and made two passes, managing to set one of the engines on fire. The Argentinian pilot stuck with his machine until it was clear he could do no more then ejected and it crashed.

Later that afternoon Lt Cmdr Neil Thomas and Lt Cmdr Mike Blissett of 800 Sqn saw four Skyhawks in a tight V-formation about to enter San Carlos Water. The Sea Harriers went straight into the attack, and at the sight of the Harriers the Argentinian pilots jettisoned their bombs and pulled hard right, going low and changing into a wide, long, echelon formation covering over a mile. The two Harriers approached from behind. Blisset locked on a Sidewinder and fired first, then Thomas fired from behind him at another. Thomas's target made for cloud with the missile following and it hit inside the cloud, falling out on fire; Blisset's hit its target which exploded immediately.

In the early afternoon 'Fred' Frederiksen and Lt Andy George were flying CAP when Capt. H. Gonzalez led a flight of four Daggers, but as they approached at medium level they were seen on radar by HMS *Brilliant* as they came in across West Falkland. The Daggers crossed the coast in two pairs as the Harriers saw them from 2,500 feet above and Frederiksen went into a diving turn to get behind them while George dropped back, waiting to see if there were any escorts behind. Frederiksen went for the left-hand pair. George, having checked that there were no escorts, then followed him down and lined up behind the right-hand pair. Frederiksen was lined up on the wingman in the left-hand pair just as the Argentine pilot saw George on the way down. He looked in his mirror and saw Frederiksen right in his six o'clock just as

Frederiksen fired a Sidewinder, which hit seconds later and the Argentine pilot ejected before the Dagger ploughed into the ground. Frederiksen then lined up behind the leader of the left-hand pair and opened up with his 30 mm cannon, but they escaped the Harriers by climbing into cloud, letting down later over Falkland Sound to attack HMS *Ardent*. They went in high enough to allow the bombs to arm properly and flew into a hail of anti-aircraft fire. One bomb hit and several others exploded nearby. The Lynx helicopter and its hangar were blown off, as was the Sea Cat launcher, killing and injuring several crew members. More Skyhawks followed and she was hit again in the stern, but she continued to fire back with her 20 mm guns.

Meanwhile, 'Sharkey' Ward was flying CAP over a wide, flat valley close to Mount Maria on West Falkland, with Steve Thomas as wingman. Their mood was grim. As they had flown in to take up their position they had crossed Falkland Sound and seen *Ardent* limping northwards, smoke billowing from her damaged superstructure. Over the valley they started flying the race-track pattern. At each corner they turned towards each other first to check each other's six o'clock. As they turned at the southern end of the patrol Ward saw the familiar triangular silhouettes of Mirages, flashing along the far side of the valley, a mile away, in close formation, about 100 feet above the ground. Ward reported their position to Thomas, then rolled out of the turn, put on full power and flew straight at them, passing through their formation seconds later. He expected the Mirages to continue towards Falkland Sound so broke hard right, intending to turn through 180 degrees to get on their tail, but they were nowhere to be seen. He realised why when he saw Thomas's aircraft overhead, heading west. Instead of continuing east to their targets, the two Argentine pilots had turned round and were heading west, towards home. They had not seen Thomas who was now right behind them. He fired a Sidewinder and the Argentine pilot either received an audio warning that a missile was approaching or he saw it because just before it hit the canopy blew off and he ejected as it hit. Ward checked the rear as Thomas locked on to the second Mirage, which was still trying to escape to the west in full afterburner. Thomas then fired a second 'winder which chased the Mirage, and just as it seemed the missile might run out of fuel, and the Mirage lifted towards some low cloud, the proximity fuse detonated the warhead under its wing – it was later confirmed as a kill.

At that moment a third Mirage arrived from the north, having exited from Falkland Sound. He fired at Ward but missed, but did not stay to fight, diving below Ward and heading west for home. Ward broke right and down, flying very close to the ground while tracking the brown and green camouflaged shape over the boggy ground ahead. He selected a Sidewinder, heard the growl in his headphones which told him it had locked on and fired. It hit and blew the Mirage to smithereens, large pieces of it immediately hitting the ground at full speed; the pilot did not eject.

Looking towards Falkland Sound, Ward then saw Skyhawks approaching and gave a warning over the radio. They were Navy A-4s, and the pilots were trained to attack ships with American 'Snakeye' bombs with fins which popped out after release, retarding the bomb and giving the aircraft time to get away from the blast. Three of them attacked the crippled *Ardent*, damaging her further, just as Lt Morrell and Flt Lt John Leeming arrived, having been alerted by Ward's call. They saw the bombs explode and dived at full throttle towards the Skyhawks which were trying to escape over the Sound, flying very close to the water. The last of them raised the alarm when he saw the Harriers coming down and all three jettisoned their external fuel tanks and bomb racks, but the Harriers still gained on them, Leeming going for the one at the rear while Morrell went for the leader. Morrell locked on with a Sidewinder and fired, and it exploded just behind the A-4; the pilot ejected. He then went for the second in line, opening fire initially with cannon then switching to Sidewinder which locked on but failed at the last moment, falling away into the sea. Leeming was also using his gun against the last in the line which was just above the water. He fired several short bursts but the FAA pilot did not react until the rounds started hitting the water around him, when he broke right, reducing the range to Leeming to about 200 yards, when he opened fire again and hit, the Skyhawk disintegrating in the air, showering debris in Leeming's path and forcing him to pull up to avoid it. The third Skyhawk had been badly holed by gunfire and was leaking fuel. Unable to make it back to the mainland, the pilot went for Stanley, ejected over the water and was picked up by helicopter.

The FAA lost 12 aircraft on the first day of the fighting over Falkland Sound: 5 Daggers, 5 Skyhawks and 2 Pucaras; plus 1 Chinook and 2 Puma helicopters. The Royal Navy and RAF lost 2 helicopters and 1 Harrier, all to ground fire. HMS *Ardent* was also lost: she had been hit by seven bombs and 22 members of the ships company had been killed and 30 injured. HMS *Argonaut*, with two bombs inside her which had failed to explode, was towed further out to sea where they were defused. The warships had done their job in drawing fire from the transports, and by nightfall on 21 May 3,000 British soldiers and 1,000 tons of supplies had been put ashore and were moving inland to establish a beachhead. With no helicopters to move them, and no air cover, the Argentinian Army did not counter-attack. The FAA had missed its opportunity by not concentrating its attacks, coming in flights of three and six aircraft and arriving at intervals, giving the air defences time to breathe. There was no doubting the courage of the FAA pilots, but they were outclassed in the air, technically and tactically. The Royal Navy also outclassed the FAA in serviceability and sortie rate.

By dawn on 22 May there were more Blowpipe and Rapier anti-aircraft systems in place around San Carlos, adding to the Argentinian difficulties, but bad weather meant that only two sorties could be mounted from the mainland: two Skyhawks flew through the Sound but did not drop bombs. The British were equipped for, and were used to, bad weather, and the Harriers could and did operate in near nil visibility which would have been impossible with a conventional fighter.

The second major attack came on 23 May but with better defences only half the raids reached their targets. A flight of Skyhawks went for HMS *Antelope* and one hit her mast after dropping its bombs, flying very low. Another dropped its bombs and was then hit by a Sea Wolf missile from HMS *Broadsword* – it blew up and the pilot was killed. On 24 May only 12 AAF aircraft got through the defences and 4 of them were lost: 1 Skyhawk and 3 Daggers.

The following day, 25 May, was Argentina's national day, and Admiral Woodward expected attacks to be heavy, moving the two carriers west to within 150 miles of the beaches to give the Harriers more time over the operational area. He was right. At 2 p.m.

six Skyhawks attacked HMS *Broadsword* and *Coventry*. Steve Thomas was flying CAP and was alerted, but as he approached he was warned off because *Broadsword*'s missiles were going to engage the Skyhawks, but at the critical moment its missile computer and radar system 'sulked', and both ships were hit: *Coventry* capsized and 19 of her crew were killed.

That evening two CANA Super Etendards took off from Rio Grande to launch the third and fourth of its five Exocets at the Task Force. They did not take the shortest, most obvious route, but used in-flight refuelling from the C-130 to fly well to the north of the Task Force and attack around the defensive screen of frigates. They launched the missiles at thirty miles and turned for home, but the frigate HMS *Ambuscade* had picked up the radar emissions and sent a warning to the rest of the Task Force. Both carriers and other ships fired chaff rockets and launched Lynx helicopters with decoys. It seems that the defences were effective in preventing the Exocets from hitting the carriers, but one hit the *Atlantic Conveyor*, which was sailing with the Task Force while unloading stores from Ascension Island. Fortunately the Harriers it had been carrying had already been flown off, but a number of helicopters had to be abandoned and a great many spares for the existing aircraft on *Hermes* and *Invincible* were lost.

Between 21 and 25 May the two RN carriers, which had 30 Harriers between them, had flown some 300 sorties, a huge testimony to the men keeping them flying. The FAA and CANA, with vastly greater numbers of aircraft and a land-based maintenance system, free from threat of attack, could only manage 180 sorties over the same period. Argentina's national day, 25 May, marked the high point of sustained air activity and in that period Argentina lost 19 aircraft. Britain lost one destroyer, two frigates and one supply ship, with damage to another destroyer, two frigates and two supply ships, but by the end of 25 May 5,500 troops and 5,000 tons of supplies were ashore and British soldiers and Royal Marines started their epic yomp across East Falkland towards Port Stanley.

On 27 May, Sqn Ldr Bob Iveson and Flt Lt Mark Hare were tasked with flying close support for the 3rd Battalion, The Parachute Regiment, as they advanced against the much larger and more heavily armed garrison at Goose Green. On their first pass they were unable to identify any targets for the cluster bombs, but on the second they dropped them on well-dug-in troops. Then they came back for a third pass to strafe the Argentinian positions with 30 mm cannon fire, but the anti-aircraft gunners had now found their mark and hit Iveson. The controls went completely sloppy and he ejected, landing almost immediately. Iveson evaded capture for three days before being picked up by helicopter, and he was flying again a week later.

On 28 May the weather was very overcast, but it did not stop the few remaining Pucaras from attacking the Paras with napalm and cannon fire. The battle for Goose Green had been going on all night and into the morning when the CO, Lt Col. H. Jones, was killed. The Paras were coming under attack not only from Argentinian artillery but also from the 35 mm Oerlikon anti-aircraft guns being used against infantry, and advancing to take Goose Green was clearly going to be very difficult. The new CO, Maj. Chris Keeble, called for air strikes against the anti-aircraft guns and the artillery, and a flight of three RAF GR.3 Harriers was despatched, Sqn Ldr Peter Harris, Flt Lt Tony Harper and Sqn Ldr Jerry Pook, carrying a mixture of cluster bombs and 2 in. rockets. They let down through the cloud and under direction from a forward air controller on the ground went in between fifty and a hundred feet towards a small promontory to the east of Goose Green where the guns were based.

They achieved complete surprise and hit the positions with cluster bombs and rockets. It was a decisive attack, just at the right moment in the battle, lifting the Paras' morale at a sticky moment and damaging Argentinian morale. The battle continued through the following night but, shorn of much of their heavy weapons, the Argentinians will to fight diminished, and by the morning Maj. Keeble had opened negotiations for the surrender of the garrison, which was much stronger than his force.

The weather continued to be very poor, with high seas battering the Task Force. On 30 May Lt Cmdr Mike Broadwater was preparing for take-off from *Hermes* when his Sea Harrier slid off the side of the ship; he ejected and was rescued. The same day the CANA decided to use the weather to launch its last Exocet in the hope of hitting one of the carriers, which they hoped would have a decisive effect on the course of the conflict now clearly swinging in Britain's favour. It was an elaborate plan involving two Super Etendards, the second aircraft to be there in case of a radar failure on the missile-carrying aircraft, two C-130 tankers and four FAA Skyhawks to follow up any successful Exocet attack.

They took off from Rio Grande and clearly there was a British intelligence operation, either SAS or submarine, which detected the raid because the Task Force was put on action stations, expecting an Exocet attack. The raid went south of the Falklands at low level. When they reached the southeastern waters around the islands the Super Etendards detected ships twenty-four miles ahead on radar, locked on, fired, then turned for home. The Skyhawks followed the smoke trail as the missile disappeared into the distance. The target was not the *Invincible*, as the Argentinians had hoped, but the destroyer HMS *Exeter* and the frigate HMS *Avenger*, which were on radar piquet duty twenty miles from the carriers. The warships picked up the Super Etendards' radar and alerted the whole Task Force, firing large numbers of chaff rockets to confuse the Exocets. They succeeded, and the missile fell harmlessly into the sea, then the ship's radar locked on to the Skyhawks, and the first two were shot down by Sea Darts. The other two followed through the smoke generated by the missiles, the ships themselves and the chaff dispenser rockets, and dropped 500 lb bombs which narrowly missed *Avenger*. The Skyhawk pilots were convinced that the ship was a carrier and that the smoke indicated the Exocet had hit it and that is what was reported back at base to great jubilation, which turned out to be ill founded.

On 1 June one of the C-130s, which had been regularly flying into Port Stanley with supplies, was returning to Argentina at low level when the crew decided to climb high enough to gather some intelligence about activity in Falkland Sound; it doing so, it came above the radar horizon and was picked up by radar. 'Sharkey' Ward was flying CAP and was directed to the Hercules; the transport was helpless and Ward riddled it with cannon fire and it crashed into the sea.

On the same day Ian Mortimer was flying an armed reconnaissance to the south of Port Stanley at 12,000 feet when he saw a Roland missile fired at him from the ground. He went into a climb and was trying to outrun it when it hit. He ejected and landed in the sea, where he spent nine hours in a dinghy before being rescued by a Sea King from *Invincible*.

On 5 June a major development in providing close support for the troops as they advanced on Stanley took place when a small airstrip, hewn out of the bog by army engineers with no heavy earth-moving equipment and paved with aluminium matting, was opened above San Carlos Water. It was called Sid's Strip, after Sqn Ldr Sid Morris who commanded it, and it had enough room for four Harriers, fewer than it should have done because most of the aluminium matting had been lost with the *Atlantic Conveyor*. It was just the kind of improvised landing ground for which the Harrier had been conceived in the first place, and it increased the time which the Harriers could spend over the operational area by a factor of nearly four.

On 8 June the Royal Navy was putting ashore the Welsh Guards at Bluff Cove near Fitzroy. The landings were in full view of Argentinian observation posts, which saw the advance parties putting Rapier SAMs around the landing area. A force of eight Skyhawks and six Daggers took off from the mainland. Three of the A-4s failed to refuel and turned back, and one of the Daggers had an oil leak and also turned back, leaving ten for the mission. Sid's Strip was out of action because of a hard landing by a Harrier GR.3 that day so the ground attack Harriers were back on the carriers, which were far out to the east, so CAP could only be sporadic.

The Daggers approached through Falkland Sound, but as they flew up the Sound the frigate HMS *Plymouth* saw them and, robbed of surprise, they decided to attack it instead. They dropped their bombs and four hit *Plymouth*, but none of them exploded; Sea Harriers on CAP detected them but failed to catch them.

The Skyhawks were now down to five and they found the landing ships *Sir Galahad* and *Sir Tristram* off Bluff Cove in the middle of the landings in broad daylight with no air cover. They had time and space to approach from the right altitude and hit both ships with 1,000 lb bombs, setting both ships on fire. Fifty-one soldiers were killed and 46 were injured in the worst single incident for the British forces.

The Sea Harriers immediately mounted CAP over Bluff Cove and at dusk David Morgan and Lt David Smith were patrolling at 10,000 feet when they saw a landing craft from HMS *Fearless* come under attack in Bluff Cove from four more Skyhawks. Morgan dived on them, reaching practically supersonic speed, approaching the Skyhawks from behind; he locked a Sidewinder on to the last in the formation which went straight home and blew it to bits; the others did not see their comrade go down. Morgan then turned on a second Skyhawk with another Sidewinder. This time the pilot saw it coming and reversed his turn, trying to throw the missile off course, but it had a good lock-on and hit, breaking the Skyhawk just in front of the fin and sending it straight into the water. Morgan then opened up with cannon fire on the two Skyhawks still in front of him until he ran out of ammunition. Smith, behind, could not fire his Sidewinder because it might have locked on to Morgan so Morgan then went into a vertical climb to get out of the way. Smith locked on to one of the remaining A-4s and the Sidewinder went straight in as it hit. Three pilots were killed; the fourth dropped his tanks and managed to escape. It all took less than two minutes. Flying top cover at 35,000 feet were Mirages with air-to-air missiles, one of the rare occasions they made it over the islands after the first day. Ward and Thomas were patrolling at 20,000 feet and set off after them, but the Mirages thought better of it and went home.

After heavy fighting, by 13 May British troops were surrounding Stanley and the game was clearly up. Skyhawks did attack General Jeremy Moore's HQ on 13 May but did little damage. The next day the Argentinian commander on the Falklands, General Menedez, surrendered. At sea on the carriers there was little elation because they waited to hear that the government on the mainland was not going to go for one last strike.

It was Britain's first real air war since Suez and the first time the FAA and CANA had fought any kind of air war. Both sides had to play fine judgements with the range of their aircraft and the danger they would be in, all the more acute for the British because their resources were so small in the first place. Seven British ships were lost, and several more severely damaged, accounting for many of the British casualties in the conflict, but despite those losses the British pilots, with the missile operators both on board ships and on land, accomplished their mission to protect the Task Force and provide close support for the soldiers on the ground. The low-flying skills of the Harrier pilots, the result of a great deal of very unpopular training at home, were at a premium in hitting targets. It showed that the traditions of excellence and aggressiveness among the pilots of the two British services, the Royal Navy and the Royal Air Force, were among the best in the world, and it showed what a small, quality force could achieve against a much larger, badly trained and largely obsolete force, even though they had no airborne radar to rely on. After their experiences in aerial combat on the first day, the FAA made no further real attempt to fight it out with the Harriers for superiority over the islands.

The Harrier acquitted itself very well in its first combat. Given that they had no airborne radar and had to fly standing patrols, which took a huge toll on parts and serviceability, the sortie rate was all the more remarkable. The Sea Harrier and the GR.3 Harrier operated in weather conditions which would have been impossible for conventional aircraft-carriers.

The war showed again how vulnerable ships were to air attack without air superiority and how vulnerable to attack by modern sea-skimming missiles. The Exocet sank two ships and became a worldwide bestseller as a consequence, even though one had failed to explode and three had been effectively decoyed by chaff and missed. It was the threat of the Exocets that kept the Task Force at a distance, drastically cutting down the effectiveness of the Sea Harrier patrols because of the range. Had the Argentinians had more Exocets, and more training with them, and had they made concentrated attacks, the outcome of the war could have been very different.

As the fighting ended, a whole range of improvised and hastily built high-technology equipment began to be available to the British forces. An improvised ECM pod, known as 'Blue Eric', to counter Argentinian ground defences and radar was built by Marconi and the RAF, and was fitted to four Harriers which went to Ascension Island and would have been deployed on *Hermes* had the conflict continued. Two Sea King helicopters were equipped with the Searchwater radar normally fitted in the Nimrod. The modifications were carried out from scratch in eleven weeks and the two Sea Kings did deploy to the area after hostilities had ended. The Royal Navy subsequently converted more Sea Kings to the AEW role.

The conflict lasted seventy-five days as a whole, and in that time there were only seven days of intensive aerial combat: 1, 21–5 May and 8 June. The Harriers shot down 32 aircraft of all types, 19 of them plus three probables with AIM-9L and a further 6 with cannon, all for no loss in aerial combat, although 5 were lost to ground-based air defences. The all-aspect AIM-9L Sidewinder was the killer: it gave the RN pilots a huge advantage, both in combat and psychologically, because the Argentinian fighter pilots knew they were up against a far superior missile, making them tentative in combat and reluctant to get within its range. A total of 26 AIM-9Ls were fired in 23 separate engagements and they accounted for 73% of all air-to-air victories. Very few of the FAA pilots saw what had hit them.

Argentina's FAA and CANA planned 505 missions, of which 445 were actually flown as sorties and only 280 reached their targets. Seventy-five per cent of the bombs they dropped failed to explode. Argentina lost 101 aircraft of all types in the war: 63 FAA, 13 Navy, 3 Coastguard, 22 Army – 36 of them in combat, 2 of them to friendly fire. Twenty-six were abandoned on the Falklands and only 3 of the light attack aircraft based on the Falklands went back to Argentina.

The RN and RAF Harriers represented a tiny amount of air power, but they represented a 1980s air force and, the Super Etendard/Exocets aside, the FAA was a 1960s air force without modern equipment, without the understanding of aerial warfare or the experience to get the best out of their numerical advantage. The British were operating a long way from home, without the radar cover on which much of their training and doctrine was based, without the support of land-based fighters and without the smart weapons which the RAF would have used in a land war in Europe. What they did have was just enough of a technical advantage to give them the edge when it mattered. Above all, they had the training, individual skills and the will to win, despite the odds.

CHAPTER TEN
Instant Thunder

In 1989, forty years after the formation of NATO and the start of the Cold War, the Soviet Union collapsed from within, bringing the Warsaw Pact and much of the communist world down with it. The Cold War was over, and the capitalist West, in the guise of NATO, had won. It was the end of a discreet period in history characterised by stability on the one hand, arising from the stand-off between two superpowers, both of them in a permanent state of readiness for a war which they knew they could never fight, and instability on the other in the form of so-called 'post modern war', war by proxy, as hundreds of local and regional conflicts simmered along the ideological fault lines of the world, occasionally boiling over into fighting in which the superpowers invariably backed different sides.

The collapse of the Soviet Union was due in large measure to the economic burden of keeping up with the USA in defence technology, in particular the Strategic Defense Initiative (SDI), more popularly known as Star Wars, a whole range of space-based, computer-controlled weapons systems, giving the USA a defence against ICBMs and a possible first strike advantage over the Soviet Union. The Berlin Wall came down, East and West Germany were reunited after forty-five years, the countries of Eastern Europe held elections and turned their backs on communism, some of them even asking to join NATO. The Soviet Union broke up into its component nations, with Russia, Ukraine, Belorus, Georgia, Moldova, Kazakhstan and Turkistan turning in on themselves, on their own economic and social problems. The tight integration of Soviet armed forces and its arms industry was weakened to the point where they no longer posed a serious threat to the West.

Far from being the end of history, as one commentator put it, the end of the Cold War simply marked the end of one period in history and the beginning of another. Just as the brave new world that followed the defeat of Nazi Germany had its own character so the brave new world ushered in by the collapse of Soviet communism quickly took on a character of its own, a world in which ideology gave way to nationalism, global systems gave way to local fragmentation and Cold War stability gave way to uncertainty as old scores, many of them forgotten during the decades of power bloc mentality, were renewed with all the vigour brought on by years of hidden frustration. The conflict which marked the transition from one era to the next, from post-modern war to a new form of war, often called infowar, like so many Cold War conflicts, took place in the Middle East.

Kuwait is a small, rich country at the head of the Persian Gulf where the Tigris and Euphrates Rivers run into the sea. It achieved full independence from Britain in 1961, having been a protectorate since 1899. Among the world's top oil producers, Kuwait's almost feudal ruling family provided a high standard of living for most of the population just over 2 million, with a modern infrastructure based on education, housing and health care. Kuwait's southern border is with Saudi Arabia; to the north, its border is with Iraq, and a narrow strip of Iraq, containing the strategically important Shatt al Arab Waterway, separates Kuwait from another powerful neighbour – Iran. During the Iraq–Iran War, Kuwait supported its co-religionist Sunni Muslim neighbour, Iraq, against largely Shi'ite Iran, providing huge loans to finance the war, but Iraq never recognised Kuwait as an independent country, claiming it as its own 19th Province, a claim based on a time when both countries were part of the Ottoman Empire.

Iraq won that war in 1988 under the leadership of Saddam Hussein who then felt militarily strong enough to throw his weight around in the Middle East. To pay for the war and sustain his armed forces, Saddam relied on oil revenues, and he was outraged when other OPEC states, particularly Arab states, would not cut back on production to force up the price of oil to help him. On 16 July 1990 Iraq accused Kuwait of encroaching on its oil reserves in the border area and demanded $2.5 billion in payment. Kuwait declined so Saddam upped the stakes, demanding that Kuwait write off loans of over $5 billion, restating Iraq's claims to two Kuwaiti islands, Warba and Babiyan. Working on the assumption that he had the tacit approval of the USA, whose ambassador had said that the USA had no opinion in the inter-Arab dispute, Saddam began massing troops on the Kuwaiti border. Even though Iraqi plans to invade Kuwait had existed since 1961, Western intelligence had failed to detect the seriousness of the moves and most thought it was bluster, but early in the morning of 2 August 1990 Saddam Hussein ordered the Iraqi army to invade.

Iraq had by far the largest armed forces in the Middle East, including an air force with 700 aircraft, 550 of them combat aircraft, and a small number of Tu-22 Backfire bombers, far larger than the Gulf States could muster between them. Kuwait's tiny armed forces could put up only token resistance and the country was swiftly overrun. Kuwait's ruler, Sheik Jaber Ahmed al-Sabah, fled to Saudi Arabia with as many Kuwaitis as could flee, and by the end of the day Saddam was in control of Kuwait. The Iraqi Air Force (IAF) attacked Kuwaiti air bases, but some Kuwaiti pilots managed to escape with their aircraft, mainly A-4 Skyhawks, and fly south to Royal Saudi Air Force (RSAF) bases.

The United Nations Security Council met in emergency session and passed a Resolution demanding Iraqi withdrawal. Iraq refused, but while diplomatic efforts continued, with little effect, the worry in Western capitals was that if the invasion was tolerated Saddam would not stop at the Saudi border and that a majority of the world's oil supplies could come under Iraqi control. RSAF Tornados and F-15 Eagles established combat air patrols along the Kuwaiti border immediately but they would not have been able to resist a full-scale attack by Iraq. Something had to be done, and on 6 August King Fahd of Saudi Arabia invited other countries to help defend his country. A Coalition was formed around NATO forces, under US leadership, to do so if diplomacy failed.

On 7 August 1990 President George Bush ordered the deployment of US forces to defend Saudi Arabia in Operation 'Desert Shield'. Moving ground troops would take time so the initial response was with US air power, and the first sign Saddam Hussein had that the West was serious about defending Saudi Arabia came the same day when 48 F-15 Eagles flew direct from Langley, Virginia, to the RSAF base at Dahran on the northeastern coast of Saudi Arabia, opposite Bahrain in the Persian Gulf. They flew in eight flights of six aircraft, ready to fight, guns loaded and underwing strongpoints bristling with AIM-7 and AIM-9 missiles. After a 15-hour flight, involving six in-flight refuellings, they arrived overhead Dharan tactically, coming in at intervals carefully timed so that as one flight landed another patrolled overhead. Their stated job was to protect Dharan and other RSAF airfields from Iraqi attack, and after a day of rest the pilots were back in the air, mounting round the clock patrols: 2 pairs, flying three-hour sorties in a race-track pattern at 20,000 feet over northern Saudi Arabia under control from RSAF AWACS. Under their Rules of Engagement they were not allowed to cross the border into occupied Kuwaiti airspace.

The Iraqi pilots clearly had similar orders, with the result that both sides flew to within a few miles of the border, watching each other on radar. Occasionally, USAF F-15 pilots locked their long-range Sparrows on to Iraqi fighters across the border in a process of deliberate, aggressive intimidation, letting the Iraqis know what was in store for them if they came south. Other F-15 pilots flew CAP to protect USAF and RSAF E-3 Sentry AWACS aircraft which also patrolled over northern Saudi Arabia, scanning deep into Iraq looking for threats from the IAF and ready to co-ordinate any response. At any one time four AWACS were airborne on 16–18 hour missions, three covering different sectors of Iraq or occupied Kuwait and one as a 'spare in the air' in case anything went wrong.

Desert Shield was not simply defensive. Over the horizon, three thousand miles south of the Gulf in the Indian Ocean on the tiny British island of Diego Garcia, beyond the reach of the IAF, USAF

B-52 strategic bombers started arriving on 8 August and went straight on to alert. Days later USAF 4th TFW F-15E Strike Eagles, the two-seat, attack version of the original F-15, deployed to Taif on the western side of Saudi Arabia. The US Navy sailed for the Middle East, too, deploying four battle groups, two in the Red Sea and two for the Gulf. The USS *John F Kennedy* sailed on 15 August with 20 F-14 Tomcats, 20 F/A-18 Hornet, 12 A-6E Intruders, including some KA-6 tankers, 4 EA-6B Prowler and 4 E-2C Hawkeye AEW aircraft. On 21 August the first of 22 of the most advanced military aircraft in the world, which had only been unveiled in public that year, the F-117A 'Nighthawk' Stealth fighter of 415 TFS/37 TFW, were deployed to Khamis Mushait air base in the south of Saudi Arabia. On 23 August the US Air National Guard was mobilised.

British participation was much smaller but no less immediate. Within days of the invasion, three RAF Nimrod maritime patrol aircraft were despatched to Seeb, in Oman, right at the mouth of the Gulf, where they assisted the Royal Navy and other NATO navies in blockading the Gulf to shipping destined for Iraq. On 9 August the RAF deployed the first Tornado fighters, F Mk 3s of 5 Sqn, which joined the F-15s at Dharan, followed by GR Mk 1 strike versions with JP233 airfield denial weapons, Jaguar GR Mk 1 ground attack fighters and Buccaneer S Mk 2B with laser designators and precision guided weapons, supported by VC-10, Tristar and Victor tankers, all of which went to a base built for the RAF in the 1950s, now renamed Sheik Isa air base, on Bahrein, where the RAF shared Bahrein's facilities with US Marines Corps F/A-18 Hornet and AV-8B Harriers.

The French government signed up to the Coalition with reservations. France had strong links with Iraq as one of Saddam Hussein's arms suppliers. To avoid direct involvement in Saudi Arabia, L'Armée de L'Air sent its Mirage F1C, Mirage 2000C and Jaguars to its ex-colony Djibouti on the African coast opposite Aden first, and they did not arrive in Saudi Arabia until October.

The Iraqi Air Force suffered from many deficiencies compared with the Coalition. With few exceptions, its aircraft were a generation older and their electronics were greatly inferior to the latest NATO inventory. The basic design of many of its combat aircraft, such as the MiG-19, Su-7 and even some Hawker Hunters in the ground attack role, dated back to the 1950s, while most of the ground attack force was MiG-23B Floggers of 1970s vintage. The ground-controlled interceptor force was largely made up of MiG-21s and F-7As, a Chinese copy of the MiG-21, armed with AA-2 Atolls, backed up by a small number of MiG-25A Foxbats used mainly for reconnaissance, and for air superiority Iraq had recently purchased 113 Mirage F1Cs from France. The centrepiece of the IAF fighter force was 35 MiG-29 Fulcrums, the Soviet Union's versatile answer to the F-15, all backed up by Soviet Adnans AEW & C aircraft and Midas in-flight refuelling tankers. In all there were 15 different types of fighter in the IAF, bought without a coherent plan from USSR, China and France at various times, and the sheer variety of machines created a huge maintenance problem. The IAF was large but it was not very effective. It flew second-rate fighters under a system based on Soviet doctrines of tight ground control, and in training, experience and attitude Iraqi fighter pilots also lacked the skills and understanding of air combat to make proper use of what they had. Iraq's ground-based air defences were based on the Soviet model, with the IAF operating SA-2, SA-3 and SA-6 systems and the Iraqi Army equipped with SA-7 and some 1,200 anti-aircraft guns, including the mobile ZSU-23-4 and ZSU-57-2. The importance of co-ordination of air defences in battle, relying on computers, a high level of training, effective IFF systems, real-time intelligence, all linked through good command, control and communications systems, had been one of the strongest themes of the electronic revolution of the 1970s and 1980s, and Iraq was sadly deficient in managing those systems over the battlefield, a deficiency which had been vividly illustrated in the Iran–Iraq War where 75% of all Iraqi losses in the air had been to Iraqi ground-based air defence.

Air defence apart, command, control, communications and intelligence-gathering systems are especially important for a ruthless military dictatorship like Iraq. Saddam Hussein was at the centre of a highly centralised political, economic and military culture, and final control of most things, especially military decisions, was vested in the President. The promotion of military officers was largely determined by Saddam Hussein's paranoia about power seeping away from him, rather than by the recognition of any real ability, and there was very little room for individual initiative or flexibility in thinking. Saddam Hussein had controlled the Iran–Iraq war and, though one million soldiers had died, Iraq had won. It had been a very low-technology war with victory based on a doctrine of attrition on the ground, and the IAF had played only a relatively small part. That was the kind of war that Saddam wanted to fight against the Coalition. He believed that NATO, the West in general and the Americans in particular would not stand for the kind of casualties he imagined he could inflict on them, and in a famous phrase he promised the West 'the mother of all battles'. That was not what the Coalition had in mind. NATO had moved from a doctrine of attrition to the idea of the AirLand battle which relied on smaller, flexible forces led by officers picked for their initiative, and relying heavily on air superiority and the flexibility that would give them.

By the end of August 1990 the Coalition, backed up by systems designed for NATO to combat the Warsaw Pact in a high-technology war in Europe, had deployed enough of that high-technology air power to make it impossible for Saddam to go further south without exposing himself to devastating air attack. He had missed his chance to push south into Saudi Arabia, if he had ever intended to, and while US, RSAF, RAF and Free Kuwait Air Force fighters, and some from the Gulf States, too, patrolled the northern border of Saudi Arabia, the biggest airlift in history, from the USA and Europe, began the build-up of a land army which was not only superior technically, but also numerically.

As the ground forces built up through the autumn, Combat Air Patrols along the border gave the Coalition commander, Vietnam veteran US General Norman Schwarzkopf, time to plan and train to retake Kuwait while his ground troops acclimatised. It was important work but not the best preparation for combat and the fighter pilots wanted to 'put some gs' on their bodies – get used to the feeling of the violence of air combat. To keep their skills up, impromptu Top Gun courses were established for them to practise ACM against dissimilar aircraft in which the L'Armee de L'Air Mirage F.1s were especially popular because the IAF had them too. As the USS *John F Kennedy*, the flagship of Admiral Riley Mixson, a fighter pilot with 250 A-7 missions in Vietnam behind him, sailed through the Mediterranean he arranged for its Tomcats to have simulated combat with RAF Phantoms based on Cyprus.

Secrecy was paramount as General Schwarzkopf's plan took shape, and Iraqi aerial reconnaissance had to be prevented. Coalition AWACS almost immediately established electronic superiority along the border: as soon as an Iraqi fighter took off from its base it would be observed and a howling would start in the IAF pilot's headphones, letting him know that he had been spotted, that he was being followed and targeted. Coalition fighters were sent to intimidate them further, and there were unconfirmed reports that some IAF fighters flew towards the AWACS, only to get an even more urgent warning in their ears telling them that the F-15 escorts had locked on to them at long range with AIM-7 Sparrows, a process the US fighter pilots called 'burning his ears'. Crossing the border meant certain attack by F-15s and the Iraqi pilots invariably fled back to their bases. Reconnaissance MiG-25s could have tried to make photographic sorties south of the border, but they knew that if they did they would almost certainly be shot down.

Such cat and mouse tactics left Saddam Hussein and his generals without any reliable intelligence about what Schwarzkopf was planning and they were also part of the moral value of air power in preparing the enemy for defeat, creating a climate of helplessness and fear. It worked. USMC F/A-18s carried out the CAP role in the northern Gulf and when the IAF sent attack aircraft, often as many as 12 MiG-23s or Mirage F1s, to threaten Coalition warships, possibly with Soviet sea-skimming, anti-ship missiles, the Hornet pilots would move up and lock on with their radar, occasionally burning Iraqi ears at maximum missile range, and the Iraqis invariably turned and fled back to their own airspace, never even getting to visual range.

The Coalition used its superior position during the build-up, not just to prevent Iraqi intelligence-gathering but actively to gather as much as they could for Schwarzkopf. Among the first aircraft to be deployed in August 1990 were three RC-135 Rivet Joints. SAC operated them from Riyadh and probably from bases in Turkey, too, covering Iraq's northern border. The RC-135, a converted 707, can stay airborne for up to twenty-four hours, and they had been used for years to collect Electronic Intelligence (ELINT) and Communications Intelligence (COMINT) by eavesdropping on Soviet radio communications from just outside Soviet airspace, part of the infowar. To avoid just such eavesdropping the Iraqis had laid thousands of miles of cable across the desert to provide a secure system of communication, much of it fibre-optic cable capable of carrying many telephone conversations at once. So, to help the Rivet Joints, US and British special forces were dropped into the desert, well inside Iraq, to cut the lines, forcing the Iraqis to use radios which could then be monitored.

The technique of using high-speed runs by fighters towards the borders meant that the Iraqi early warning system either had to ignore them, and stay silent, or switch on their radar, giving away priceless information about reaction times, operating frequencies and the behaviour of Iraqi procedures and even individual behaviour. For example, the Rivet Joint radar operators noticed that whenever F-4G Wild Weasels flew along the border and switched on their radar, the air defence systems, knowing that the Weasels carried Shrike and HARM missiles, would switch off their systems very quickly, giving away a specific fear they had and indicating a weakness. By this process, the ground-based air defences were intimidated by the electronic power and superiority of the Coalition and they mentally started preparing for defeat, like the fighter pilots.

Eavesdropping was the passive side of the infowar, but as the time for hostilities approached, the Coalition went on to the offensive in that war by jamming and otherwise interfering with Iraqi military communications. The USAF had another specialised aircraft for the job, the EC-130H Compass Call, a C-130 Hercules transport from which the operators prepared to take the Iraqi electronic systems apart, using very powerful scanners. During the build-up they recorded voice communications for later analysis, then when hostilities opened they could jam the frequency with a continuous wailing sound. If the Iraqis switched to another frequency, they used the scanner to switch to it and jam that too, or it could transmit bogus Iraqi communications, further confusing the enemy.

The latest addition to the US electronic surveillance capability was the Grumman E-8 Joint Surveillance and Target Attack System, J-STARS, a battlefield control system which was still at an experimental stage as Desert Shield started. Like AWACS, it was based on the 707 and in the same way that AWACS gathered intelligence on, and then controlled, the air-to-air war, so J-STARS did the same for the air-to-ground war, identifying high value targets, such as convoys of vehicles or tanks, or headquarters where there was a lot of traffic to and from them, then vectoring ground attack pilots to them using its Norden AN/APY-3 phased array radar. The radar operated in two basic modes. The Moving Target Indicator (MTI) mode was used to cover a wide area, looking for anything that moved on the ground, and a separate pulse-Doppler radar sharpened up the images. If the moving targets stopped, then the pulse Doppler radar could not track them any longer so the operator could then turn to Synthetic Aperture Radar (SAR) mode, which could take over from 300 miles away, giving a high-resolution radar map of an area of 30,000 square miles and picking out the targets with a resolution of three feet, though some reports put the resolution down to one foot. The information was then displayed on any one of ten consoles to give the big picture of the battlefield – the position of the Iraqi army, its tanks, convoys, helicopters, fuel dumps, artillery emplacements, SCUD missile sites – in real time, day and night. Two prototype J-STARS were rushed to Saudi Arabia before they were fully operational where, like other large, vulnerable aircraft which were high-value targets, they had to be protected around the clock by fighters, leading to a new acronym HavCAP for High-value Combat Air Patrol.

The build-up of intelligence-gathering aircraft continued at another RSAF base far away from the border area at Taif, in south-western Saudi Arabia near Jeddah, in a very secret operation with high-altitude reconnaissance aircraft, including the venerable U-2R and TR-1A. The TR-1As could monitor large troop movements and concentrations, giving the commanders at the main HQ in Riyadh details of the deployment of enemy ground forces through photographs, backed up by COMINT. The U-2s were able to monitor COMINT and transmit information from high above Iraq via a secure satellite link straight back to Riyadh in real time.

AWACS, COMPASS CALL, RIVET JOINT, J-STARS, U-2 and TR-1 were at the hub of an information-gathering and -processing network which then supplied it to attack aircraft such as the USAF EF-111A Ravens, the US Navy's E-2C Hawkeyes, EP-3E Aries, EA-6B Prowlers, EA-3B Skywarriors, the US Army's OV-1D Mohawk, RC-12 and RV-1D Quick Look aircraft and EH-60A helicopters and

USAF F-4G Wild Weasels. The full weight of a system designed to take on the Warsaw Pact in Europe was brought to bear on a much smaller and less sophisticated enemy, and such close observation made it virtually impossible for the Iraqis to move men and equipment on the ground without the Coalition knowing what they were doing. The electronic warriors were doing exactly the same as the fighter pilots: as well as gathering valuable information and slowly building up a very comprehensive picture of the enemy's command and communications network, they were getting ready to destroy it in the early part of the fighting while intimidating the Iraqi operators and their commanders who knew that most of their systems and a great deal of what they were saying was being monitored.

The strategy for Desert Storm, the hostile phase of the war which was to follow if diplomacy failed, was based on air power – air power used much more than simply as a supporting arm of the ground campaign. It was almost the other way round – that ground forces would eventually play a secondary role to the air forces. The USAF bomber generals of the Second World War and early Cold War, who had controlled the thinking in the 1950s and 1960s, had been largely replaced by a generation of fighter generals who had grown up with the ignominy of failure in the Vietnam War. They were determined to end the twenty-five years of pessimism which had followed Vietnam, and the basic plan, which was formulated by the USAF, had at its heart a statement about how to fight it: it was called Instant Thunder, a repudiation of Rolling Thunder and the whole concept which went with it, sending a message to any politician who wanted a graduated response to be wary.

That plan revolved around first taking command of the airspace and the electronic spectrum over the whole of Iraq and Kuwait, then attacking relentlessly and accurately with the simple and clear intention of crippling Iraq's ability to take any form of offensive air action, or air action of any kind for that matter, isolating Iraqi ground forces in Kuwait from air support by the IAF, and isolating the commanders on the ground from each other, and from HQ in Baghdad.

Its purpose was unashamedly to paralyse Iraqi air forces in Kuwait and Iraq first, then wreck the army's communications, their supply routes and their fortifications as quickly as possible, and kill their troops, and only when air power had reduced Iraq's ability and will to fight would the troops go in on the ground, limiting Coalition casualties by dismembering the enemy first. Instant Thunder incorporated the doctrine of air superiority, using high-technology strike packages, and many aspects of it were based on the Israeli operation in the Bekaa valley a decade earlier. The Gulf War was the first real test of the USAF since Vietnam, and the men who led it, and flew its aircraft, were determined that it would be a success.

It had taken five and a half months to plan, but by mid-January 1991 everything was in place. The Coalition consisted of the USA, UK, France, Saudi Arabia, Canada, Italy, New Zealand, Australia, Bahrain, Free Kuwaitis, Qatar, UAE and South Korea, and with so many different countries, air forces, ground troops and navies, a high priority was given to integrating command and control. By far the greatest contributor was the USA, with over 3,600 aircraft, of which 750 were USAF combat aircraft and 650 USN and USMC. On the ground there were 600,000 troops with 4,000 tanks from the same countries, as well as Egypt, and at sea there were 150 warships, the most powerful military force assembled anywhere in the world since D-Day, 1944. The last ultimatum to Saddam Hussein expired at midnight on 16 January 1991. Diplomacy had failed, and in the early hours of 17 January 1991 Desert Shield became Desert Storm; for the next thirty-five days it was purely an air war conducted by some of the best-trained and -equipped pilots in the world.

The first Coalition mission was to neutralise two air defence radar sites which were part of the air defences near Baghdad: eight AH-64 Apache attack helicopters, armed with Hellfire laser-guided missiles, rockets and cannon, opened up on them at 2.30 in the morning, and completely destroyed them. Once the helicopters had cleared the area, F-117A Nighthawk stealth fighters, able to work in the face of the electronic defences, loiter over their targets, getting it just right, moved in and without the need for the huge levels of support and fighter protection of a conventional strike package rained precision guided weapons on other targets in the air defence system while remaining invisible to it. As the explosions alerted the air defences so they started firing back in an unco-ordinated way, lighting up the night sky over Baghdad with tracer but leaving the unseen attackers unscathed. Next came Tomahawk cruise missiles fired from warships in the Gulf against headquarters and communications centres in the capital as the world watched on television.

While the initial attacks on Baghdad hit the nerve centre of Iraq's command and control system, the main Coalition strike packages were forming up in the air, a huge choreography of different types of attack and support aircraft, protected by fighters from USAF, USN, USMC, RSAF, RCAF, RAF flying CAP. The AWACS, RC-135 Rivet Joint, J-STARS and COMPASS CALL aircraft and over 50 tankers were in the air, positioned to supply their protective shield of fighters and the strike package aircraft with fuel and information. The first air casualty came in unusual circumstances. An unarmed EF-111A Raven was carrying out an electronic jamming mission west of Baghdad when an IAF Mirage F1 got on his tail and launched an AAM. The Raven pilot released chaff and flares to confuse the missile, then went into a diving turn, going very low and using his Low-Altitude Navigational Targeting Infra Red for Night system (LANTIRN) to fly just above the ground. The Mirage followed, but without any such system the Iraqi pilot could not manage the low-level flying in the pitch black night that the Raven could, and he flew straight into the ground.

Iraqi airfields were the first targets for the strike packages. One, heading for an airfield near Baghdad, consisted of attacking F-15Es and F-111s supported by F-4G Wild Weasels with Shrike and HARM with EF-111As, for jamming, protected by F-15Cs. One four-ship from the 71st TFS, led by Capt. Steve Tate, consisted of two pairs on counter-rotating patrols, one pair low, the other high, covering each other's six o'clock. Tate was passed a message from an AWACS, identifying a bogey heading for the high pair above him. He locked on to it with an AIM-7 Sparrow and once it had been positively identified as a bandit, using IFF, he fired at twelve miles range. Seconds later the night sky was lit up by a huge explosion as his missile hit an Iraqi Mirage 1 F.1 four miles away.

Against small, precise targets, such as the hardened aircraft shelters (HAS) which housed Iraqi fighters, F-111 and F-15Es used LANTIRN to find their targets at night then dropped Paveway precision guided weapons (PGMs), which had come a long way since the days they had been used in Vietnam. The system relies on one aircraft using its air-to-ground radar to identify the target, passing the target information to a second, attacking aircraft, which uses a Pave Tack laser designator and range-finder with infrared sensors to mark the target; the signals are bounced back off the target in a shape like an upturned cone above the target. The weapon is then released at the optimum height and range and its sensors pick up the coded signals from the reflected laser which guide it, using moveable fins on the tail of the bomb, right on to the target, regardless of what the aircraft does after release. The PGM was part of the answer to the HAS which had made the pre-emptive strike against air forces on the ground more difficult, and they were used to great effect by F-117As, F-111s and F-15E Strike Eagles. If the IAF stayed on the ground, the Coalition attacked them on their airfields in their HAS with smart weapons, and if they left the bunkers and flew, they entered the realm of the ever-vigilant AWACS who followed their every move and vectored the F-15 'cappers'.

That night the IAF offered scant opposition in the air and, consequently, it was forced to take its punishment on the ground. The RAF Tornado GR.1's job on the first day was to attack IAF airfields with JP233 airfield denial bombs. The first strike was against Tallil airfield, north of Basra. The strike package included F-16s who carried out a high-speed attack first to suppress the anti-aircraft fire, followed by F-4G Wild Weasels to deal with SAMs while EF-111A Ravens jammed and F-15Cs and Tornado F.3 fighters flew CAP. The four Tornados arrived over the airfield well under 200 feet at high speed and discharged two JP233s each, spraying hundreds of bomblets over the main runways and taxiways. Flak was criss-crossing the airfield but none of the Tornados was hit and the package went home intact. As dawn broke a second Tornado strike hit Shaibah airfield south of Basra in similar fashion. The Tornados carried Sidewinder missiles for self-defence and one of them was hit by flak and exploded, damaging the aircraft seriously. The pilot, Flt Lt John Nicholl, and his navigator, Flt Lt John Peters, had to eject; both were captured and severely mistreated by the Iraqis before being paraded for the television cameras in Baghdad.

At around 3.00 in the afternoon of the first day Capt. Charles Magill USMC, on exchange with the USAF, was leading a flight of eight F-15Cs as escorts to a strike package of F-16s with F-4G

Wild Weasel and EF-111A jammers to hit Al Taqaddum airfield to the west of Baghdad. The strike package was in the middle of refuelling when an AWACS warned of two bogeys some eighty miles to the north on CAP southwest of Baghdad, flying a north–south pattern in the path of the strike package. Magill accelerated ahead of the package, splitting his flight into two: a four-ship led by him to take on what turned out to be two MiG-29 Fulcrums, while the other four-ship continued to search the area for any other hostile aircraft.

Nearer to the target a SAM system fired several missiles at them and they dropped their external tanks to make them more manoeuvrable, put on power and went into immediate violent evasive manoeuvres, successfully avoiding the missiles. Then, as they closed to under forty miles, the MiGs turned north on their patrol, away from the F-15s, back towards their airfield. Magill increased speed again and lowered the nose as the MiGs began to turn. Instead of returning to their airfield, they turned south once again, into the path of the F-15s at about fifteen miles range. There is no evidence that either of the MiGs managed to lock on to the F-15s, but Magill and his No. 3, Capt. Rhory Draeger, USAF, both locked on AIM-7 Sparrows, one on to each of the Fulcrums, and they fired almost simultaneously, Magill firing two and Draeger one. All three missiles hit and both MiGs exploded with no sign of ejection by either pilot. Coming in behind them, the F-16s saw plenty of flak ahead, but it was uncoordinated. There were protective SAMs but as they switched on their radar so the F-4G Wild Weasels, who were flying behind the F-16s, fired HARM missiles over the top of them, and when they arrived over the airfields to drop their bombs the SAM sites had already been hit.

Up to midnight on the first day, Coalition aircraft flew 2,107 sorties and the Iraqis flew 24; the IAF lost eight aircraft in the air, including 3 MiG-29 Fulcrums and 3 Mirage F1s; the Coalition lost none.

On the second day Saddam Hussein attacked Israel with SCUD surface-to-surface missiles. One landed in Tel Aviv, causing casualties and four others landed harmlessly in open countryside. Another was fired towards Dharan in Saudi Arabia but was shot down by a US Patriot anti-missile. The SCUDS were armed with conventional explosive warheads, but there was also a possibility that Saddam Hussein might use them with either nuclear, biological or chemical weapons. If Israel entered the war to protect itself there could have been a split between the NATO element in the Coalition and the Arabs so the Coalition was keen to keep Israel out of the war in order to hold the Coalition together, and that meant hunting out the SCUDS and destroying them. The SCUD launchers were mobile launchers and they became high-priority targets for the Coalition. The aircraft used to hunt them down were mainly F-111s and F-15Es using LANTIRN at night armed with PGMs.

On the third day, 19 January, the IAF flew 55 sorties, the high point of its activity, and they lost six aircraft, four of them in air to air combat: two MiG-25s to AIM-7, one MiG-29 to AIM-7 and one MiG-29 through manoeuvring. The IAF had 66 airfields at the start of Desert Storm, 24 of them 'main bases'; within a week it could only operate from 5 of them. The IAF had been bombed or intimidated into virtual inactivity. As the Coalition effort continued, its air forces flew 3,000 sorties a day while the IAF could manage fewer than 40, and those that did venture to resist the Coalition air forces were met by air superiority fighters of vastly higher quality, both technically and in pilot skill. Many Coalition fighter pilots remarked, some with some apparent sadness, that each time they were given 'bogeys' to investigate by AWACS, and they manoeuvred to attack, the IAF fighters turned and fled.

The war against the Iraqi electronic defences was equally formidable. The Coalition started systematically taking them apart as soon as hostilities started. Unmanned RPVs, BQM-174Cs and ADM-141s were also used to simulate waves of Coalition aircraft approaching Iraqi territory, forcing the radar to light up and become instant targets for the F-4G Wild Weasels with their AGM-45 Shrike and AGM-88 HARM anti-radiation missiles, pre-briefed with intelligence about SAM sites and the frequencies their radar were likely to use, gathered during Desert Shield. The Wild Weasel crews' job was to fire their HARMs before the SAM operators could fire their missiles, and to saturate the defences while a second wave of Wild Weasels launched their HARMs over the top of the first wave.

The seven EC-130H COMPASS CALL aircraft in the theatre started jamming Iraqi communications from Day 1, leaving SAM batteries deprived of target information from the main air defence radar and forcing them to light up their own radar to search for targets. Around 200 Iraqi radar sites were knocked out in the first 72 hours, and in the first week of Desert Storm Iraqi radar activity had virtually ceased for fear of attracting attacks, leaving the airspace above the intended battlefield in southern Kuwait under Coalition control. Voice communication also virtually ceased, as did the flow of information within the Iraqi command structure, and commanders in the field did not receive any orders or communications of any kind for days on end. Saddam Hussein's army was without eyes or ears and that had its own, huge, demoralising effect.

Under an air superiority umbrella provided by F-15s on CAP and F-4Gs loitering over the area, ready with HARMs if any radar lit up, Coalition ground attack aircraft bombarded the Iraqi army in its defensive positions along the Saudi Arabian–Kuwaiti border. F-16s attacked the air defences around Kuwait City, Tornados, F-111s, Buccaneers and F-16s blew up bridges over the Euphrates to the rear of Iraqi forces in Kuwait in Iraq proper and attacked sites known to contain nuclear, biological and chemical warfare plants and SCUD launchers, and J-STARS crews co-ordinated F-16, AV-8B, A-10 and Jaguar fixed-wing attack aircraft and helicopters such as Apache on to a whole range of targets in the battlefield area. On 22 January a 60-vehicle Iraqi convoy was seen approaching Coalition forces in a potential outflanking movement. An air strike was ordered and 58 Iraqi tanks were destroyed. In the whole of Desert Storm, the two prototype J-STARS flew 49 sorties, averaging $10\frac{1}{2}$ hours each, and proved that the concept amounted to little short of a breakthrough in battlefield intelligence. Air force and army commanders could see their vast battlefield laid out before them in real time. It was as if the 'fog of war', the virtual blindfold which had afflicted commanders throughout history once the battle had started, had been lifted. Gen. Merrill McPeak, the Coalition air forces commander, said of J-STARS: 'We will not ever want to fight a war without a J-STARS kind of system.'

For Vietnam veterans it was never again to be the stop-go policies of Rolling Thunder. Air power was used unrelentingly against Iraq, never giving the enemy time or space to breathe, regroup or think, keeping up the pressure around the clock. The post-Vietnam intensive training programmes which were designed to improve skills were evident throughout USAF squadrons, but one unit stood out in the air-to-air war, the 33rd TFV, which scored 17 of the total of 32 air-to-air kills under the command of Col. Rick Parsons, who shot down two Su-22 Fitters himself.

Its pilots had a particular knack of being in the right place at the right time, and its maintenance crews had the aircraft ready, fully armed and fully serviced. It seemed to get everything right, being simply the best in every department, rather like Col. Robin Olds of the 8th TFW in Vietnam. Of the 36 pilots in the squadron, 12 scored kills, 4 of them double kills. One man who did stand out was Capt. Rhory Draeger, who had scored his first kill on Day 1 with Capt. Magill. On 26 January he was leading a flight of four F-15s on HavCAP and had just finished refuelling when an AWACS called up and passed information that four aircraft had just taken off from H2 airfield near the Jordanian border, nearly 100 miles north of their position. The enemy aircraft were heading northeast, away from the F-15s, but, ever eager, Draeger asked for clearance to go after them. The AWACS agreed and gave Draeger and Capt. Tony Shiavi a heading to intercept them. The F-15 pilots put on all the speed they could, but still could only close the gap slowly and realised that they would be out of fuel if they went on.

Just at the point where they had to consider turning back, the AWACS announced that four more had taken off from H2. The Americans feared a trap, that by going for the easier targets, the aircraft just taking off, they might find themselves sandwiched between two flights and at a numerical disadvantage, but when the AWACS reported that the first flight was off the screen the F-15 pilots realised they were in a perfect position for the new targets and started to close on them swiftly. The contacts were MiG-23 Floggers flying at low level. The Americans closed quickly, and one of the MiG-23s turned back to H2. At twenty miles Draeger's flight decided which one of them was going to go for which target and they lock up AIM-7 Sparrows. Draeger locked on to the leader, Shiavi on to the No. 2 and the other two F-15s in the flight both locked on to the third Flogger. Once inside range, all three F-15 pilots fired AIM-7 Sparrows and had to wait briefly before all three Floggers disintegrated and smashed into the ground. Draeger called the AWACS, 'Splash three Floggers'.

AWACS was the lynchpin of modern aerial combat. In Desert Storm the four AWACS airborne all the time orchestrated 3,000 carefully interwoven sorties each day. Great emphasis has been placed on the technology involved, but wielding that technology were men, airborne radar operators on the edge of the battle zone, thinking, reacting and giving the big picture to the fighter pilots who reacted almost as by invitation rather than an order to participate. Much has been written and speculated on regarding the integration of technology and people as the basis of what has been called 'cyborgs', short for cybernetic organisms. Ever since fighter pilots first started fighting each other in 1915, the fusing of men and machines has been part of their experience, and the best fighter pilots have always been at one with the technology which surrounds them. Mastering that process, and staying on top of the technology, has always been the mark of the most successful fighter pilots, and it was no different in the Gulf War.

Of the 32 air-to-air kills, F-15s were responsible for 30 of them, 28 to USAF pilots, 2 to Capt. Ayehid Salah al-Shmrani of the RSAF and 2 to US Navy pilots flying F/A-18s. There were no gun victories – all fell to missiles, 9 to all-aspect 'heaters, the evergreen Sidewinder in its AIM-9M and P variants, the remaining 23 to the longer range AIM-7 Sparrows which was the killer, the ultimate guardian of the air superiority in Desert Storm.

Air-to-air kills accounted for just one in nine of Iraq's 270 losses of combat aircraft. Intimidation had worked, and very few Iraqi fighters fought in the air, so the vast majority were destroyed on the ground, often in their hardened shelters where they fell victim to PGMs. After two weeks of pounding the Iraqis realised that there was no escape in Iraq and if they stayed there the entire IAF would be destroyed. Rather than face combat and virtually certain destruction, Iraqi fighter pilots chose to escape, flying to airfields in Iran, Iraq's former enemy. Demoralised and sensing defeat, a total of 148 pilots flew their aircraft to Iran, including 115 combat aircraft, until Coalition fighters intensified patrols along the border and closed off that escape route, too.

Gen. Tony Peak, Chief of Staff of the USAF, is philosophically generous to the IAF: 'I think they did rather well under the circumstances. They're a pretty good outfit; they happened to be the second best air force in the fracas. Having the second best air force is like having the second best hand in poker – it's often the best strategy to fold early. I think they folded early.'

Infowar systems and air power had been used to 'prepare the battlefield', a mixture of brainpower, high technology and brute force. Much has been made, and rightly so, of the success of the PGMs against specific targets, from bridges and HAS to underground command bunkers, but, with little danger from either air or ground based air defence systems, the B-52s from Diego Garcia in the Indian Ocean, and from bases in Britain, rained iron bombs on the Iraqi defences in Kuwait, accounting for half of all the bombs dropped in the war and killing many thousands of Iraqi soldiers in their fortified positions.

After thirty-five days Gen. Schwarzkopf started the ground war on 24 February 1991. With such a high level of control and the IAF grounded and unable to gather any intelligence on the movement of Coalition forces, he was able to use surprise to maximum effect, and he made good use of this freedom to move a huge force west, much of it by air in transports such as C-130 and in helicopters, moving men and supplies quickly into position to make an armoured thrust around the enemy's right flank. The plan was a complete surprise – one thrust going straight for Kuwait City, while the armoured thrust outflanked the Iraqi defences to the west. The ground war lasted four days, and after weeks of aerial bombardment large numbers of Iraqi soldiers surrendered without firing a shot.

On 26 January Saddam Hussein realised it was all over and announced that he had ordered the Iraqi army to withdraw from Kuwait. It left Kuwait City and started streaming north along the road to Basra inside Iraq, in what the J-STARS operators, who saw it all on their screens as a brightly illuminated, continuous thread of contacts, called 'the mother of all retreats'. They marshalled attack aircraft to mount a relentless attack on the dense traffic in what started out as merciless carnage, similar to that which had happened in Korea in 1950 when the North Koreans retreated without air cover, and in the Mitla Pass in 1967 when the Egyptian army was caught without air cover. One column of Iraqi vehicles was watched by J-STARS until it was well clear of Kuwait City, when USMC F/A-18s mined the road in front of it, bringing it to a halt. Flights of eight F/A-18s then queued up for 15-minute slots in the 'killing zone'. The Basra road was soon blocked with the burning wrecks of soft and armoured vehicles, loot which the Iraqi soldiers were taking back with them and dead bodies.

At the UN, Iraq asked for a cease-fire and promised to implement all of the UN Resolutions, but nobody in the Coalition trusted any Iraqi statement. That night a pair of F-111s of the 492 TFS/49 TFW, flown by Lt Col. David White and Lt Col. Kenneth Combs, took off from Taif air base in Saudi Arabia, armed with two completely new PGMs which had been developed during the war and rushed out that day from the USA after testing the same morning in New Mexico. They were designated GBU-28, and were made out of 20-foot lengths of used artillery barrels stuffed with 4,700 lb of high explosive with a Paveway laser-guidance system in the nose. Their target was an underground command bunker at Al Taji airfield north of Baghdad which the Iraqis believed was immune from attack. In tests the GBU-28, inevitably dubbed Deep Throat by the men who built it, had pierced 22 feet of reinforced concrete without difficulty, and through intelligence sources the precise position of the bunker was known. White and Combs dropped the two bombs right on target and video footage showed evidence of a small explosion coming out of one of the entrances, followed by a fierce secondary explosion. It was a demonstration that the mixture of high technology and good intelligence, allied to plenty of high explosive, could find enemy commanders deep in their bunkers where they had previously felt safe.

Saddam Hussein had ordered a withdrawal from Kuwait, but on 27 February his Republican Guard was still fighting hard against US and British armoured forces and he had not personally agreed to the UN Resolution so the air attacks continued throughout the day, including many by A-10 Warthogs against Iraqi tanks, and by evening most of the Iraqi army's fighting capacity had been destroyed. Only then did politics intervene: Iraq was defeated, and before the Gulf War turned into a pointless massacre a cease-fire was announced by President Bush.

The Gulf War had been planned around air superiority. Saddam Hussein was quoted as saying that 'no air force has ever been the decisive factor in a battle in the history of warfare'. Command of the air, achieved and maintained by skilled aircrews using highly capable aircraft with high-technology systems, had not only been decisive but had beaten his ground army. Air power could not have done it alone, ground forces would always have had to fight through what was left of the defences, to occupy and hold the ground, and in emphasising the central role of aircraft nothing should detract from the success of the ground and naval forces. But co-ordinated, concentrated air power made victory on the ground possible, victory achieved with an extraordinarily low level of Coalition casualties: with over half a million Coalition soldiers in the theatre, only 200 died. Saddam Hussein had wanted a war of attrition, 'the mother of all battles', on the ground. He believed that the Coalition would never have tolerated the level of casualties that a war fought on his terms would have created – a slogging match in the desert along the lines of the Iran–Iraq war, a war in which he could inflict enough casualties to make the Coalition fold its tent and go home. Instead, the Coalition used its overwhelming superiority in men and machines in the air to set its own agenda, then fight the war on its own terms, seeking to maximise any advantage. The result was that for the first time a field army had been soundly beaten by the surprise, flexibility and destructiveness of air power, something which had been the subject of debate ever since air warfare had first become a reality, and something which many, including Saddam Hussein, believed would never be possible. The Iraqis, and the rest of the world, had been taught just how far air warfare had advanced in the two decades since the Vietnam and previous Arab–Israeli wars.

The strategy had been right: Coalition air forces flew 114,000 separate sorties, over half of them, 65,000, flown by US aircraft; they lost 60 aircraft, none of them in aerial combat. There were mistakes – 21 British soldiers were killed by USAF A-10s through mistaken identification, a B-52 was damaged by a HARM missile which locked on to its electronic counter-measures; some Iraqi targets were hit more often than necessary because of the lack of enough photo-reconnaissance aircraft, but by any military standards the war was a resounding success, if not a triumph, for the Coalition. Instant Thunder had been shown to be a better policy than Rolling Thunder, and the USAF went home with its status much enhanced, both at home and abroad, many of the ghosts of Vietnam expunged. The F-117A, which dropped the first bomb of the war on an air defence control centre, had shown the value of stealth technology and how valuable independence from support aircraft could be. F-117As represented 2.5% of the strength of Coalition combat aircraft, but achieved 31% very accurate hits with PGMs, 1,271 combat sorties without a scratch.

The West's newest air-to-air missile, the AIM-120 AMRAAM, was not ready in time for the conflict, and though several examples were rushed out before the end of hostilities none of them was used in combat. Ironically, nearly two years after the Gulf War, on 27 December 1992, the AMRAAM was used for the first time in anger over Iraq. Following the war, the USAF, RAF and L'Armée de L'Air were tasked with imposing No-Fly Zones over northern and southern Iraq, operating from bases in Turkey and Kuwait. When an Iraqi MiG-25 Foxbat poked its long nose twenty miles into the southern zone, a USAF F-16 engaged from long range with an AIM-120 and shot it down, the first hostile use of the AMRAAM.

In the Gulf War as a whole, 1,300 AGM-88 HARMs were fired and 250 radar sites were destroyed; the highest scorer was Capt. Vince Quinn with Maj. Ken Spaar in the back of the F-4G Phantom who fired 30 missiles and knocked out 12 sites. The role of Suppression of Air Defences (SEAD) was not as glamorous as air-to-air combat, and there is no benchmark for becoming an ace, but their role is every bit as important in securing air superiority.

Although it is deeply unfashionable in some quarters to say so, winning a war remains something to celebrate, and there was a great deal of celebration, both among NATO countries and in the Middle East, at the Coalition victory. Whatever view one takes on the politics of the Middle East, like Argentina's invasion of the Falkland Islands on a much smaller scale, many countries and the UN had shown that invading one's neighbour would bring retribution, and victory in that context was undeniably welcome to most people, especially those with worrisome, belligerent neighbours.

The danger is that the wrong conclusions are drawn from the Gulf War. The fourth generation of NATO jet fighters, designed for confrontation in Europe, had fought and won their first battles in the Persian Gulf. Desert Storm was a victory for NATO air power, but it was against a much smaller, inherently inferior air force whose equipment was a generation behind, following a doctrine of tight control which had been shown to be second best when confronted with highly flexible air forces operating at the front edge of technological progress. It was an appropriate response to the problem, but against a much larger, more determined enemy, with a range of aircraft and weapons closer to that of the Coalition, the result could have been very different. The air campaign in the Gulf War was based firmly on the idea of superiority. The whole point was to be superior, to make every effort to be the best, not to fight with restraint but to fight to win, be proud of it and not apologise for it. That lesson should not be forgotten.

CHAPTER ELEVEN
Pinball Policemen

On 19 June 1995 the tear-stained face of an American fighter pilot stared out from the front cover of *Time* magazine; his name was Capt. Scott O'Grady, USAF. He had been plucked from semi-obscurity to international acclaim, not for having won in aerial combat but for having been shot down over Bosnia. Two weeks earlier, on 2 June, O'Grady had been flying an F-16 over Bosnia as part of Operation Deny Flight, a UN peace-keeping operation using NATO air power to deny the Bosnian Serbs use of air power in the civil war between Serbs, Muslims and Croats in Bosnia, which followed the break-up of Yugoslavia. O'Grady had been flying over an area between Banja Luca and Bihac, which NATO intelligence regarded as free from Serbian SAMs, when his flight leader, Capt. Bob 'Wilbur' Wright, saw his wingman's aircraft explode. O'Grady's F-16 disintegrated before Wright could see whether his colleague had ejected or not. He had, in fact, ejected, and he landed by parachute in an area heavily populated and patrolled by Bosnian Serbs. For six days he evaded capture, hiding in scrub and moving at night, trying to find a place where he could use his personal radio to bring in a rescue helicopter. He had a personal locator beacon that emitted a constant signal which was picked up intermittently by other NATO aircraft patrolling the area, but for several days it was unclear whether it really was him or whether the Serbs had captured him and were using the bleeper to lure the rescue helicopters into a trap.

After six days the NATO headquarters at Aviano airbase in Italy decided that on the balance of the evidence it could be O'Grady, and mounted a huge intelligence operation involving satellites, AWACS and reconnaissance aircraft to pinpoint his position and make certain. In the early hours of 8 June an F-16 pilot from O'Grady's own wing, Capt. Thomas Hanford, heard him calling over his radio, using his personal call sign. Hanford asked him questions about the squadron in which he had served in Korea, which only O'Grady could have answered. He did, then Hanford reported his position to an AWACS which in turn alerted the commander of the 24th Marine Expeditionary Unit aboard the USS *Kearsage* in the Adriatic. By dawn the rescue was under way: 51 Marines on board two CH-53E Super Stallion helicopters, one for the rescue, one as back-up, escorted by two USMC AH-1W Super Cobra helicopter gunships, and two AV-8B Harrier VSTOL fighters riding shotgun. A second, identical, force was put together in case something went badly wrong. To guard against SAM attack, two USN EA-6B Prowler SEAD aircraft were launched and they in turn were escorted by two Marine F/A-18D Hornets and two USAF A-10 Warthogs in case there were any Serbian tanks – 18 aircraft in all, and well over 120 personnel, not including all the AWACS and other recce aircraft, to rescue one US fighter pilot.

The leading rescue team reached the area around 6.35 that morning. As soon as he saw it, O'Grady set off a yellow flare and the helicopter pilot homed in on it immediately. O'Grady broke his cover, ran towards the waiting machine and jumped in before any of the Marines had even got out, and they were soon on their way. On the return flight to the Adriatic coast, the helicopter pilot used evasive tactical flying techniques, throwing everybody around in the back; they did come under fire from SA-7 shoulder-launched missiles which missed, but they were hit by small-arms fire before arriving back on board the *Kearsage*.

Huge resources had been used to save O'Grady from capture. The news was flashed to the White House where President Clinton was so relieved he reportedly smoked a cigar to celebrate. For a few weeks a single fighter pilot seemed to symbolise the power of the USA. When he arrived back in the USA he was given a hero's welcome and held a televised press conference, which only magnified his status as a national symbol. There was the humanitarian issue, which anybody would understand; there was also his value as a trained F-16 pilot which, though considerable, was small alongside the psychological value of not letting him fall into Bosnian Serb hands. His tenacity in evading capture and the skill of the team that rescued him, all transmitted immediately round the world on television, were symbolic of American prowess in the air. That view, though understandable, was misplaced. The rescue to some extent obscured the fact that he had been shot down in the first place, and that had been due to a failure by NATO intelligence to fully appreciate the danger of SA-6 in the area. It was a vivid illustration of the fine dividing line between being on top of the situation and being on the defensive, between imposing air superiority and accepting something less, between the need to operate unfettered by political constraints and the realities of the political situation.

Air power was used very differently in Bosnia-Herzegovina to the Gulf War. An Air Exclusion Zone had been established in 1992 by UN Resolution and it became effective in March 1993, but, unlike the Gulf, where the enemy, the battlelines and the objective were clear, the map of Bosnia was a patchwork of Serb, Muslim and Croat enclaves, some of them safe areas protected by UNPRO-FOR, the UN force with the unenviable task of trying to make peace between the warring parties while delivering humanitarian aid. The USA had argued for the use of air strikes to bring the belligerents, particularly the Serbs, to the conference table, but European governments and the UN had resisted them, pointing out that the USA did not have troops on the ground and that provoking the Serbs would result in harassment of their troops, or worse. UNPROFOR was a small international force without a war-fighting capability, and even without provocation it was constantly being humiliated on the ground by having to deal with Serb, Muslim and Croat militias who erected road blocks to stop the convoys of humanitarian aid which the troops were protecting.

Operation Deny Flight was designed to stop combat aircraft of the ex-Yugoslavian Air Force, largely in the hands of the Serbs, from either intervening or attacking UNPROFOR, and NATO resolve had been demonstrated on 28 February 1994 when six Serb G-4 Super Galeb light attack aircraft attacked a Muslim warehouse. They were detected by a NATO AWACS which vectored a flight of F-16s to the area. After visual identification and a radio warning, one of the F-16 pilots locked on an AIM-120 AMRAAM, fired and hit one of the G-4s. The F-16s were now close enough to engage with AIM-9 Sidewinders and the same pilot fired two, bringing down two more G-4s, then a second F-16 pilot shot down a fourth. It was the first military action by NATO forces operating as NATO in the Alliance's 45-year history.

The harassment of UNPROFOR on the ground continued into 1995. Cease-fires came and went, and the Serbs in particular shelled UN 'safe areas', killing Muslim civilians in Sarajevo and Bihac. The UN was unwilling to allow unfettered use of air power to restrain the Serbs and insisted that any response should be 'proportionate', usually a counter artillery barrage and occasionally an air strike against the guns. In April 1995 the Serbs were warned that they faced harsher consequences, and when Serb artillery fired on a safe area in May, and the deadline for the withdrawal of the guns passed with no response, NATO aircraft bombed an ammunition dump near the Bosnian-Serb capital, Pale. As had been predicted, the Serbs responded by taking 300 UN soldiers hostage, showing them on television chained to other potential targets for NATO air strikes.

The hostages were eventually released, but tension on the ground grew, and it was against that background that O'Grady's flight was made on 2 June. Whether bringing down an F-16 was part of the retaliation for the air strike on Pale is not known, but there is evidence that the Serbs had laid a trap for the NATO air forces, and had successfully taken O'Grady, Wright and the huge electronic monitoring effort which surrounded Deny Flight by surprise. It appears they carefully monitored the regular routes taken by the Deny Flight aircraft, which were pretty difficult to vary in such a small piece of airspace, then moved an SA-6 system into the area, which they had previously kept clean of SAMs, at the last minute.

They then used separate acquisition and target tracking radar in case they were detected, before firing the missile from directly beneath O'Grady; it needed only twenty seconds to reach him.

Had they killed or captured him, it would have been a huge propaganda coup which could have influenced international public opinion, already against the air strikes, and US policy. The European media were largely against air strikes and the debate continued, as did the anarchy on the ground, but through July and August NATO resolve grew, and there was as much debate in its circles about what the response should be. Many senior officers believed that the only way to proceed was to establish air superiority by destroying the Bosnian-Serb air defence system before it did any more damage. That was impossible under the terms of the UN Resolution so, in the meantime, they ordered that flights over Bosnia should have increased SEAD support. There was a total of around 250 aircraft involved in Deny Flight, 150 of them fighters, the rest supporting those operations, including 20 USAF EF-111A Ravens and USN EA-6B Prowlers for air defence suppression. In July they were joined by eight specialised F-16Cs equipped with AGM-88 HARMs and ASQ-213 HTS, HARM Targeting System, an underwing pod which turned the single-seat F-16 into a Wild Weasel.

NATO already had AWACS deployed in the area, but in July 1995, to bolster the intelligence-gathering powers, the USA deployed its latest UAV, Predator, a small aircraft about the size of a motorcycle, which operated initially from Albania from where the CIA was already using an earlier system, Gnat 750. Predator had an endurance of 40 hours, giving it the ability to loiter over Bosnia at altitudes up to 25,000 feet, or low down, using video cameras, SAR and other sensors to build up a clear picture of the Serbian air defences and other potential targets. Among the first jobs for its operators was to follow the mobile SA-6 batteries as they were moved around the country. USAF commanders longed to take out the anti-aircraft systems, but instead they used EF-111 Ravens, Prowlers, F-16C HTS and Predators to create 'SEAD windows', periods which intelligence showed were as safe as possible for the patrolling fighters.

Everything changed on 28 August 1995 when artillery shells rained down on a busy Sarajevo marketplace, killing 37 people and wounding 85 more. In a thoroughly dirty war, with many atrocities, it was an atrocity too far, and while Serbs and Muslims blamed each other for the shelling, NATO experts were sure it was the Bosnian Serbs who fired on the city. The USA proposed bombing the Serbs until they agreed to a cease-fire, and European resistance, weakened by the wave of revulsion which the television pictures of the bodies in the marketplace produced, eventually crumbled. The UN gave NATO the green light to bomb the Serbs to the conference table and at 2 a.m. on 30 August Operation Deny Flight became Operation Deliberate Force.

NATO fighters, 60% of them American, hit 90 targets, starting with the Bosnian-Serb integrated air defence system but including command centres, ammunition dumps and artillery positions, pre-selected inside specific zones of action agreed with the UN. The attacks were made in the knowledge that they could be delivered with great accuracy, arising from the huge amount of intelligence which had been gathered and the certainty which PGMs gave of hitting the target. When the pilots were briefed in Italy they were shown the latest video footage of their targets, shot from Predator UAVs, so that when they arrived over the Sarajevo area they were immediately familiar with the terrain and where their targets were in it, enabling them to set up and drop their PGMs on the first pass and deliver them with pinpoint accuracy, causing maximum damage to the intended target while minimising collateral damage. The attacks went on for two days, destroying the Bosnian-Serb air defences and a great many ammunition dumps, command centres and artillery emplacements. They were stopped on 2 September to give the Serbs a chance to talk but when they refused it started again on 5 September and continued until 14 September, including attacks on bridges and warehouses, using Tomahawk cruise miss-iles, until the Serbs agreed to sit round the conference table.

In all, 3,500 sorties were flown, 750 of them by attack aircraft, the rest in support, and in the course of the attacks one French Mirage 2000 was shot down and its crew captured. Later analysis on the ground showed that 80% of the strikes had been on target.

The talks took place at Wright Patterson AFB near Dayton, Ohio, where the parties were forced to hammer out a detailed agreement to end the fighting. A cease-fire was agreed on 21 October and the final Agreement was signed on 14 December. In January a new peacekeeping force, IFOR, including 60,000 US troops, moved in, and as part of the agreement the two French airmen shot down in August were released.

Three years of hesitation by the UN and most European governments had resulted in the worst atrocities since those of Nazi Germany, and they were brought to an end by the Serbs capitulating in the face of the overwhelming force of NATO air power. Once again, as in the Gulf, though this time it was against even weaker opposition, air power had achieved a positive result for the UN/NATO in the new, uncertain world order. The NATO fighters were virtually unopposed, which cannot be assumed in future conflicts, but Deny Flight showed that even in peacekeeping operations, while troops are needed to hold the ground, air superiority remained the key prerequisite to carrying out ground operations without unacceptable casualties, and that air power, if applied robustly and very precisely, could establish control over even very complicated situations by 'imposing peace from 15,000 feet'.

Deny Flight in Bosnia and the No-Fly Zones in Iraq are demonstrations of the versatility of air power. The precise conditions which applied in the Gulf and the Balkans may not arise again, but existing NATO equipment, with its emphasis on high technology and on highly skilled pilots and systems operators, though designed and built for high-intensity war, can be adapted to the needs of what are now termed 'operations other than war' (OOTW). The main lesson is not to misuse it, either by emasculating it with political constraints or by using it simply to massacre weaker opponents.

Peacekeeping OOTW is one of the themes of the 1990s, but planning for full-scale war remains the primary role of NATO and the air forces of the world's most advanced countries. During the Cold War each side responded to the technical developments of the other, almost regardless of cost. In 1989, as the Iron Curtain crumbled, so procurement and planning slowed on both sides and all Western armed forces had their budgets cut. Senior USAF commanders, long imbued with the idea of quality above all else, took a conscious decision to counter the effect of budget cuts by training smaller numbers of the best people and giving them the best technology they could afford, keeping their edge rather than keeping up numbers. The USAF was reduced by a third, and as it contracted, on 1 June 1992, SAC and TAC, the old commands which reflected the bomber and fighter view of the world, were rationalised and fused together into Air Combat Command (ACC). ACC is divided into composite groups with fighters, strike aircraft and jammers. The changes were being planned well before the Gulf War, and it came out of that war very well, blowing away most of the ghosts of the muddle which had led to ultimate defeat in Vietnam.

Air power is central to NATO's war-making ability and to US power projection. Any threat would be met with a massive *ab initio* attack on the enemy – getting in first, using every advantage to the full and being ruthless in using air power to paralyse the enemy, particularly its command structure and communications. Unmanned aircraft, often working with manned aircraft, already play a significant role in intelligence-gathering in the initial phase of any operations. During Desert Storm, US UAVs, particularly Pioneer, flew over 500 missions gathering valuable information and others were used as decoys to deceive and disrupt the Iraqi integrated air defence system.

In the attack phase the pilots' job is to fight to open a gap in the enemy's Forward Line of Troops (FLOT) so that other aircraft can go through and strike at targets in the rear while others support ground operations, at the same time denying that same space and ability to the enemy, very similar to the basic job defined on the Western Front in 1918. In this phase, the 'cappers' and SEAD aircraft are mutually supportive, the fighters protecting the Weasels from the air threat while the Weasels defend the cappers from the SAM threat. Soft targets such as AWACS, J-STARS, Rivet Joint and tankers are kept well away from the FLOT, protected by HavCAPs, then move forward as air superiority is established. The next job is to prise that gap apart, widening and deepening the corridors and breaking down the overlapping integrated air defence system. As a basic doctrine, it worked in the Bekaa in 1982 and in the Gulf in 1991.

In the post-Cold War world, the USA, Israel and the European countries continue to use the latest technologies to give their air forces the edge, no longer regardless of cost, but the philosophy continues to be the search for the best even if programmes have slowed down and some have been abandoned. The economic impact of the collapse of the Soviet Union had a greater effect on the Soviet Air Force, which was already going through change before 1989 as policy shifted from relying on large numbers of tightly controlled, role-specific aircraft to combining that with the need to match NATO in highly capable, more autonomous fighters and moving away from the inflexible GCI system. Part of the post-Cold War world order was negotiated force reductions on both sides which meant that, even putting economic considerations aside, the SAF would no longer be able to rely on weight of numbers where it lacked technological parity. In 1990 the Soviet Union had 6,500 combat aircraft; by 1994 Russia, as the biggest member of its successor, the Commonwealth of Independent States (CIS), had reduced that number to 2,500, and even those statistics hid the true picture. According to the Chief of Staff, General Deynekin, due to Russia's worsening economic position, by 1995 the SAF was only getting 30% of its smaller budget, reducing R&D to a snail's pace and cutting back on already low levels of maintenance and training. In an ideal world fighter pilots should get 200–250 hours in the air every year; in 1995 Russian pilots were getting between 30 and 40, leading to a higher accident rate, which in turn added to costs. To try and compensate, the SAF and the aircraft industry was encouraged by the Russian government to earn hard currency by operating as a business and exporting to supplement its budget.

The Soviet Union's move towards more autonomous, multi-role fighters along Western lines, the MiG-29 and Su-27, with pilot training to match, was a reaction to seeing its client states beaten by US-backed states, especially by Israel in the Middle East. At the same time it clung to the pure interceptor tradition with a derivative of the MiG-25 Foxbat, the two-seater, Mach 2.4 MiG-31 Foxhound which was first deployed in 1983. It had a combat radius of 1,300 miles, a ceiling of 100,000 feet, but no dogfighting capability. Its big radar had a 190-mile range with a look down shoot down capability and, to make them more autonomous and free them from the constraints of GCI, the crews created their own AWACS by clubbing together, flying four MiG-31s in line abreast, 125 miles apart, so that their combined radar covered a 550-mile-wide front, then swapping information between the fighters on a data link. It was armed with up to eight AAMs, four AA-8 Aphid and four AA-9 Amos and was designed to take more advanced AAMs such as

AA-12 'Amraamski' and the KS-172 long-range missile which could be fired from 250 miles. Its role remained defence against strategic bombers, but its look down shoot down capability also gave it a role against low-flying cruise missiles such as Tomahawk, and it could engage NATO strike packages from above, in particular searching for the high-value aircraft such as AWACS, tankers, J-STARS, Rivet Joints and their HavCAPs operating well behind the FLOT.

With the collapse of the Soviet Union, the veil of secrecy that surrounded the Soviet aircraft industry was partially lifted, and the full extent of the effort which had taken place behind the Iron Curtain in the closing years of the Cold War became evident in the early 1990s. New fighters were put on display, not at May Day parades but at the Western commercial air shows in Paris and Farnborough, demonstrating that the latest Russian fighters were not only as good as the West's, if not better in some aspects, but also available for export for hard cash rather than ideological brotherhood.

Western intelligence had always believed that the MiG-29 Fulcrum and the Su-27 Flanker, which entered service in 1985 and 1984 respectively, were not much more than large copies of the YF-17 Cobra and the F-15 Eagle and therefore ten years behind. They were wrong, and Western experts were startled, and the public thrilled, as they gave a dazzling display of their power and agility for the first time in the West at the Farnborough Air Show in 1990, in particular the spectacular tail-sliding aerobatic manoeuvres known as the Hook and Cobra, designed to confuse hostile radar. The MiG-29 had a thrust to weight ratio of 1.35:1, giving it an initial rate of climb of 65,000 feet, twice the height of Everest, in a minute. It clearly did represent a completely new breed of Soviet fighter, finely engineered and more durable than its predecessors, if rather large. Its electronic systems were greatly improved, though still behind NATO equivalents, and the initial admiration for the MiG-29 in the West has worn off as Western experts have had opportunities to see them up close and even to fly them, as happened in Germany when the Luftwaffe inherited large numbers of them following the collapse of the Berlin Wall. The Luftwaffe found its radar and radar warning systems unreliable and export versions were eventually offered with Western avionics.

The Su-27 Flanker, the Russian equivalent of the F-15, was impressive. It is the most powerful fighter in the world, and is likely to remain so into the next century. With a total of 55,000 lb of thrust, its outright performance is greater than the MiG-29, and it snatched a total of 31 time-to-height records. It is inherently unstable with full fly-by-wire controls, a 150-mile radar with an integrated fire control system on the lines of the F-15, the full range of the latest Russian AAMs, IR sensors, with information from them all either projected into the pilot's helmet or on to a wide-angle HUD. The Su-27 is the basis of a Sukhoi family of air superiority fighters, culminating in the Su-35 which will have vectored thrust, giving short take-off capability, high man-oeuvrability and a much improved radar with a range of 250 miles. In computer-simulated combat with the latest F-15 in the USA, the Su-35 showed that it was the equal to, if not slightly ahead of, the American fighter, though the comparison ignores the fact that the F-15 is now twenty years old and the Su-35 is not yet oper-ational; it should go into service in Russia before the end of the century.

The MiG-29 and Su-27 are still armed with a cannon, but their new missiles, the AA-10 Alamo, a Sparrow equivalent, and the AA-11 Archer all-aspect heat-seeker, are examples of a new gen-eration of AAMs which are coming into service in the 1990s. The AA-11 is initially slaved to the fighter's radar and Infra Red Search and Track (IRST) system which scans a wide field of view and points the missile's seekers in the right direction. Once a target has been acquired, it is then switched to the pilot's helmet sight to cue a lock-on in the much narrower heat-seeker cone by moving his head through 180 degrees rather than by manoeuvring the whole aircraft, then launching it without moving the aircraft to point at its target first. The AA-11 has overtaken the venerable US AIM-9 Sidewinder, as have both the Europeans and the Israelis in close quarter air combat missiles. A BAe-led consortium with Hughes in America, in which BAe makes the missile and Hughes the Imaging Infra Red (IIR) homer, has produced the short-range AIM-132 ASRAAM which is also slaved to the pilot's helmet sight. ASRAAM is tail-steered, making it very agile, and its homer trans-mits a picture of the target which the pilot can use to choose a particular area of the target aircraft to hit. It should enter service on RAF Harrier GR.7s in the late 1990s. The Israelis' IIR short-range AAM with helmet sight, the Python III, is similar.

Now over fifty years old, the last major development in the AIM-9 was the all-aspect L model, which did very well in the Falklands and in the Middle East. Later models are slaved to the fighter's radar for target acquisition, but not to the pilot's helmet. Sidewinder has not been developed at the same pace as the radar-based missile in the USA, the AIM-120 AMRAAM on which R&D has focused for many years as an eventual replacement for the AIM-7 Sparrow. The AIM-120 is as small as a Sidewinder but much longer-range, with a radar seeker that enables the pilot to engage several targets at once and fire several missiles at once against different targets. Once it has been fired, the AIM-120 can be forgotten; it has all the homing and guidance radar on board, unlike the Sparrow which relies on the fighter's radar to supply data about the target while in flight. Russia has an equivalent to AIM-120 in development, the AA-12 Adder, known less officially within NATO circles as 'Amraamski', which should be in service before the end of the century.

The next generation of Sidewinders is scheduled to come into service in 2002, the AIM-9X, which is linked to an Agile Eye helmet sight, and beyond that there is a Sidewinder in development for internal storage in the next generation of clean-lined, stealthy US fighters, which, like the AA-11, ASRAAM and Python III, can be fired without pointing the aircraft at its opponent.

The US Navy, which originated work on the Sidewinder, leads the world in long-range AAMs with the AIM-54 Phoenix which can be fired from up to a hundred miles away at a small target, or up to 240 miles for larger, bomber or AWACS-sized aircraft, using the F-14 Tomcat's new AN/AWG-9 radar which can track 24 separate targets at once.

The job of the new Russian fighters is to take on the strike package and win, and there are concerns in NATO fighter circles that if enough MiG-31s, MiG-29s, Su-27s and Su-35s survive the *ab initio* air attack with their new Short, Medium and Long Range missiles, they could blunt the effectiveness of the strike package. The idea of the Hook and Cobra manoeuvres demonstrated at Farnborough was not meant for tangling with F-15s, but to avoid detection by the AWACS and their escort fighters' own intercept radar by sudden moves which would interrupt the Doppler effect for just long enough for the hostile radar to lose contact for a time.

One tactic, which has emerged from talking to Russian pilots, is for two pairs of Su-27s to fly towards a strike package from a distance, the wingman 25 metres or so behind the leader and just far enough to one side to avoid the jet efflux and vortices. When the Su-27 RWR warns the pilot that the AWACS radar has made contact with him, the two leaders execute a Hook or Cobra, shifting position so quickly they create a tiny window of confusion for the AWACS and its computers during which the two leaders then dive for the deck, leaving the AWACS radar to lock back on to the two wingmen who continue to fly at the same height and speed as if nothing had happened. The two leaders meanwhile have hit the deck and now attack from low level, using IRST to search for the AWACS at long range, then firing a salvo of KS.172 AAMs which penetrate the HavCAP fighter shield and hit the high-value target.

There is always the spare ready in the air, but NATO doctrine has become so reliant on the command, communications, control, intelligence and data-processing role of these huge and vulnerable aircraft that shooting them down would cause widespread confusion, and they cannot operate in an area where air superiority has not been established, and establishing it without them, or by pushing them back too far from the FLOT, would make establishing that superiority much more difficult in the first place.

The one big difference is that the Russian doctrine, though now closer to that of the West, is still essentially defensive, reacting to events rather than setting the agenda with offensive action of its own. Air power is essentially offensive, hence the reliance by the West on an *ab initio* attack to paralyse the defences and the communications first. The strike package relies on suppressing the enemy's ground-based air defences which in turn relies on SEAD operations. The cost of having a dedicated Wild Weasel aircraft is very high; the F-4Gs have been retired and the EF-111 Ravens are near the end of their lives, but instead of replacing dedicated SEAD aircraft the USA is converting F-16Cs into instant Wild Weasels by attaching a HARM Targeting System (HTS) pod, known in the trade as 'weasel in a can', which can be hung on quickly with the latest AGM-88 anti-SAM missile which, once it has locked on to SAM's radar, if the radar is switched off, an inertial navigation system (INS) stores details of the target so that AGM-88 can continue to the target. Beyond HTS there is the Precision Direction Finder (PDS), which will turn the single-seat F-15 into a Weasel.

There has been a long debate about the effectiveness of single-seat Weasels, a job which has traditionally relied heavily on backseater expertise. Weasel crews work together, and one of the problems of handing over to a single-seater is that the intimacy of that relationship, and the intuition which backseaters develop about how enemy radar operators will react in the subtleties of an electronic battle of wits – the ability to use the human mind to analyse the enemy's tactics, consider what may or may not be decoys, ploys and ruses, to get inside the mind of the enemy in a way that the computer cannot, to override computers, to avoid friendly fire incidents, to outwit the enemy – will be lost, and once it is lost it will be very difficult to replace. The single-seat Weasel means that the lone fighter pilot will inevitably rely more on computers.

The other view is that the backseater can be safely replaced by electronics and computers, including a system called Pilot's Associate, an electronic buddy based on artificial intelligence which has been developed for the next generation of fighters that monitors the aircraft systems and alerts the pilot to any potential problems and to any changes in the overall air battle which could affect his position, offering him potential solutions which he can accept or reject. Resistance to machines replacing craftsmen is centuries old, and while the craft of the Wild Weasel backseater is only just over thirty years old its passing into history now seems as certain as the way electronics have replaced navigators, bombardiers and flight engineers over the last fifty years.

New technology continues to change the environment of aerial combat profoundly, but many of the basic principles of air warfare endure. Oswald Boelke's first dictum, to 'secure all possible advantage before attacking', remains as true as it has always been, and the determination and aggressiveness implied by the second, 'always carry through an attack once you have started', remains equally true. The biggest change that technology has brought about in the last fifty years is in the size of the aerial battlefield, which has grown prodigiously. With closing speeds well over Mach 4, fighters need a huge piece of sky in order to manoeuvre for advantage, and with the advent of more powerful and longer range radar and missiles the battle starts with electronic contact between opposing fighters up to 130 nautical miles apart, well Beyond Visual Range (BVR).

Of all Boelke's dicta, only open fire at very close range' is the one that has changed completely. Today fighters work with AWACS to establish 'BVR kill boxes', huge, three-dimensional chunks of sky defined by radar and the range of missiles where all aircraft are assumed to be hostile. 'Always keep your eye on your opponent' is difficult with BVR, but applying the same rule to maintaining radar contact with all threats is the modern equivalent. 'Always attack your enemy from behind', though not obligatory thanks to 'all-aspect' AAMs, remains the favoured tactic, and even in today's smaller number of hostile aerial encounters 80% of all victories are from the six o'clock position, and few pilots who are hit see their opponent in time. 'Always turn to meet your opponent' remains equally true – the head-on shot is still the most difficult – and 'remember your line of retreat' is also true in an ever more hostile environment including SAMs.

Formation flying and the wingman principle, which Boelke first identified as the most effective way to fight in the air, remain at the core of the fighter pilot's *modus operandi*. The tactical formation has continued to widen, and while the wingman's job is still to protect his leader's tail the wider 'Kette' formations favoured by Adolph Galland and his Me 262 pilots and the even wider 'Loose Deuce' of the Vietnam era have given way to a separation of up to three miles, with the wingman either slightly higher or lower than the leader, making the pair less easy to spot visually. Wider formations take several miles to turn, but they are a less vulnerable target for IADS and they leave both pilots more room to use their ever more powerful ECM and radar to scan ever more airspace for potential threats.

After the size of the battlefield, the next most profound change is in the amount of information which a fighter pilot has to process about many different kinds of threats, potential targets, his own weapons, the position of friendly forces, navigational information, fuel states – the list is endless. Voice communication between fighter pilots, and between fighter pilots and AWACS, is giving way to secure data links which constantly swap information and add to situational awareness, updating the on-board computers and displaying the 'big picture' not only right in front of the pilot on screens but, increasingly, straight into his helmet.

Some of the major problems with the increased size of the aerial battlefield and BVR kill boxes, and the increased amount of information being processed, are target acquisition and identification and making the decision to fire when the target has not been identified visually. AWACS, the 'Big Eye', is the hub of the network of airborne computers that form the brain of the battle. The basic means of identifying targets remains IFF, a small transmitter that broadcasts a continuous code identifying an aircraft as military or civil, with special secure codes available in time of war. In many engagements short of all-out war, for various reasons, visual identification has been required, but this is contrary to the optimum use of the new long-range radar and missiles whose sole purpose is the BVR kill. Systems currently available for AWACS use computers to take the radar signals that come back from a contact and match the modulation from the fan blades of a jet engine to identify the aircraft as friendly or hostile, but it still relies on a computer for positive identification. AWACS and J-STARS console operators are beginning to get information in a form and at a time when allocating the target to a fighter will come long before the fighter pilot can see the opponent, which raises a major dilemma: who decides to fire, console operator or fighter pilot, computer or Mk 1 Eyeball?

Reliance on computers nearly led to a major disaster in January 1994 when an AWACS picked up a contact flying in the southern No-Fly Zone in Iraq which it decided was a bandit and authorised a pair of US Navy F/A-18 Hornets to shoot it down at BVR. The Navy pilots decided to wait for a visual identification, which was fortunate because when they saw the bandit it turned out to be a Sudanese airliner. Three months later, over the northern No-Fly Zone, an AWACS picked up what its computers decided were two Iraqi Mi-24 Hind helicopters attacking a Kurdish village in defiance of the cease-fire arrangements. There were no IFF signals so the target was passed to two US F-15Cs, who also failed to get a friendly IFF, locked on and fired missiles without making visual contact, shooting down the two helicopters. They turned out to be US Army UH-60A Blackhawks operating with the United Nations as part of Operation Provide Comfort on an inspection flight who had switched off their IFF because it was overheating. Twenty-six UN personnel died. These incidents underlined one of the main arguments against unmanned fighters with their inherent reliance on computers, namely that even in the heat of full-scale war when the human condition is at its most ruthless, let alone in peacekeeping and OOTW, there is a troubling response to the idea of giving a computer the final say in whether to unleash lethal weapons.

Finding the enemy and seeing him first, then identifying him as hostile, either by eye or by radar, is a problem as old as air warfare, and ever since the Second World War the principal means of looking for the enemy has been radar. Making aircraft invisible to radar offers a huge advantage, and the search for stealth aircraft during the Cold War was part of the technological revolution of the 1970s and 1980s.

The operational aircraft nearest to the future is the F-117A Nighthawk, the Stealth Fighter. The USA is the only country with stealth aircraft, and it proved its value in the opening hours of the Gulf War by operating over Baghdad without the massive SEAD and ECM back-up of a conventional strike package, but in the endless dialectic between new technologies and competing military applications the F-117A gave up manoeuvrability for stealth and concealment. It is not really a fighter at all – it is an attack aircraft with smart bombs and missiles stored internally rather than hanging off the wings where they would disturb the stealth profile. If it was intercepted by even the most lowly air superiority fighter, it would have little or no ability to fight its way out of the engagement; hence it can only operate at night. To maintain its invisibility to radar, it must fly in radio silence and must not manoeuvre in the combat zone for fear that a change in its profile in relation to the radar gives it away. Relying so completely on concealment, if a new radar detection system were able to detect the F-117A, that would make it obsolete overnight.

Apart from the lack of manoeuvrability, the biggest difference for the pilot compared with a conventional fighter is that while an F-15 or F-16 is designed around high visibility from the cockpit, the F-117A pilot rarely looks out of the cockpit, getting all his information from three computer screens which are fed with data from on-board computers, from data links, from satellites and from a Forward-Looking Infra-Red (FLIR) 'ball' in the nose, which constantly tracks the aircraft's position and that of potential targets, displaying all the information on the screen rather like a video game. It has a top speed of 650 m.p.h., but is not that thirsty and has a range of 1,200 miles. It has no gun, but can carry Sidewinders internally for use against enemy AWACS by creeping up on them unawares. Its main bomb load consists of AGM-88 HARM and ASM-65 Maverick missiles. Nighthawk pilots need the same cool but aggressive personality, the same judgement and confidence as any fighter pilot, but they need a special affinity with computers and the ability to cope with multiple different sources of information at the same time.

In a recent anonymous interview with the man who dropped the first bomb of the Gulf War on Baghdad from an F-117A Stealth Fighter, the CO of the USAF 555th Fighter Sqn, a Lt Col., said: 'I guess I was pretty good at computer games ... in over 1,000 hours on I haven't missed a target yet, either in training or in action in both the Gulf and in Panama.'

The ex-Soviet Union took a great deal of notice of developments in stealth technology and precision weapons in the Gulf War, seeing the autonomy it offered as very much part of the future. Rostislav Belyyakov, MiG's chief designer, said that any fighter which does not incorporate stealth does not have a chance of success. Russia is undoubtedly working on stealth, and the major players in Europe, BAe and Dassault, both have versions of the Skunk Works. The combination of stealth fighters and attack aircraft, armed with PGMs, is one vision of the future, but, as ever, for every development in military technology there is always somebody looking for the antidote, and there are big commercial prizes for those who can find a stealth detection system.

The most likely, immediate vision of the future is a new generation of fighters in the highly capable tradition of the F-14, F-15, F-16 and F/A-18 and the reaction to them in Russia, improved MiG-29s and Su-27s, and the Su-35. In 1981 the Pentagon asked the US aircraft industry for design studies for the Advanced Tactical Fighter (ATF). The specification was for a fighting aircraft with increased performance levels, even more advanced avionic systems and two new characteristics in a fighter: it had to be stealthy, with a top speed of Mach 2.5, but it also had to have a high cruise speed, too, around Mach 1.4, without using too much fuel, giving it an unrefuelled range in supercruise of 700 miles. It also needed to be able to take off from much shorter runways, be highly manoeuvrable, with an operational ceiling of 70,000 feet, perfect for look down shoot down tactics; it was to have a gun, but its main armament was to be eight AAMs.

Two companies, Lockheed and Northrop, were selected to build two prototypes, the YF-22 and YF-23, each one with one of two new engines from P&W and GE, the F119 and the F120. Both incorporated vectored thrust, the ability to direct the jet efflux up and down which assisted short take-off but also to improve manoeuvrability by using engine power to tighten a turn, especially at altitude. Both were flown for the first time in 1990 and they were very different. Northrop's YF-23 was more advanced in terms of the stealth and supercruise, but at the expense of agility, and the Lockheed YF-22, which was the better compromise, was closer to the traditional qualities of a fighter, and it was chosen in April 1991.

The YF-22 showed the continuing emphasis on the use of electronics and computers to stay ahead of the opposition, which was evident in the breakdown of the cost. Based on the original order for 648 aircraft, development costs to April 1991 were $3.8 billion; further development and production costs were $60 billion, giving a total cost per aircraft of over $90 million, and around 60% of that cost was the avionics. HUD and HOTAS have been augmented by the Agile Eye helmet and a large, touch-sensitive, multi-functional display on the instrument panel with a moving map, target and navigational information and weapons availability, all filtered through the Pilot's Associate.

It is the first fighter to have a fully Integrated Electronic Warfare System (INEWS) and Integrated Communications/Navigation/Identification System (ICNIA), brought together through Very High Speed Integrated Circuits (VHSIC) which raises the data processing from 1 million characters per second, typical of contemporary fighters, to 50 million characters per second; the central computer which has 300 Megabytes of memory will grow to 650 Megabytes, and it can process 700 million instructions per second. The first production models flew in 1997 and it is scheduled to go into service in 2004, although, with the end of the Cold War, that may slip as some of the urgency goes out of the procurement process.

The Russian equivalent, the MiG I-42, has also slipped back and has yet to fly as funding has slowed to crawling pace. It has not been seen in public and the Russians are very secretive about it, making enigmatic statements such as 'a true multi-role fighter should not lose any of its flight performance for stealth'. What hard information has leaked out suggests that it is similar in size to the Su-27, that the delay has been caused by the engines, that it uses Radar Absorbent Materials (RAM) for stealth instead of relying on a Radar Absorbent Structure, such as the F-117A, that it has a phased array fire control radar, vectored thrust and large canards. In the new commercially minded Russia, Sukhoi and MiG are competitors and Sukhoi is already looking to fill the gap with further developments of the Su-27/35 family if the MiG design bureau has run out of steam after half a century of dominance in fighter design in Russia.

The cost of future fighter projects is shaping the future of the military aviation industry. The YF-22 will be built by a consortium of three of the largest companies in the world – Lockheed, Boeing and General Dynamics – and over the horizon, beyond F-22, the US industry is already working on the technology for the next generation of manned fighters. Joint Advanced Strike Technology (JAST), creating a pool of common parts and systems which can be used to meet the particular needs of each service, is already driving further amalgamations in the industry as no single aerospace company can build a modern fighter on its own.

In Europe the same criteria continue to drive co-operation between national governments and Europe's next, the EF2000 Eurofighter, which was first discussed in 1983 and now a long way behind schedule, will be built by Britain, Germany, Italy and Spain. As they agonise about the cost, especially if it continues to rise as the numbers required by the participating air forces decline, there is a large body of opinion which holds that it will be obsolete before it goes into production and that it is only being kept alive to provide employment in the hard-pressed aircraft industries of the participating countries. The prototype is flying: it is versatile, very agile, using vectored thrust, but it is not at all stealthy, and though it cannot be regarded as state of the art, on cost grounds alone it will have to be the mainstay of the RAF and Luftwaffe manned fighters force for the next thirty years.

France was part of the original Eurofighter consortium but it pulled out in 1985, the same year that the Dassault-Breguet Rafale flew for the first time and is now in production. Its primary role is as a tactical fighter, designed to replace L'Armée de L'Air Jaguars and French Navy attack aircraft. It is also designed to keep France in the business of building high-technology fighters in the future for reasons of national prestige as much as anything else. The Rafale started out as a single-seater, but in an ironic twist, following the Gulf War, the L'Armée de L'Air decided that the workload for the single-seat Jaguar pilots was too high and ordered a redesign of the Rafale to reinstate the backseater.

As fighters become more and more complex and more capable, so air forces need fewer of them, and the demand for fighter pilots decreases, but as that happens so the demands of the job have risen exponentially, and the view that the quality of the pilot remains the deciding factor as technology advances now transcends the old divide between West and East. In August 1991, following harsh criticism of the performance of Soviet equipment in the Gulf War, Col. Gen. Evgeny Shaposhnikov, the Chief of Staff of the Russian Air Force, said, in what was taken at the time as a thinly veiled criticism of Iraqi Air Force pilots, 'The effectiveness of weapons depends directly on the skills of the people manning them.'

Competition to join the élite who fly the top-of-the-range fighters in Western air forces is as fierce as ever, and the qualities of individual aggressiveness and flair are still required, but what is needed is not highly strung men, bent on glory and prone to self-destruction, or control freaks who cannot work comfortably in an electronically linked team, or obsessive types who monitor the instrument panel, chasing every detail until the displays become a barrier to considered action rather than providing assistance.

What air forces need is real talent, stable people, able to absorb huge amounts of information, with good situational awareness, who thrive under stress. One of the hallmarks of an ace down the ages is that he focuses on the essentials, prioritising effectively those aspects of the situation which matter most, and that is instinctive, part of the individual, and in the fleeting seconds when called on to make decisions, while training with good equipment is vital to maintain basic skills, no amount of training can make up for a lack of awareness, an obsessive streak which might obscure the big picture or lead to a lack of judgement under pressure. The cost of finding, training and retaining such men is high, putting more weight behind the argument for unmanned fighters in the future.

The shooting down of Capt. Scott O'Grady, a completely anonymous airman until he was shot down, brought home vividly the high political and financial risk associated with manned fighter operations. They are highly visible, high-value targets for any enemy, and their loss becomes a blow to national pride every bit as damaging as the loss of aces during the First World War. During the build-up to Operation Deliberate Force that followed his rescue, the USA deployed unmanned Predators for the first time overseas to provide assistance to the manned operations at far lower risk. Predator's 'pilot' sits hundreds of miles away in a bunker without risking his life. Each machine costs a maximum of $3 million, complete with its package of sensors and cameras, and the US Government recently nearly doubled the budget for the whole programme to $115 million, barely enough to buy one fully operational F-22 when it comes into service.

The next generation of intelligence-gathering is not far behind: Global Hawk, with a range of over 14,000 miles and endurance of 42 hours, able to send back pictures in real time; and beyond that Darkstar, which is tiny, and UAVs have become one of the central themes of debates about the long-term future of military aviation. UAVs have come a long way since the Israelis used them in the Bekaa Valley in 1982, and have proved their value in the Gulf War, the No-Fly Zones in Iraq and in Bosnia. They are difficult to detect and destroy and they are cheap to manufacture and operate, and turning them into attack aircraft and fighters is clearly an option. The Tomahawk cruise missile, which is really an unmanned, disposable bomber, whose effectiveness was shown in Baghdad in 1991, in the No-Fly Zone in Iraq and Bosnia in 1995, has shown the way forward. High technology, for so long used to sustain the fighter pilot in the fighter, is now threatening to oust him. The most recent experimental aircraft in America's X series is NASA's X-36, an unmanned fighter, the first step in using technology to take over the aerial battle completely, saving money and risking fewer lives. The technology has finally caught up with the predictions Gen. Hap Arnold made in 1945, having gazed on the

Pandora's Box of German experimental aircraft produced half a century ago.

The pilot has now become the weak point in the system because of the limitations his body imposes on the designers, just at a time when they have the means to replace him. One of the limitations comes with manoeuvring: even with the latest g-suits, which prevent the blood from sinking away from the brain under high g loads, the human body can only stand 11–12 g and that is not for sustained periods. To outmanoeuvre modern SAMs, he would need to withstand at least 15 g and Firebee and HiMAT showed twenty years ago that unmanned fighters can not only outmanoeuvre manned fighters but can sustain 20–30 g indefinitely. Pressure Breathing under g (PBG), better g-suits and reclining ejector seats are all ways of improving the ability of the pilot to withstand the forces of high manoeuvrability, and against other manned fighters they will continue to provide an advantage to the pilot who has them, but the quantum leaps required to outmanoeuvre unmanned fighters is a long way off. There are exotic solutions, including having the pilot lying completely prone in a completely virtual reality cockpit, relying on computers for all his information rather than the Mk 1 Eyeball. In that scenario, for most fighter pilots, he may as well be on the ground.

There are very few air force generals who have reached the top without pilots' wings on their chests, and even fewer who have done so with a background in computers, and while air forces are commanded by pilots, many of them fighter pilots, that day is still quite some way off, though it may be closer than some of them think, and the immediate future will see a lively debate on the matter. America, the world's only policeman with an overall policy for its armed forces of global reach, is ever less inclined to commit its armed forces to overseas wars where they might take casualties, and options to project its power based on unmanned systems are ever more attractive to the politicians who control the purse strings. However, politicians also have to ask generals to fight their wars for them when diplomacy fails, and the armed forces rarely end up fighting the wars for which they are formed, equipped and trained. If fighting for command of the air were to be consigned to computer-controlled aircraft and missiles, guided either by on-board systems or by couch-potato fighter pilots in bunkers on the ground, if the human element were taken out of aerial combat and it became one computer against another, then operations such as the Falklands, the Gulf War and the No-Fly Zones in Iraq and Bosnia would not have been possible. All too often, in all these conflicts, imagined threats have been real and vice versa, plans have changed, unexpected dangers have arisen and opportunities have developed which called for sound judgements at the last second, whether to fire or not, the 'Mk I Eyeball factor' as pilots call it, assessing the whole situation and providing what computers cannot do, at least at present – cope with the wholly unexpected.

A major part of the skill of the fighter pilot is making his opponent fight on his terms, by guile, ruse, surprise, getting in his six o'clock, by aggression, competitiveness and individualism. If the human mind can invent the ultimate military computer then it can invent the ultimate antidote – that much we know from history. In the Vietnam War the Vietcong drove buffalo drenched in human urine through the jungle to confuse the latest sensors carried by US aircraft to detect human presence. Human ingenuity will undoubtedly find novel ways of confusing future high-technology developments, and if the human factor is not there to respond in kind with equal ingenuity and imagination, if he is far away in a bunker, he will be less effective.

There is nothing new about the debate: in the 1930s it was high speeds and the almost incomprehensible problem of the sound barrier which was going to make men fighting for air superiority redundant; in the 1950s it was speed again, this time multi-sonic speeds, and guided missiles which would replace the fighter pilot, and much of Britain's aircraft industry was sacrificed to that thinking; today it is computer processing power and data links which threaten his future. So far they have all been wrong, and the successful air forces have been those who have integrated an ever more capable pilot with the new technology and insisted on the best in both. One day the fighter pilot may be as quaint and as obsolete in warfare as the knight in armour on horseback, but that day is still some way off. For the foreseeable future the quest for the latest technological advance, leading to however tiny an advantage in the air, and securing the budgets to pay for nothing but the best, will continue.

The new incomprehensible barrier to progress in military

aviation, the problem which is driving the quest for automation in its second century, is cost. In 1946 the total development contract for America's first jet fighter, the P-80 Shooting Star, was $515,000 and the first aircraft had a flyaway cost of $95,000. A quarter of a century later the F-15 Eagle development costs were $1.7 billion and the estimated flyaway cost was $8.2 million, which rose to $19 million by 1985. At up to $100 million a copy for the F-22 when it goes into service in 2004, never mind the support costs, falling military budgets, higher R&D costs, smaller production runs, the huge wasted investment if a decision is wrong, the demands of other aspects of warfare, counter-terrorism for example, and of other armed services, and the end of the Cold War – the real enemy of the manned jet fighter is the price tag when politicians and generals contemplate a UAV like Predator at $3 million, less than the price of the eight AIM-120 AMRAAMs or AIM-9X Sidewinders the F-22 will carry.

The US Navy's F-14 Tomcat, which Kleeman and Musczynski used to such good effect in the Gulf of Sirte incident, was the most expensive fighter ever built when it went into service a quarter of a century ago. The unit cost of the Tomcat in 1973 was roughly twice that of the land-based F-15, and with all toughening which is required for catapult launches and deck landings, the waterproofing and needs of storage below decks, the cost of replacing it might even be beyond the purse of the US Department of Defense. Any replacement is at least a decade or more away, and in the meantime, as its avionics are constantly updated, lengthening its operational life, the cost of keeping it in the air in an operational state goes up as one component fails for every twenty minutes in the air. Something will have to give – possibly size, maybe numbers, probably both, and certainly an ever-longer planned peacetime life. The F-86 had a fatigue life of 300 hours, the F-4 1,000 hours, the F-16 4,000 hours and the F-15 8,000 hours, giving it, at an average of 250 hours a year, a life of 30 years; they will certainly be around that long, and longer.

Looking forward to the twentieth century from 1897, when only a tiny number of enthusiasts believed that heavier-than-air machines of any kind were anything but science fiction, there were not even hazy ideas about the effect which their invention in the decade that followed would have on the conduct of war. The interaction between technological advance and the conduct of war tells us that military thinking tends to lag behind until a war forces an appreciation of the realities. Soldiers insisted on keeping cavalry long after the tank and the aeroplane had replaced it as a means breaking through enemy lines and carrying out reconnaissance. Some new device, currently only an experiment in an obscure lab somewhere – just as the aeroplane itself was in 1900, or the air-to-air guided missile was in 1950 – could rise up and challenge the aeroplane's century of dominance, and maybe aeroplanes will be replaced by electronics of as yet undreamed-of power, sophistication and reliability, with artificial intelligence to provide the flexibility; maybe they will be as redundant in warfare in the next century as horses have been in this century, but until those alternatives are clear and tested, politicians, military planners and generals should be reluctant to give up the manned fighter until that future is certain, as Cicero pointed out, at whatever the cost.

Looking forward now to the twenty-first century, the position is similar to that in 1945. The legacy of the Cold War is 'infowar' systems, stealth technology and precision guided weapons, just as the jet engine, radar, atomic weapons, rocket science and guidance systems were the legacy of the Second World War. The end of the Cold War has also ushered in another new and uncertain world order. The decline of the Soviet Union, the rise of Communist China and the Pacific Rim economies, global markets competing with politicians for power, lower defence budgets, complicated, nationalistic wars with no front line in Africa, Asia and Europe, state-sponsored terrorism, the proliferation of nuclear, biological and chemical weapons all provide ample room for surprises in world affairs and in the security of nations. As the century comes to a close, and the resources spent on defence decline, as they should, then let the reduction be in numbers not quality. Success in air warfare has been due to the combination of the best technology and the confident individualism which flourishes in Western, democratic societies, but is not as evident in ideologically or culturally collectivist societies. It comes from understanding that air power is about having the best men and machines, then using them ruthlessly to achieve supremacy when appropriate, to win, and that the cost of winning is whatever it takes to have men and machines which are simply the best.

Maj. Gen. Avihu Bin-Nun, Chief of Staff of the Israeli Air Force in 1987, a fighter pilot who fought in four air wars in different capacities, has never been in no doubt about that fundamental point: 'We must keep the balance of quality in our favour.'

Select Bibliography

Adams, Richard, and Jay Miller, *F-22* (Austin Texas: Acrofax, 1992).

Air and Space Power for the 21st Century (Washington DC: USAF, 1996).

Air Power Confronts an Unstable World, ed. Dr Richard P. Hallion (London: Brassey's New World Vistas, 1997).

Air Power: The Decisive Factor in Korea, ed. Col. James T. Stewart, USAF (Princeton, NJ: Van Norstrand, 1957).

Badsey, Stephen, *Fighters* (London: Bison, 1990).

Barron, John, *MiG Pilot: The Final Escape of Lieutenant Balenko* (New York: McGraw-Hill, 1980).

Bekker, Cajus, *The Luftwaffe War Diaries* (London: McDonald, 1967).

Beschloss, Michael R., *Mayday: Kruschev and the U-2 Affair* (London: Faber & Faber, 1986).

Birtles, Philip and Paul Beaver, *Missile Systems* (London: Ian Allen, 1985).

Bowyer, Chaz, *Gloster Meteor* (London: Ian Allen, 1985).

Broughton, Col. Jack, USAF (retd), *Thud Ridge* (Philadelphia: Lipincott, 1969).

Broughton, Jack, *Going Downtown* (New York: Orion, 1988).

Brown, Neville, *The Future of Air Power* (London: Croom Helm, 1986).

Brown, Walter J., *The Phantom in Combat* (London: Jane's, 1985).

Burden, Rodney R., Michael I. Draper, Douglas R. Rough, Colin R. Smith, David L. Wilton, *Falklands: The Air War* (London: Arms & Armour Press, 1986).

Clancy, Tom, *Fighter Wing* (London: HarperCollins, 1996).

Donnelly, Christopher, *The Red Banner: The Soviet Military System in Peace and War* (London: Jane's, 1988).

Dorr, Robert F., *Air War Hanoi* (London: Guild Publishing, 1988).

Dorr, Robert F., *F-86 Sabre: History of the Sabre and FJ Fury* (Osceola WI: Motorbooks, 1993).

Dorr, Robert F. and Warren Thompson, *The Korean Air War* (Osceola, WI: Motorbooks, 1994).

Dorr, Robert F. and Chris Bishop, *Vietnam Air War Debrief* (London: Aerospace, 1996).

Ethell, Jeffrey and Alfred Price, *The German Jets in Combat* (London: Jane's, 1979).

Ethell, Jeffrey and Alfred Price, *Air War South Atlantic* (London: Book Club Associates, 1983).

Ethell, Jeffrey and Alfred Price, *One Day in a Long War: May 10, 1972, Air War, Vietnam* (London: Greenhill, 1990).

Foreman, John and S. E. Harvey, *The Messerschmidt Combat Diary Me 262* (Walton-on-Thames, UK: Phalanx, 1990).

Forsyth, Robert, *JV44: The Galland Circus* (Burgess Hill, West Sussex, UK: Classic, 1996).

Galland, Adolf, *The First and the Last* (London: Methuen, 1955).

Griangreco, D. M., *Stealth Fighter Pilot* (Osceola, WI: Motorbooks, 1993).

Golley, John, *Whittle: The True Story* (Shrewsbury, UK: Airlife, 1987).

Gordon, Yefim and Bill Gunston, *MiG-21 'Fishbed'* (Leicester, UK: Aerofax, 1996).

Green, Michael, *US Air Power in Desert Storm* (Hong Kong: Concord, 1991).

Gulf Air War Debrief, ed. Stan Morse (London: Aerospace, 1991).

Gunston, Bill, *Modern Airborne Missiles* (London: Salamander, 1983).

Halberstadt, Hans, *Red Star Fighters and Ground Attack* (North Branch, MN: Windrow & Green, 1994).

Hall, George, *Top Gun* (Osceola, WI: Motorbooks, 1991).

Hallion, Dr Richard P., *Designers and Test Pilots* (Chicago: Time-Life, 1983).

Halperin, Merav and Aharon Lapidot, *G-Suit: Combat Reports from Israel's Air War* (London: Sphere, 1990).

Harvey, Frank, *Air War Vietnam* (New York: Bantam, 1967).

Hosking, Geoffrey, *Russia: People and Empire 1552–1917* (London: HarperCollins, 1997).

Isby, David C., *Fighter Combat in the Jet Age* (London: HarperCollins, 1997).

Israeli Air Force 1984, ed. Lt Col. David Eshel (IDA retd) (Hod Harashon, Israel: Eshel Dramit, 1984).

Jane's Weapons Systems 1985–86, ed. Ronald T. Pretty (London: Jane's, 1985).

Jane's Military Communications 1989, ed. John Williamson (London: Jane's, 1989).

Jane's Military Communications 1993–94, ed. John Williamson (London: Jane's, 1993).

Jane's All the World's Aircraft 1985–86, ed. John W. Taylor (London: Jane's, 1985).

Jane's All the World's Aircraft 1989–90, ed. John W. Taylor (London: Jane's, 1989).

Jane's All the World's Aircraft 1993–94, ed. John W. Taylor (London: Jane's, 1993).

Jane's All the World's Aircraft 1994–95, ed. John W. Taylor (London: Jane's, 1994).

Jackson, Robert, *Air War Over Korea* (London: Ian Allen, 1973).

Jackson, Robert, *F-86 Sabre: The Operational Record* (Shrewsbury, UK: Airlife, 1994).

Kelly, Orr, *Hornet: The Inside Story of the F/A-18* (Shrewsbury: Airlife, 1990).

Knaak, Marcelle Size, *Encyclopaedia of US Aircraft and Missile Systems, vol 1* (Washington DC: Office of Air Force History, 1978).

Kum-Sok, No with J. Roger Osterholm, *A MiG to Freedom* (Jefferson, NC: McFarland, 1996).

Mason, R. A., *Aircraft Strategy and Operations of the Soviet Air Force* (London: Jane's, 1986).

McDaid, Hugh and David Oliver, *Robot Warriors* (London: Orion, 1997).

Mildenhall, Charles A., *Delta Wings: Convair's High Speed Planes of the Fifties and Sixties* (Osceola, WI: Motorbooks, 1983).

Miller, Jay, *General Dynamics F-111* (Aero Publishers, 1981).

Miller, Jay, *General Dynamics F-16 Fighting Falcon* (Austin, Texas: Aerofax, 1982).

Miller, Jay, *Lockheed Martin F-117 Nighthawk* (Austin, Texas: Aerofax, 1995).

Nicholls, Cdr John, USN (retd) and Barrett B. Tillman, *On Yankee Station: The Naval Air War over Vietnam* (Shrewsbury, UK: Airlife, 1987).

Norden, Lon, *Fighters over Israel* (London: Greenhill, 1990).

O'Grady, Captain Scott, with Jeff Coplon, *Return With Honour* (New York: Doubleday, 1995).

Perlmutter, Amos, Michael Handel and Uri Bar-Joseph, *Two Minutes Over Baghdad* (London: Corgi, 1982).

Pocock, Chris, *Dragon Lady: The History of the U-2 Spyplane* (Shrewsbury: Airlife, 1989).

Quanbeck, Alton H. and Archie I. Wood with the assistance of Louisa

Tharon, *Modernising the Strategic Bomber Force* (Washington DC: The Brookings Institution, 1976).

Rendall, David, *Jane's Aircraft Recognition Guide* (London: Harper-Collins, 1995).

Rubenstein, Murray and Richard Goldman, *The Israeli Air Force Story* (London: Arms & Armour Press, 1979).

Schneider, Major Donald F., *Air Force Heroes in Vietnam* (Alabama: Airpower Research Institute, 1979).

Schofield, Carey, *Inside The Soviet Army* (London: Headline, 1991).

Scutts, Jerry, *Wolf Pack: Hunting MiGs over Vietnam* (Shrewsbury, UK: Airlife, 1987).

Shaw, Robert L., *Fighter Combat Tactics* (Cambridge, UK: Patrick Stephens, 1985).

Shield and Storm, ed. John Godden (London: Brassey's, 1994).

Smith, J. R. and Anthony Kay, *German Aircraft of the Second World War* (London: Putnam, 1972).

Smith, John T., *Rolling Thunder: The Strategic Campaign 1965–1968* (Walton-on-Thames, UK: Air Research Publications, 1994).

Soviet Military Power, An Assessment of the Threat (Washington DC: Dept of Defense, 1988).

Spick, Mike, *Fighter Pilot Tactics* (Cambridge, UK: Patrick Stephens, 1983).

Spick, Mike, *Jet Fighter Performance Korea to Vietnam* (London: Ian Allen, 1986).

Spick, Mike, *Designed For The Kill* (Shrewsbury, UK: Air Life, 1995).

The Military Balance (London: HSS, 1985).

The Military Balance (London: HSS, 1987).

The Unmanned Vehicles Handbook 1995–1996, ed. Ian Parker (Burnham, Bucks, UK: The Shepherd Press, 1995).

Thornborugh, Anthony, *Modern Fighter Aircraft Technology and Tactics* (Cambridge, UK: Patrick Stephens, 1995).

Wagner, William and William P. Sloan, *Fireflies and Other UAVs* (Leicester, UK: Midland, 1992).

Walker, Bryce, *Fighting Jets* (Chicago: Time Life, 1983).

Ward, Cmdr 'Sharkey', *Sea Harrier Over The Falklands* (London: Orion, 1993).

Weizman, Ezer, *On Eagle's Wings* (New York: MacMillan, 1976).

Wilson, David, *Lion Over Korea: 77 Fighter Squadron RAAF 1950–53* (Belconnen, Aust: Banner Books, 1994).

Wood, Derek, *Project Cancelled: The Disaster of Britain's Abandoned Aircraft Projects* (London: Jane's, 1986).

Yeager, Gen. Chuck and Leo Janos, *Yeager: An Autobiography* (New York: Bantam, 1985).

INDEX